ST. MARY
ST. MARY   MARYLAND 20686

THE RELATION OF THE QUAKERS TO THE AMERICAN REVOLUTION

Arthur J. Mekeel

Copyright © 1979 by

University Press of America, Inc.™

4710 Auth Place, S.E., Washington D.C. 20023

All rights reserved

Printed in the United States of America

ISBN: 0-8191-0792-1

Library of Congress Catalog Card Number: 79-66173

To

E.A.M.

PREFACE

The topic of this study was first suggested to me by the late Professor Raynor Kelsey of Haverford College and was carried to a successful conclusion as a doctoral dissertation under the late Professor Arthur M. Schlesinger of Harvard University. Further research on the subject and the resulting amplification of the original manuscript was made possible by the T. Wistar Brown Fellowship in Quaker Studies at Haverford College. A subsequent grant by the Friends Historical Association facilitated its final preparation for publication.

Special thanks are due the staff members of both the Quaker Collection at Haverford College and the Friends Historical Library at Swarthmore College for their ready assistance. The final form of the manuscript owes much to the attentive scrutiny of Professor William J. Frost, Director of the Friends Historical Library, who read both an earlier and the final draft of the manuscript. Professor Edwin Bronner, Curator of the Quaker Collection and Librarian at Haverford College, has given much valued counsel and advice. Barbara L. Curtis, Bibliographer at the Quaker Collection, has been a source of encouragement and helpfulness at every step of the undertaking. The perceptive critique and ever willing support of my wife have been an essential element in the successful completion of this endeavor.

Others to whom I am grateful for their valuable assistance are Jan North of the Friends Reference Library, Friends House, Euston Road, London; Treva Mathis, Curator of the Quaker Collection at Guilford College; Mary Cook, former, and Elizabeth Moger, present, Keeper of Records at the Haviland Records Room of New York Yearly Meeting; and Ruth C. Burgess, custodian of the New England Yearly Meeting Records at the Rhode Island Historical Society.

The Manuscripts Department of the Historical Society of Pennsylvania, the Library of the American Philosophical Society, and the Library Company of Philadelphia have been most helpful in putting their resources at my disposal. Other depositories of manuscript collections which deserve mention are the Rhode

Island Historical Society, the Massachusetts Historical
Society and the Houghton Library of Harvard University.

CONTENTS

KEY TO ABBREVIATIONS

Periodicals and Manuscript Depositories

BFHA   <u>Bulletin</u> of Friends Historical Association
PMHB   <u>Pennsylvania Magazine of History and Biography</u>
WMQ   <u>William and Mary Quarterly</u>

FHLSC   Friends Historical Library, Swarthmore College
HSP   Historical Society of Pennsylvania
QCHC   Quaker Collection, Haverford College

Friends Meetings Records

M.f.S.	Meeting for Sufferings	Md.	Maryland
M.M	Monthly Meeting	N.C.	North Carolina
Min.	Minutes	N.E.	New England
P.M.	Preparative Meeting	N.Y.	New York
Q.M.	Quarterly Meeting	Phil.	Philadelphia
Y.M.	Yearly Meeting	Va.	Virginia

For abbreviations of newspaper titles see Newspapers
under the Bibliography.

Chapter I

THE QUAKERS IN AMERICA IN THE EIGHTEENTH CENTURY

By the middle of the eighteenth century the
Quakers in America were one of the leading colonial
religious bodies. Their fame and prestige was largely
due to the success achieved in building what was coming
to be the most populous and wealthy province in British
North America. Imperial developments over which they
had no control were, however, destined to bring an
abrupt termination of their "Holy Experiment".

The Treaty of Paris in 1763 at the end of the
Seven Years War brought to a conclusion the long-standing rivalry for empire between France and Britain in
the New World. By its provisions Britain took possession of French Canada and the French claims to the upper
Mississippi Valley. Tensions which soon arose between
the mother country and the colonies in their conflict-
ing attempts to adjust to the new imperial situation
finally erupted in a violent confrontation which cul-
minated in the birth of a new nation.

In the course of this controversy, religious back-
ground and conviction strongly influenced many men
either to support or to oppose measures adopted to
further the colonial cause. The relationship of the
members of one religious group, the Society of Friends,
to the developing revolutionary movement and to the
war which ensued is the subject of this study.

The first Quaker missionaries had appeared in New
England and Virginia as early as 1656. (1) By 1750
there were sizeable concentrations of Friends in
Massachusetts, Rhode Island, New York, Delaware, Maryland, and North Carolina. Smaller groups also existed
in New Hampshire, Connecticut, and South Carolina.
Two decades later a Quaker settlement was established
in Georgia. (2) Since Friends had been the chief
colonizers of southern New Jersey in the previous
century, they had been and still were an important
element in that province's population, although their
political role in its affairs had declined considerably
since that time. In Pennsylvania, the colony founded
by the Quakers, they dominated the political scene and
were in the forefront of its economic life.

1

Notwithstanding the centrifugal effects of distance and difficulties of communication in a colonial, frontier society, the American Quakers maintained an unusually close and exclusive fellowship among themselves and with their co-religionists in Britain. A primary reason for this was their self-identification as a "peculiar people" who, although called upon to shun the ways of the world, were deeply involved in its activities. Their distinct mode of life and conduct, combined with a common approach in the cultural and intellectual spheres, strengthened their religious bonds and constituted a singularly cohesive force. Consequently the Friends, as individuals and as a Society, maintained a remarkably consistent course of conduct and action whenever secular affairs touched on their religious tenets and testimonies. (3)

A unique feature of the Quakers was the extent to which they attempted to apply Christian principles and ideals to the temporal world. From their origin they had considered their religious community and message as primitive Christianity revived, and as the prototype of a "City of God" upon earth. Man, they believed, is a spiritual being during his earthly life albeit a denizen of the world of matter. This eternal, spiritual nature of man is the dwelling place of the "light within" which is present to guide and enlighten every human being from birth. Therefore, it is wrong to take human life and the conduct of human relations should be based on an appeal to the spiritual nature of man rather than on the use of brute force. Violence is injurious alike to those affected by it and those employing it. Progress achieved by peaceful means may be slower, but it will be sounder and more beneficial. (4) Since the Friends lived in a world actually dominated by the rule of force, their pacifist concepts often brought them into conflict with the state. This was especially the case when tensions and disruption occurred within the empire of which they were citizens.

The Quakers advocated and practised active obedience to secular government when its rule accorded with their convictions and consciences; when its rule did not, they resorted to passive disobedience. They believed that government was divinely instituted, and therefore, they eschewed subversive plotting or cooperation with any activities intended to bring about the downfall of any regime. When opposing the demands of a government on the grounds of religious convictions they were willing to suffer for their beliefs and so

2

bear a testimony against what they considered wrong.
The Friends believed they should peacefully protest unjust and oppressive laws and government actions, while
at the same time bearing faithful allegiance to it.
This was their position under any government, whether
monarchy, republic, colony, or commonwealth. (5) On
the other hand, although they could take no part in
changing a form of government, they would support the
new as staunchly as the old when the transition had
been achieved. (6) This was their attitude toward the
King and the government of which he was the head.

A determining role in Quaker life and conduct was
the organization of church government through which the
Society effected the decisions and policies deriving
from its religious tenets. The basic unit was the
preparative meeting which functioned as the meeting for
worship, customarily held twice weekly. Several preparative meetings were comprised in a monthly meeting,
the organ of official action in any specific region
which exercised an all-inclusive jurisdiction over the
moral and social conduct of its members. It was the
monthly meeting which instituted disciplinary action
against members who failed to observe the Society's
testimonies and standards of conduct whether in respect
to business practices, social relations, or participation in warlike activities. If the individual under
discipline refused to acknowledge his error, extrusion
from the fold of the Society inevitably followed. (7)

Several contiguous monthly meetings formed a
quarterly meeting held four times a year for worship
and business. This body served as a focus of appeal
from monthly meetings, as well as a source of authority
and advice. In turn it was subordinate to the yearly
meeting, held annually for business and religious purposes. As the ultimate resort for judgments and instructions, the yearly meeting had recommendatory and
advisory authority over the quarterly and monthly
meetings. The official membership of these various
bodies consisted of representatives sent up from the
respective subordinate meetings, although any member
was allowed to attend. Each yearly meeting was an
autonomous body, although on issues affecting the
Society as a whole, action was usually taken in consultation with other yearly meetings, especially those
of Philadelphia and London, whose leadership in the
Society was well recognized.

One other organ of church government of prime im-

3

portance was the meeting for sufferings, composed of members appointed by the constituent quarterly meetings and the yearly meeting at large. This meeting carried on the business of the yearly meeting when the latter was not in session, and its decisions were as authoritative as those of the body in whose name it acted. The meeting for sufferings originated in England in the preceding century when its chief purpose was to care for Friends suffering from religious persecution. (8)

In the course of time it became vested with extensive authority, and when similar meetings were established in America, their functions were closely patterned after those of their British counterpart.

The Philadelphia Meeting for Sufferings was the first to be constituted in the colonies, in 1756. (9) Two years later, New York Yearly Meeting appointed a similar body. (10) Both were established to deal with problems arising from the war with France. In New England, Maryland, and Virginia the many difficulties caused by the Revolutionary War prompted those yearly meetings to appoint meetings for sufferings also. (11) In North Carolina, in lieu of a meeting for sufferings, standing committees of the two Quarterly Meetings, Eastern and Western, were set up in 1757 and 1778 respectively. (12) [Because of the frequent critical situations which confronted the Friends during the Revolutionary War, these bodies transacted most of the important business at that time.]

The Philadelphia Meeting for Sufferings consisted of forty members, twelve chosen at large from the yearly meeting and four each chosen by the constituent quarterly meetings. As the most important and responsible permanent body of the yearly meeting, the membership was naturally composed of the more "weighty" Friends. Those from the city were mostly well-off merchants and traders, while those from the country were well-to-do farmers, thus comprising a group which would exhibit a conservative approach in the Meeting's deliberations.

The city members were the dominant element in the Meeting for Sufferings. This situation resulted partly from their recognized status in the Society and partly from the fact that the meetings of this body were held in Philadelphia, rendering it more difficult for country members to attend when urgent business required sittings to be held on short notice. The three

4

Pemberton brothers, who belonged to one of the wealthiest and most influential families in the city, were all members of the Meeting for Sufferings, and one of them was almost always its clerk or presiding officer during the Revolutionary years. (13)

Another determining factor in the life of the colonial Quakers was that they and their British coreligionists were citizens of the same political entity the British Empire, and the Friends on both sides of the Atlantic saw themselves as members of one religious family. The Quaker movement had originated in England; and Pennsylvania, Delaware, and southern New Jersey had been largely settled by a direct migration of Friends from Britain with resulting strong ties with British Friends. Therefore, the colonial Quakers considered seriously the advice and counsel of English Friends, especially when British Government policies and actions affected the interests and testimonies of the Society.

The attitude of the British Quakers, on the other hand, was especially important in the case of Pennsylvania because of the English Friends' long-standing concern for and involvement in the affairs of the province. From the early years of its foundation, Pennsylvania had been an object of their paternal care, and the London Meeting for Sufferings had often exerted its influence with the various ministries and Parliament in the colony's behalf. (14) Influential Friends throughout the colonies and in England were in close touch. Transatlantic intervisitation and correspondence, both official and private, were comparatively frequent, and annual epistles were exchanged between the American and London Yearly Meetings. Consequently the English Quakers knew more about colonial conditions than most of their countrymen.

Developments within the Society of Friends previous to the Revolutionary years also had a decisive influence on its subsequent role and conduct. By the 1750's the rapid economic growth of Pennsylvania and the ramifications of political responsibility had begun to affect the mode of life of many Friends. The accumulation of great wealth in the hands of the Quaker merchant class, together with the influence of the mores and life-style of the expanding non-Quaker constituency of the province, resulted in an increasingly worldly way of life on the part of many members of the Society. Awareness of the danger of too great an involvement in worldy affairs was further strengthened

5

by the controversy in the Pennsylvania Assembly in 1755-56 over taxation measures to provide for the defense of the western frontier against the French threat. Because of this Quaker opposition, the British government, spurred on by the opponents of the Quakers, considered the adoption of legislation requiring an oath of allegiance from all colonial office holders, thereby effectively disbarring the Friends from office in Pennsylvania. At the urging of the London Friends who were mediating in the matter, most of the Quaker members of the Assembly resigned and during the immediately succeeding war years the Pennsylvania Friends remained out of politics. (16)

This experience served to disillusion many Quakers as to the validity of achieving their ideal of the "Holy Experiment" and prompted them to turn their attention to purifying the inner life of the Society. Changes in the leadership of Philadelphia Yearly Meeting in this period gave impetus to this movement. In March 1755 the general spring meeting of the Ministers and Elders of the Yearly Meeting issued an epistle of advice, calling on the membership to have their minds "sufficiently disentangled from the surfeiting cares of this life and redeemed from the love of the world." (17) The increasing sentiment for reform led to the adoption of a revised Book of Discipline in 1762 and a general tightening up of the requirements that members of the Society faithfully observe their peculiar testimonies as applied to daily life and conduct. Consequently the succeeding years witnessed a significant increase in the number of disownments for failure to adhere to the prescribed Quaker way of life. Between 1760 and 1775 the Pennsylvania meetings disowned what was probably the equivalent of twenty-two percent of the yearly meeting membership as it stood in 1760. (18)

These developments in Pennsylvania were soon followed by similar action on the part of the Quakers in the other colonies. Spiritual reform was strongly encouraged by the visitations of Samuel Fothergill, an English Friend, accompanied by various American Friends to meetings throughout the colonies. In 1760 New England Yearly Meeting adopted a revised Book of Discipline which greatly enhanced the authority of the yearly meeting to oversee the conduct of the membership. By 1770 the monthly meetings had set up committees to work for a purification of the life of the Society, and they began to investigate members who

6

deviated from the proper observance of the Quaker testimonies. (19) New York Yearly Meeting, following the lead of Philadelphia, made significant changes in its disciplinary requirements in 1760 and 1762. (20)

This movement for spiritual revitalization and stricter observance of their peculiar testimonies was bound to influence the overall relationship of the Friends to society in general. It strengthened their group solidarity and laid a firmer basis on which they could consistently face the tests and tensions of the Revolutionary years.

(1)   Jones, Rufus M., assisted by Isaac Sharpless and
      Amelia M. Gummere, The Quakers in the American
      Colonies (London, 1911), 28,266.
(2)   By 1775 there were six yearly meetings in America
      comprising eighty monthly meetings. These were:
      The Yearly Meeting of Friends for New England,
      commonly called New England Yearly Meeting, with
      fourteen monthly meetings, eight in Massachusetts,
      four in Rhode Island, and two in New Hampshire;
      New York Yearly Meeting with five monthly meetings;
      The Yearly Meeting for Pennsylvania and New Jersey
      and the Provinces Adjacent, commonly known as
      Philadelphia Yearly Meeting, with thirty-eight
      monthly meetings, twenty-one in Pennsylvania, ten
      in New Jersey, two in Delaware, two in Maryland,
      and two in Virginia; The Yearly Meeting for Mary-
      land (known today as Baltimore Yearly Meeting)
      with four monthly meetings; Virginia Yearly Meet-
      ing with six monthly meetings; and The Yearly
      Meeting for North and South Carolina and Georgia,
      commonly known as North Carolina Yearly Meeting,
      with twelve monthly meetings, nine in North
      Carolina, two in South Carolina and one in Georgia
      A small monthly meeting at Charleston, South
      Carolina affiliated with London Yearly Meeting was
      laid down toward the end of the 18th century and
      the property was sold to Philadelphia Yearly Meet-
      ing. All the monthly, quarterly and yearly
      meeting sessions sat as mens' and womens' meetings
      separately. Therefore, the minutes referred to
      are minutes of the men's meeting since the problem
      related to the war which came before the various
      meetings concerned men Friends. Points of parti-
      cular concentration of Quakers aside from Penn-
      sylvania, New Jersey and Delaware were: Rhode
      Island, Nantucket, and the eastern towns of Mass-
      achusetts, in New England; Westchester County,
      the Hudson River Valley, New York City and western
      Long Island in New York; and in the south the tide
      water areas of Maryland, Virginia and North
      Carolina, and the upper piedmont regions of North
      and South Carolina and Georgia.
(3)   For an illuminating account of the unity of colo-
      nial Quakerism see Henry J. Cadbury's "Inter-
      colonial Solidarity of American Quakerism", PMHB,
      v. 60 (1936), 362-374. The close relationship
      between English and American Quakers is discussed
      in Frederick B. Tolles' Quakers and the Atlantic

Culture (New York, 1960), chap.2.

(4) A succinct account of Quaker beliefs is given in
Isaac Sharpless' A History of Quaker Government
in Pennsylvania(2vols.,Philadelphia,1899),v.1,9-14.
A more recent and extensive discussion of the religious and philosophical principles on which the
organic structure of the Society of Friends is
based and operates is Howard H. Brinton's Divine-
Human Society (Philadelphia, 1938).

(5) In 1755 Philadelphia Yearly Meeting urged its
members to follow the example of the early Friends
as follows:

> ...it is well known to have been their
> constant and uniform practice to comply
> with the Laws of Government under which
> they lived in every Case not contrary to
> the Laws and Doctrine of our Supreme
> Lord and Lawgiver and when anything was
> required of them which was forbidden by
> Him they patiently suffered not believing
> it to be allowed to the followers of Christ
> by force and violence to oppose the Ordi-
> nances of Magistrates...(Phil,Y.M., Min.,
> v.3, 76.)

(6) For the British aspect of this question see
William C. Braithwaite's The Second Period of
Quakerism (2nd ed., Cambridge, 1961), chap. 21,
and W. A. Cole's The Quakers and Politics (unpublished Ph.D. thesis, Cambridge University,
1955), 32-36. For the viewpoint of the American
Quakers compare "The Ancient Testimony and Principles of the People Called Quakers," Phil.M.F.S.
Min. v. 2, 54-59, with "An Address to the President of the United States", Phil.Y.M., Min. v.4,
163-65. Both are quoted in Sharpless, op.cit.,
v. 2, 125-28, 220-22.

(7) A concise account of the machinery of church government is given in Sharpless, op.cit., v. 1, 21-
31 and in J. William Frost's The Quaker Family in
Colonial America (New York, 1973), 3-5. For a
discussion of the disciplinary procedures of the
monthly meeting see Frost, op.cit., 53-61.

(8) Braithwaite, op.cit., 281-82.

(9) Bowden, James, The History of the Society of
Friends in America, (2 vols., London, 1854), v.2,
283.

(10) Jones, op.cit., 259.

(11) N.E.Y.M., Min. v.1, 310; Md.Y.M., Min. v.3, 102,

Va.Y.M., Min., 1702-1843, 150.

(12) Western Q.M., Min., 1760-1900, 137. The minutes of the Standing Committee of the Eastern Quarter begin in 1757. Those for the Standing Committee of the Western Quarter have, unfortunately, been lost

(13) See Phil.M.f.S., Min., for the period of 1765-1780 passim.

(14) From 1750 on, the London Meeting for Sufferings assumed almost complete responsibility for protecting colonial Quaker interests. In 1755, when Parliament was considering a bill requiring an oath of allegiance from Pennsylvania office holders, the London Meeting for Sufferings acted as an intermediary with the government in obtaining a withdrawal of the proposition. (Dr. John Fothergill to Israel Pemberton, July 8, 1755; same to same March 6, 1756, in Chain of Friendship, Selected Letters of Dr. John Fothergill of London, 1735-1780, ed. Betsy C. Corner and Christopher C. Booth (Cambridge, 1971), 173-77, 178-180.) In 1764-1765 when the British Government was considering the advisability of changing Pennsylvania from a proprietary into a crown colony, the London Meeting for Sufferings informed the Philadelphia Friends:

> ...we shall watch with great Attention and do everything that lies within our power to secure your civil and religious liberties on their ancient foundation.

(London M.f.S. to the Phil.M.f.S., Feb. 15, 1765, quoted in "The Society of Friends in Pennsylvania and New Jersey, 1764-1782", The Friend (Philadelphia), v. 20, 1847, 62). See also Ann Gary Pannell's The Political and Economic Relations of the English and American Quakers, 1750-1785 (unpublished Ph.D. thesis, St. Hughs College, Oxford, 1935), 32ff., 87-94. Pannell takes the position that the attitudes and actions of the American Quakers during the Revolutionary period were dictated by the London Meeting for Sufferings and the advice of prominent British Friends. She gives little consideration to the impact of local colonial conditions, political and otherwise, or to the differences between the various American Quaker groups.

(15) In Virginia, South Carolina and parts of New York the Friends were subject to the payment of tithes until the Revolution. In North Carolina they were

10

at times subjected to certain civil disabilities.
In 1746 a temporary law, made permanent the following year, exempted the Quakers from supporting
the state church in Massachusetts. (Jones, op.cit.
153-58, 227-28, 317-18, 350-53; Weeks, Stephen
Bureauguard, The Southern Quakers and Slavery
(Johns Hopkins Univ. Studies in History and
Political Science, extra v.15,(Baltimore, 1896).
161, 167-68; Ramsay, David, The History of South
Carolina, (2 vols., Charleston, 1809), v. 1, 2;
The American Revolution in New York, prepared by
the Division of Archives and History of the State
of New York (Albany, 1926), 243.

(16) For a full discusson of this controversy and its
effect on the Society of Friends in Pennsylvania
see: Boorstein, Daniel J., The Americans: The Colonial Experience (New York, 1858), 56-60; Bronner,
Edwin B., "The Quakers and Non-Violence in Pennsylvania," Pennsylvania History, v. 35 (1938), 1-
22; Crossfield, George, Memoirs of the Life and
Gospel Labors of Samuel Fothergill (Liverpool,
1843), 219, 232, 247, 255-56; and Jack D. Marietta
"Conscience, the Quaker Community, and the French
and Indian War," PMHB, v. 95 (1971), 3-27.

(17) Tolles, Frederick B., Meeting House and Counting
House, The Quaker Merchants of Colonial Philadelphia, 1682-1763 (Chapel Hill, 1948), 235-36. For a
full discussion of this development see "Reformation in the Society", ibid., 234-43.

(18) Marietta, Jack Donald, Ecclesiastical Discipline
in the Society of Friends, 1682-1776 (unpublished
Ph.D. thesis, Stanford Univ.,1965), 148-50.
Marietta also discusses the development of this
reform movement in his "Conscience, the Quaker
Community and the French and Indian War", loc.cit.
See also Richard Bauman's For the Reputation of
Truth (Balt., 1971), chap. 3. Rayner W. Kelsey
discusses the revised Book of Discipline of 1762
in "Early Disciplines of Philadelphia Yearly
Meeting", BFHA, v. 24 (1935), 20-23.

(19) Worrall, Arthur J., New England Quakerism, 1656-
1830 (unpublished Ph.D. thesis, Univ. of Michigan
1970), 56-8.

(20) N.Y.Y.M., Min., 1746-1800, sessions of 1760 and
1762, passim.

11

Chapter II

PROBLEMS OF EMPIRE

By the Treaty of Paris in 1763 Great Britain had vastly extended her trans-Atlantic domains. The acquisition of Canada and the trans-Appalachian regions inexorably thrust the problem of imperial administration before the attention of the Ministers at Whitehall. The urgency of the siutation was soon greatly accentuated by Pontiac's Indian uprising, prompted by discontent over the loss of French support coupled with suspicion as to British intentions. At one time the Indian attacks threatened to drive the British forces back to the coast. (1)

The British government now faced the task of providing an appropriate and durable imperial administration which would effectively combine the older colonies with the new acquisitions, regulate relations with the Indians, and provide a suitable defense against further Indian attacks. In order to achieve these goals, as well as to enhance the enforcement of existing trade regulations, the Ministry decided to expand the corps of imperial officials in America and to station a standing army of 10,000 troops at strategic points in the colonies for internal, defensive purposes. (1) Such a program would obviously be costly, an unwelcome prospect for the country already harnessed with the highest national debt in its history as a result of the late war. Without raising the current heavy incidence of taxation it would be impossible to finance the new undertakings. Therefore many government officials and many members of Parliament thought it was only fair that the colonies share this increased burden. So George Grenville, the new Chancellor of the Exchequer, decided to resort to direct taxation of the colonies. (3)

In adopting such a course of action, the Government failed to consider sufficiently the prevailing colonial situation and conditions. The political institutions and ideals of the colonies, as well as their commercial development, had become well established and self-sufficient to such a degree that any interference from the mother country was bound to

12

cause resentment and resistance. (4) The colonies re-
garded themselves as integral parts of the British
Empire and as loyal subjects of the Crown. But during
the colonial period a concept of their constitutional
relation to Great Britain had evolved which was quite
different from that entertained by most of the members
of the Government, and probably by most Englishmen.
This divergence was starkly revealed when the British
Parliament began to exert an authority over the colonies which it had not previously exercised.

During the period 1763 to 1775, increasing fric-
tion between the mother country and her colonies grew
to the point of conflagration. Certain colonies stood
out as leaders of radical action or moderation according to their particular economic interests, religious
configuaration, political philosophy, and the ethnic
composition of their population. The fact that Pennsylvania was the leader of the moderates was due in
large part to its Quaker inhabitants. Because of
their traditional participation in public affairs and
their dominant position in the mercantile life of the
province, the Friends were unavoidably involved in the
imperial dispute from the beginning.

Since the Quakers in Pennsylvania constituted the
largest and most influential section of the Society of
Friends in America, their advice and action gave the
cue for the conduct and attitudes of other colonial
Friends. In the other colonies the political role and
economic interests of the Quakers were not such as to
induce them to participate in resistance measures. The
chief concern of the Society in those areas was to preclude its members from taking part in such activities
as might compromise their religious testimonies. Not
until the event of warfare would those Friends face the
necessity of charting their particular courses of action according to their respective situations, and even
then they would look to the pronouncements of Philadelphia Yearly Meeting for guidance. Until the outbreak of war in 1775, therefore, the role of the
Friends in the colonies' reaction to British colonial
policy centers for the most part on the Pennsylvania
Quakers.

Despite the fact that most Friends in the Pennsylvania Assembly had surrendered their seats in 1756
at the time of the war with France and had refused to
serve as assemblymen until peace was restored, and
that the ties between Meeting House and State House

13

were no longer so close as in former times, the Quakers still considered themselves as the natural guardians of the interests of the province. The so-called "Quaker System" which was run on the basis of "an undenied prior authority in the realm of government" (5) operated through the Quaker Party. This political alignment, which by the later 60's consisted of the Quakers, many Anglicans and most of the Germans, together with other conservative elements, dominated the government until the end of the colonial period. (7) This conservative configuration desired to maintain the political and social status quo of the province.

A dominating fear of the conservatives, especially the Quakers and Anglicans, was that the Presbyterians, increasingly strong in the under-represented western counties, by combining with other anti-Quaker groups, would gain sufficient influence to foster fundamental changes in the policies traditionally maintained by the Friends and their allies. The Quakers had a religious aversion to the idea of Presbyterian domination in view of the harsh treatment Quaker missionaries had received in Massachusetts a century earlier and of the subsequent continuing struggle for religious freedom. These apprehensions had recently been intensified by the violent conduct of the Scotch Irish Paxton boys who marched on Philadelphia in 1764. On their way east they had massacred a group of Christianized Indians at Conestoga and had threatened similar action against other Indians in the environs of Philadelphia. (8)

This antipathy and fear was one of the chief reasons for Franklin's efforts in the 1760's to have Pennsylvania converted into a royal province. Thomas Wharton clearly voiced these feelings when he said that the "natural increase of the Presbyterians and the vast number yearly arriving among us" made it imperative to seek royal government to escape a Presbyterian domination. (9)

Early in 1765, John Reynell, a leading Philadelphia Quaker merchant, indicated the Quaker attitude even more forcefully in a letter to his English correspondent, James Shirley, to whom he declared that if the Pennsylvania Calvinists gained the upper hand, religious freedom might well disappear in Pennsylvania and the Friends suffer persecution again. (10)

The emergence of the current imperial problem had

14

a profound effect on this situation. The Scotch-Irish in the western counties harbored anti-British sentiments because of their inherited mistrust of the British government. (11) The fact that this back-country population was under-represented in the Assembly, lacked adequate roads, and felt it lacked adequate protection against the Indians, laid the basis for a growing discontent. Eventually the sentiments and feelings of these inhabitants of the back-country led them to cooperate with other elements in the province who came to resent the political monopoly of those in power and who joined in the growing opposition to the actions of the British government. The leadership of this revolutionary movement was largely Presbyterian. (12)

The rapid economic growth of Pennsylvania had much to do with the rise of a powerful socio-economic class in the colony. By 1760 Philadelphia was the leading commercial center of the colonies and was firmly under the control of a merchant aristocracy, largely dominated by well-to-do Quaker families. (13) The economic interests of many leading Philadelphia Quakers were dependent on their participation in the mercantile life of the British Empire. On the one hand, as merchants they would oppose imperial policies bearing unfavorably on trade, while on the other, they would be strongly conservative with regard to any movement affecting the constitutional status quo of the province.

Such firms as James and Drinker, Reynell and Coates, the Pembertons, Stephen Collins, and Thomas Clifford maintained close contacts with Quaker merchants in London who dominated the trade with North America. Prominent English Quakers in this category were David Barclay, Daniel Mildred, Hinton Brown and Capel Hanbury, all of whom were members of the London Meeting for Sufferings. (14) Religion and commerce afforded strong bonds of common interest between British and American Friends, thereby reinforcing the aversion of American Quakers to any idea of armed conflict with, or separation from, Britain. By the same token, the London Quakers sympathized more deeply with the colonists than did many of their compatriots. This close relationship afforded an excellent basis for concerted action and cooperation in efforts to induce the British government to change its colonial policies on the one side, and on the other, to urge the Americans to modify the virulence of their oppos-

15

ition./

/Thus fear of internal revolution, economic interests, a religious testimony against violence and war,
as well as close ties with the British Quaker community
combined to render the American Friends persistent
opponents of a break between the colonies and the
mother country/ Consequently they exerted themselves
vigorously whenever possible to promote a peaceful solution to the imperial dispute.

Soon after the inauguration of the new British
colonial policy, opposition was voiced by two prominent Friends, Stephen Hopkins, governor of Rhode Island
and Dr. John Fothergill, a prominent Quaker physician
in London. Even before becoming governor in 1764,
Hopkins had published "An Essay on the Trade of the
North American Colonies" in the Providence Gazette.
Its purpose was to show the economic damage which
would ensue to Rhode Island by the newly instituted
procedures for the enforcement of the regulations governing the importation of molasses and sugar from
freign sources. (15)

When rumors reached American in November 1764 that
Parliament was considering levying a stamp duty in the
colonies, the Rhode Islanders took early action. Governor Hopkins drafted a statement on the constitutional
aspects of the proposed legislation, published under
the title The Rights of the Colonies Examined. (16)
In his argument Hopkins rejected the authority of
Parliament not only to tax the colonies but even to
legislate for the colonies in any way, except as such
acts were passed for the general good of the whole
empire. (17)

Meanwhile the Rhode Island Assembly prepared a
petition to the King, expressing alarm over the proposed stamp tax, and despatched Hopkin's statement to
the colony's agent in London, instructing him to have
it printed and circulated to the other colonial agents
if it should "be advantageous to the colonies." (18)
It was published in England under the title The Grievances of the American Colonies Candidly Examined and
was presented to Lord Dartmouth, then president of the
Lords Commissioners of Trade and Plantations. (19)

In the succeeding years Hopkins played a prominent
role in the opposition to British policy. He was a
leading spirit in the establishment of the Sons of Lib-

16

erty in Providence, and he was chairman of the Rhode Island Committee of Correspondence. James Otis and Samuel Adams were his close correspondants, and his writings in behalf of the colonies appeared frequently in the columns of the Providence Gazette. (20)

The passage of the Stamp Act in the spring of 1765 also prompted Dr. Fothergill to take up his pen in behalf of the colonies. (21) The support which he and other leading English Quakers gave to the colonial cause reflected in part the attitude of many Englishmen toward the glaring deficiencies in the existing mode of Parliamentary representation. Leaders in the industrial revolution and prominent members of the merchant class in England were calling for reform of a system which left many localities and large sections of the British population unrepresented and which put all effective power in the hands of the land-owning classes. In their opinion, representation in the legislature of the kingdom was the basis of constitutional liberty and all legitimate government. Without it government was nothing but usurpation. (22)

It was this system with its deeply entrenced corruption which George III and his ministers subsequently employed to gain control of Parliament and thereby assure the implementation of their proposals to deal with colonial problems. Liberal minded Englishmen sensed the implications of this situation, and many of them despaired for the future of liberty in England. On the eve of the American Revolution, the belief that England was on the brink of disaster was entrenced in the minds of many on both sides of the Atlantic. As a result, associations were formed in London and other parts of the kingdon to promote the cause of reform. (23)

In August 1765 when the controversey over the Stamp Act was at fever heat, Dr. Fothergill wrote to his friend Lord Dartmouth at the Board of Trade, pleading the cause of the colonies. He proposed that commissioners be sent to America to confer with representatives of the colonies on the current problems. He argued that if the colonies did "aspire to Independency" as had been asserted, making it their interest to obey would avoid such an event, while attempts to teach obedience might well make them "wish for such a situation". (24)

Somewhat later he sent Dartmouth a copy of his Considerations Relative to the North American Colonies

17

in which he declared:

> A British Parliament has certainly
> Power to do many things which they have
> no Right to do. They have the Power to
> enact what Laws they think fit, res-
> pecting any Part of the Brittish Sub-
> jects; but still it is to be remembered,
> that Reason is the supreme Law, and any
> thing inconsistent with it, is void in
> itself. (25)

Distance precluded the Americans from being represented
in Parliament; and subjecting them to laws in whose
making they had no voice struck at the root of the
Constitution.

Fothergill fully realized that one of the chief
reasons for the general British attitude toward the
colonies was ignorance about them."How many People
are there," he queried, "and those too of no small
Figure, who know no Difference between the Inhabitants
of North America, and those of the West India Islands?" (26) As one remedy for this deficiency he
proposed a plan to grant scholarships to Americans to
attend the British universities, the government granting free passage on the King's ships for those going
to England to study. The result of such a policy, he
argued, would be to unite the two parts of the Empire
more firmly.

> The Americans, by mixing with our Youth
> at the University, will diffuse a Spirit
> of Enquiry after America, and its affairs;
> they will cement Friendships on both Sides,
> which will be of more lasting Benefit
> to both Countries, than all the Armies
> that Britain can send thither. (27)

In Fothergill's opinion, there were three possible
lines of action for the British Government; to enforce,
suspend, or repeal the Stamp Act. If the first course
were adopted, the result would be bloodshed and the
King would lose the affection of the colonists. Implementation of the second alternative would seem
like holding a yoke of disgrace over them and would
lead to quicker strides toward independence. The last
recommendation, repeal of the act, was the only means
of convincing the Americans of the equity and moderation of the Administration, and of dispelling their
suspicions of "design against their freedom, privel-

18

eges or interests". (28)

An English Quaker merchant, Thomas Crowley, also espoused the American cause. In letters to the press and to Ministers in the Government such as Grenville, Bute, and the Marquis of Rockingham early in 1766, he insisted that the colonists had the right as Englishmen to be consulted when taxes were levied upon them. Rather than punishing them for protesting, the government should remedy their grievances. He proposed that the Stamp Act be suspended for three years. In the meantime each colony should be invited to send from one to five representatives, according to population, to sit in Parliament where they could plead their cause. (29) Sitting in such a manner, Parliament could either repeal or reinstitute the Stamp Act. Under this plan the colonies would retain all power over internal affairs, while Parliament, when composed of representatives from both Great Britain and the Dominions, would legislate on imperial matters such as defence.

In February 1766, Crowley published "The Controversy between Great Britain and her Colonies briefly Analyzed" under the pseudonym Amor Patriae. His thesis was that the colonies did not have virtual representation in Parliament, as did the large mass of non-voting Englishmen, since those who made the laws for the colonies were not themselves subject to them. Thus there was no defense against arbitrary, exhorbitant and unfair taxation which could take away "a quarter, a half, or a larger part of their estates". (30)

The Americans viewed the passage of the Stamp Act as the culmination of a new British policy of trade regulation which had been operating to their detriment for over a year. (31) In September 1765, the Pennsylvania Assembly of which the Speaker, Isaas Norris, and almost one-third of the membership were Quakers, passed a set of resolves maintaining the indisputable privelege of British subjects to be taxed only by their own consent, and claiming that the only legal representatives of the province were the annually elected assemblymen. (32) In October, representatives from most of the colonies met at the Stamp Act Congress in New York and sent addresses to both Houses of Parliament and the King, stating the colonial position. (33) Opposition to the act soon erupted in riots and tumults in many parts of the colonies, and in Boston this resulted in the destruction of Lieutenant Governor Hutchinson's home. In Philadelphia, threats to deal like-

19

wise with the official stamp consignee, John Hughes,
induced him to promise not to execute his duties unless
other colonial agents did do. (34)

The reaction of Friends to the Stamp Act controversy was somewhat varied. Many joined Thomas Clifford
in supporting the constitutional protests of the colonists. At the time of the Stamp Act Congress, Clifford
denounced the refusal of Parliament to receive the
American petitions for a change in policy, declaring
it was inconsistent with the tradition of the British
Constitution to condemn men unheard. (35) The day on
which the Stamp Act went into effect he declared to
some English correspondents: "America is doing all
they can to avert this heavy blow at Liberty." (36)

Meanwhile, the official bodies of the Friends were
concerned lest some of their members become involved in
the protest actions in a manner contrary to their religious testimonies. At its sessions in September 1765
Philadelphia Yearly Meeting addressed an epistle to the
New England Friends which cautioned:

> ...as many of these Provinces seem
> filled with rumors, noises, & confusion
> from without, on the account of Human
> policy and affairs of Government, which
> shows the fluctuating and unstable
> situation of minds principally intent
> on the concerns of this world, may we be
> watchful to keep out of those things...(37)

Throughout the tumult occasioned by the Stamp Act
affair, merchants both in England and America, especially those involved in the North American trade, exerted their best efforts to obtain the repeal of the
act. Since the goal of the commercial classes was to
persuade the mother country to comply with the colonial
objections through peaceful means, many Friends considered such a procedure justifiable and proper and not in
conflict with their religious tenets.

Six days after the Stamp Act went into effect, the
merchants of Philadelphia met and concluded a non-importation agreement. (38) Over eighty Friends signed,
of whom eight were members of the Philadelphia Meeting
for Sufferings. (39) The merchants also appointed a
committee of eleven, including six Friends, to obtain
subscriptions and to oversee the enforcement of the
terms of the agreement. (40) It was this committee

20

which addressed a memorial to the London merchants soliciting their interposition with Parliament for the removal of the burdens and restructions imposed by the late act. (41) In drafting the memorial the Quaker committee members used their influence to temper its language, while most of the other members were so violent "that it required patience & steadiness to persuade them to accept it" in its final moderated form.(42)

In response to this appeal the Londoners, spurred on by the English Quaker merchants, took action. Among the most influential merchants were David Barclay, Daniel Mildred, and Capel Hanbury, all of them close collaborators with Franklin. A committee of the London merchants, on which Barclay and Mildred represented the merchants trading with Philadelphia, intervened with the Administration to obtain the repeal of the Stamp Act. It solicited the support of several Ministers and others in the Government, and received assurances of their assistance in this effort. Circular letters were also sent to the merchants and manufacturers in all parts of the kingdom, requesting their support.(43)

Capel Hanbury, the leading merchant in the colonial tobacco trade, was instrumental in obtaining the support of the Merchants Venturers of Bristol who controlled the election of two members of Parliament. Hanbury's cousin, William Neave, Master of the Merchants Venturers in 1765-1766, was sent to London to present a petition to Parliament. Neave worked closely with Hanbury in interviewing personally members of Parliament to obtain the repeal of the act. (44) In the course of the Parliamentary debates on the repeal proposal, Hanbury was examined for two hours before the bar of the House of Commons and David Barclay was questioned for a shorter period. "All came off with reputation," Dr. Fothergill later wrote to James Pemberton. (45)

The chief concern of the American Quakers at this time was that the disorders accompanying opposition to the Stamp Act would more likely bring reprisal than repeal. James Pemberton feared that unless some expedients were soon found, the colonists would unavoidably be reduced to confusion and distress. He wrote Dr. Fothergill that he hoped nothing had been done in Pennsylvania and West Jersey for which their inhabitants would "share in the censures to which these riotous proceedings deservedly expose the perpretators of them..." (46) As for the Stamp Act Congress, he placed

21

little reliance on its proceedings since it had "not been conducted w^t that Concord and unanimity wch the Occasion required." (47)

To enlist the support of Friends in behalf of restraint, the Meeting for Sufferings in Philadelphia issued a letter of advice to the constituent meetings in February 1765, copies of which were sent to Friends in other provinces. (48) This urged all members to act according to "the Practice and advice of faithful Friends in all times of tryal and Difficulty, Particularly of our Honourable and faithful Elder George Fox who in an Epistle to Friends in the year 1685 thus Expresseth himself 'whatever bustling & Troubles or Tumults or outrages Should rise in the World' keep out of them..." (49)

The effort of the Pennsylvania Quakers to restrain the protest actions of their fellow subjects had some success. Whatever incidents occurred were blamed on the Presbyterians. According to General Gage, that sect was "as ripe for outrage as they can be, but the contrary Party composed of Quakers and their Friends, tho' complaining of the hardship of the Stamp Act, have been for complying with the Law; And have found Means to keep Peace and Tranquility..." (50) The Philadelphia Friends confirmed to the English Quakers that the relative freedom from riots and tumults in Pennsylvania and New Jersey as compared with their northern neighbors was largely due to the Quaker influence. (51)

The Quakers in England, were meanwhile watching closely the proceedings of Parliament. Late in February 1766, Mildred and Roberts informed John Reynell that they had been "wholly employ'd attending Parliament" and that a bill had been brought in for repeal of the Stamp Act. (52) Thomas Crowley wrote Israel Pemberton that the House of Commons had passed the repealing act and that similar action was expected in the House of Lords. He hoped that this outcome would remove every appearance of discord between the two parts of the King's dominions, and that they would be joined in "indissoluble Bonds of Union by a just & equitable representation for the Americans in the Parliament of Great Brittain..." (53) He suggested that informing the newspapers on the status of repeal might "work for the public welfare".

In view of the violent tone of the colonial protests against the Stamp Act, Dr. Fothergill was con-

22

cerned about possible disorderly and disrespectful celebrations on its repeal. He complained that nothing had created such difficulty for the friends of America in Britain, and furnished their opponents with so many arguments against them, as did the tumultuous behavior of persons of all ranks in the colonies. He further voiced the apprehension that:

> If the people of America give the loose
> to intemperate Joy, the Parliament will
> doubtless consider it as a triumph on
> your part, and if an ensuing session act
> according to such an opinion, and which
> they most certainly will if your opponents
> come into power, what then becomes of
> the publick safety, mutual security,
> and the common good...(54)

Fothergill urged James Pemberton that if the Pennsylvania Assembly were in session when this letter arrived it should act at once to acknowledge the gracious action of the mother country and that such action should strictly avoid discrimination between America's friends or enemies in England. William Pitt should not be crowned King of America for his support of the colonies nor should George Grenville be "hanged in effigy at every town's end." He stressed that "the M of Rockingham, Secretary Conway, and all the active part of the administration deserve your grateful acknowledgements," which should however, be given with discretion and not at the expense of opponents. Subsequently Fothergill also advised the Americans with regard to the Declaratory Act which accompanied the repeal of the Stamp Act and which asserted the supreme authority of Parliament to legislate in all cases whatsoever. He urged them to take notice of it but to "suffer it to die away in the obscurity it deserves". (56) Mildred and Roberts wrote in a similar vein to John Reynell. (57)

In compliance with Fothergill's suggestion, Pemberton imparted the most important parts of the letter to the principal magistrates of Philadelphia and such other persons as would have some influence with the people in general. The printers were persuaded "to avoid murmuring, or inflammatory publications," and to publish an extract of the letter. (58) Pemberton also submitted the letter to the governor of New Jersey, who agreed that the publication of certain sections might have a good effect. (59) Thus he was able to inform Dr. Fothergill that before the news of the repeal act

23

reached America "a favorable opportunity was had of preparing the minds of the people, to keep their demonstrations of joy within bounds..." (60)

As the day for public rejoicing approached, several prominent Friends visited the chief magistrates of Philadelphia and solicited their help in inducing a moderate popular behavior. Although the officials felt the public would be discontented with a total prohibition of such a celebration, they promised to exert themselves in preserving the peace. These efforts seem to have been successful since "no tumults were raised, or violence Committed on those who would not join therein... (61) Subsequently the London Meeting for Sufferings expressed its approbation that the Friends in Pennsylvania and New Jersey had acted "so consistent a part in the late trying & disturbed Situation of Affairs", and it commended them on their instrumentality in restraining the behavior of others. (62)

Quaker influence also modified the actions of the Pennsylvania Assembly. James Pemberton, who had accepted nomination for assemblyman only after consultation with several friends, and only with the intention of representing the interests and viewpoint of the Friends, was now a member. (63) Early in June 1766, the Assembly appointed a committee of fourteen, of whom six were Friends, including Pemberton, to frame addresses of thanks to the King and Parliament for the repeal of the Stamp Act. Dr. Fothergill had already advised Pemberton that if the Assembly took such action, it should address the King only, since many in Parliament had opposed repeal. Moreover, the King was the head of the empire, and an address to him would reflect credit on the friends of the colonies in England. (65) As a result the committee only proposed an address to the King for the Assembly's approval, and the Council took similar action. (66) Subsequently the Assembly passed a resolution which proclaimed its loyalty to the crown and which declared that whenever the province was called upon for aid in a constitutional manner, it would consider it an indispensable duty to grant such sums as the safety of the colonies required and the ability of the province allowed. (67)

In a final letter to Pemberton toward the end of the year Fothergill insisted that credit for the outcome of the controversy was due not so much to Lord Chatham as to "the steadiness of the late administration, under providence and to a few (other) individuals here..." He complained that the colonists overlooked those who had actually served them and were "erecting statues to a man, who however he may deserve it on other occasions" had less merit in this matter than they imagined. (68)

(1) Morgan, Edmund S., and Helen M., The Stamp Act
      Crisis (Chapel Hill, 1953), 21-23.
(2) Alvord, Clarence V., The Mississippi Valley in
      British Politics (2 vols., Cleveland, 1917), v.1,
      chap. 6; Beer, George Louis, British Colonial
      Policy, 1754-1765 (New York, 1907), chap. 9.
(3) Van Tyne, Claude H., The Causes of the War of
      Independence(New York,1922),138-139;see also
      Gipson, Lawrence Henry, The Coming of the
      Revolution, 1773-1775 (New York, 1854), chap. 5.
(4) Van Tyne, op.cit., chap. 2 gives a good brief dis-
      cussion of the institutional and political condi-
      tions of the colonies in 1763. For the commercial
      aspect of the situation see Gipson, op.cit.,
      chap. 2.
(5) In its annual epistle to the London Friends in
      1764, the Philadephia Yearly Meeting indicated its
      divorce from any official participation in the
      affairs of government, declaring that its endeav-
      ors had "not yet been so effectual as to prevent
      a number of our profession from accepting seats in
      the House of Assembly" and that the Friends had
      avoided every occasion which might give grounds
      to be charged with "a connection with them."
      (Phil.Y.M.,Min., v.3, 203-205.
(6) Pole, J.R., Political Representation in England
      and the Origins of the American Republic (Berkley,
      1971), 122.
(7) Lincoln, Charles H., The Revolutionary Movement in
      Pennsylvania (Publications of the Univ. of Penn-
      sylvania, Series in History,No.1,Philadelphia,1901),
      25 n. For some decades there had been a Quaker
      Party but whereas in the 1740's the stress had
      been a Quaker Party but whereas in the 1740's the
      stress had been on Quaker, in 1765 it was on
      Party. (Rotherman, Dietmar, The Layman's Progress.
      Religious and Political Experience in Colonial
      Pennsylvania, 1740-1770(Philadelphia,1961),130.
(8) Fisher, Sydney George, Pennsylvania: Colony and
      Commonwealth(Philadelphia,1897),248;Wellenreuter,
      Hermann, Glaube und Politik in Pennsylvania 1681-
      1776 (Koeln, 1972), 374, 385.
(9) Cited in Thayer, Theodore George, Pennsylvania
      Politics and the Growth of Democracy 1740-1776
      (Harrisburg, 1953), 104. See James H. Huston's
      Pennsylvania Politics 1746-1770(Princeton, 1972)
      for an extensive discussion of this effort and its
      repercussions on Pennsylvania politics. In a note

to Lord Hyde, Secretary of State, Franklin's friend Peter Collinson wrote:

> I presume my dear Lord is no stranger to the commotions in which the riotous Presbyterians by illicit acts and contrivances have jockeyed out of the Assembly my ingenious friend, Mr. Franklin...They have still the Oliverian spirit, I find, in them, and if ever a revolution is attempted to set themselves up independent of their Mother Country, it will arise from the prevailing Presbyterian faction."
> (Peter Collinson to Lord Hyde, Nov. 11, 1764, cited in Brett-James, Norman G., The Life of Peter Collinson (London, 1926), 183-84.

(10) John Reynell to James Shirley, May 14, 1765, quoted in Carol Leroy Romanek's, John Reynell, Quaker Merchant of Philadelphia, (unpublished Ph.D. thesis, State Univ. of Pennsylvania, 1969), 139. Evidence of this feeling is also seen in James Pemberton's remarks to the London Quaker Dr. John Fothergill on the conduct of the New Englanders in the Stamp Act affair:

> ...the public papers so fully demonstrate the disposition of the people in the Eastern provinces that it requires no particular remarks further than that we have reason to apprehend the same temper & principles must Under the administration of Government in Such hands be very oppressive and dangerous...

(James Pemberton to Dr. Fothergill, March 1, 1766, in the Pemberton Papers at HSP, v. 34, 140.)

In reply Dr. Fothergill queried:

> By what means can the increase of P.b.y.n. power in America be most effectually checked consistently with the liberty of conscience and the genious of Brittish freedom: I see that sometime America will be P.b.t.n. a persuasion altogether intolerant, and I would wish to retard it, as long as possible.

27

(Dr. Fothergill to James Pemberton, May 10, 1766,
Etting Pemberton **Pap.**,v.2,54, at HSP.

(11) Lincoln, op.cit.,33.

(12) Hawke, David, The Colonial Experience (Indianapolis, 1966), 506; Nelson, Russel Gage, Back-
country of Pennsylvania 1709-1774, The Ideals
of William Penn in Action (unpublished Ph.D.
thesis, Univ. of Wisconsin, 1968), 210-11,214,318.

(13) Schlesinger, Arthur M., The Colonial Merchants in
the American Revolution (Columbia Univ. Studies
in History, Economics and Public Law, v. 78,
no. 182, New York, 1918), 27-28. See Carl and
Jessie Bridenbaugh's Rebels and Gentlemen (New
York, 1942), 179-184 for a discussion of the rise
of this class in colonial Philadelphia.

(14) London M.f.S., Min., v.32, 31-34, passim.

(15) Lovejoy, David S., Rhode Island Politics and the
American Revolution 1760-1776 (Providence, 1958),
31-2.

(16) Ibid., 73. The statement is printed in full in
Rhode Island Colonial Records (v. 1-7 of Records
of the Colony (and State) of Rhode Island and
Providence Plantations, 1636-1792, ed. John
Russell Bartlett, 10 vols., Providence, 1856-
1865), v. 6, 416-427. Also see Lovejoy, op.cit.,
chap. 4. Hopkins'views doubtless reflected the
economic and political thinking of an important
group of Rhode Island and New England merchants
and politicians rather than his religious convictions.

(17) The publication of The Rights of the Colonies
Examined provoked an extended controversy with
Morton Howard, Jr. of Newport who upheld the full
authority of Parliament over the colonies. It
was then that Hopkins retreated from his original
extreme position and merely denied the power of
Parliament to tax the colonies, probably because
he did not wish to arouse the rancour of the
British government. (Lovejoy, op.cit.,77-8.)

(18) R.I.Col. Rec., v.6, 412-13.

(19) Pannell, Political and Economic Relations of
English and American Quakers, 244. Hopkins,
Stephen, The Grievances of the American Colonies
Candidly Examined (London, 1766).

(20) Foster, William E., Stephen Hopkins (Rhode Island
Historical Tracts, No. 10, Providence, 1874), 44-5
48, 49n., 51, 56-7, 72. Hopkins was disowned by
the Friends in 1773 for owning a slave.

(21) Dr. John Fothergill was a member of the Royal
Society as well as physician to and friend of

several members of Parliament and the Cabinet,
among them Lord Dartmouth, at various times
Secretary of the Board of Trade and a Secretary
of State for the Colonies. He was also for many
years a leading member of the London Meeting for
Sufferings and served at times as its clerk. In a
letter to James Pemberton he explains his interests in America as follows:

> For my own part, Having from my infancy
> been attentive to America more than others-
> the several visits of my Father to that
> extensive country, of my brother, of my
> most valued Friends – the Acquaintance I
> have had with some of the most sensible,
> intelligent, judicious persons in all
> provinces – a forty years correspondence
> with persons in that country of every party,
> denomination, province and situation – I
> cannot give up, on slight grounds the
> opinions I have formed of them, of their
> rights and of their power likewise. (Dr.

John Fothergill to James Pemberton, Nov.3,1775,
Pem.Pap., v. 34,170).

(22) Price, Richard, A Discussion on the Love of Our
Country (London, 1879), 39.
(23) Ibid., 41.
(24) Dr. John Fothergill to Lord Dartmouth, Aug.29,
1765, Chain of Friendship, 248-49.
(25) Fothergill, Dr. John, Considerations Relative to
the North American Colonies (London, 1765), 16.
(26) Ibid., 35-6.
(27) Ibid., 48.
(28) Ibid., 45.
(29) Crowley, Thomas, Letters and Dissertations on
Various Subjects by the Author of the Letter
Analysis A.P. on the Dispute between Great Britain
and America (London, 1776), 7-15. In 1774 Crowley
was disowned for supporting the payment of tithes
for the support of the Church of England. (Devonshire House M.M., Min., Aug. 4, 1773; Feb.9,1774.)
(30) Crowley, op.cit., 16-18.
(31) The letters of a number of the Philadelphia Quaker
merchants indicate that they were opposed not only
to the Stamp Act, but also to several preceeding
ones such as the Sugar and Colonial Currency Acts
of 1764. See James Pemberton to Dr. John Fothergill, Dec.17,1765, Pem. Pap.,v.24,137; Thomas
Clifford to Thomas Pennington, Nov.23,1765,
Thomas Clifford Letter Book 1759-1766; and same to

Hide and Hamilton, Nov.23,1765, in _ibid_.

(32) Almon J., _A Collection of Papers, relative to the Dispute between Great Britain and America_ (London 1777), 21. The Friends in the Assembly were Isaac Norris the Speaker, Joshua Ash, George Ashbridge, John Fairlamb, Samuel Foulke, John Jacobs, John Norton, Isaac Pearson, Nathaniel Pennock and William Rodman. (The members are listed in _Votes and Proceedings of the House of Representatives of the Province of Pennsylvania, 1683-1776_ (6 vols., Philadelphia, 1775-1776), v.5, 373. Foulke, Jacobs, Pearson, Pennock and Rodman were later disowned for participating in the Revolution. (Darby M.M., Min., 1763-1783, 214-18; Middletown M.M., Min., 1755-1800, 403; Newgarden M.M., Min., 1768-1778, 340, 344; Richland M.M., Min., 1767-1786, 12/16/1779, 5/18/1780; Uwchlan M.M., Min., 1776-1795, 10,14.)

(33) Gipson, _op.cit._, 98-100.

(34) Morgan and Morgan, _op.cit._,127,248,252.

(35) Thomas Clifford to Harper & Hartshorne, Oct.8,1765 Letter Book, _lcc.cit._

(36) Same to same, Nov.1,1765, in _ibid_, _loc.cit._

(37) Phil.Y.M. to N.E.Y.M., Sept.,1765, in the South Kingston Papers in the N.E.Y.M. records at the Rhode Island Hist.Soc., Providence.

(38) Schlesinger, _op.cit._,79;Pa. Jnl., Nov.14,1765; John Reynell to Mildred and Roberts, Nov.8,1765, Letter Book, 1762-1767.

(39) As far as can be determined those who were Friends were: John Armitt, David Bacon, Joseph Baker, John Baldun, Isaac and Moses Bartram, John Bell, David Beveridge, Clement and Owen Biddle, Elijah Brown, Samuel Bunting, Thomas Clifford, Stephen Collins, John Cox, Benjamin Davies, David Deshler, John Drinker,Jr., James Eddy, George Emlen, Jr., Samuel Fisher, William and Joshua Fisher, Hugh Forbes, William Stores Fry, Marcy Gray, Reuben Haines, James Hatley, John Head, Benjamin Hooton, Peter Howard, John Ladd Howell, Samuel Howell, Richard Humphreys, Caleb and Owen Jones, Benjamin Kendall, Thomas Lawrence, Thomas Lightfoot, William Lloyd, Benjamin and Christopher Marshall, Samuel Meridith Jonathan and Thomas Mifflin, Abraham Mitchell, Cadwalader and Samuel C. Morris, Samuel Morris,Jr. John and Samuel Morton, Richard Parker, Isaac Pachall, Israel and James Pemberton, Samuel Pleasants, David Potts, John Reynell, Francis Richardson,Jr., Joseph Richardson, Hugh and George Roberts, Thomas Robinson, Jacob Shoemaker, Jr.,

Samuel Smith, Richard Stevens, Benjamin Swett,Jr.,
Peter Thomson, Joseph Trotter, Robert Waln,
Jeremiah Warder, Thomas and William West, James,
John, Joseph and Thomas Wharton, James White,
Daniel Williams, William Wilson, Daniel Wister,
and Jonathan Zane. A complete list of the signers
is given in J. Thomas Scharf and Thompson Westcott's History of Philadelphia (2 vols., Philadelphia, 1884), v.1,412-413.

Twenty-two of these Friends were disowned for
various reasons connected with the Revolution:
Moses Bartram, Clement and Owen Biddle, John Cox,
William Fisher, Jr., Reuben Haines, Samuel
Howell,Jr., Richard Humphreys, Benjamin Marshall,
Jonathan Mifflin,Jr., Samuel Cadwalader Morris,
Samuel Morris,Jr., George Roberts, Thomas
Robinson, Jacob Shoemaker,Jr., Peter Thomson,
Joseph Trotter, James, John, and Joseph Wharton,
James White and Jonathan Zane. (Phil.M.M., Min.,
1771-1777,331-393;passim;ibid.,1777-1782,175-302;
passim;ibid., 1782-1789,12,87,88;Phil.M.M.No.Dist.,
Min.,1772-1781, 166-482,passim;Phil.M.M.So.Dist.,
Min.,1770-1780,113-155,passim.

Those who were members of the Meeting for
Sufferings during part or all of the decade 1765-
1775 were: David Bacon, Benjamin Hooton, Owen
Jones, Thomas Lightfoot, Israel and James Pemberton,
John Reynell, and Hugh Roberts. Israel Pemberton
served as clerk of the meeting in 1767, James in
1766,1770-1771,1774-1775, and their brother John
in the remaining years.

(40) They were Samuel Mifflin, Samuel Howell, Samuel
Wharton, John Fisher, Joshua Fisher, and Abel
James. (Pa. Gaz., Nov.14,1765;Pa.Jnl.,Nov.14,1765.)

(41) Schlesinger, op.cit., 79;James Pemberton to
Henton Brown and Dr. Fothergill, Dec. 17,1765, Pem.
Pap., v.34,37.

(42) James Pemberton to Dr. Fothergill, Dec. 18,1765,
Pem.Pap.,v.34,138.

(43) Mildred and Roberts to John Reynell, Dec. 12,
1765, Coates Reynell Pap., bx. 13(1766-1767).

(44) See Pannell, op.cit., 245-250 for an extensive
account of the involvement of the British Quaker
merchants in behalf of the colonies. Chapter 2
entitled "The Machinery of Political Influence",
describes the efficient lobbying system which the
British Quakers employed in dealing with Parlia-

ment.

(45) Dr. Fothergill to James Pemberton, April 25,1766,
     Ett. Pem. Pap., v.2, 51.
(46) James Pemberton to Dr. Fothergill,Dec.18,1765,
     loc.cit.
(47) Ibid.
(48) There is a copy of this epistle in the So. Kings-
     ton Pap.
(49) Phil. M.f.S., Min., v.1., 262.
(50) General Thomas Gage to Secretary Conway, Jan.1,
     1766, The Correspondence of Thomas Gage (ed.
     Clarance Edwin Carter, 2 vols., New Haven, 1931-
     1933), v.1,82-83.
(51) Phil.M.f.S. to London M.f.S., Feb.20,1766, Phil.
     M.f.S., Min., v.1, 261.
(52) Mildred and Roberts to John Reynell, Feb.27, 1766,
     Coates Reynell Pap., loc.cit.
(53) Thomas Crowley to Israel Pemberton, Feb.24,1766,
     Pem.Pap.,v.18, 102.
(54) Dr. Fothergill to James Pemberton, Feb.25,1766,
     Ett.Pem.,Pap.,v.2, 51.
(55) Ibid.
(56) Dr. Fothergill to James Pemberton, April 8,1766,
     Ett.Pem.Pap., v.2, 53.
(57) Mildred and Roberts to John Reynell, May 10, 1766,
     Coates Reynell Pap., loc.cit.
(58) James Pemberton to Dr. Fothergill, June 7,1766,
     Pem.Pap., v.34, 144. Extracts were published in
     both the Pa. Gaz.and the Pa. Jnl. on May 8,1766.
(59) The Governor of New Jersey to John Smith, May 3,
     1766, Pem.Pap., v.8, 130; John Smith to James
     Pemberton, May 4, 1766, in ibid., 130.
(60) James Pemberton to Dr. Fothergill, June 7, 1766,
     loc.cit.
(61) Ibid.; Gordon, Thomas F., The History of Penn-
     sylvania (Philadelphia, 1829), 444; Pa. Gaz.,
     May 22, 1766.
(62) London M.f.S. to Phil.M.f.S., Aug. 22, 1766,
     Phil. M.f.S., Misc.Pap.,box.13 (1766-1773).
(63) James Pemberton to Dr. Fothergill, Dec.18,1766,
     loc.cit.
(64) Votes and Preceedings of the House of Representa-
     tives of the Province of Pennsylvania 1683-1776
     (Pennsylvania Archives, 8th Ser.,ed. Charles F.
     Hoban and Gertrude Mckiney, 8 vols., Harrisburg
     1931-1935, v.7) 5880,5882.
(65) Dr. Fothergill to James Pemberton, April 4, 1766,
     Ett.Pem.Pap., v.2, 53. Extracts of this letter
     were published in the Pa. Gaz., June 19, 1766.
(66) Minutes of the Provincial Council,1762-1771

(Colonial Records of Pennsylvania, 1683-1790 ,
16 vols., Phil., 1852, v.9), 313-16.
(67) Votes and Proc.Pa. Arch., 8th Ser., v.7, 5885.
(68) Dr. Fothergill to James Pemberton, Sept.30,1766,
Ett.Pem.Pap., v.2, 55. A statue of Lord Chatham
still stands in Charleston, S.C. erected by the
citizens of the city at that time.

Chapter III

THE QUAKERS TAKE ALARM

Relative peace and tranquility reigned in the relations between England and America for a time, but
the pressing need for more money to finance the expenses of empire still remained. In the fall of 1767,
Charles Townsend, Chancellor of the Exchequer, secured
the passage of new enactments to raise revenue, this
time from colonial trade. These laws provided for the
levy of import duties on certain goods such as glass,
paint, lead, and tea on their arrival at colonial
ports. (1) Although the acts complied with the colonial protest against taxes levied internally in the colonies, such as the stamp tax, and instead called for
duties to be paid externally on goods in imperial commerce, the Americans were not slow in sensing their implication. Resistance was thus inevitable and the
Quaker merchants could not escape involvement.

Coincidentally with the outbreak of the imperial
controversy, a struggle was in progress in Pennsylvania
between the proprietary party lead by John Dickinson
and the anti-proprietary or Quaker party headed by
Joseph Galloway. The Quakers had for some time been
disillusioned with the policies of the proprietors and
their adherents in the government of the colony. This
situation was in large measure due to the fact that
Penn's descendents were no longer Friends and had no
interest in the ideals of the founder. They rather
viewed the province solely as a source of income. This
was one of the reasons why some of the leading Quakers
had supported Franklin's earlier proposal to transfer
the province to crown control. The struggle between
these two groups was most obvious in the legislature
where the proprietary supporters controlled the Council
and the Quaker party the Assembly.

One of the more ardent opponents of the proprietary party was Thomas Wharton, a Quaker merchant who was
also deeply interested in western land schemes. He had
already established a company for the implementation of
such plans and was doubly anxious that good relations
be preserved between the crown and the colony, since
the British government controlled those areas. (2) In

34

an effort to give the most effective support to the anit-proprietary forces, as well as to confute the arguments of the nascent radical element which he held responsible for the recent public commotions, Wharton joined forces with Joseph Galloway in launching the Pennsylvania Chronicle with William Goddard as publisher. The first issue appeared in January 1767, and although it was intended to be conservative in tone, before the year was out the paper had become famous for its publication of John Dickinson's "Farmer's Letters", much to the chagrin of the owners. (3)

In November the Townsend Acts went into effect and the following month the first of the "Farmer's Letters" appeared. In succeeding issues Dickinson argued forcefully for the constitutional rights of the colonies and pointed out the threat to them in prevailing British policies. At the same time he advocated the cultivation of a spirit of conciliation on both sides and considered a resort to armed resistance justified only in case the annihilation of American liberty became a certainty. (4)

Although Wharton, like most Friends, agreed in general with the basic content of Dickinson's argument, he was irritated with Goddard for publishing the "Letters". He considered them inflammatory and the editor "imprudent" to have printed them "at such a time." (5) In this opinion he was joined by Samuel Rhoads who viewed the "Letters" as "calculated to excite the passions of the unthinking "and believed that their appearance would do "naught but render a just and friendly union with the parent state more difficult." (6) Some of the other Quaker merchants, however, were more forceful in expressing their opinions as to British policy. Shortly after the publication of the "Letters" Thomas Clifford wrote to a friend in England:

> We find fault with the British Parliament
> for passing unconstitutional Acts res-
> pecting our trade, laying burdens on it
> & prohibiting Legislatures from issuing
> paper currency. (7)

In the political sphere the resentment of the colonies against the implementation of recent imperial regulations was soon apparent. In October 1767, Boston supported by other Massachusetts towns, started a non-consumption movement. Early the next year, spurred on by the passage of the Townsend Acts, the Massachusetts

Assembly issued a circular letter addressed to the other colonial assemblies protesting the British government's infringement of the rights of the colonies and stating its opinion that colonial representation in the British Parliament was not a realistic proposition. (8)

In Pennsylvania the Assembly, firmly in the hands of the Quaker party, pursued a more moderate course. Its committee of correspondence instructed the colony's agents in London, Franklin and Jackson, to cooperate with other colonial agents in any "decent and respectful applications to Parliament" in protesting the Townsend Acts, provided other agents took the initiative. (9)

Inevitably tensions soon began to mount, and renewed violence broke out in June when the customs officers at Boston seized the sloop Liberty for violation of the trade laws. A riot ensued, the crown officials retired to the protection of Fort William, and British troops and war vessels were then sent to Boston. (10) Thus the sparks of discontent were being fanned into a threatening conflagration of resistance.

The merchants, as before, were the spearhead of the movement to persuade the British government to change its policies by means of economic pressure. Such action had to present a united front if it were to be successful, and therefore Boston and New York, whose merchants had agreed on a non-importation program, appealed to the Phialdelphia merchants to join them. The Philadelphians, however, were disinclined to enter into such an arrangement, and despite the eloquent urgings of Dickinson at two meetings of the merchants in March and April 1768 they remained unmoved. Since the state of their econmony was relatively favorable, they preferred to move with caution rather than take immediate action. (11)

The British Quakers were closely following the course of events, and Dr. Fothergill wrote to James Pemberton approving the moderate position taken by the Pennsylvanians. He felt all the colonies should practise the greatest possible economy in the guise of prudence and not rebellion. (12) In his opinion the Americans had right sentiments but were acting unwisely. As for the Bostonians, they were "not to be vindicated, and should they push matters to extremity, they must be chargeable with the fatal consequences." Although the taxes complained of were unjust, force was not the proper instrument by which to obtain relief. Talk of resistance aroused "the whole mastiff spirit of John Bull..., and if it were his only brother, and by whose benevolence he subsisted, pride and passion would carry him headlong into battle and violence..." (13)

Pennsylvania should stand on its own in this matter, he contended. It should not submit silently to the imposition in question but should remonstrate in decency and firmness. All violent conduct toward the mother country should be avoided "till -- oppression without prospect of redress -- but this is not your case yet, " he argued. His final advice was:

> Soft language, conduct not servile --
> patience repeated -- prudent application,
> will make those your Frds who know that
> pride and ignorance are your enemies,
> and will enable those who would serve
> you from just principle to do it effect-
> ively. (14)

During the summer of 1768 the radicals mounted a campaign in the newspapers against the slowness of the merchants in entering a non-importation agreement, even threatening those who refused to support a boycott of British goods. Both Dickinson and Charles Thomson joined the fray. (15) In order to arouse the population and bring pressure on the lawmakers, a meeting of the citizenry was called at the State House in July, at which time a resolution of sympathy for Boston was adopted. Even more important, the meeting formulated instructions to the city's representatives in the Assembly, calling for the presentation to both houses of Parliament of remonstrances against the Townsend Acts. (16) Subsequently John Reynell informed Mildred and Roberts that the Philadelphia merchants might well feel obliged to accept the invitation from Boston to join a non-importation agreement unless there were some prospect of repeal of the offensive acts. (17)

When the Assembly reconvened in September, it was faced with two critical issues, one of which was the demand for more forceful action regarding the Townsend Acts. The other one was a demand from Lord Hillsborough for the Assembly's dissolution in case it considered the Massachusetts Circular Letter. Simultaneously a message was received from the Speaker of the Virginia House of Burgesses recounting their proceedings in rejecting Hillsborough's instructions. (18)

The Assembly was not long in acting on both matters. It appointed a committee of twelve, including
James Pemberton and three other Quakers, to draft petitions to the King and both houses of Parliament asking for repeal of the Townsend Acts. (19) The committee not only drafted the petitions as directed, but it
also replied to Lord Hillsborough's threat in two resolutions stating the Assembly's right both to sit
upon its own dissolution and to correspond with any of
the American colonies relative to grievances affecting
their general welfare. (20)

The merchants, on their part, although preferring
to await the outcome of the legislative petitions before entering into any inter-colonial agreement, (21)
were as strongly opposed to the revenue laws as their
compatriots. The Quaker Samuel Coates expressed the
merchant's sentiments forceably in a letter to William
Logan in London in the early fall of 1768 when he said:

> Your M--rs have administered a loathsome
> Pill, a bitter dose to ye colonies indeed,
> and such a one I firmly believe they will
> never allow... (The acts were) calculated
> to enforce a slavish submission to ye
> B-r-sh P-m-t...

and to such the colonists were "unswervingly opposed."
(22) Even William Allen, Chief Justice of the province, a prominent Presbyterian and a leader of the
opposition to the Quaker party, wrote to Thomas Penn
in England that although Pennsylvania was the most moderate of the colonies,

> [...none are more fixed than we are in not
> giving up the right of being taxed by our
> own representatives...The Quakers in their
> way are as zealous in claiming their right
> as their neighbors.] (23)

Somewhat later in the fall the Philadelphia merchants began to take action. John Reynell, a member
of the Meeting for Sufferings, headed a committee of
ten merchants, including four Friends, which addressed
a memorial to the British merchants and manufacturers
requesting their assistance in obtaining the repeal of
the Townsend Acts. The memorial not only pointed out
the baneful economic effects of former and current

38

parliamentary legislation affecting trade and commerce, but it also stressed the unconstitutional aspects of the acts in question. (24) Reynell later boasted of having been the first to sign the memorial, declaring his opposition to the Townsend Acts on the basis of the rights of the colonists as Englishmen. (25)

In its reply to the solicitations from Philadelphia, a committee of the London merchants which included David Barclay and Daniel Mildred promised that as soon as opportunity offered, since Parliament was not then in session, "nothing on our parts will be wanting, to obtain, as soon as 'tis possible, Relief from the late Revenue Act". (26) In an accompanying letter, David Barclay requested the Philadelphia merchants not to publish any of the communications from London for fear of the prejudicial effect in England. (27) There was now a lull in the non-importation agitation since the signers of the merchants' memorial had pledged further action the next spring if their appeals proved unavailing. (28)

One of the important motives behind the delaying tactics of the Quaker merchants at this time was revealed by James Pemberton in an account he sent to Dr. Fothergill in November, detailing the events of the past few months. An underlying fear of the Quakers was that the Presbyterian element in the province was exploiting the present situation to gain control of affairs. According to Pemberton:

> ...the weak state to which our old antag-
> onists ye P-T-ns are reduced by the frantic
> attempts of some of them to disturb the
> public tranquality...has convinced them
> of ye incapicity to effect ye aspiring
> views yet which their brothers in New
> England have brought such a scourge on
> themselves by ye rashness of their con-
> duct...(29)

In conclusion he expressed his conviction that only if the British government would "dispassionately attend to reason and justice" and pursue measures truly consistent with the real interest of all the British dominions could the colonies hope for redress of their grievances and a restoration of harmony.

By the early months of 1769 there was a general belief that the merchants of Boston and New York would again attempt to obtain an inter-colonial non-importation agreement. If Parliament wholly rejected the application of the colonies for relief, James Pemberton believed that the arguments by which such action was avoided the preceeding year would be fruitless. (30) According to a reporter from London, the Philadelphians were preparing for such an eventuality. "The Quakers (chiefly) in Philad^a," he said, "have imported their Spring goods which sail next week, & then I apprehend they will come into the resolutions of N.Y. & c." (31)

Although the Pennsylvanians had stood aloof from any inter-colonial commitments for the time being, they followed a program of frugality and economy. In this the Quakers were among the most active. Early in February 1769, John Reynell wrote that his wife had bought a new spinning wheel and was spinning her own cloth. Rather than have the American cause fail, he would give up his "beloved Article of Tea, & put on a leather jacket". (32)

It was at this time that the merchants, realizing the increasingly critical juncture of affairs, appointed a committee of twenty-three, including ten Friends, to watch events and formulate an appropriate course of action. (33) When news arrived in March of the failure of the British merchants to achieve any progress in behalf of the American cause, the Philadelphia merchants informed their colleagues in Boston and New York of their readiness to enter into a non-imporation agreement to remain in force until the Townsend Acts were repealed. They declared that they were fully united with the people of all the colonies in opposition to Parliament's attempt to tax them unconstitutionally and that the reason for their delay in undertaking non-importation had been to wait until all other efforts to obtain redress failed. Their reaction to the London merchants' suggestion that an appeal to Parliament should be based on expediency rather than constitutional right, was that they would "never hazzard such a step" since the Americans were so jealous of their liberty. (34)

A few months later John Reynell explained the situation to his English correspondents in greater detail. He assured them that the repeal of the duties on paper and glass would not satisfy the Americans, since the Tea Act was just as much intended to raise a revenue in America. Let the people of Great Britain think as hard of the Americans as they would, the lat-

40

ter would never agree to being taxed by a parliament in which they were not and could not be represented, a point of English liberty they could not consent to surrender. (35) The Philadelphia merchants' committee wrote in a similar vein to the London merchants. (36) Subsequently Reynell requested his London agents to use their influence to prevent the English merchants from making any shipments contrary to the non-importation agreement, since such attempts might render it difficult to maintain peace and quiet in the colonies. (37) In response the London Quaker merchants Mildred and Roberts expressed hearty approval for the measures the Americans had taken. (38)

Throughout the imperial dispute the colonial cause found active support not only in merchants' lobbying in the halls of Parliament but also in pleaders in its behalf in the public press. In August 1768, an anonymous Friend published an open letter to the King in the London Gazette and Daily Advertiser, defending the American cause. (39) Having followed the controversy between England and America from its beginning, the writer had come to the conclusion that if there was "any right in human policy", it lay with the Americans. In part he argued:

> With whatever views the Americans trans-
> ported themselves, it is certain they went
> fully satisfied, that notwithstanding
> their vast distance, they were to be
> under the mild and noble legislation of
> Englishmen. They went out at a vast ex-
> pense of money and labour to cultivate
> and to flourish; England reaped a prodigious
> advantage from their prosperity; and indeed,
> the benefits between the mother and her
> daughter were mutual.

Whether or not the idea of freedom entertained by the colonists was correct, they had enjoyed it for over a century and were now being deprived of it by "an arbitrary judgement", and they did not possess the same privileges they had before the Stamp Act. All the remonstrances of the Americans had been clear and respectful. Although the King might not be able to grant all their liberties, he could certainly grant some.

Thomas Crowley also raised his voice in a series of appeals to high government personages as well as to the public, in which he endorsed the constitutional

position of the colonies and advocated a plan for solution of the imperial problem. In a letter to the
Duke of Grafton and the Earl of Halifax he argued for
colonial representation in Parliament and urged an
amendment to the protested legislation to provide for
it. (40) In a letter to the London Public Ledger he
declared that "the maxim is uncontrovertable, no representation no taxation". The right of representation
must be granted to the colonies or they must be exempted from taxes imposed without their consent. Those
colonials who opposed the idea of being represented in
Parliament on the basis of impracticality or the danger
of being imposed upon only evidenced the desire to be
excused from taxation. In a union of the colonies with
Britain in Parliament, the Americans should be able to
cooperate with their "countrymen on this side of the
water" in enacting necessary imperial regulations. (41)

However, at this point Crowley parted company with
his fellow Quakers. In a letter to William Pitt he advocated firmness against violent and rebellious acts on
the part of any colony. The Americans should either
accept representation in Parliament or be content to
be taxed without representation or propose some measure
to "share in a just and proportionate expense of general protection and defense". It was "needful to avoid
every appearance of unconstitutional measures on one
side, and of disregard of duty...on the other". (42)
In a later appeal "To the Administration", he advocated
a combination of responsiveness and firmness in reply
to colonial protests. Terms of accomodation should be
offered to the colonies, accompanied by "the appearance
of irresistable force" such as the closing of New England ports. He further warned that "now or never is
the time to lay the foundation of a better mutual confidence and security and if this occasion be neglected,
it will be too late". (43)

In October 1768, Crowley published his Observations and Propositions on Accomodation between Great
Britain and Her Colonies setting forth his ideas and
presented a copy to the King. In this treatise he
repeated his advocacy of an act of union providing
for colonial representation in Parliament. He proposed
that such an act designate the precise mode and extent
of interanl taxation as applied to the colonies and
that it also preclude parliamentary taxation in any
other manner than the one prescribed. (44)

With the object of reaching the public in the

colonies directly, Crowley sent copies of his letter
in the Public Ledger and of the Observations and Propositions to Governor Samuel Ward of Rhode Island, requesting that they "be inserted in your Gazettes
immediately". (45)

The official bodies as well as individual members
of the British Society of Friends had grave misgivings
over the trend of events. In the fall of 1768 the
London Meeting for Sufferings, having been "greatly
affected" by the critical situation in America, communicated its concern to the Philadelphia Friends. In
what seems to be a veiled reference to British government officials, it expressed its "earnest desire that
the hearts of all concerned in directing the public
councils may be touched with a great sense of the
importance of their deliberations on the present juncture, and that they may be inclined to true wisdom and
moderation". (46)

The following March, after the Philadelphia merchants had joined the non-importation agreement, the
English Friends became anxious about possible future
developments in America. In an epistle to the Philadelphia Meeting for Sufferings they urged the Pennsylvania Quakers to maintain their peaceful conduct
and to heed the advice of George Fox in his epistle
to Friends in 1685 when he advised them to keep clear
of all riots and tumults. (47) In an accompanying
letter, Daniel Mildred requested that copies of the
epistle be distributed to the members of the yearly
meeting. He declared the Friends in England were
"very tender of giving particular advice" but at the
same time they could not but sincerely desire "that
such conduct may be observed by every individual as
becomes our Christian Society..." (48) At its annual
session in May 1769, London Yearly Meeting issued an
epistle "to all Friends, in every Place". It reminded
them of their duty and affection to the King and
charged them:

> ...not only to demean themselves as
> becomes good and faithful Subjects, both
> in Word and Conduct, but also to promote
> the like Sentiments of Duty and Affection
> among those over whom their Influence may
> extend; and that they avoid being ensnared
> by the Animosities of contending Parties,
> or anything unbecoming the Stability and
> Uprightness of our Profession...(49)

Dr. Fothergill, whose hand was constantly on the pulse of public events and who was more of a proponent for action, albeit restrained action, than the Meeting for Sufferings of which he was a member, was deeply disturbed by the attitude of British government leaders. He warned his American friends:

> We have people at the Helm that seem to like violence more than peace and would rather command obedience than genuine affection. They are deaf to any other arguments than those of necessity, and where the contest will end, no body knows... (50)

Unless the Americans tried to live another year without importing any goods from England, the best procedure would be "to depute some cool sensible men from each colony to come over to join their agents here, and the few American merchants who...are your Friends" in soliciting the members of Parliament at its next session. With regard to the non-importation resolutions, he urged the colonists either to "not resolve or go through stick and adhere to their resolutions". Those who were adverse to the colonies said they were weary of them already, that the English merchants were indifferent, and that "the M--ry know you too well to be in pain about any of your combinations". (51)

Events of the next few months in Philadelphia caused some Friends to fear lest their participation in the proceedings of the merchants would compromise their religious principles. Apprehension as to the political implications of those activities also haunted them. When the non-importation agreement was initiated a committee was appointed to implement its provisions and correspond with the cooperating merchant groups in the other colonies. Because of the general confidence in the Quakers, eight were chosen as members, and John Reynell was appointed chairman. (52) The Friends accepted this appointment with the purpose of "prevailing by their advice to have such measures pursued as would be consistent with the public interest without violating the rights of individuals". (53) Reynell believed it was necessary to remain in control of the situation until the protested acts were repealed. (54)

As the spring progressed, however, the Meeting for Sufferings became increasingly alarmed. During the month of June it held weekly meetings to consider the

44

state of public affairs "the consequence of which may affect our religious liberties". Many of its members were greatly concerned that measures publicly proposed in "support of our civil liberties" would lead some Friends into activities inconsistent with their religious testimonies. (55) Israel Pemberton, an influential member in the Meeting and the leader of the conservative wing among the Quakers, was already aroused over the activities of John Reynell as a member of the non-importation committee. (56)

About the middle of July, the _Charming Polly_ arrived from Yarmouth, England, with a shipment of malt for Amos Strettel. When the captain applied to some members of the committee to enforce the non-importation agreement for permission to land the cargo, they were at first inclined to allow him to do so. But it was finally referred to a general meeting of the committee which decided, contrary to the advice of the Quaker members, to convene the city's inhabitants at the State House to determine the matter. At this public meeting which Reynell chaired, the brewers, attending in a body, presented an agreement signed by all of them, including three Friends, promising not to buy any of the malt in the cargo. (57) After some discussion, it was unanimously voted that the shipment was contrary to the non-importation resolution of the preceeding March and that whoever countenanced its being unloaded was an enemy to his country. Soon thereafter the _Charming Polly_ set sail for Ireland. (58)

Before the ship sailed, Philadelphia Monthly Meeting appointed a committee to confer with the captain of the vessel, the consignee of the shipment, Mr. Strettel and those Friends who were serving on the merchants' non-importation enforcement committee. The latter, already fully convinced of the inadvisability of calling the citizenry together, "the greater part of whom were incapable of judging prudently on a matter of so great importance", promised not to assent again to such a proposal. (59) The conference with the captain was intended to disabuse him of any resentment he might have against the townspeople. He was assured "of the anxiety and pain friends in general, and the more considerate and judicious of all denominations were under on his Acct." On the advice of the Friends he again applied to the merchants' committee for permission to land his cargo, but his request was rejected. (60)

Following these events, the merchants' committee

called a general meeting of all parties to the non-importation agreement, at which further resolutions in support of their actions were adopted. Some Friends on the committee were opposed to these decisions, and Philadelphia Monthly Meeting advised its members to withdraw wholly from the committee. It took this position, as it later explained to the London Friends, to avoid further occasions which might "subject us to any censure from our superiors, as we desire to approve ourselves both in principle and practice dutiful, affectionate and loyal Subjects to the King, and peaceable members of civil Society..." (62)

The action of the merchants' committee to which the Quakers especially objected was the calling of a meeting of the city's inhabitants. Israel Pemberton expressed this concern in a letter to his brother:

> If thou seeth the papers thou wilt find they have been so wild as to collect ye inhabitants, and by their resolve oblige an honest man from Yarmouth with a cargo of malt...to take back his cargo.(63)

As Charles Thomson latter said: "The Quakers had an aversion to town meetings & always opposed them". (64) In the opinion of many Friends, especially the more conservative ones such as Pemberton, the result of such meetings in New England where the radical elements had employed them as a means to instigate opposition to the government was a profitable object lesson. A similar procedure in Pennsylvania might lead to domination by elements whose rule would threaten the liberties which the Quakers had so long enjoyed. Public meetings would also make it difficult to restrain violent actions and thus alienate the good will of the British authorities.

The Philadelphia Meeting for Sufferings soon sent an account of these disturbing occurrences to the Friends in London. (65) It also issued an epistle of advice to Friends in Pennsylvania and the adjacent provinces, exhorting them to avoid conducting themselves inconsistently with their religious profession "by joining with the measures publicly proposed for the support of civil liberties". It further emphatically declared:

> Should any now deviate from the example and

46

> practice of faithful friends at all
> times..., as to manifest a disposition
> to contend for liberty by any methods
> or agreements contrary to the peaceable
> spirit and temper of the Gospel... we
> must declare that we cannot join with such,
> and that we truly believe a steady uniform
> Conduct under the influence of that Spirit
> will most effectually tend to our relief
> from every kind of Oppression and would add
> a convincing force to the reasoning
> necessary to be used in support of our
> civil liberty and rights. (66)

The meeting ordered two thousand copies to be printed
and distributed to the membership of the Society.

The state of affairs in New York also became a
matter of special concern to the Pennsylvania Quakers
at this time. In the autumn of 1769, the conservative
party gained control of the New York Assembly and proceeded to carry out the provisions of the late Quarter-
ing Act by supplying the British garrison in the province with all the supplies they requested, (67) a
policy vigorously denounced by the radical elements.
Fearing lest some Friends there become involved in the
popular agitations, the Philadelphia Meeting for Sufferings expressed their apprehensions to their New
York brethren in an epistle of February 1770. It
advised the New York Quakers to maintain the principles
of their profession faithfully, since by so doing they
might influence others to follow a more peaceful course.
It recommended their holding a general meeting of
all Friends in the city to strengthen and unite them and
to caution them "against attempting to maintain or
defend our Rights and privileges" by inconsistent measures. (68)

Both the Philadelphia and London Meeting for Sufferings communicated a similar concern to the Maryland
Quakers regarding the conduct of Friends in the currently disturbed situation. In its annual epistle of June
1770, the Yearly Meeting for Maryland assured the
London Quakers that most members had kept clear of any
public agitations. Those who had not would, it hoped,
"be careful of being active therein as they are now
informed the solid body of Friends appear concerned to
Caution & advise against these measures." (69)

The Society of Friends had by this time begun to

question seriously the propriety of its members participating in seemingly peaceful measures to obtain redress of colonial grievances. The employment of economic sanctions to this end had at first seemed to be a
plausable device. By now, however, a gnawing fear
persisted that the trend of events carried a threat
to the inherited and proper balance of political control by which the charter and the liberties it guaran-
teed were safeguarded. Religious, economic, and political considerations all played an important role in
determining the attitude of the Pennsylvania Quakers.
Possible effects on their commercial interests and
the future stability of the Quaker merchant class were
important factors contributing to the increasing alarm
over the state of affairs. Thus many Pennsylvania
Friends, and to a certain degree other colonial Quakers,
were becoming convinced that the constitutional connection with Britain must be maintained as a bulwark
against the overturn of the political and governmental
status quo.

Radicals

Notes for Chapter III

(1) Gipson, <u>The Coming of the Revolution</u>, 172-175.
(2) Lincoln, <u>The Revolutionary Movement in Pa</u>., 158n.
(3) Schlesinger, Arthur M., "Politics, Propaganda, and
     the Philadelphia Press, 1767-1770",<u>PMHB</u>,v.60(1936),
     310,314.Wharton was one of the Quakers exiled to
     Virginia under suspicion of treason in September,
     1777, (See chap.10). He was later proscribed as
     an enemy of his country and his estate was confis-
     cated. (Wharton, Anne H., <u>Geneology of the Wharton</u>
     <u>Family of Philadelphia, 1664-1880</u>, (Philadelphia,
     1880), 12.
         Despite his birth into a Quaker family, Dic-
     kinson's father early withdrew from the Friends
     and the young Dickinson was not reared as a member
     of the Society. (Jacobson, David L., <u>John Dickin-</u>
     <u>son and the Revolution in Pennsylvania, 1764-1776</u>
     (Univ. of California Publications in History, v.78,
     Berkley, 1965), chap. 1.
(4) For an excellent discussion of the <u>Farmer's</u>
     <u>Letters</u> see Stillé, Charles J., <u>Life and Times of</u>
     <u>John Dickinson</u>, <u>Memoirs</u> of the Hist. Soc. of
     Pennsylvania, v.13 (Philadelphia, 1891), 81-89.
(5) Goddard, William, <u>The Partnership</u> (Philadelphia,
     1770), 16.
(6) Dickinson, John, <u>The Writings of John Dickinson</u>,
     <u>Political Writings, 1764-1774</u>, ed. Paul Lester
     Ford, <u>Memoirs</u> of the Hist. Soc. of Pennsylvania,
     v.14, (Philadelphia, 1895), 280n.
(7) Thomas Clifford to Launcelot Cowper, March 31,
     1768, Letter Book, 1767-1773.
(8) Lincoln, <u>op.cit</u>., 144-145.
(9) Houston, James E., "The Campaign to Make Pennsyl-
     vania a Royal Province, 1764-1770", <u>PMHB</u>,v.95
     (1971), 41.
(10) Gipson, <u>op.cit</u>., 185-187.
(11) Schlesinger, <u>Colonial Merchants</u>, 115-119; Jensen,
     Arthur L., <u>The Maritime Commerce of Philadelphia</u>
     (Madison, 1963), 173-174.
(12) Dr. Fothergill to James Pemberton, July 5, 1768.
     Ett.Pem.Pap., v.2, 57.
(13) Same to same, Sept. 16, 1768, Ett.Pem.Pap., v.3,
     58.
(14) <u>Ibid</u>. Dr. Fothergill further advised:

         Have no glance to the other colonies. And

be not hasty in remonstrating. The
conduct of Boston by soliciting the aid
of the other provinces has given great
disgust without necessity...They have
raised prejudices everywhere against
them, and as they have intimated resistance I should not wonder if they
are put to a bitter trial; and all
America suffer for their intemperate
Zeal. (Ibid.)

(15) Romanek, John Reynell, 151; Schlesinger,op.cit.,
     118-120.
(16) Brunhouse,R.L., "The Effects of the Townsend Acts
     in Pennsylvania," PMHB v.54 (1930), 362.
(17) John Reynell to Mildred and Roberts, Aug. 25,1768,
     Letter Book, 1767-1769, at the HSP.
(18) Votes and Proc, Pa. Arch., 8th Ser.,v.7, 6181-6184
     6188,6189.
(19) Ibid.,6193. The Quakers were Pemberton, Livezey,
     Rodman and Ashbridge.
(20) Schlesinger, op.cit., 126. See also the letter to
     the Pennsylvania agents in London, Votes and Proc.,
     6278. The petitions are in ibid., 6271-6277.
(21) Schlesinger, op.cit.,127.
(22) Samuel Coates to William Logan, Sept. 24, 1768,
     Samuel Coates Letter Book, 1763-1781, at the HSP.
(23) Jensen, op.cit., 178.
(24) Schlesinger, op.cit., 127-28.
(25) John Reynell to William Henry Reynell, May 15,
     1769, Letter Book, 1769-1770, at the HSP.
(26) London Merchants to John Reynell et al., Jan. 4,
     1769, Coates Reynell Pap., bx.14 (1767-1771).
(27) David Barclay to John Reynell, Jan.28, 1769,
     Coates Reynell Pap., Correspondance 1763-1784.
(28) Schlesinger, op.cit., 129.
(29) James Pemberton to Dr. Fothergill, Nov.20,1768,
     Pem.Pap., v.34, 154.
(30) Same to same, Jan. 30, 1769, Pem.Pap., v.34, 156.
(31) Dennys de Berdt to Richard Cary, Feb.2, 1769,
     "Letters of Dennys de Berdt, 1757-1770", Colonial
     Society of Massachusetts, Publications, v.13
     (Transactions, 1910-1911), 357.
(32) John Reynell to Andres Henry Grath, Feb.2, 1769,
     Letter Book, 1767-1769.
(33) Papers of the Committee of Merchants of Philadel-
     phia, Feb. 6, 1769-Dec. 19, 1769, Sparks MSS,
     v. 62, sub-vol. 7, 174-75. The list of the com-
     mittee members is on 175n. The Friends were James
     Pemberton, Joseph Richardson, John Reynell,

Jeremiah Warder, Samuel Howell, Abel James, Thomas Fisher, Thomas Mifflin, Henry Drinker and George Roberts.

(34) Romanek, op.cit.,154-55.

(35) John Reynell to Mildred and Roberts, May 17, 1769, Letter Book, 1769-1770.

(36) Papers of the Committee of Merchants, loc.cit., 190-92.

(37) John Reynell to Mildred and Roberts, June 6, 1769, Letter Book, 1769-1770.

(38) Mildred and Roberts to John Reynell, July 7, 1769, Coates Reynell Pap., 1767-1771, loc.cit.

(39) Pa. Jnl,Oct. 26, 1769, 1.

(40) Crowley, Let. and Diss., 70-72.

(41) Ibid., 61-2.

(42) Ibid., 65-70.

(43) Ibid., 50-1.

(44) Ibid., 85-6; Crowley, Thomas, Observations and Propositions on Accomodation between Great Britain and Her Colonies, London, 1768.

(45) Both items are in the John Carter Brown Library, endorsed as having been received by Governor Ward on January 29, 1769.

(46) London M.f.S. to Phil. M.f.S., Oct. 14, 1768, London M.f.S., Letters to and from Philadelphia.

(47) Same to same, March 10, 1769, Phil. M.f.S., Min. v.1, 288.

(48) Daniel Mildred to John Pemberton, March 10, 1769, Phil. M.f.S., Min., v. 1, 289.

(49) London Y.M., General Epistle of 1769, Epistles from the Yearly Meeting held in London, 1675-1850 (2 vols., London, 1760, 1850), v.2.

(50) Dr. Fothergill to James Pemberton, May 16, 1769, Ett.Pem.Pap., v.2, 60.

(51) Ibid.

(52) The Quakers were John Reynell, William Fisher, Abel James, Henry Drinker, Thomas Mifflin, Jeremiah Warder and Thomas Fisher (the full list is given in Papers of the Merchants' Committee, loc.cit., 192,194,197). Schlesinger, op.cit., 192; Phil. M.f.S. to London M.f.S., Aug. 5, 1769, Phil. M.f.S., Min., v.1, 293-94.

(53) Phil. M.f.S. to London M.f.S., Aug. 5, 1769, loc.cit., 294.

(54) Romanek, op.cit., 159.

(55) Phil. M.f.S., Min., v. 1, 290-91.

(56) Thayer, Theordore, Israel Pemberton, King of the Quakers, (Philadelphia, 1943), 206.

(57) Pa. Jnl., July 20, 1769, 3. The list of the signers is given in Scharf and Westcott, Hist.

of Phil., v. 1, 282. The Friends were Anthony
Morris, Jr., Anthony Cadwallader Morris and
Isaac Howell, all later disowned for active sup-
port of the Revolution. (Phil. M.M., Min., 1771-
1777, 361, 404, 408, 420; Phil. M.M. No. Dist.
Min., 1772-1781, 202, 213).

(58) Phil. M.f.S. to London M.f.S., Aug. 5, 1769,
loc.cit., 294; Pa. Jnl., July 20, 1769; Pa. Gaz.,
July 20, 1769.

(59) Phil. M.f.S. to London M.f.S., July 29, 1769,
London M.f.S., Letters to and from Philadelphia.

(60) Ibid.

(61) Phil. M.M., Min., 1765-1771, 337, 343.

(62) Phil. M.f.S. to London M.f.S., Aug. 5, 1769,
loc.cit., 295.

(63) Israel Pemberton to his brother, July 24, 1769,
cited in Lincoln, op.cit., 151.

(64) Charles Thomson to W.H. Drayton, cited in Stille,
op.cit., 344.

(65) Phil. M.f.S. to London M.f.S., July 29, 1769,
loc.cit.

(66) Phil. M.f.S., Min. v.1, 290, 296-97.

(67) Fisher, Sydney George, The Struggle for American
Independence (2 vols., New York, 1908), v. 1, 135.

(68) Phil. M.f.S. to N.Y. M.f.S., Feb. 15, 1770, Phil.
M.f.S., Min., v.1, 306-07.

(69) Md. Y.M. to London Y.M., June, 1770,Md.Y.M.,
Misc. Pap.; Epistles to London Y.M., v. 4 (1758-
1778), 277.

Chapter IV

THE BREAKDOWN OF NON-IMPORTATION AND THE CHALLENGE TO QUAKER POLICY

The year 1770 was a turning point for the better in Anglo-American affairs. When Parliament convened that winter, the colonial situation was one of the most important questions before it. The English merchants were still pressing for repeal of the Townsend Acts, and Daniel Mildred, speaking for the Quaker merchants, promised his American friends they would give the effort "every Assistance" in their power. He was dubious of the outcome, however, because of the Administration's determination not to give up the duty on tea. (1)

By this time two prominent American Quakers, Robert Murray, a leading New York merchant, and Abel James, the Philadelphia merchant, had arrived in London and were working with the London merchants for the hoped-for repeal. Finally, late in January, the London merchants presented a petition to Parliament requesting the repeal of the protested acts. (2) As a matter of fact, the government had now come to see the necessity for such action, and Lord North, the new Prime Minister, used the opportunity offered by the merchants' petition to introduce a bill to repeal all the acts but the tax on tea. (3) A few weeks later the bill passed Parliament, and the King signed it in April. (4)

Both the American and British Quakers were skeptical as to the motives for this action. Mildred and Roberts declared that the Ministry was strongly set against complete repeal because of the influence of pensions, placements, etc. (5) Abel James expressed his opinion to Henry Drinker that colonial protests were "not in the least degree ... the means of taking off the Duties on Glass Paints & Paper". Parliament had not acted "from a principle of justice to the Colonies, but because it was bad policy to tax the Manufacturers of the Kingdom". As long as the present ministry continued in office, all efforts for complete repeal would be in vain. (6)

In their analysis of the situation, the Quakers'

opinions were correct. Since the time of the Stamp Act
affair five years previously, the political configuration of Parliamentary alignments had shifted sharply.
Although always dominated by the landed gentry, Parliament had customarily supported mercantile interests on
the basis that a healthy commerce would assure the
economic welfare of the country. Conditions had now
changed, however, and though this consideration still
carried some weight, the merchants no longer had the
same ready ear in Parliament. Not only were members
of Parliament very sensitive to the rapidly mounting
financial problems of the government, but even more
important, their response to ministerial wishes had
been assured by the distribution of offices, the purchase of parliamentary seats, and the buying of votes
in contested elections, developments which had been
greatly facilitated by the extensive resources of the
crown to which the government's supporters in Parliament were fervently loyal. Consequently most members
of Parliament looked upon colonial opposition to ministerial policies as tantamount to treason. (7) Only
on convincing evidence that the economic situation of
the kingdom was adversely affected by colonial taxation
would they support a change in policy, and not because
of the colonial protests, especially when they were
presented on the basis of constitutional rights. Whereas it had taken the English merchants only a few months
to obtain the repeal of the Stamp Act, it now took
three years to accomplish repeal of the Townsend
Acts. (8)

The news of partial repeal of colonial duties
created a new problem for the Americans. If Parliament had repealed all of the taxes, non-importation
would have ceased immediately. But since the duty on
tea remained in effect, the demands of the colonists
were not completely satisfied. Already divisions of
opinion had begun to appear in the ranks of the colonial merchants over continuance of the restrictions on
which they had agreed. Henry Drinker, for one, doubted
the sincerity of the motives of many merchants and
questioned how long public spirit and patriotism would
hold out. He suspected that such sentiments were only
skin deep, in view of breaches in the agreement by
many of those who first promoted it. (9) Although Abel
James wrote home enthusiastically about the return of
cargoes rejected in America, he also feared that the
subscribers to the non-importation agreement would not
remain firm, and that even at Boston a general importation would be allowed. (10)

James was both surprised and impressed by the attitude of many Englishmen toward America at this time. On a visit to Bath he had found that "the inhabitants generally are on the side of Liberty and the colonies". (11) He wrote to his friend, Laurence Cowper:

> ... the firmness of the Americans amazes all ranks of people here, I wish they may act wisely and that their present virtuous efforts may be crowned with the desired success... (12)

While the colonies were passing through this period of uncertainty, Dr. Fothergill was actively supporting the American cause in England. In several interviews with the Speaker of the House of Commons he convinced him of the probable unhappy results of ministerial measures under consideration to strengthen the military detachment at Boston. He presented some of Abel James' ideas as to possible courses of action, which prompted the Speaker to request an interview with their author so that he might be "fortified with some good arguments for adopting a different policy toward America". (13) Before the appointed meeting Fothergill and James met with Franklin to prepare for the discussion. The chief point which they decided to stress was the necessity of giving a working basis to those elements in the colonies which favored conciliation. As long as the Tea Act and other offensive measures were continued, improvement would be difficult. In Pennsylvania the influence of Friends and other religious groups which supported the Quaker policy would decrease as the irritation of the Americans rose. Unless the cause of the dispute were removed, it was not likely that the union and confidence of the two countries would be restored. (14)

In an effort to encourage the search for means of mutual accomodation in the imperial dispute, the London Meeting for Sufferings wrote the Philadelphia Friends that the English Quakers would cooperate to their utmost if there should be any opportunity of devising conciliatory measures. The conduct of the American Friends was looked on "in a very favorable light, by those in authority ... as well as by judicious persons of every Rank". (15)

In transmitting this epistle to James Pemberton, clerk of the Philadelphia Meeting for Sufferings, Dr.

Fothergill proposed that Pemberton and "a few solid judicious friends" draw up a petition to be presented in their behalf to the Throne. This should contain "a clear concise pertinent account of the hardships and difficulties to which Friends are and will be unavoidably exposed to by the non-importing scheme". Done in this fashion, Fothergill believed it might "have some good effect in bringing about a better temper" in England. All petitions and remonstrances which had thus far been received had "carried that in their Front which defeated their own purposes, an assertion of right". He advised the Philadelphians:

> With this you have no business. What
> you feel, what you clearly see, that
> you may declare, leaving both the right
> and the means of redress untouched. (16)

Among the merchants in New York and Philadelphia there was much division of opinion as to the appropriate steps to be taken in response to the partial repeal of the Townsend Acts. This controversy resulted partly from a provision in the Maryland merchants' agreement allowing the importation of coarse woolens which were vital to the trade with the Indians. Consequently the Maryland merchants were engrossing this trade at the expense of their northern neighbors. (17)

Finally, in the middle of March 1770, a special effort was made to secure the attendance of all the members of the Philadelphia non-importation committee, since several, including the three Friends Henry Drinker, Jeremiah Warder and John Reynell, had not attended for some months. At that time it was decided to hold a general meeting of all the subscribers to the agreement on April 1, and Henry Drinker was appointed to a committee to make the arrangements. (18)

After some consideration, Henry Drinker decided to attend neither the committee nor the subsequent general meeting, since he found himself in a "streight". Although the lifting of the boycott of British imports would benefit the shopkeepers who were suffering for lack of supplies, he could not think of deserting a measure planned to secure and support the liberties and rights of the colonies. He felt that such a step would invoke the contempt and indignation of the other colonies as well as the derision and exultation of the mother country. (19) When Providence and Newport later dropped non-importation, Drinker considered that the "little dirty Colony of Rhode Island" had "shamefully broken faith" with the merchants of the other colonies. (20)

Another factor influencing Henry Drinker against participating in public affairs was the fear that he might be involved in activities whose mode of action was inconsistent with his religious principles. Consequently he announced his determination to refuse nomination for any public office or appointment. (21) His action was indicative of the misgivings of many of the leading Quakers who had strong convictions about, and had participated actively in, the recent controversial developments.

After postponing the general meeting of merchants twice, the planning committee finally held it on June 5. (22) This delay was caused by a division of opinion over whether to recommend a continuation of the present agreement or to adopt a partial non-importation. In preparation for the second alternative two lists of goods were prepared, one containing those items considered to be superfluous, and the other indicating those items agreed on as necessary and therefore to be imported. (23)

Upon the initiation of the non-importation program several of the Quaker merchants had advocated the idea of partial non-importation. Abel James had preferred this, but he had been overruled by the agrument that it was impossible to agree on what articles should or should not be imported. (24) Another Quaker of the same opinion was Thomas Gilpin, one of Franklin's correspondents. He had been in favor of the partial program on the basis that the colonies would weaken their cause by adopting too rigorous measures which they would eventually be compelled to rescind. (25)

Two weeks before the merchants' meeting, the mechanics, artisans, manufacturers, and tradesmen held a mass meeting and resolved that non-importation should be continued. They also decided to attend the general meeting of the merchants on June 5. Shortly afterward a "Lover of Liberty and a Mechanic's Friend" published a statement, arguing that a response to unconstitutional taxation was an issue of "general public concern and not the private business of a few merchants". (26) It was obvious that the mechanics and artisans, now realizing how their economic interests differed from those of their former political allies, the Quaker

merchants, and lacking any political leverage, had
determined to exert their influence by the only means
at hand, extra-legal association and action.

The tactics of the mechanics and artisans evidently succeeded, for at the general meeting at the State
House on June 5 it was decided not to alter the existing non-importation agreement. (27) According to the
advocates of alteration, among them the more influential Quakers, Charles Thomson and his radical
associates were responsible for this decision, since
they had introduced a "body of disaffected mechanics
among the subscribers" to the agreement and thereby
succeeded in carrying the day for complete non-importation. Many of the merchants resented "this artifice",
contending that their consultations were not free and
that their hands had been forced. (28)

Boston and New York had already agreed to continue
non-importation for the time being. When the news of
their decision reached England, Abel James wrote to his
friend Launcelot Cowper expressing a feeling of patri-
otic pride mingled with doubts as to what the future
attitude of the Friends would be.

> How shall I glory in being a Native of a
> Country where partiotism is so prevalent
> & the public good so much preferr'd to
> private Interest & Convenience ... shall
> we doubt this being the Golden Age -
> And that the N Americans take Rank in
> it - (29)

As far as Pennsylvania was concerned he believed

> that a certain Society there will be
> very watchful of their Members least
> by their taking a Lead the Credit &
> reputation of the whole Body sho.
> suffer here, where I know that a certain
> Society have ever wished to stand fair. (30)

On his part he hoped the colonies would adopt a
more moderate policy of trade "on principles of prudence & good economy". They should reject such articles as they could do without or manufacture themselves.
He admitted that such action would probably not obtain
the repeal of the tea duty, but at least it would encourage the growth of American industry. (31) Complete
non-importation, he wrote to Henry Drinker, not only

injured many worthy people who depended on commerce
with England, but it would also turn such trade to
Montreal, Rhode Island, Maryland and Virginia. "Had
a broader bottom been taken at first as Maryland and
Virginia", there would never be need for "a shameful
retreat wch now one can't help fearing must be the
Case". (32)

As James and others feared, it was not long before
the colonial policy of non-importation underwent extensive modification. The change began in July 1770,
when the New York merchants decided to reopen their
trade with England in all but taxed articles. (33)
Agitation for an alteration of policy was thereupon revived in Philadelphia where the merchants were not at
first inclined to follow the New York plan. (34) However, it soon became obvious that the New Yorkers would
profit at the expense of their southern neighbors. On
September 12, therefore, fourteen merchants informed
the merchants' committee of their dissatisfaction with
the state of affairs and suggested a reopening of trade
in all articles except tea. (35) Although the committee refused to take the opinion of the merchants individually, as requsted by the complainants, it promised to call a general meeting of the subscribers to
the old agreement. (36)

Fearing a recurrence of what had happened at the
last general meeting, the dissenters called a meeting
of the subscribers which fewer than half attended. The
merchants' committee also attended this meeting and
appealed for a continuation of the existing agreement.
The majority of those present, however, voted to adopt
the New York plan of general importation, barring
taxed articles, and consequently the committee resigned. (37)

This action was in accord with what many of the
Quaker merchants had desired for some time. Samuel
Coates, for one, thought that if this had been done on
the partial repeal of the Townsend Acts, it would have
been more timely. In his opinion the Boston merchants
had betrayed New York by arranging importation on
their own behalf to Montreal and Quebec, thereby
stealing the Indian trade. Although New York, to its
honor, had held out and had finally broken only under
the pressure of Boston's action, he felt the New York
merhcants should have consulted the Philadelphia merchants before opting so quickly for partial importation. (38)

The decision of the merchants had far-reaching
political effects, since it resulted in an open split
among the supporters of the Quaker party. Continuation
of non-importation was in the interest of the mechanics,
artisans, and small tradesmen, and they blamed the
merchants for its demise. In the elections of October
1770, the mechanics responed to the appeal of the more
radical elements whose leaders, mainly from the Presbyterian element, had vigorously supported non-importation on political as well as economic grounds. The
result was the defeat of the Quaker party leader
Joseph Galloway who stood for election from Philadelphia County. This shift has been termed one of the
most important events in the history of the province,
for it created the nucleus of a patriot faction or
party and led to the eventual seizure of power by
the radicals. (39)

At its sessions in September 1770, Philadelphia
Yearly Meeting drafted an epistle of advice to the
other American yearly meetings regarding the recent
events. This cautioned Friends against entering
into associations or supporting measures to assert
their civil rights and liberties which would produce
consequences "inconsistent with the nature of the
Gospel, and our peaceable Testimony thereto". Friends
in all places were encouraged "to live near the Divine
principle which ... will preserve us in a conduct becoming our Holy Profession". (40) New York, New
England, and Maryland Yearly Meetings all communicated
the contents of the epistle to their members. (41)

The next three years were a period of comparative
calm, and the Quakers breathed a sigh of relief. Early
in 1771 the Philadelphia Meeting for Sufferings wrote
to the English Friends:

> It hath been & is a cause of Reverent
> thankfulness that after the Commotions
> with which many have been agitated, Friends
> in general here are preserved in such a
> state of unity & Concord, that the in-
> fluence of their example, is considered &
> acknowledged by others; and that the en-
> deavors used to guard our Brethren
> against any attempts to contend for Civil
> Liberty or Priviledges in a manner unbecoming
> our peaceable profession were salutary &
> seasonable...(42)

Later that spring James Pemberton shared his
analysis of the situation with Dr. Fothergill. Despite
the unhappy reactions of the colonies against the policies of the British Government, he hoped that if the
Americans now conducted themselves with prudence, the
Ministry would surmount its resentment and act for
the interest of Britain and the Dominions. As for
Pennsylvania, from the "noise and clamour discovered in
ye temper of their (the Ministry's) opponents we have
reason to think that power would not be much safer in
their hands". Among them there were too many "clamorous
men...who with the greatest vociferations for Liberty,
have under a temporary power, given proofs of the most
tyrannical disposition. "(43)

like colonists

(1) Mildred and Roberts to Thomas Clifford, Feb. 9,
     1770, Clifford Pap., vol 5, 153; same to John
     Reynell, Feb. 8, 1770, Coates,Reynell Pap., bx.15
     (1772-1773).
(2) Dennys de Berdt to Thomas Cushing, Feb.2, 1770;
     same to Edward Sheafe, Feb. 2, 1770, "Letters of
     Dennys de Berdt", loc.cit., 396,398.
(3) The Cambridge History of the British Empire,ed.
     J. Holland Rose, A. P. Newton, E. A. Benians (8
     vols., New York and Cambridge, 1929-1959), v.1,
     668-69.
(4) Fisher, Struggle for American Independence,v. 1,
     132.
(5) Mildred and Roberts to John Reynell, March 14,
     1770, Coates,Reynell Pap., bx. 14.
(6) Abel James to Henry Drinker, June 25, 1770, Abel
     James Letter Book, 1770, in the Jonah Thompson
     Collection, at the HSP.
(7) Dickerson, Oliver M., The Navigation Acts and the
     American Revolution (Philadelphia, 1951), 163-64.
(8) Ibid., 166.
(9) Henry Drinker to Abel James, Feb. 12, 1770, James
     and Drinker Correspondence, 1759-1775, Jonah
     Thompson Col.
(10) Abel James to Pigon & Booth, April 26, 1770, Let-
     ter Book; same to Launcelot Cowper, June 15, 1770,
     in ibid.
(11) Abel James to Dr. Evans, May 2, 1770, in ibid.
(12) Same to Launcelot Cowper, July 2, 1770, in ibid.
(13) Same to Henry Drinker, July 20, 1770, in ibid.
(14) Ibid.
(15) London M.f.S. to Phil. M. f. S., Aug 24, 1770,
     Phil. M. f. S., Min., v. 1, 328-29.
(16) Dr. Fothergill to James Pemberton, Aug. 15, 1770,
     Ett.Pem.Pap.,v.2, 63.
(17) Schlesinger, Colonial Merchants, 217-18; Abel
     James to Henry Drinker, July 5, 1770, Letter Book;
     Samuel Coates to William Logan, Sept. 26, 1770,
     Letter Book, 1763-1781.
(18) Henry Drinker to Abel James, April 29, 1770, cited
     in Drinker, Henry, "Effects of the Non-Importation
     Agreement in Philadelphia", PMHB, v. 14 (1890),43.
(19) Ibid.
(20) Henry Drinker to Abel James, May 26, 1770, ibid.,
     44.
(21) Same to same, May 16, 1770, ibid.
(22) Schlesigner, op.cit., 219.

(23) Abel James to Launcelot Cowper, June 18, 1770,
     Letter Book.
(24) Abel James to Samuel Elam, June 27, 1770, in ibid.
(25) Thomas Gilpin to Benjamin Franklin, Feb. 6, 1769,
     cited in Gilpin, Thomas, "Memoir of Thomas Gilpin",
     PMHB vol. 49 (1925), 303; same to same, May 17,
     1770, ibid., 311.
(26) Olton, Charles S., "Philadelphia Mechanics in the
     First Decade of the Revolution, 1765-1775", Jour-
     nal of American History, v. 59, (1972-1973), 321.
     Non-importation had been a stimulant to local
     manufacturing, much to the advantage of the
     mechanics and artisans.
(27) Schlesinger, op.cit., 219; Pa. Gaz., June 7, 1770.
(28) Samuel Coates to William Logan, Sept. 26, 1770,
     Letter Book. Lieutenant Governor Colden of New
     York blamed the Quakers erroneously for this out-
     come.· He informed his superiors in England that
     when the duties on glass and paper were removed,
     the Philadelphians had decided upon a general im-
     portation of all articles except tea. Soon
     thereafter, a letter had arrived from a "Gentle-
     man in England, on whom the Quakers in Pennsyl-
     vania repose the greatest confidence", advising
     strict adherence to the original agreement
     until every internal tax was renounced. This had
     altered the decision of the Philadelphia merchants
     (Lt. Gov. Colden to the Earl of Hillsborough,
     July 7, 1770, Documents Relative to the Colonial
     History of New York,(15 vols., Albany,1853-1887),
     v. 8, 216; same to Anthony Todd, July 11, 1770,
     ibid., 218. The gentleman referred to was
     evidently Benjamin Franklin as indicated in
     Schlesinger, op.cit., 219-220.
(29) Abel James to Launcelot Cowper, June 20, 1770,
     Letter Book.
(30) Ibid.
(31) Abel James to Dr. Evans, June 23, 1770, in ibid.
(32) Abel James to Henry Drinker, July 5, 1770, in ibid.
(33) Schlesinger, op.cit.,225-227;New York Merchants to
     the Phil.Merchants,July 10,1770,Pa. Jnl., July 12,
     1770.
(34) Philadelphia merchants to the New York merchants,
     July 11, 1770, Pa. Jnl., July 12, 1770.
(35) Schlesinger, op.cit.,231; Pa.Gaz.,Sept. 20,1770,
     Pa. Jnl., Sept. 20, 1770. Among the complainants
     were John Reynell, James and Drinker, Clement
     Biddle , Jeremiah Warder and Thomas Fisher.
(36) The Quakers still on the committee were William

Fisher, Samuel Howell, Thomas Fisher and George
Roberts, three of whom were later disowned, as
indicated in chap. 2, note 3, above.

(37) Schlesinger, op.cit.,231; Pa. Gaz., Sept. 27, 1770
Pa. Jnl., Sept. 27, 1770.

(38) Samuel Coates to William Logan, Sept. 26, 1770,
Letter Book.

(39) Huston, James H., Pennyslvania Politics 1746-1770.
(Princeton, 1972), 235-236, 240-243; Ryerson,
Richard Alan, Leadership in Crisis (unpublished
Ph.D. thesis, Johns Hopkins Univ., 1972), 109.

(40) Phil. Y.M., Min., v.3, 271-72.

(41) N.Y.Y.M., Min., v. 1, 63-4; Md. Y.M., Min., v.3,
43; Epistle from Phil. Y.M. to N.E.Y.M., 1770,
So. Kingston Pap.

(42) Phil. M.f.S. to London M.f.S., Feb 21, 1771,
Phil. M.f.S., Min. v. 1, 331.

(43) James Pemberton to Dr. Fothergill, May 3, 1771,
Pem.Pap., v. 24, 159.

Chapter V

THE TEA CRISIS AND ITS SEQUEL

The peaceful lull in the imperial controversy
which followed the cessation of non-importation soon
proved to be but a short-lived and deceptive calm. The
one item of the Townsend Acts left unrepealed in 1770,
the tax on tea, was destined to precipitate a new
struggle between the mother country and her insistent
colonies. According to imperial mercantile legislation,
Britain was the only lawful source for the importation
of colonial tea. Before the passage of the acts of
1767, all tea imported into England from India or elsewhere was taxed one shilling per pound, a sum passed on
to the colonial merchants. Dutch tea, therefore, was
less expensive, and there was widespread smuggling
from Holland, with proportionate losses for the East
India Tea Company which held the monopoly of the
British tea market.

In order to increase the sale of tea to the colonies, Parliament had allowed in the Townsend Acts a
complete drawback for five years of the shilling per
pound tax on all tea transshipped to America, provided
the Company compensated the government for any resulting loss in revenue. In place of the former shilling
tax, a three penny duty per pound was to be levied on
the arrival of the tea in the colonies, a device intended primarily to assert Parliament's authority.
This reduction of the tax on tea put English imported
tea on a more equal footing with foreign imports and
even made the price for the American consumer about
one-half of what was paid in Great Britain. But the
colonists continued the boycott of the British tea,
considering the duty required as unconstitutional
parliamentary taxation. This in turn encouraged smuggling, to the benefit of many merchants. (1)

Smuggling had long been widely practised by the
colonial merchants to thwart the restrictions of the
trade and navigation laws. Evasion of the imperial
customs regulations by trading with the French, Spanish
and Dutch possessions in the New World had proven
highly profitable. For this reason the British government in 1764 inaugurated a far-reaching program to im-

prove the enforcement of the trade laws at colonial ports, a step which soon became a chief cause of discontent among American merchants.

Since many Friends, especially in Pennsylvania and Rhode Island, were engaged in mercantile pursuits, they were subject to great temptation to indulge in illegal trade. Obedience to the law was one of the chief tenets of the Society, and therefore most American yearly meetings had incorporated an article on the subject in their Books of Discipline. Philadelphia, Maryland, New York, Virginia, and New England Yearly Meetings had all done so, and Philadelphia's query, typical of the others, read:

> Do you maintain a faithful Testimony...
> Against defrauding the King of his dutys,
> or Buying or vending of goods unlawfully
> Imported, or prize Goods...?

New York Yearly Meeting had condensed this query to "defrauding the King of his Dues". (2)

The Philadelphia Friends were especially concerned over the maintenance of this testimony. At its annual session in 1771 the Yearly Meeting urged its members to manifest "our Faithfulness and Allegiance to the King" and to give no countenance "to any thing that has a tendency to defraud him of his Customs and dues, which it is feared some professing among us have not been so attentively concerned to discourage as our duty requires..." (3) Answers to the queries which were read periodically in the monthly and quarterly meetings indicate that this testimony was not sufficiently adhered to, and one of the chief offenses in this connection was the use of tea unlawfully imported. In September 1772, Shrewsbury and Rahway Quarterly Meeting reported: "...all are not clear of Buying goods unlawfully imported". (4) The following year the quarterly meeting specifically mentioned the use of tea as one type of deviation. (5) Chester Quarterly Meeting reported similar difficulties. (6) Late in 1774 it stated that "a scruple" had arisen among the members "respecting the use of Tea, as being an article unlawfully imported". (7) Philadelphia Monthly Meeting in its answer to this query declared that "most of those in the use of Tea, are not clear..." (8)

In New England, the Rhode Island Quakers faced the same problem. In the spring of 1772 Rhode Island

66

Quarterly Meeting issued an epistle of advice to the
subordinate monthly meetings, emphasizing this particular query. Reports received indicated there were

> some among Friends (nothwithstanding the
> present advice of friends to the Contrary)
> who do not maintain a faithful testimony
> against Depriving the King of his Dues. (9)

The epistle urged the monthly meetings to inspect the
conduct of their members carefully in this respect "and
deal with the offenders...according to the Discipline".

The following year a similar instruction was sent
out to the monthly meetings stating that there were
some members who were in the "practice of Running
Goods". This activity was the cause of many of the
current disturbances, and participation in it would
render the Friends "odious in the sight of the world
and Ill'y bespeake our Gratitude to the King under
whose Government we enjoy so many Priviledges". The
monthly meetings were directed to testify against dis-
obedient members without unnecessary delay. (10)

Because of the refusal of the Americans to drink
tea imported from England, the East India Tea Company
had by 1773 accumulated a large surplus in its store-
houses in London which, together with some unwise financial actions, had brought the Company into dire financial straits. The British government, deeply concerned about the Company's difficulties because of its
importance in the imperial commercial system and its
key position on the Indian sub-continent, attempted to
ameliorate its fiscal problems by allowing it to lower
the price of tea to the colonists, thereby inducing
them to buy more English tea.

As already noted, the Townsend Acts had provided
that the Company compensate the government for losses
in revenue due to the complete drawback of English
import duties on tea transshipped to America. In 1772
a three-fifths drawback was instituted, compensated
for by elimination of liability for losses in revenue
occasioned thereby. Since this alteration had not resulted in a significant increase in the sale of tea,
by the Tea Act of 1773 Parliament restored a complete
drawback and provided that the Company could ship its
tea directly to consignees in the colonies. In this
way, middlemen's profits were eliminated, and the price
to the Americans could be made more attractive. The
only duty left was the three pence tax, to be collected

67

at the colonial ports. (11) Despite a strong move in
Parliament to abolish the remaining tea tax, Lord North,
at the behest of the King, insisted on its retention as
a sign of Parliamentary authority. (12) This action
proved to be the fatal step which, by the succession of
events which it induced, rendered reconciliation between Great Britain and the colonies virtually impossible and led ultimately to war.

The colonists did not take kindly to the new
arrangement. The merchants stood to lose because of
the East India Tea Company's monopoly of the colonial
tea market, while the American objection to Parliamentary taxation remained unappeased. Colonial discontent
was further instensified by the fact that as a result
of the new procedure, the colonial merchants could no
longer boycott the importation of tea from England by
refusing to buy it on the London market. Thus the
British government could circumvent that unique weapon
of colonial protest.

During the fall of 1773, measures were taken in
all the colonial ports to prevent the landing and sale
of tea shipped under the provisions of the revised law.
On October 18 the Philadelphians held a public meeting
of protest at the State House and adopted resolutions
branding the law as taxation without representation
and declaring those countenancing its operation to be
enemies to their country. (13)

By this time some prominent Philadelphia Friends
had become involved in implementing the Tea Act. The
large and influential firms of James and Drinker, and
Thomas and Isaac Wharton had accepted commissions as
agents of the East India Tea Company. A committee
appointed by the State House meeting of October 18
waited on them and eventually obtained their resigna--
tions, although the delay of James and Drinker in
complying with their request somewhat irritated the
radicals. (14) At the same time some other Friends
were participants in the popular movement to resist
the enforcement of the Tea Act.

Before the State House meeting, the overseers of
the three Philadelphia Monthly Meetings, greatly concerned over the effect of the public agitation on
their fellow members, met to consider appropriate
action. At a second meeting which included other
weighty Friends, it was decided to call a general
meeting of all male members of the Society in Phila-

delphia on the 17th, the day preceeding the State House
assembly. On that occasion the advice of George Fox
to the Friends of his time to avoid "bustling &
Troubles or tumults", the cautioning epistle from the
London Meeting for Sufferings of 1769, and a similar
cautioning minute of the recent Yearly Meeting sessions
were read. Various Friends then spoke to the gathering
"exciting to a due Consideration of the Nature of our
Religious Profession which requires us to keep quiet
and Still both in respect to Conversation & Conduct on
such public occasions". (15) It was not therefore surprising that the Quakers generally abstained from
attending the State House gathering.

Subsequently James Pemberton wrote to the English
Friends informing them of the events which had trans-
pired, and assuring them that as far as he knew, no
Quakers had participated. In conclusion he stated the
position of the Philadelphia Friends as follows:

> Altho: we are not insensible of the
> Incroachments of Powers & of the value of
> Civil Rights yet in matters contestable
> we can neither join with nor approve the
> measures which have been too often proposed
> by particular persons and adopted by others
> for assertg and defending them, and such is
> the agitation of those who are foremost
> in these matters it appears in Vain to
> interfere. (16)

Although Pemberton did not approve of the actions
of his fellow citizens, he called for a recognition of
Britain's provocative actions. In a letter to Mildred
and Roberts he declared the British government should
consider how unreasonable was its attempt to govern a
people with severity "when gentle methods and constitutional laws would procure their affection and allegiance" in a most effectual manner. (17)

Meanwhile the British Friends were exerting their
influence to avert harsh treatment of the colonies.
Patience Wright, a Quaker and a friend of the well
known member of Parliament, Colonel Barre, spent nearly
two hours with the King discussing the American situation. (18) The London Meeting for Sufferings, several
of whose members were active in the same cause, advised
the Philadelphia Friends not to be discouraged if no
immediate advantage resulted from such applications
and urged:

> Let us rather be induced to watch
> carefully the times, and as Providence may
> stir on the minds of any, and make way for
> them, to those in Authority, let us
> faithfully discharge Our Duty in this
> respect, and so...be made the Instruments
> of averting the Calamities which...
> overtake those who are harried...into
> hurtful Excesses. (19)

Thomas Crowley now came forward again with his plea for colonial representation in Parliament, although the colonies had generally rejected the idea. During 1770 Crowley had consistently appealed to Lord North in behalf of such a plan, and had even presented "A Memorial and Plan of Union" to the King, his Ministers, and a Privy Council. (20) He now published "A Receipt ot Mediate the Very Dangerous Differences between the Mother Country and her Numerous Colonies"(21) In this treatise he proposed that Parliament pass an act granting the colonies representation in Parliament, and that the only colonial taxes levied by such a body would fall on Englishmen and colonials alike, thereby guaranteeing security against unilateral and arbitrary taxation of the colonies. Little attention, however, seems to have been paid to these appeals.

A new turn of events occurred early in December 1773 with the arrival at Boston of two shiploads of tea. Both ships were owned by Quakers, the Dartmouth by Francis Rotch of New Bedford and the Beaver by William Rotch, the leading Friend on the island of Nantucket. Francis Rotch was in Boston when the ships arrived, and when he saw the temper of the people who were protesting the landing of the tea, he did his utmost to obtain clearances for the ships to leave Boston and return to England. But neither the crown-appointed customs officers nor the royal governor would grant him such permission, with the result that the mob finally took over and unloaded the tea shipments into the harbor. (22)

Furious at the destruction of property and the flaunting of Parliamentary acts, the British government decided to resort to coercive measures. Early in 1774 Parliament passed the so-called Coercive Acts, closing the port of Boston until the destroyed tea was paid for, and reorganizing the government of the colony so as to bring all governmental functions into the hands of crown-appointed officials. In May General

Gage arrived as governor to supervise the enforcement
of the acts. On the day of his arrival, the Bostonians
held a town meeting which denounced the action of
Parliament and called on the other colonies to join in
a strict non-importation and non-exportation agreement. (23)

The Bostonians then sent Paul Revere to Philadelphia to obtain the support and cooperation of their
fellow colonists. On reaching his destination, Revere
immediately consulted with Joseph Reed, Charles
Thomson, and Thomas Mifflin, the leaders of the Philadelphia radicals, who decided to call a meeting of the
more prominent citizens of the city. (24) In an effort
to assure a favorable outcome of such a meeting, it was
decided to obtain, if possible, the backing of the
leading Friends, or at least to assure they would refrain from blocking measures the radicals desired to
see adopted.

Through the intermediation of John Dickinson who
was now in the confidence of may of the Quakers and
associated closely with them, several of the leading
Friends attended the appointed meeting. After
extensive discussions it was resolved to request the
governor to convene the Assembly to consider the
current emergency. A committee of nineteen, of whom
six were Quakers, was appointed to execute the resolve, and it was authorized to call a general meeting
of the city's inhabitants in case the governor refused
to act. (25)

Events were now progressing toward the point when
the Friends would face the necessity of disciplining
members who refused to observe the Society's position
regarding the type of protest increasingly employed by
the radical leaders and their followers. An indication
of the trend in this direction appeared in connection
with the public fast day observed on June 1, the day
the Boston Port Act went into effect, as an expression
of sympathy for the Bostonians. On May 30 representatives of the various religious denominations in Philadelphia met and decided that all business should cease
on June 1. (26) The Quakers, hearing of this action,
held a meeting in their schoolhouse on Chestnut Street
and formulated a statement published later in the
Pennsylvania Gazette, declaring that no one had been
authorized to represent them in the aforesaid meeting,
and that if anyone had pretended to do so he had acted
contrary to the religious principles of the Society.

71

They emphasized their sympathy with the distressed Bostonians but stated that although they fully realized the value of their religious and civil rights, they felt it their duty "to assert them in a Christian spirit". (27)

Despite the request of the committee of nineteen, the Governor refused to convene a special session of the Assembly. Thereupon the committee decided to call a general meeting of citizens and invited representatives of each religious group in the city to assist them in making plans. Of six Quakers invited to attend, only four came: Owen Jones, James Pemberton, George Roberts, and Thomas Wharton. (28) They at first had had grave doubts as to the propriety of participating in the project, and had finally decided to attend only on the advice of several Friends in the hope of exerting their influence "to correct if not prevent ill timed & rash proceedings". (29)

The proposed planning conference was held on June 10. Mr. Dickinson produced a number of resolves which after some debate were adopted, the harsher parts having been eliminated at the insistence of the Quakers present. (30) Despite this success, these Friends became convinced of the inconsistency of their "meeting in such a milieu to confer on matters of this kind". After offering such opinions as they deemed proper they refrained from attending any further meetings. (31) Nevertheless the committee adopted several of their suggestions, especially the one requiring the submission of the speeches to the presiding officers before the general meeting, in order to avoid inflammatory harangues which might incite the public. (32) Also, the conferees appointed James Pemberton, along with Dickinson and Thomas Willing as presidents for the proposed public meeting. (33)

Two days before the State House gathering, the Philadelphia Meeting for Sufferings convened. After careful consideration of the trend of events, it declared that for the Friends as a religious society the most consistent conduct was to

> keep from mixing with the people in their
> Public Consultations, as snares & dangers
> arise from meetings of that kind, however
> well disposed particulars be to mitigate
> & soften the violent disposition too
> prevalent...(34)

72

The Meeting also agreed to meet weekly "to watch every opportunity wherein ffrds may be useful in the present trying Circumstances..." (35)

The public meeting at the State House on June 18 passed resolutions denouncing the Boston Port Act and recommending the calling of a congress of all the colonies. The submission of speeches to the presidents had evidently had a moderating effect, especially in the case of Provost Smith who, more restrained than usual, urged the people to temperate action. (36) A Committee of Correspondence was appointed for the city of Philadelphia to keep in touch with other cities and colonies. Twelve of the members were Friends, including Thomas Wharton, James Pemberton, and Edward Pennington. (37)

Pemberton's name had been approved without obtaining his consent, and in view of the position taken by the Meeting for Sufferings of which he was a member, he refused to serve on the committee. (38) Wharton and the other Friends, however, accepted their appointments. Although Wharton had not participated in public affairs for some years, he had decided to cooperate with this endeavor at the solicitation of a number of his fellow citizens who shared his desire "to keep the transactions of our City within the points of moderation & not Indecent or offensive to our parent State". (39)

The new committee met at Carpenters' Hall on June 27 and resolved that the Assembly should meet not later than August 1 to consider the current state of affairs. It also directed that letters be sent to the counties of the province, recommending the establishment of county committees to act in conjunction with the one in Philadelphia. (40)

A few days after the State House meeting, the Meeting for Sufferings again convened. Alarmed over the participation of members of the Society in the recent public proceedings, it appointed a committee to visit the Quaker members of the Committee of Correspondence and inform them of its opposition to their action in serving. The committee subsequently reported its failure to induce the Friends concerned to withdraw. (41)

Events now moved rapidly. On July 11 a meeting of tradesmen of the city met and expressed the hope that a colonial congress would draw up a uniform non-

73

importation agreement for the colonies to adopt. Four days later a convention of delegates from the counties of the province met in Philadelphia to discuss the current crisis. The convention adopted a resolution which declared the Coercive Acts passed by Parliament against Massachusetts to be unconstitutional, called for the meeting of a colonial congress to obtain redress of colonial grievances, and expressed the delegates' intention to cooperate with a cessation of all trade with Britain if such a congress so decided. (42)

In addition to encouraging direct action, those who supported a more vigorous policy of colonial protest subsequently moved to silence their opponents by threat and inuendo. It therefore became increasingly difficult, and even at times somewhat dangerous, to express opposition or to question their methods and activities. (43) Shortly after the above mentioned events, resentment against this deprivation of freedom of debate and expression of opinion on the burning issues of the day was expressed by John Drinker, a member of the Meeting for Sufferings. In two articles in the Pennsylvania Journal signed "A Tradesman of Philadelphia", and later published under the title Observations on the Late Popular Measures offered to the Serious Consideration of the Sober Inhabitants of Pennsylvania by a Tradesman of Philadelphia, Drinker complained that the freedom of the press had been interfered with by the illegal menaces of a "prevailing party" resulting in two newspapers turning down his articles. The editor, William Bradford, appended comments disavowing Drinker's charge, especially as it concerned the Pennsylvania Journal. (44)

While supporting the rights of the colonies, Drinker called for the utilization of the established governmental procedures in obtaining redress of grievances, and he implied that law-defying, smuggling interests were playing a strong hand in the current radical movement. He declared that "the devoted colonies had been under tyrannical proscription" during the eight years since the Declaratory Act of 1766. And now, he continued, the latest act of the British Government had been to grant authority to the East India Tea Company to export its tea directly to America "subject to that obnoxious duty". (45) He accused the British Government of driving over the rights and privileges of the colonies "under the colour of punishing a flagitious conduct, a conduct which we cannot justify".

74

Whatever the situation was, however, Drinker claimed it was the "right of every free man" to question the expediency of placing public confidence in such politicians as were instrumental

> in exposing us to the hand of oppression,
> both ministerial, parliamentary and
> popular, and who, by prefering money and
> popularity before honesty have made it
> their interest to lead us out of the
> path of order and honour. (46)

In conclusion he proclaimed his own convictions on this issue:

> I am jealous for the honour of my
> countrymen in whom I wish a righteous
> zeal to prevail,...a zeal for that liberty
> which is essential to human happiness,
> and not a liberty which is destructive
> of it, a license to tread down common
> right on the pretence of opposing the
> invaders of it. (47)

Jabez Fisher, another Quaker merchant and strong proponent of the American cause, unable to obtain a hearing in the Philadelphia press, published an open letter under the name of Veritas in Rivington's New York Gazeteer of July 15. In this he denounced the manner in which Charles Thomson and the radicals were employing unfair and abusive tactics to silence their opponents, and he complained that "the presses in Philadelphia were held under an undue influence". He stated his apprehension as follows:

> I wish unanimity firmness and moderation.
> An over-heated violence or an unbounded
> zeal will not effect the purposes aimed
> at...and the destruction of public
> confidence will end in the destruction of
> liberty. (48)

In a subscript to the letter he stated:

> The Gentleman who hands this to the Printer,
> is desirous to know why this subject has
> not been discussed with equal freedom in
> the Philadelphia newspapers...And does not
> the sending it here to be published imply
> either partiality or fear in the Printers?
> (49)

75

It is obvious that the proponents of a vigorous protest action against British policy while claiming that theirs was a struggle for liberty, were in the anomalous position of depriving their fellow subjects of their civil liberties.

In communicating these developments to the London Meeting for Sufferings, the Philadelphia Friends pointed out that since their membership in the province was numerous, some deviation of opinion was to be expected with regard to the recent public activities and resolutions. Some Friends had attended public meetings and served on committees, and although in no case had they approved of the measures undertaken, their participation in such bodies had, regretfully, rendered them parties to whatever actions resulted. (50)

The Philadelphia Quakers also stated their official attitude toward the current crisis. Their basic thesis was that their forefathers had extended invaluable religious privileges to all denominations of the province by the constitution under which the government of the colony was established. These privileges had been preserved "thro' the kindness of Divine Providence and the clemency of the kings who presided over the British Dominions". The most grateful acknowledgements were due for this favor, and any means proposed or pursued which were inconsistent with the government's authority as established by the charter and laws of the colony were a cause for alarm. Therefore the Friends could not approve "the Peoples collecting at town meetings for the debating & determining on matters of important concern", a procedure they feared might endanger their "Civil & Religious Liberties". Nevertheless they intended to wait patiently for some opportunity "wherein we may be mutually Instrumental to engage the attention of those in power for Conciliating the differences, and averting the scourage threatening both countries". (51)

Friends in other parts of America were also feeling the reprecussions of the events transpiring in New England. In the youngest and most southerly province of Georgia there was early reaction against the Boston Port Act and the other coercive measures. A Quaker settlement had been established there in 1768 under the patronage of the royal governor, Sir James Wright, hence the name Wrightsboro. It had now grown to about two hundred families, and a monthly meeting had been set up. (52)

In August 1774 a group of citizens from the various parishes of the province met in Savannah and adopted a series of resolutions denouncing the action of the British government. When the Wrightsboro community learned of this, the Quakers joined with others in issuing a protest against the resolutions. This statement declared that the steps taken in Savannah as representing the province had been undertaken only by "a few acting for a whole" and without the latter's knowledge. Such proceedings they "apprehended as being contrary to the rights and privileges of every British subject". Among the first to sign were two leading Quakers, Joseph Maddox and Jonathan Sell. (53)

At its sessions the following October, North Carolina Yearly Meeting, of which Wrightsboro Monthly Meeting was a constituent meeting, issued an epistle of advice to its subordinate meetings, "Relating to the Commotions now Subsisting between Great Brittain, and America". It exhorted all Friends to maintain their traditional conduct of "Passive Obedience, or Submission to our Superiours", and declared

> ...we cannot Joyn with things that we
> do not know in what or where they will
> End, and therefore we do think it will be
> adviseable and Safe for Friends to keep
> Clear of Joyning in things that may End in
> Distress and Confusion. (54)

Increasingly disturbed over the mounting rancor of the imperial dispute, the Friends in the mother country were concerned that the American Quakers maintain their pacifist testimony and remain aloof from internal colonial controversies. At its sessions in May 1774, London Yearly Meeting addressed epistles of advice to all the American yearly meetings with particular reference to the current state of affairs. Several of the epistles urged the colonial Quakers to conduct themselves "with circumspection in matters of public concern", to keep "free from all tumults and commotions", and to "manifest to the world we are under the government of His spirit who is the Prince of Peace." In their epistle to the Philadelphia Friends the English Quakers expressed great satisfaction that their conduct during the recent agitations in the colonies "hath been very acceptable to the government here and hath tended to promote a favorable disposition towards you". (55)

Because of the particularly critical course of events in New England, the English Friends were especially anxious about the situation of the Friends there. The London Yearly Meeting epistle of May 1774 to the New England Yearly Meeting expressed the hope that their New England brethren would be preserved from taking part in any of the Commotions and Disturbances" which might occur. (56) Later in the year the London Meeting for Sufferings addressed a special epistle of concern to the New England Friends, conveying the "brotherly sympathy we feel for you under the present trying occasion" and urging them:

> When ye shall hear of wars and rumors of wars, see that ye be not troubled...Mix not in the various outward Consultations, dwell alone...(57)

This epistle was read in the Friends Meetings and distributed to Friends families throughout the confines of the Yearly Meeting. (58)

(1) Fisher, <u>Struggle for American Independence</u>, v.1,
     164. Samuel Wharton in his unpublished treatise,
     Observations upon the Consumption of Teas in
     North America, London 1773 (in the HSP), claims
     that an even more important reason for the colon-
     ists buying tea in the Netherlands was that the
     Americans could always exchange their grain and
     flour for tea at any time in the Dutch ports
     whereas they were not acceptable in London where
     specie, of which the colonists had little, was
     required.
(2) Phil.Y.M.,Min., v.3 (1747-1779), 215; Md. Y.M.,
     Min., V. 3, 20; Va. Y.M.,Min. (1702-1843), 140;
     N.Y.Y.M., Min., v.1 (1746-1800), 95; N.E.Y.M. MS
     Book of Discipline, c.1760, 115-120, in the QCHC.
(3) Phil.Y.M., Min., v.3, 279.
(4) Shrewsbury and Rahway Q.M., Min., 1757-1828,
     Aug. 17, 1772.
(5) <u>Ibid</u>., Aug. 16, 1773.
(6) Chester (Concord) Q.M., Min., 1768-1813, Aug. 10,
     1772.
(7) <u>Ibid</u>., Aug. 8, 1774.
(8) Phil.M.M., Min., 1771-1777, 256.
(9) Epistle from R.I.Q.M. to the subordinate monthly
     meetings, April 9 & 10, 1772, in the So. Kingston
     Pap.
(10) Same to same, Jan.7 & 8, 1773, So. Kingston Pap.
(11) Schlesinger, <u>Colonial Merchants</u>,250-51, 262-63.
     For a discussion of the problems of the East India
     Tea Company see Labaree, Benjamin Woods, <u>The</u>
     <u>Boston Tea Party</u> (New York, 1964), chap. 4.
(12) Labaree, <u>op,cit</u>., 72-3. In the parliamentary de-
     bate, Lord North indicated there were "political
     reasons...of such weight, and strength" that he
     was very unwilling to support the abolition of the
     tea tax.
(13) Schlesinger, <u>op,cit</u>., 279, 281.
(14) Labaree, <u>op.cit</u>.,96-103; Taylor, Thomas B., "The
     Philadelphia Counterpart of the Boston Tea Party",
     <u>BFHA</u>, v. 3 (Feb., 1909), 30: Stone Frederick D.,
     "How the Landing of Tea Was Opposed in Philadel-
     phia by Colonel William Bradford and Others in
     1773", <u>PMHB</u>, v. 15 (1891), 389.
(15) James Pemberton to Dr. John Fothergill, Jacob
     Hagen, and David Barclay, Oct. 30, 1773, Pem.
     Pap., v. 34, 169; Phil.M.f.S., Min., v.1, 398.
(16) James Pemberton to Dr. John Fothergill et al.,

Oct. 30, 1773, loc.cit. There were those who
accused the Quakers of complicity in the commotions.
Joseph Reed informed the Earl of Dartmouth that
although they did not appear "openly in the
present opposition, they have given it every private encouragement". (Mr. Reed to the Earl of
Dartmouth, Dec. 27, 1773, cited in William B.
Reed's Life and Correspondence of Joseph Reed,
2 vols., Philadelphia, 1847, v.1, 55).

(17) James Pemberton to Daniel Mildred, Jan.3, 1774,
Cox, Wharton, Parrish Papers at the HSP.

(18) William Forster to his sister Elizabeth, Oct.7,
1773, Journal of the Friends' Hist. Soc. (London),
v. 20 (1923), 95,96. Col. Barré was a strong
supporter of the colonies.

(19) London M.f.S. to Phil.M.f.S., Dec.10, 1773,
Phil.M.f.S., Min., v.1, 409.

(20) Crowley, Thomas, Lett.and Diss., 136, passim.

(21) Ibid., 220.

(22) Larabee, op.cit., 118-125, chap.7; Stackpole,
Edouard A., The Sea Hunters, The New England
Whalemen During Two Centuries, 1635-1835 (Phila-
delphia, 1953), 62-65.

(23) Fisher, op.cit.,v.1, 175-176, 182-183; Schlesinger,
op.cit.,313.

(24) Charles Thomson to William Henry Drayton, Thomson
Papers, Collections of the New York Hist. Soc.,
v. 11 (1878), 275. Mifflin, as before mentioned,
was a Quaker.

(25) Ibid., "Joseph Reed's Narrative", Thomson Pap.
op.cit., 270; Schlesinger, op.cit., 343-344.
Charles Thomson expressed the attitude of the
radicals toward the Friends when he said: "...
they were principled against War, saw the storm
gathering, (and) were industriously employed to
prevent anything being done which might involve
Pennsylvania further in the dispute". (Charles
Thomson to William Henry Drayton, loc.cit.)
        The Quakers on the Committee were Edward Pen-
nington, Samuel Howell, Thomas Mifflin, Benjamin
Marshall, Jeremiah Warder, Jr., and John Cox. A
full list of the members is in Horace Weymess
Smith's Life and Correspondence of the Rev.
William Smith (2 vols., Philadelphia, 1879), v.1,
492.

(26) Gordon, Hist. of Pa., 485.

(27) Ibid.,486, 486n.; Amer.Arch., 4th Ser., v. 1, 365-
366; Marshall, Christopher, Diary 1773-1793, May
31, 1774, at the HSP. Christopher Marshall was

disowned by Philadelphia Monthly Meeting in 1751 for insufficiency of acknowledgement in the charge of intimate association with men engaged in forgery and the passing of false currency, and not for revolutionary activity as is often stated. (Phil. M.M., Min., 1745-1755, 3/31/1751).

(28) Bolles, Albert S., _Pennsylvania, Province and State_ (2 vols., Philadelphia and New York, 1892), v. 1, 421; Thomas Wharton to Samuel Wharton, July 5, 1774, Thomas Wharton Letter Book, 1773-1784, at the HSP.

(29) James Pemberton to Dr. Fothergill, July 1, 1774, Ett.Pem.Pap., v.2, 68. Thomas Wharton's viewpoint on the issues at hand probably represented the thinking of many Friends. In letters to various relatives and friends, he indicated his opinion that since the colonists could not be represented in Parliament, it was inconsistent with the "Spirit of our Constitution" for the property of an Englishman to be taken without his consent. This principle he applied to the tea tax or any other import duty. At the same time, he believed that the East India Tea Company should be reimbursed for the tea destroyed at Boston.

As a means of solving the current imperial problem he advocated a union between Great Britain and her colonies "whereby a lasting cement will be effected". The British government would appoint a supreme magistrate to reside in America. He together with a fixed number from each colonial assembly would form an upper house of a legislature whose function would be to control the general affairs of the continent and be a "proper check to the forward ambitious views of any one colony" - (Thomas Wharton to Anthony Ladd, April 5, 1774, Letter Book, 25-27; same to Samuel Wharton, May 3, July 5, 1774, _ibid._,29,51; same to Thomas Walpole, June 10, 1774, _ibid._, 47.

(30) Thomas Wharton to Samuel Wharton, July 5, 1774, _loc.cit_.

(31) James Pemberton to Dr. Fothergill, July 1, 1774, _loc.cit_.

(32) Ford, Paul Leicester,"The Adoption of the Pennsylvania Constitution of 1776", _Political Science Quarterly_,v.10, (1895),428;Charles Thomson to William Henry Drayton, _loc.cit_., 278; Thomas Wharton to Samuel Wharton, July 5, 1774, _loc.cit_.

(33) Charles Thomson to William Henry Drayton, _loc. cit_., 278.

(34) Phil. M.f.S., Min. v. 1, 414-15.
(35) James Pemberton to Dr. Fothergill, July 1, 1774,
     loc.cit.
(36) Schlesinger, op.cit.,346-47; Gordon,op.cit.,489;
     Fisher, Pennsylvania, 303. In preparation for the
     public meeting, Dickinson consulted James Pember-
     ton. On June 13 he sent Pemberton a note express-
     ing the desire to discuss a matter "Of great
     Importance to the public". Since their intimacy
     was known, he suggested that Pemberton call upon
     him "to avoid any suspicion of our concerting a
     Plan between us". (John Dickinson to James Pember-
     ton, June 13, 1774, Cox, Wharton, Parrish Pap.)
(37) Gordon,op.cit., 489; Smith, op.cit., 494-495.
     Both give the complete list of members of the
     committee. The Quakers were, besides those
     mentioned, Samuel Howell, George Roberts, Thomas
     Mifflin, John Cox, Anthony Morris, Jr., Jeremiah
     Warder, Jr., Reuben Haines, Benjamin Marshall and
     Isaac Howell.
(38) James Pemberton to Dr. Fothergill, July 1, 1774,
     loc.cit.
(39) Thomas Wharton to Samuel Wharton, July 5, 1774,
     loc.cit.Wharton believed that if the "Freedom of
     America were taken away, that of England would
     not continue long". At the same time he and other
     Friends were convinced that "decent & loyal
     Expressions, with a firm Attachment to the Consti-
     tutional Principles of an Englishman would better
     become (the Americans), than any other mode that
     could be adopted". (Thomas Wharton to Thomas Wal-
     pole, Aug. 2, 1774, Letter Book.)
(40) Lincoln, op.cit., 173.
(41) Phil. M.f.S., Min., v.1, 415; James Pemberton to
     Dr. Fothergill, July 1, 1744, loc.cit.
(42) Labaree, op.cit.,245; Ford, loc.cit.,428-29.
(43) Ryerson, op. cit.,15.
(44) Drinker, John, Observations on the Late Popular
     Measures (Phil., 1774), 11. See also the Pa. Jnl.
     Supplement for August 17, 1774.
(45) Drinker, op.cit., 11.
(46) Ibid., 7.
(47) Ibid., 22.
(48) Riv.'s N.Y. Gaztr., July 14, 1774.
(49) Ibid.
(50) Phil. M.f.S. to London M.f.S., July 21, 1774,
     Phil. M.f.S., Min., v. 1, 418-19.
(51) Ibid., 419-420.
(52) De Brahm, John Gerar William, History of the
     Province of Georgia with Maps of the Original

Survey, 1772 (Wormsloe, Ga., 1849), 25; Wrightsboro M.M., Min., v. 1, 1.

(53) The Revolutionary Records of the State of Georgia,
comp. by Allen D. Candler (3vols.,Atlanta, 1908),
v. 1, 13-7, 27-8. Maddox and Sell later became
loyalists and left Georgia with the British at the
end of the Revolution.

(54) N.C. Y. M., Min., v. 1, 130-34.

(55) London Y.M., Min., v. 5, 6-16 passim.

(56) London Y.M. to N.E.Y.M., 1774, So. Kingston Pap.

(57) London M.f.S. to N.E. M.f.S., November 4, 1774,
London M.f.S., Min. v. 33 (1771-1775), Oct. 7,
Nov. 4, 1774; a copy of the same is in the So.
Kingston Pap.

(58) N.E. M.f.S. to London M.f.S., Aug. 13, 1776,
Epistles to London Y.M., v.4, 430.

Chapter VI

THE QUAKERS CAST THEIR LOT

The Quakers and their allies were so apprehensive about the future actions of the Philadelphia radicals that they were prepared to employ any appropriate tactics to prevent the situation from getting out of control. Therefore, when the public meeting of July 15 threatened to convene a provincial congress unless the government acted, the governor summoned a special session of the Assembly on the pretext of considering an Indian outbreak on the frontier. (1) .

Joseph Galloway was now Speaker of the Assembly and its most influential member. He was strongly supported by the Quakers both because they agreed on the proprietary question and because he was a leader of the moderates in the dispute with the mother country.(2) At this time there were in the Assembly eleven Quaker members, decribed by a contemporary as "a parcel of Countrymen sitting with their hats on, great coarse cloth coats, leather breeches and woolen stockings in the month of July", who,with the support of the Anglicans, made Galloway's control of the House possible. (3)

In order to forestall action by a provincial congress, the Assembly resolved unanimously that a colonial congress should be held to obtain redress of American grievances. It appointed seven delegates to attend such a congres, among them three Friends, Rhoads, Mifflin, and Morton. (4) Galloway headed the delegation, the Assembly having accepted his condition that it approve instructions which he had drafted. (5)

The recent rapid course of events had demonstrated how swiftly the balance of political forces in the province was changing. The artisans and mechanics who had been staunch supporters of the Quakers in the previous decade were now being pulled into the train of the more radical and militant elements. They had organized the Patriot Society; they were in the forefront of the new protest movement which emerged in 1773-1774; and they had made their voices heard in the June public meetings. (6) It was evident that the lower middle and working classes were pursuing their own economic interests in demanding non-consumption of British imported goods and the encouragement of dom-

estic manufacturing. Their reaching out for a greater
role in the life and politics of the city was a disturbing development for the conservative and wealthy
classes which up to then had been in control. Evidence
of this change in the leadership of the revolutionary
movement is seen in the fact that whereas two thirds
(67%) of these signing the non-importation agreement
of 1769 were merchants, of which 39% were Quakers, in
1774 the merchants comprised only 50% of the movement's
leaders, of which only 29% were Quakers. Thus, the influence of both the merchant and Quaker elements had
declined, indicating a most significant alteration in
the occupational and religious character of the revolutionary leaders. (7)

In this last category were the well-to-do Quaker
merchants who were torn between opposition to British
colonial policy, which they considered both unjust and
unwise, and grave apprehension of the measures being
undertaken in retaliation. They feared that the
result of the latter would be separation from the mother country and political upheaval in the colony, accompanied by bloodshed and economic ruin. (8) This
anxiety of the Quakers over the future of their beloved
province had now led them to the point of appearing to
be more concerned about stemming the tide of radicalism
at home than resisting tyranny from abroad. Thus they
viewed the deliberations and outcome of the First Continental Congress in Philadelphia in the fall of 1774
with much trepidation.

In contrast to the apprehensive attitude of the
Philadelphia Friends toward the proposed congress,
Dr. Fothergill was inclined to be rather optimistic.
In his opinion, the delegates were "men of whose
penetration, judgment and stability he had reason to
think most favourably", and he trusted that a wise plan
of procedure would be adopted. (9) He hoped that the
congress would appoint a committee to go to England
immediately and that in the meantime the Americans
would observe "the most perfect submission to authority", avoiding all inflammatory publications and non-
importation schemes which their enemies could use to
their disadvantage. The primary task of such a committee would be to lobby extensively in both Houses
of Parliament, urging "with great moderation, yet
proper firmness,...their attention to the mutual,
reciprocal interests of a great empire". It was
imperative that the colonies prefer their immediate
interests to what they had the right but not the power

to demand. "Petitions, memorials, addresses," he
declared, "with whatsoever cogency of reason they are
composed, will be totally inadequate. They will be
treated as your Agents, as ex-officio businesses - and
they will soon have their quietus's". (10)

If such a course were followed, Fothergill was
sure that the more prudent Englishmen would be impressed by the moderation of the colonies and the
justice of the American cause. In case the government
insisted on pursuing an oppressive policy, the colonists would then be free to provide for their safety
and would have "all the people of sense and moderation"
on their side.

At the very time that the First Continental Congress was convening in Philadelphia in early September 1774, the Quakers attempted to influence the King
to adopt a milder policy toward the colonies. Jacob
Hagen, a member of the London Meeting for Sufferings
who became clerk of London Yearly Meeting in 1775, submitted to the royal cabinet, under condition of strict
confidentiality, a letter from some prominent Philadelphia Friends concerning the imperial dispute. The
letter, conveyed to the King by the Prime Minister,
Lord North, prompted a declaration of royal policy
burdened with unhappy consequences for the colonies.
The King's comments to North stated that the Quakers
in Pennsylvania had retained

> that coolness which is a very strong charac-
> teristic of that body of people; I was in
> hope it would have contained some declara-
> tion of their submission to the Mother
> Country; whilst by the whole tenor they seem
> to wish that England give in some degree,
> way to the opinions of North America;
> the dye is now cast, the colonies must
> either submit or triumph; I do not wish to
> come to severer measures but we must not
> retreat...(9)

The sessions of the First Continental Congress
lasted from September 5 until October 26. During this
time an incident occurred which clearly indicated an
important reason for the Pennsylvania Friends' fear
of a colonial union independent of Britain. On October 13 Stephen Hopkins, "a Wet Quaker", and Samuel
Ward, "a Wet Anabaptist", (12) informed John Adams

that a number of gentlemen from different parts of
America wished to confer with him on the proposition of
colonial union. Accordingly a meeting was arranged for
the following evening in Carpenters Hall. (13)

When John Adams arrived at the appointed time and
place, he found the "great Quakers, the Pembertons, the
Drinkers and the Shoemakers, &c" all there, about fifty
of them, with Israel Pemberton, "the great Belweather
of the Flock", at their head. A number of Baptists
were also present under the leadership of Isaac Bacchus
of New England. Bacchus opened the conference by
complaining about the unjust treatment of the Quakers
and Baptists by the legislative and judicial authorities of Massachusetts. (14) After some discussion,
Israel Pemberton arose and said that "the Conference
was not intended so much to inquire after particular
Facts and individual Cases, as into general Principles".
The Congress was planning a union of the colonies, but
there were difficulties in the way. He and his friends
were concerned over the establishment of religion in
Massachusetts, and they had arranged the interview in
order to induce the delegates from that province to
bring about the abolition of all such laws. (15)

In the subsequent discussion between Adams and
Pemberton, the latter asked the pointed question which
indicated the chief concern of the Quakers when considering colonial union: "Would you not allow your Brethren in the other Colonies Liberty of Conscience?" Although Adams was satisfied that the Quakers and Baptists were "hushed and abashed", and the "reasonable
conscientious part of them...convinced" that their
apprehensions were baseless, (16) he had conceived a
profound dislike for Pemberton. He later declared that
"Old Pemberton was rude and his rudeness was resented".
In his opinion,"this artful Jesuit...was endeavouring
to avail himself of this opportunity to break up the
Congress, or at least to withdraw the Quakers and the
governing part of Pennsylvania" from the support of
the other colonies.(17) Thereafter they detested the
name of Adams "and at all elections propagated far
and wide that John Adams was a Presbyterian, had
established Presbyterianism in the United States and
compelled Quakers, Baptists, and all other Denominations to pay Taxes to Support the Presbyterian
Church". (18)

Philadelphia Yearly Meeting held its annual session while the Continental Congress was sitting. More

disturbed than ever over the course of events, it issued a general epistle of advice to Friends throughout America. (20) This epistle pointed out that in case of past revolutions of government (21) their ancestors had consistently remonstrated against the oppression of rulers and their unjust laws, and that their avoidance of plots and conspiracies against any government had added a "convincing Force to the reasons they offered in support of their Rights and Liberties". Since under the present cirucmstances the Friends were indebted to the King for the enjoyment of the liberties they possessed in America, they were obligated to manifest their loyalty and allegiance to him. It waa therefore their duty to discourage any attempt "to excite dissaffection or disrespect to him", as well as manifest their dislike to "all such Writings as... may be published of that Tendency..." Included was a special exhortation against defrauding the King of his customs and dealing in or using goods unlawfully imported. (22)

The epistle aroused great displeasure on the part of the "friends of freedom and liberty". (23)   Ezra Stiles of Newport, Rhode Island, noted a month later that it was read in the Friends Meeting there, and he supposed that it had been procured by ministerial influence.   In his opinion, the ministry and its supporters were making special efforts to detach the Quakers and Baptists in America from the colonial cause.   The actions of the Quakers were dictated by London Yearly Meeting, he declared, and as long as that was the case, there was no hope for them "until the Seat of Empire (was) transferred or erected in America. " (24)

On the other hand, the Friends also had their defenders.   "A Lover of Peace" sent an excerpt from the epistle to the New York Gazette and the Weekly Mercury with the accompanying comment:

> The following paragraphs of an epistle
> from the annual meeting held in Phila-
> dephia, dated the first inst. express
> sentiments which do honour to that society
> and deserve to be considered by every
> man..." (25)

During the sessions of the Continental Congress, Joseph Galloway became the leader of the conservative faction, and in the course of the debates he proposed his plan for a union between Great Britain and the

colonies. (26) In line with Dr. Fothergill's suggestion, which James Pemberton had communicated to him,
he also unsuccessfully attempted to obtain the appointment of a deputation to go to England and present "a
regular State of Grievances complained of, enforced by
such Arguments as would manifest that the Colonies had
no views but to retain the most perfect harmony &
Connection with the mother country". (27) Both moderate suggestions were defeated.

The most important accomplishment of the Congress
was the adoption of an agreement or "Association", establishing the most complete non-importation, non-exportation, and non-consumption program yet attempted.
It was signed by all the members of the Congress on
October 20 and was a virtual declaration of economic
war on England. Stringent non-importation was to begin
on December 1, 1774, and non-exportation on September
10, 1775. Profiteering was forbidden, and local
economy was the order of the day. Anyone who refused
to sign the Association or who violated its provisions
was to be declared an enemy to American liberty. In
order to achieve the strictest observance, committees
were to be chosen in every county, city, and town by
those qualified to vote for the legislature to enforce
the necessary compliance. (28)

As a result of the adoption of the Continental
Association, the Philadelphia Committee of Correspondence which had been chosen the preceding June called
a public meeting for November 12 to select a new committee to oversee the implementation and enforcement
of the Association and to exercise the functions of the
old Committee of Correspondence. The radicals, anxious to encourage the appearance of legitimate action,
called a public meeting for the 7th where it was proposed that the new committee be elected by ballot by
wards, a method of selection which was adopted. (29)

The Quakers were opposed to these measures for
two reasons. First, they feared that the actions of the
Congress would encourage moves toward open resistance
to the mother country, and secondly, they considered
that placing the power to enforce the Association in
the hands of extra-legal authorities would almost sure-
ly result in violence. In order to prevent members of
the Society from becoming involved in these activities,
Friends in Philadelphia held several conferences in
the first week of November, followed by a general meeting for all Friends in the city on the 10th, three days

after the public meeting of the 7th at the State House.
At this last gathering all Friends were charged to refrain from participating in any public proceedings
which might be considered inconsistent with their religious profession. (30).

There were a number of Friends who did not support the steps which had been taken and who feared
the Society was going too far in its opposition to
the colonial proceedings. Samuel Sansom spoke for
this group in a letter to one of the Pembertons in
which he questioned the propriety of having held the
meeting of November 10. He stated he had no objection
to advising Friends against acting contrary to their
principles, but he dreaded the consequences of issuing
testimonies against the current public measures. (31)

According to contemporary reports, less than one-
sixth of the qualified voters voted in the election
which had been called, and the Committee of Sixty-Three
which was elected was a complete victory for the radicals. (32) Several Quakers were on this new committee,
among them Owen Biddle, Thomas Mifflin, and Joseph
Wetherill. (33) These Friends accepted their appointment despite the advice issued by the Society on November 10 because of their strong commitment to the colonial cause.

In England there was some division of sentiment
among the Quakers with regard to events in the colonies. James Freeman, a nephew of Dr. John Fothergill,
wrote to John Bartram that the resolves of the Congress
seemed "to be not hastily, but deliberately adopted",
and he hoped they would be "steadily abode by even if
the Mother sho'd repent her severity towards her
children & again restore to them their Natural Rights".
(34) William Forster thought the members of Congress
had "acted constitutionally & their resolves & whatever violent measures" they had engaged in, they had
been forced into "by our arbitrary illegal proceedings". (35)

There were others, on the other hand, such as
Morris Birkbeck, who did not approve of the measures
of the Congress. (36) Dr. Jonathan Binns of Liverpool was skeptical of the course being pursued by the
colonies. He expressed grave concern over what the
outcome of a possible conflict between Britain and
her colonies might be. Although he was optimistic
enough to believe that after a few skirmishes and some

90

bloodshed the colonists would accept the measures of
the British government, if they should

> attempt to stand on <u>vi & armis</u> & shou'd
> even get the better of our forces (of
> which I have not the least apprehension)
> what will be the next law passed in our
> Parliament? Wou'd not thou expect to
> hear of some other of your ports block-
> aded?...you will find that you are not
> yet able to withstand the power of Great
> Britain, or as you perhaps think of it
> little Britain tho' you will in time I have
> no doubt...(37)

In his opinion, the colonies should "bear a hand towards our revenue".

When the proceedings of the Continental Congress
were laid before the Pennsylvania Assembly, there was
some debate over accepting them. Galloway led the
opposition, but through the exertions of Mifflin and
Dickinson the Quaker members deserted him and the
House voted unanimous approval. (38) This was evidence that there was not unanimity among Friends as to
the results of the Congress, and it caused many to
believe incorrectly that the Quakers were swinging over
to the colonial side. At the same time, although
direct Quaker responsibility cannot be proven, when it
came to military preparations the Assembly refused to
provide a quantity of fire-arms and ammunition or to
repair the soldiers' barracks. (39)

The New Jersey Provincial Assembly also approved
unanimously the actions taken by the Continental Congress. The Quakers there, however, qualified their en-
dorsement by "excepting...such parts as seem to wear
an appearance, or may have a Tendency, to Force (if
any such there be) as inconsistent with their religious
Principles". (40)

When the approval by the Pennsylvania Assembly became known, the Meeting for Sufferings soon took action
since it considered some of the resolutions of the
Congress to be "very contrary to our Christian Profession & Principles". (41) Many Friends feared lest
the example of the Quaker assemblymen in approving the
proceedings of the Continental Congress lead to a division of sentiment and a difference of conduct within
the Society. In an effort to prevent such a develop-

ment and to influence the Quaker members of the Assembly to desist from participating in the future in any measures which might impinge on the religious testimonies of the Society, the Meeting for Sufferings appointed a committee to admonish the Quaker assemblymen. After several consultations with the persons concerned, the committee reported that the assemblymen were too little aware of their deviations "& little sensible of the Grounds of Friends Concern" on that account, although a few were convinced of their error. (42)

By the end of 1774, measures were in full swing to implement the resistance program adopted by the Continental Congress. Accordingly, tensions within the Society of Friends over the appropriate position for the Society to take with regard to these developments were becoming more and more acute. Many Quakers who had traditionally been associated with the political life of the province and who were vitally concerned over its fate, linked the welfare of the colony, of Philadelphia Yearly Meeting, and of their own economic interests. This group, strongly attached to the charter and its institutions, consisted largely of the Philadelphia Quaker merchants and wealthy Quaker farmers who had long dominated the Meeting for Sufferings and played a leading role in the affairs of the yearly meeting. They were averse to any cooperation with the radicals whom they rightly suspected of being opponents of the traditional constitutional relationship with Britain. Conversely, they were inclined to be outspoken in behalf of loyalty to the legitimate constitutional authorities, a stand which greatly irritated the radicals.

A second smaller group, also politically motivated but less attached to the religious and constitutional traditions of the colony, was strongly committed to the colonial cause and believed that the Society should not oppose the colonial program of resistance of Britain and should not interfere with its members' active participation therein. Thomas Mifflin, Owen Biddle, Joseph Wetherill and most of the Quaker members of the Assembly represented this group. Their weakness, however, lay in the fact that many of their sympathizers were nominal Friends and had little interest in the maintenance of the Society's testimonies. As Anthony Benezet explained to Patrick Henry who was puzzled over the differences he noted in the attitudes of many Friends:

> ...many of them had no other claim to
> our principles, than as they were children
> or grandchildren of those who professed
> those principles...(43)

A third element, small but quite influential, was
represented by the so-called reformers who believed
the Society should not become involved in the current
political controversy on either side and should abstain from taking an official position "against the
general proceedings of the People". (44) A number of
these Friends had doubted the propriety of holding the
general meeting of November 10, fearing it would take
on a political tone and the Friends involved might
through "their Zeal be carried beyond the Bounds of
true knowledge". (45) Their chief concern was to maintain and promote the spiritual integrity of the Soc-
eity. Therefore they exerted every effort to avoid
the contaminating effects of any political partisan-
ship.

In the middle of December 1774 the Pennsylvania
Assembly appointed a delegation to attend the Second
Continental Congress which was scheduled to meet in
Philadelphia the following May. The prospect of another Congress,the threat of internal difficulties
in the province, and the disagreements manifest among
Friends prompted Philadelphia Monthly Meeting to hold
adjourned sessions on December 30 and January 2 where
there were heated arguments. In the end the dominant
conservative element prevailed, and all the members
were strictly enjoined not to concern themselves in
the public dispute or to interfere with any of the
King's officers in the discharge of their duty. Moreover, they were not to join any city, county, provincial, or general committees which were being established, under threat of disownment.(46)

By this time it was obvious that the Society's
leadership, aroused over the actions of the Friends
in the Assembly and the nomination of a number of
Quakers to public committees, was deeply concerned
about the need for establishing officially a strict
canon of conduct for the membership with a prescribed
penalty for non-observance. On January 5, 1775, the
Meeting for Sufferings issued an epistle of advice and
warning to the members of the yearly meeting, pointing
out that some Friends had accepted public appointments,
while others had agreed to public resolves whose "nature and tendency were contrary to our religious prin-

ciple", and urging those Friends to reconsider their
conduct.   In case others should depart from their religious principles by "manifesting a disposition to
contend for liberty by any methods or agreements contrary to the peaceable spirit and temper of the Gospel",
their respective meetings should deal with them as pre-
cribed by the Book of Discipline. (47)

Only ten years before at the time of the Paxton
riots the Philadelphia Quakers had been shocked by the
number of Friends who had taken up arms. None were
ultimately disowned despite their openly voiced support
for the defensive bearing of arms. Under the present
circumstances it was imperative that the Society make
its position promptly and decisively clear and to act
accordingly. (48)

The interest of the public at large in whatever
position the Quakers took regarding the current measures of colonial resistance is indicated by the fact
that the epistle was published in full in Rivington's
New York Gazeteer. (49) This same notice was reprinted
subsequently in the Boston Evening Post and the Salem
Essex Gazette. A comment in the Massachusetts Spy, reprinted in the Essex Gazette, claimed erroneously that
the epistle was actually issued ten years earlier at
the time of the Stamp Act and that "the Friends, to
the Southward and elsewhere, are as much against the
measures now pursuing by the Crown as any set of men
whatever". (50)

Two weeks later, the Meeting directed a covering
letter to the constituent monthly and quarterly meetings in Pennsylvania and New Jersey, regarding the
"Instability of some Members of our Religious Society
in divers Places in this Time of public Commotions".(51)
It declared that the acts of the recent Congress were
"in their Nature and Tendency...manifestly repugnant
and subversive of the Laws & order of the Government
under which we live..." Because of the conduct of the
Quaker assemblymen in approving the decisions and resolutions of the Congress, an action which "may ensnare
others to their own hurt, & the further wounding of the
Testimony of Truth", the meeting (had issued) the previous epistle of "renewed Caution & Advice". It
therefore considered it necessary "earnestly to entreat
& exhort" the elders and overseers to deal with any who
should be concerned as committeemen in promoting and
executing those resolutions, and if any should persist
therein, "the Judgement of Truth must go out against
them". (52)

Just at this time a direct challenge to the position of the Friends occurred. The new Committee of
Sixty-Six arranged for the meeting of a Provincial
Congress in Philadelphia on January 23 which immediately unanimously endorsed the Association and pledged
to obey its provisions. (53) Since the Assembly had
refused to authorize any military preparations, there
was much agitation to have the Congress bypass the
legislature and direct the people to arm themselves
and train. (54)

The Meeting for Sufferings deemed the situation so
critical as to require an attempt to deter such a move.
According to Christopher Marshall, there were "meetings
of the Quakers daily", and tempers evidently ran high.
James Pemberton called all those siding with the Congress rebels, and Joseph Wetherill was threatened with
disownment if he did not desist attending public committee meetings in the city and the suburbs. (55)
Finally on January 24, the day following the meeting
of the Provincial Congress, the Meeting for Sufferings
issued the "Testimony of the People Called Quakers"
which James Pemberton believed was successful in check-
ing the warlike measures proposed by many. (56)

The Testimony stressed that members of the Society
had been advised repeatedly to keep clear of public
resolutions which increased contention and produced
discord and confusion. Since the religious principles
of the Friends led them to discountenance measures
tending to disaffection to the King, they entirely
disapproved of recently published addresses and political writings whose "spirit and temper was destructive
of the peace and harmony of civil society". The best
means of obtaining relief and establishing the rights
of the people were decent and respectful addresses
from those in legal authority. The course the colonists had thus far pursued, argued the Testimony, was
more likely to produce bloodshed and to subvert
constitutional government and liberty of conscience
than to obtain the remedy desired. It concluded:

> We are therefore, incited by a sincere
> concern for the peace and welfare of our
> country, publicly to declare against
> every usurpation of power and authority,
> in opposition to the laws and government,
> and against all combinations, insurrections,
> conspiracies and illegal assemblies...(57)

There was not complete unanimity on publishing the Testimony. During the session of the Meeting for Sufferings which decided to issue it, one Friend advised and entreated the other members not "to mix politics and religion", asserting that they were "distinct and separate things". (58) This sentiment reflected the growing concern of a number of Friends that the leadership of the Society might well prejudice the religious nature of its peace testimony by publicly stating a position in the current political controversy. Although Pemberton felt it had been more favorably received than he had expected, he conceded that it had not escaped severe censure from some. (59) A Philadelphian wrote his friend in New York that "many of (the Friends), perhaps most of them" disapproved of it, an obviously exaggerated statement. (60)

Samuel Wetherill, Jr., denounced the publication of the Testimony in a letter to Anthony Benezet. (61) Subsequently, he explained his position to James Pemberton. He said he had found that many non-Friends as well as some Quakers believed Friends "were joining with a Corrupt Ministry", and that the Testimony was directed against the merits of the colonial cause. This idea was being fostered by imprudent members of the Society who publicly stated that the present situation was a just retribution for rebellion. Wetherill thought that the Society "ought to be as a Watchman on the Walls, and that there was something due from the Friends both to the King and to the Publick Cause." (62)

Soon after the publication of the Testimony a counterstatement appeared entitled <u>An Earnest Address to such of the People Called Quakers as are Sincerely Desirous of Supporting and Maintaining the Christian Testimony of their Ancestors</u>. The author maintained that the only proper course for Friends was to decline taking part "on either side in ay political contention". The conduct of some of the leaders of the Society would expose it to the just censure of the world.

> If the Gospel directed us to give up
> a part of our rights rather than to enter
> into contention about it, much more does it
> command us not to strike hands with the
> oppressor...(63)

A righteous and just man might defend his property, but he was a villain "who either attempted unjustly to de-

96

prive him of it, or abetted the man who did". (64)

The Testimony was widely circulated outside as
well as within the Society and was translated into
German for distribution among the German sects, esp-
ically the Mennonites who had already sent a delegation
to confer with Friends in Philadelphia. (65) The day
after publication, the Testimony was printed in the
Pennsylvania Gazette (66) and early in February appeared in Rivington's New York Gazeteer, the Massachusetts
Gazette and the Boston Post Boy, the Boston Evening
Post, the Salem Essex Gazette, and in some of the
Virginia newspapers. (67) Lieutenant Governor Colden
of New York sent a copy to the Earl of Dartmouth, and
it was laid before both Houses of Parliament. (68)

In the public at large there were varying opinions and attitudes regarding the Testimony and the
motives for publishing it. Friends of the Society
attempted to interpret the Testimony in the best
light possible, although in doing so they gravely misinterpreted its content and purpose. The Philadelphia
merchant Stephen Collins, a friend of Sam Adams and a
strong supporter of the colonial cause, contended that
although the Testimony did not represent the sentiment
of the whole Society of Friends, it was a "very fair,
clear and just explanation" of the Society's position
which no member could "contradict as not being consistent with the conduct and practice of the Society
from the beginning". He believed, moreover, that the
admonitions contained "could not and ought not to be
applied to the present continental measures against
the tyranny of Great Britain", and he could see "no
injury to the grand and righteous cause". (69)

An apology for the Testimony appeared in the
Pennsylvania Journal and Weekly Advertiser on February
1 signed by B. L. (70) The writer argued that the
Friends did not intend to cast any disrespect on the
cause of public liberty or to create division and discord.

> Taken in its true and proper light,
> it is calculated to point out those rocks
> of licentiousness and outrage which often
> lay concealed under the smooth surface
> of the fairest pretensions, and have
> proved fatal to the fairest of causes.

He emphasised that there was no mention of Parliament

and that advocating loyalty and obedience to the King
and his government referred only to

> ...a Government bounded and limited by
> law, and founded upon the two great prin-
> ciples of the <u>English</u> Constitution, which
> entitles the governed to dispose of their
> own property, and to partake in legis-
> lation. This is the government for which
> America is contending, in which our duty
> to our King and our own rights are so
> happily blended.

Further, the Testimony's condemnation of "riots, routs,
illegal combinations and assemblies", did not include
the Congress and the committees set up according to its
directives.

A month later a citizen who signed himself Amicus
Veritatis persuaded the <u>Pennsylvania Gazette</u> to re-
publish these same comments, as it was the paper most
likely to be read by the Sons of Liberty. (71) He
evidently hoped thereby to disabuse them of their
strong prejudice against Friends.

Edward Stabler wrote from Virginia that the moderates there approved of the Testimony and that the Governor had commended the action of the Friends. (72)
On the other hand, William Hooper of North Carolina,
then attending the Continental Congress in Philadelphia, declared that the Quakers were attempting "to
restrain the other Sects in their Spirited Conduct".
He and others charged that their action encouraged the
British government in its coercive measures against
the colonies.(73)

At this point a decided divergence of opinion
appeared between the Pennsylvania Friends and the
British Quakers. The effect of the Testimony in
Britain caused much consternation to the Friends there.
David Barclay informed James Pemberton that he and
other leading Friends feared it was being "made a
handle of, to the disadvantage of the (Quaker) community - the language of the Court being that they have
the Quakers approbation of their measures". (74) He
further complained that it contained

> some <u>hard</u> words that we could have
> wished had been omitted, as they seem to
> convey that which we hope is not in your

>hearts, an Inclination to obtain
>favour at the expense of <u>others</u>.

In conclusion Barclay strongly advised that the Philadelphia Friends take this expression of the British
attitude into consideration before deciding on any
further such action. (75)

Dr. Fothergill was as concerned about the situation as any and laconically remarked:

>We have seen the Testimony given out by
>Friends and the nation hath seen it.
>We doubt not but that it was thought
>right and proper such advice should be
>given. (76)

He advised the American Quakers not to "lean to the
violent; nor...join the obsequious...your all in this
life is at stake,...life, liberty and property". He
was convinced that:

>If America relaxes, both you and we are
>undone; I wish Frds would studiously
>avoid every thing adverse either to
>admᵗ here on one side – or the Congress
>on the other. Submission to the prevailing
>power is the general voice of America.(77)

In commenting on the sharp difference of views between the British and Philadelphia Friends at that
point, Fothergill wrote William Logan that he could
"only say at present that we are quite of opposition opinions on the present subject, a case that has not
hitherto happended..." (78)

Both official bodies of the British Friends, the
Meeting for Sufferings and the Yearly Meeting, subsequently expressed the same concern over the relationship
of the Pennsylvania Quakers to the course of events in
the colonies. Toward the end of March 1775 the Meeting
for Sufferings, apprehensive over the "increasing ana-
mosities which seem to threaten the liberties America
hath hitherto enjoyed", urged the Friends in Philadelphia to

>give no just cause for offence to lawful
>superiors, by contending for our just
>rights and liberties, in any other way
>than by a patient submission, and proper

> respectful remonstrances; neither to
> seek occasions of manifesting an intem-
> perate opposition to those who think them-
> selves engaged to pursue different meas-
> ures. (79)

At its sessions the following May, London Yearly
Meeting addressed an all-inclusive epistle "To Our
Friends and Brethren in America "; expressing anxious
sympathy for the American Quakers and an earnest desire for their"preservation amidst present confusions".
(80) Their advice to the American Friends was:

> It will add much to your safety in every
> respect...to keep out of the spirit of
> parties and to cherish in your hearts the
> principle of peace and good will to all.

It was obviously difficult for the English Quakers
to realize the local tensions under which the Friends
in Pennsylvania labored. In this particular instance
an action undertaken to meet a local Pennsylvania
situation, and intended primarily for the domestic
constituency, was viewed in quite a different light
when it appeared in the British political context and
was accordingly misinterpreted and misused. Under the
circumstances the British Friends naturally felt that
their efforts to support the American cause had been
seriously undercut.

This interpretation seems to be born out by James
Pemberton's attempt to relieve the apprehensions of the
English Quakers. In a letter to Dr. Fothergill he contended that the results feared by the English Friends
were quite contrary to the intention of the Philadelphians. He believed that the reports received in
England were not entirely true and that they had arisen
from misrepresentations and calumniations spread abroad by certain members of the Society, thereby giving
"a handle" to the Quakers' adversaries. (81)

It cannot be denied that the position taken by
the Meeting for Sufferings in the Testimony put the
Pennsylvania Friends squarely against what was becoming an openly militant movement of opposition to
Great Britain. The action of the Philadelphia Quaker
leaders, although based on religious grounds, was
obviously weighted with political implications. Those
Friends who were opposed to the publication of the
Testimony were convinced that the Society was thereby

100

entering the political realm where it did not belong as a religious body.

Meanwhile the Quakers in the other colonies had taken steps to assure that their members abstain from any participation in the public commotions. In the latter part of November 1774, Henrico Quarterly Meeting in Virginia advised its members "to avoid being concern-ed in signing any such resolutions and Associations, or putting in Execution such of them" as might be incon-sistent with their principles. It also cautioned the Friends to refrain from "unnecessary conversation res-pecting these disputes". (82) Shortly afterward Edward Stabler the prominent Virginia friend informed Israel Pemberton that as far as he had heard the Quakers in Virginia had kept clear of the popular agitations. (83)

In New York City as well as in Philadelphia, some Friends had become participants in the popular resis-tance measures. (84) Throughout 1774 there had been a continuing conflict between the radicals and the conservatives in the city as to the proper course to pursue in protesting British policy. Several committ-ees followed each other in rapid succession in an attempt to placate all factions. Finally, in November 1774, a Committee of Sixty was appointed consisting of representatives from both groups. On it were two Quakers, Lindley Murray, a prominent New York merchant, and Lancaster Burling. (85)

Needless to say, the New York Friends were dis-turbed by this turn of events. They were spurred to action by a letter received from the Philadelphia Meeting for Sufferings early in December, recounting steps taken to persuade those Friends who were serving on public committees to refrain therefrom. The letter concluded:

> ...it will afford us real Satisfaction
> to hear the like Care and Concern hath
> engaged you to use your Endeavors to
> the same good purpose...(86)

The New York Friends appointed a committee to deal with members who were serving on public committees. (87) They reported subsequently to their Philadelphia bret-hren that they had adopted measures to deal with the situation and hoped

> to convince those who Names appear on

101

public Committees of the Danger of
being active in the Prosecution of
Measures inconsistent with our peaceable Principles, This may probably
occasion more frequent Meetings & open
the way to a more frequent Communication of Sentiments in a brotherly
Correspondance between your Meeting &
ours". (88)

Two months later the committee reported to the
New York Meeting for Sufferings that as a result of
their efforts several of those interviewed had been "so
much convinced in their Judgements as to decline taking
any further active part" in the public committees. (89)
However, the two Friends Lancaster Burling and Lindley
Murray continued to serve on the Committee of Sixty.
At first they promised "to send in writing their reasons for non-attendance to the Chairman" of the Committee of Sixty, but late in March the committee reported:
"...there appears less encouragement to hope their declining an active part (in that committee)..." (90)

The New England Friends, according to all reports,
generally abstained from participating in the public
agitations and activities. (91)

A serious problem now facing Friends was their relation to the enforcement of the provisions of the
Continental Association. Differences of viewpoint and
action with regard to compliance with the articles of
the Association soon appeared among the Quaker merchants in Pennsylvania, Virginia, and New York. In
December 1774, several Friends in Philadelphia refused
to surrender goods received from England to the committee of inspection. (92) In April 1775, both James &
Drinker and Samuel Shoemaker attempted to load vessels
for Newfoundland but were stopped by the city committee. (93)

In Virginia, on the other hand, Robert Pleasants
complied with the regulations on non-importation.
Early in January 1775, he received a shipment of goods
from England and turned it over to the committee of
Henrico County to be disposed of according to Article
X of the Association. (94) Soon afterward both Henrico
Quarterly and Henrico Monthly Meetings issued state-
ments of advice to their members. The Quarterly
Meeting directed those Friends who were requested to
sign the Association to reply that because of their re-

102

ligious testimony against "all war (as to us) unlawful"
they could not sign since they could not "act in any
matters which (might) have a tendency to the shedding
of blood". At the same time they considered it their
duty "to comply with the laws and regulations of Government under which (they lived) in all cases not interfering with tender scruples of conscience". Therefore
they would "submit to all regulations of trade" and
whatever else would "in a peaceable way..promote the
true interest of the community in general." (95)
Henrico Monthly Meeting followed suit in giving similar advice to its members. (96)

The Virginia Quakers thus elected to follow a more
neutral policy than that adopted by the Philadelphia
Friends, a course in line with the position of the
British and New England Quakers. Despite their moderate stand, their refusal to subscribe completely to
colonial policies brought the disfavor of the more radical elements upon them. Edward Stabler was haled before the committee of his county for refusing to sign
the Association and was threatened with interdiction
by the community. (97)

In New York City the firm of Robert and John
Murray defied the non-importation agreement for purely
economic reasons. In March 1775, a cargo of goods
arrived from England at Sandy Hook where John Murray and
his clerk met the ship. Part of the shipment was
transported to Elizabeth Town in New Jersey to be disposed of there. When the committee of inspection in
New York discovered this infringement, the offenders
were called before it and finally made a full confess-
ion. The case was taken before the New York Provincial
Convention which, on the promise of the Murrays to
abide thereafter by all the regulations in force, restored their full commercial privileges. As compensation for their action they donated the sum of ₤200 for
the rebuilding of the hospital at Elizabeth Town which
had recently been destroyed by fire. (98) This affair
received wide publicity in the colonial press from
New England to Virginia. (99)

When one reviews the reaction of the Friends,
especially in Pennsylvania, to the proceedings of the
First Continental Congress and the subsequent events
throughout the colonies, it is clear that the crisis
of decision for the Quakers came in the fall and
winter of 1774-1775. They fully shared the constitutional convictions of their fellow citizens and be-

103

lieved that colonial grievances should be rectified. As long as peaceful measures were employed to obtain a satisfactory settlement of the quarrel with the mother country, there was no obstacle to individual Friends participating in such action. As the influence of the radical groups became more prominent in the direction of affairs, with resort to violent and repressive acts and extra-legal procedures to by-pass legitimate governmental institutions, the Pennsylvania Friends increasingly feared internal revolution in the province and eventual open conflict with Britain. Proportionately, the official bodies of the Friends, largely dominated by the more conservative element of the Society, exerted increasing moral pressure on those members who were supporting and participating in the popular proceedings to desist therefrom. This was especially true from the summer of 1774 on.

When it became clear that the forces of moderation were no longer effective and that there were a number of Friends whose association with the radical measures was causing confusion within and without the Society as to its official position, the Society acted to forbid its members to become involved in the colonial resistance measures. In pursuing this policy, the Friends in Pennsylvania were the first to take action because of their peculiar internal situation. Although in the critical period 1774-1776 they adopted a somewhat less neutral stance in the controversy than did the Quakers in other colonies, such discrepancies never assumed serious proportions.

The three monthly meetings in Philadelphia were the first to institute dealings with their members who were serving on public committees, and Chester Monthly Meeting followed suit soon afterward. (100) In all cases the offenders, some of whom later joined in military activities also, were eventually disowned. The Friends in New York City were the only other ones to institute dealings with members who participated in public protest meetings.

(1)   Labaree, The Boston Tea Party, 247.
(2)   Ryerson, Leadership in Crisis, 187-88.
(3)   Ford, "The Adoption of the Pennsylvania Constitu-
      tion of 1776", loc.cit., 429; Keith, Charles P.,
      The Provincial Councilors of Pennsylvania (Phila-
      delphia, 1883), 228. The Quakers were Joseph
      Parker, Samuel Rhoads, Thomas Mifflin, Joseph Elli-
      cott, John Foulke, Benjamin Chapman, William Rod-
      man, Isaac Pearson, John Jacobs, John Morton, and
      Joseph Pennock. (Votes and Proceedings, Arch. of
      Pa. 8th Ser.,v. 8, 7024.) Chapman, Parker and
      Foulke were later disowned for active support of
      the American cause. (Phil.M.M., Min., 1771-1777,
      361,394; Richland M.M., Min., 1767-1786, 11/18/
      1779, 6/15/1780; Wrightstown M.M., Min., 1734-
      1790, 246-47.
(4)   Ford, loc.cit., 430; Votes and Proc., 7098. Rhoads
      was soon afterward elected mayor of Philadelphia
      and resigned his appointment ot he Continental
      Congress. (Stillé, Dickinson, 118.)
(5)   Keith, op.cit., 228.
(6)   Olton, Charles S., "Philadelphia Mechanics",
      loc.cit.,322-3.
(7)   Egnal, Marc, and Ernst, Joseph A., "An Economic
      Interpretation of the American Revolution",WMQ,
      3rd Ser., v. 29 (1972), 29; Oakes, Robert F.,
      Philadelphia Merchants and the First Continental
      Congress," Pennsylvania History,v. 40 (1973), 151,
      158-160.
(8)   Jensen, The Maritime Commerce of Philadelphia, 219.
(9)   Dr. Fothergill to James Pemberton, Aug. 23, 1774,
      Ett.Pem. Pap., v. 2, 69. In this letter Fothergill
      made some interesting comments on the attitude
      of the crown officials in America.
      He felt it was unfortunate for the colonies that
      it had been "the interest and inclination of too
      many persons in office on your side the water, to
      represent the people there, just in the light,
      that too many here wish to view them - as
      hostile in their intentions to their mother coun-
      try, and the objects of correction and restraint.
      Perhaps a remembrance that the Ancestors of most
      now in power, were a century ago sufficiently
      humbled by the progency of those, whom they now
      look upon with a vindictive detestation. Their
      dependents are catching, or affect to have catched

the like resentment to America; and every little
ebullition of Pariotism on your side is worked up
into a studied rebellion - I suspect that this is
one secret unheeded motive to that unparalleled
act of oppression in respect to Boston".

(10) Ibid.
(11) King George the Third to Lord North, Sept. 11,
1774, The Correspondence of King George the Third,
ed. by Sir John Fortescue (6 vols., London, 1928),
v. 3, 130-31. This document, if still in existence, has not been published and therefore the
names of th subscribers are not known.
(12) Adams later defined a Wet Quaker as follows:"Soak
a Piece of Buckram in Water. All, or at Least
some of the Stiffness will be taken out. Sponge
a Piece of glossy Broadcloth in Water and all the
outside beauty, will be destroyed. A Wet Quaker
is a Soaked Buckram, and a Sponged Cloth.,i.e. a
Quaker relaxed a little by Reading and Experience
from the rigidity of their Principals, and consequently read out of their Meetings,i.e. ex-
communicated". (John Adams to Adrian Van der
Kemp, May 20, 1813, John Adams Letters, 1781-1825,
at the HSP.)
(13) John Adams to Adrian Van der Kemp, March 18, 1813,
loc.cit.
(14) Ibid. Despite the earlier relieving legislation,
it was reported five years earlier that five
Quakers had been imprisoned in Worcester for refusing to pay taxes for the support of the ministry in Massachusetts. (Nwp. Mer.,Jan. 15, 1770).
(15) John Adams to Adrian Van der Kemp, March 18, 1813,
loc.cit.,Adams, John, Diary(Works of John Adams
with a Life of the Author,ed. Charles Francis
Adams, 10 vols., Boston, 1856, v.2), 398.
(16) John Adams to Adrian Van de Kemp, March 18, 1813,
loc.cit.
(17) John Adams to James Warren, Oct., 1775, Warren-
Adams Letters, Collections of the Massachusetts
Hist. Soc., v. 72 (1917), 168.
(18) Adams, Diary, 397, 398, 399.
(19) John Adams to Adrian Van der Kemp, March 18, 1813,
loc.cit. Nelson Rightmyer in his "Churches under
Enemy Occupation, Philadelphia 1777-1778", (Church
History,v. 14 (1945),54-55), points out that the
Quakers knew from bitter experience that the New
England conception of freedom had not included
freedom for Quaker consciences. The Friends had
had religious freedom under the Crown but they

could not be assured of it under a government dominated by New Englanders.

(20) Phil.Y.M., Min., v.3, 316,366-367. In recording
this event Adams says: "The Quakers had their general meeting last Sunday and are deeply affected
by the complexion of the times. They have recommended to all their people to renounce tea..."
(John Adams to William Tudor, Sept. 29, 1774, Adams,
John, Correspondence, Works v.9, 347.) See also
Thomas Clifford to Thomas Frank, Oct. 11, 1774,
Letter Book, 1773-1789.

(21) The revolutions here referred to are obviously
those of 1660 when the monarchy was restored under
Charles II and 1688 when James II was dethroned
and replaced by William and Mary.

(22) Phil.Y.M., Min., v.3, 366.

(23) Marshall, Diary, Sept. 24, 1774.

(24) Stiles, Ezra, Literary Diary (Franklin Bowditch
Dexter, ed., 3 vols., New York, 1901), v.1,490-
491.

(25) N.Y.Gaz., Oct. 31, 1774.

(26) Van Tyne, Causes of the War for Independence, 440.

(27) James Pemberton to Dr. Fothergill, Nov. 5, 1774,
Ett.Pem.Pap., v.2, 71.

(28) Van Tyne, op.cit., 442. The full text of the
Association is given in Schlesinger, Colonial
Merchants, 607-613.

(29) Schlesinger, op.cit., 456-458.

(30) Marshall, Diary, Nov.5, 1774; James Pemberton to
Dr. Fothergill, Nov. 4, 1774, loc.cit.;Phil.M.f.S.
to London M.f.S., Nov. 5, 1774, Phil.M.f.S., Min.,
v.1, 431. The Meeting for Sufferings also informed the English Friends that they had refrained
from participating in the relief of Boston lest
it "should subject us to be considered approvers
of their conduct".

   Both Thomas Wharton and Thomas Clifford expressed disapproval of the actions of the Congress.
Wharton's chief objection was that it had not "made
such, an offer to G. Britain as would at once have
proved that (America) did not wish a separation
but a Constitutional Connexion preserving (her)
rights & Priviledges". He wished that cooler and
more temperate measures had been adopted "whereby
an Opening would have been afforded to the Friends
of America (in England), to have Exerted their
influence for the repeal of (those) Unjust

Acts, which had so apparently widened the Breach".
(Thomas Wharton to Samuel Wharton, Nov. 7, 1774,
Letter Book, 97; Same to Walpole & Ellison, Jan.2,
1775, Letter Book, 127.) Thomas Clifford believed
that a more equitable plan could have been devised
by the Congress. Many Americans who were strongly attached to the parent state desired to avoid
any action which might increase the present difficulty would, on the other hand, support every reasonable measure for the preservation of their
civil and religious liberties. (Thomas Clifford to
Thomas Frank, Feb. 5, 1775, Letter Book, 1773-
1789.)

(31) Letter to Samuel Sansom, Nov. 5, 1774, Pem.Pap.,
v. 27, 9.
(32) Schlesinger, op.cit., 457 n., 457-458.
(33) Ryerson, Leadership in Crisis, 263.
(34) James Freeman to John Bartram, Dec. 18, 1774,
Darlington, William, Memorials of John Bartram and
Humphrey Marshall (Philadelphia, 1849), 462-463.
(35) William Forster to Elizabeth Forster, Feb. 20,
1775, BFHA, v. 14 (1925), 74-75. With regard to
the situation in Parliament, Forster said he had
the "honor to be of Chatham's and Camden's Opinion, and tho' I think we never engaged in a more
unchristian wicked exertion of despotic power than
at present, yet I am much pleased to find there
are honest men in both Houses who will exert themselves for the Welfare of their Country, & show a
venal and corrupt Ministry that their whole proceedings must every way terminate to their Confusion, and in this Opinion I am also rejoiced to
find the most of our valuable Friends".

With reference to the proceedings in the House
of Lords, he said: "Thou hast, I suppose seen...the
Debates in the upper House, where the sly Mansfield
so jesuitically defends his Cause; where Lyttleton
prostitutes his abilities in defaming and attempting to ridicule a brave People in setting Affairs
in a false Light; where the whole Bench of hire-
ling Bishops, always alarmed at the Abridgment of
any of their privileges, appear asleep while the
Liberties of others are destroying; except in
giving their Voice for it; where Chatham, Camden,
Rockingham, & Shelburne expose them & their Intentions, their proceedings and the futility of
their attempts".

William Forster was a land agent and suveyor
from Tottenham near London and an esteemed Friend.

(Biographical Catalogue, London, 1888, 222.)

(36) William Forster to Elizabeth Forster, Feb. 20, 1775, loc.cit., 74. Morris Birkbeck, father of Morris Birkbeck who founded New Albion, Illinois, was a prominent Friend from Wanborough, Surrey. (Biographical Catalogue, 95.)

(37) Dr. Jonathan Binns, Jr., to Dr. Parke, October 7, 1774, Pem.Pap., v. 26, 163-64.

(38) Votes and Proc., 7162; Stillé, op.cit., 149. The number of Friends in this session of the Assembly was the same as in the previous one, Robert Kirkbride of Bucks Co. having taken the place of William Rodman, (Votes and Procs.,7148.)

(39) Joseph Reed to the Earl of Dartmouth,Dec. 24, 1774, Reed, Life and Correspondence of Joseph Reed v. 2, 89.

(40) Fisher, Edgar Jacob, New Jersey as a Royal Province, 1738-1776 (Columbia Univ. Studies in History, Economics and Public Law, v. 41, New York, 1911), 448-49; Votes and Proceedings of the General Assembly of the Province of New Jersey, session beginning January, 1775 (Burlington, 1775), 16.

(41) Phil.M.f.S.,Min, v. 1, 435.

(42) Ibid., 437; James Pemberton to Dr. Fothergill, Feb. 15, 1775, Pem.Pap., v. 27, 75.

(43) Anthony Benezet to Samuel Allinson, Oct. 23, 1774, Brooks, George S., Friend Anthony Benezet,(Philadelphia, 1937), 322.

(44) Letter of Samuel Sansom, Nov. 5, 1774, Pem.Pap., v. 27, 9.

(45) Ibid. See Bauman, op.cit., chap, 4, for a different grouping.

(46) Marshall, Diary, Dec. 30, 1774; Jan. 2, 1775.

(47) Phil.M.f.S., Min., v. 1, 438, 440-42.

(48) For a full discussion of the effect on the Society of the numerous military deviations at the time of the Paxton riots see David Sloan's "A Time of Sifting and Winnowing", Quaker History, v. 66, no. 1 (Spring , 1977), 3-22.

(49) Riv.'s N.Y. Gaztr., Jan. 26, 1775.

(50) Ev. Post,Feb. 6, 1775; The Essex Gaz., Feb. 14, 1775.

(51) Phil.M.f.S., Min., v· 1, 443-45.

(52) Ibid., 445.

(53) Schlesinger, op,cit., 460.

(54) Thomas Wharton to Samuel Wharton, Jan. 31, 1775, Letter Book; James Pemberton to Dr. Fothergill, Feb. 15, 1775, loc.cit.

(55) Marshall, Diary, January 24, 1775.

(56) James Pemberton to Dr. Fothergill, Feb. 15,
1775, loc.cit. The text of the Testimony is given
in Phil.M.f.S., Min., v.1, 446-448.

> At this juncture the Quakers were anxious not
> only to keep their own members from supporting
> the growing radical movement but also to rally
> those opposed to the current public proceedings.
> Thomas Wharton spoke for many Friends when he
> wrote:

>> ...the thoughtful among us cannot help
>> asking, what is to be the next step if
>> England should be overcome? This question
>> sinks deep in our friends, for although we
>> think our parent wrong with respect to some
>> acts of Parliament, yet we have reason to
>> believe she will ever redress our grievances
>> when properly stated; but what redress is
>> to be expected, what civil or religious
>> liberty to be enjoyed, should others gain
>> the ascendency.

> (Thomas Wharton to Samuel Wharton, Jan.31, 1775,
> loc.cit.)

(57) Phil. M.f.S., Min., v.1, 448.

(58) An Earnest Address to Such of the People Called
Quakers as Are Sincerely Desirous of Supporting
and Maintaining the Christian Testimony of Their
Ancestors (Philadelphia, 1775), 19. A possible
author is Samuel Wetherill.

> There is some justification for the thesis
> that the epistle was imposed on the Society by a
> small group of wealthy, conservative men jealous
> of Quaker predominance in the province. See
> Bauman, For the Reputation of Truth,152.

(59) James Pemberton to Dr. Fothergill, May 6, 1775,
Pem.Pap., v.27, 138.

(60) Amer. Arch., 4th Ser., v.1, 1270.

(61) Marshall, Diary, Jan., 24, 1775.

(62) Samuel Wetherill to James Pemberton, Feb. 4, 1775,
Pem.Pap., v.27, 67. Wetherill was later disowned
for taking a loyalty test to the new government
and assisting in the publication of a book causing
dissension among Friends. (Phil.M.M., Min ,1777-
1782, 131, 133.

(63) An Earnest Address, 6. This tract was translated
into German and distributed throughout Lancaster
County.

(64) Ibid., 8.
(65) James Pemberton to Dr. Fothergill, Feb. 15, 1775, loc.cit.
(66) "To the Printers of the Pennsylvania Gazette", Amer. Arch., 4th Ser., v. 2, 80.
(67) Riv.'s. N.Y. Gaztr.,Feb. 2, 1775; Mass. Gaz., Feb. 6, 13, 1775; Ev. Post., Feb. 6,1775;Essex Gaz., Feb. 14, 1775; Edward Stabler to Israel Pemberton, May 16, 1775, Pem. Pap., v. 27, 144.
(68) Lieutenant Governor Colden to the Earl of Dartmouth, Feb. 1, 1775, Doc. Rel. to the Col. Hist. of N.Y.,v. 8, 532: Journals of the House of Lords, (60 vols., London n.d.), v. 34, 341; Journals of the House of Commons,(90 vols., London n.d.), v.35 171.
(69) Stephen Collins to William Tudor, Feb. 17, 1775, Stephen Collins Letter Book, 1773-1775. (Stephen Collins Papers, Library of Congress.)
(70) Pa. Jnl., Feb. 1, 1775.
(71) Amer. Arch., 4th Ser., v. 2, 80-1.
(72) Edward Stabler to Israel Pemberton, May 16, 1775, loc.cit.
(73) William Hooper to Samuel Johnston, May 23, 1775, Colonial Records of North Carolina (vols. 1-10 of Colonial and State Records of North Carolina ed. William Saunders and Walter Clark, 26 vols. Goldsboro, 1886-1907), v. 9, 1280. James Pemberton to Dr. Fothergill May 6, 1775, loc.cit.
(74) David Barclay to James Pemberton, Feb. 2, March 18, 1775, Pem.Pap., v. 37, 101-104.
(75) Ibid. This reaction of the British Friends is understandable in view of the fact that at that very time they were in the midst of a most intensive lobbying campaign with both the Ministry and the Parliament in behalf of the colonies. This effort is fully discussed in Chapter VII below.
(76) Dr. Fothergill to James Pemberton, March 17, 1775, Pem.Pap., v. 34, 173.
(77) Ibid.
(78) Dr. Fothergill to William Logan, Mar. 18, 1775, William Logan Fox Collection, at HSP.
(79) London M.f.S. to Phil. M.f.S., Mar. 24, 1775, London M.f.S., Min., v. 34.
(80) Epistles from London Yearly Meeting, v. 5 (1774-1790), 25-7.
(81) James Pemberton to Dr. Fothergill, May 6, 1775, loc.cit.
(82) Henrico Q.M., Min., 1745-1783, Nov. 27, 1774.
(83) Edward Stabler to Israel Pemberton, Dec.9,1774,

Pem.Pap., v. 27, 36.

(84) N.Y. M.f.S., Min., v.1 (1758-1796), 15.

(85) Becker, Carl Lotus, <u>History of Political Parties
in the Province of New York, 1760-1776</u> (Bulletin
of the Univ. of Wisconsin, no. 286, History Series
II, No. 1, Madison, 1909), 112-16,131-32,167-68
gives a full account of these developments. The
list of the Committee of Sixty is given in Becker,
op.cit., 168n. and in <u>Amer. Arch., 4th Ser</u>., v.1,
330. Lancaster Burling was later disowned for
continuing to participate on the public committees;
(Flushing M.M., Min. 1771-1776, 85; 1776-1781,1.)

(86) Phil.M.f.S., Min., v.1, 433; N.Y. M.f.S., Min.,
v. 1, 15.

(87) N.Y. M.f.S., Min., v. 1, 15.

(88) Phil. M.f.S., Min., v.1, 449.

(89) N.Y.M.f.S., Min., v. 1, 19.

(90) <u>Ibid</u>., 21- 23.

(91) James Pemberton to Daniel Mildred, Dec. 6, 1774,
Pem.Pap., v. 27, 30; Phil.M.f.S. to London M.f.S.,
March 25, 1775, Phil.M.f.S., Min., v. 1, 454.

(92) Israel Pemberton to John Pemberton, Dec. 8, 1774,
Pem.Pap., v. 27, 31.

(93) Marshall, Diary, April 29,30,1775.

(94) <u>Va.Gaz</u>., Feb. 11, 1775.

(95) Henrico Q.M., Min., 1745-1783, Feb. 2, 1775.

(96) Henrico M.M., Min., 1757-1780,222.

(97) Edward Stabler to Israel Pemberton, May 16, 1775,
loc.cit.

(98) Marshall, Diary, March 22, 1775. Extensive docu-
mentation on the Murray affair is given in
<u>Amer. Arch., 4th Ser.</u>,v. 2, 145-48.

(99) <u>N.Y. Jnl</u>.,March 23, June 15, 1775; <u>Nwp.Mer.</u>,March
20, 27, 1775; <u>Essex Gaz</u>., March 28, 1775; <u>Pa. Mer</u>.,
June 16, 1775; <u>Pa.Ldg.</u>,March 25, 1775; <u>Md. Gaz.</u>,
March 30, 1775; <u>Va. Gaz</u>.,April 8, 1775.

(100) Those disowned in Philadelphia were: Owen Biddle,
Benjamin Marshall, Thomas Mifflin, William Robinson and Joseph Wetherill. (Phil.M.M., Min.,
1771-1777, 288,299, 313-314, 355,393; Phil. So.
Dist. M.M., Min., 1770-1780, 82,83, 102, 103.)
Mifflin later became a general in the American
army. Those disowned by Chester Monthly Meeting
were: David Lewis, Isaac Eyre, Nicholas Fairlamb,
and Samuel Fairlamb, (Chester M.M., Min., 1745-
1778, 422-424.)

Chapter VII

CONCILIATION EFFORTS OF THE BRITISH QUAKERS

While the Pennsylvania Friends were acting vigorously to prevent members of the Society from participating in the increasingly militant opposition to the
coercive measures of the British Government, the British Friends were exerting every effort to induce the
Government to adopt a more lenient approach to the
colonial problem and thereby stay the tide of movement
toward violent congrontation. As has already been
indicated, because of the close relationship with and
interest in the colonies, the Friends, to a greater
extent than any other particular segment of British
society, strongly supported the colonial constitutional
position. Because of that relationship and the Quaker
testimony against all war, they contemplated the idea
of an imperial conflict with dread and sorrow.

The friends of America in England, of whom there
were not a few, looked especially to the Quakers as
the only influential body in a position to influence
the Government ot modify its course of action. As
early as April 1774 the Kentish Gazette (Canterbury)
declared that both England and America were praying
for steadfastness on the part of the Quakers, since "it
rests with them to absolutely save the country". If
the Quakers stood firm, it would have far more effect
than "all the things yet written or said for America."
(1) In like vein Attakullakulla in the London Packet
pled with the Quakers to shake off their lethargy
and step forth as the saviors of America. (2) There
were also reports that the Ministry was greatly alarmed at their action and was trying to buy them off. (3)

The idea that England and America would be saved
if the Quakers firmly supported the colonial cause was
still the sentiment in various quarters a year later,
as indicated by statements in both the London Chronicle
and the Gentlemen's Magazine in March 1775. (4) The
basis for such highly exaggerated notions was the
currently accepted belief as stated in the London Packet that the Quakers "hold great sums of money in our
funds and are in possession of most of the ready cash
that circulates in and among the colonies." (5)

The first move to initiate steps toward colonial conciliation was undertaken by Dr. Fothergill and David Barclay at the instigation of Lord Dartmouth, Secretary for the Colonies. Soon after the conclusion of the First Continental Congress, Dartmouth, who was considered by Dr. Fothergill to be a good friend of America,(6) decided to resort to extra-cabinet means in an attempt to "lay the storm". At his suggestion Lord Hyde, Chancellor of the Duchy of Lancaster, known for his American sympathies, proposed to David Barclay that he and Dr. Fothergill approach Franklin for his ideas on how peace might be restored. (7) During the course of events which followed, Dartmouth remained behind the scenes receiving reports on the negotiations being carried on by Barclay and Dr. Fothergill. Although his cabinet position was of strategic importance, the fact that he was the step-brother of the Prime Minister, Lord North, gave his role added significance. (8)

David Barclay as the leading North American merchant in London frequently consulted Franklin and other colonial agents on affairs relating to the colonies. On December 1, 1774, shortly after the opening of the winter session of Parliament, he conferred with Franklin on the possibility of the North American merchants presenting a petition to Parliament regarding the state of the relations between Britain and America. He then took the opportunity to implement Lord Hyde's suggestion of enlisting Franklin's cooperation in proposing steps which might lead to a reconciliation between the two parts of the empire. In Barclay's opinion Franklin's knowledge of both countries, together with his influence and abilities, admirably fitted him for such an undertaking.

Franklin was inclined to believe that the attitude of the Cabinet precluded any such move, but Barclay considered his judgment too harsh. He contended that not all of the Ministers were unfavorably disposed and that the majority would gladly welcome such terms as might extricate them from the present difficulties, provided that the honor and dignity of the Government were at the same time preserved. Franklin finally consented to think the matter over. (9)

Barclay's viewpoint was supported at a meeting a few days later by Dr. Fothergill who urged that there was good reason to believe there were those who desired some accommodation in the current dispute. If Franklin would draw up a plan to achieve this end, he and David

114

Barclay would have it communicated to the more moder-ate Ministers. Franklin yielded to their soliciations and promised to present something for their consider-ation at another meeting two days later. (10)

At the appointed time Franklin produced a copy of his "Hints for the Conversation, upon the subject of Terms that may probably produce a durable union between Great Britain and the Colonies." (11) Among the chief points in this paper were the following: all control over the internal affairs of the colonies to be turned over to them; all acts restraining colonial manufact-uring to be repealed; all duties levied to regulate trade with the colonies to be turned into the colonial treasuries; the appointment of all colonial officials, with the exception of certain crown functionaries, to be in the hands of the colonies; in royal provinces the judges to hold office on good behavior and to be paid by the particular colonies; the governors to be granted their salaries by the colonial Assemblies; the extension of the act of Henry VIII, whereby persons charged with treason were to be extradited to England for trial, to be disclaimed by Parliament; and in time of war the Americans to comply with requisitions from the King, to be levied by the colonists on themselves on a proportional basis according to the manner of assessing taxes by Parliament in England.

These points were accepted as a basis of dis-cussion, but on three other points there was some dis-agreement. These were: that the Tea Act be repealed; that all customs collections made under the Act should be repaid to the treasuries of those provinces where they had been made; and that Parliament should dis-claim authority to legislate on internal colonial matters. On Franklin's insistence the first item was allowed to remain. Dr. Fothergill and David Barclay strongly objected to the other two, and Franklin allow-ed them to be expunged. (12)

Shortly after this meeting Dr. Fothergill handed a copy of the "Hints" as finally agreed on to both Lord Dartmouth and Sir Fletcher Norton, Speaker of the House of Commons, who very strongly favored steps being taken toward conciliation. Sir Fletcher con-sidered that the terms as outlined were too severe and that it would be very humiliating to Great Britain to accept them. Dr. Fothergill's rejoinder was that Great Britain had been unjust and that she must bear the consequences of her conduct. The pill might be bitter but it would be salutary to swallow it, for sooner or later similar measures would have to be adopted or the empire would fall apart. (13)

David Barclay, meantime, transmitted a copy of the "Hints" to Lord Hyde who was in contact with some of the other Ministers. About a week later Hyde informed him that the terms as they stood were too hard and should be moderated, and Barclay passed these comments on to Franklin. (14)

Toward the end of December the Howe family, all of them staunch friends of America, entered the affair. Lord Richard Howe, who advocated sending a commission to America to treat with the colonies, offered to serve as intermediator to Lords Dartmouth and Hyde.(15) When news of the resolutions of the Continental Congress calling for a trade embargo against Britain reached England, however, the King became more adamant and opposed the idea of such a commission. (16) The whole matter was then dropped to allow further time to consider the actions of the Congress and the contents of the "Hints".

With the opening of the New Year, David Barclay undertook to organize a mercantile lobby in behalf of the colonial cause. In this effort he acted as liaison with the colonial agents, especailly Franklin and William Lee of Virginia. (17) On January 4, 1775, he presided over a meeting of three to four hundred merchants at the Kings Arms Tavern to consider the dispute between the mother country and the colonies. Barclay opened the discussion by declaring that the meeting was not a manoeuver of the Government, as some claimed, but that it was an independent action on the part of those concerned. He then proposed two resolutions for consideration: first, that the alarming state of trade with America made it expedient to petition Parliament for redress of American grievances; and second, that a committee be appointed to prepare a petition to this end, addressed to the House of Commons. (18)

The resolutions were adopted, and a committee was appointed to draft a petition to Parliament to be approved by the merchants at their next meeting. The petition as finally presented to Parliament pointed out the effect of the imperial dispute on trade, urged that the problem be more thoroughly examined before any further action was taken, and requested that representatives of the merchants be allowed to present their

views on the matter. (19)   The petition was subsequently rejected by Parliament, and the merchants, now convinced of the futility of this course of action, presented a petition to the King. (20)   These proceedings
of the London merchants were reported in the colonies
in several of the New England newspapers. (21)

Dr. Fothergill, by now greatly aroused over the
intransigence of the Government, appealed directly to
Lord Dartmouth in behalf of some move in the direction
of conciliation.   In a letter of January 12, 1775, he
forcefully pointed out the situation as he saw it:

> America is now grown too great to be
> humbled by this country without such an
> exertion of force as might thus bring on
> such an Hemoptae as would end in a fatal
> consumption. We might harrass, vex, dest-
> roy a large territory, many people, re-
> tard their progress toward greatness, but
> never, never hope to subject them to
> Great Britain. This is, at least, my
> firm belief founded on what appears to
> me indubitable evidence...Do, my noble,
> much esteemed Friend, forget the little
> trifling quarrels fomented by mischievous
> people for the ruin of this great Empire
> and give America all she asks... Violent
> measures will ruin us both, partial
> condescension will pave the way to future
> and worse misunderstandings. A generous
> mind will open itself to the liberal plan
> of human felicity and regulate its actions
> accordingly. (22)

Somewhat later Fothergill informed the Philadel-
phia Friends of the various initiatives of the London
Friends in behalf of the colonies.   In a letter to
James Pemberton he said in part:

> Whatever may be the result of these affairs,
> we have none of us been wanting, as opport-
> unities offered, to render the best services
> we could to our Friends in America as
> well as to the inhabitants of that vast
> region in general, by endeavoring to con-
> vince those we had access to that however
> some warm spirits might have erred both in
> expression and in act, yet that the
> generality deserved the generous confidence

117

of the British nation. (23)

Despite these efforts, he was, however, pessimistic as
to the outcome of the imperial dispute. In explaining
the difficulties faced in working for a change in the
Government's attitude on colonial policy, he declared:

> There is a part of Administration which
> we believe has the King's confidence most,
> who are utterly averse to temperate
> measures and who will leave no stone unturn-
> ed to engage both countries in hostilities.
> They are the descendents of those people
> who in every reign since James I adhered to
> unlimited monarchical principles, adverse
> to civil and religious liberty. Too
> many of these are about the King and have
> been so from his earliest infancy. People
> of these principles prevail in the cabinet.
> (24)

David Barclay was meanwhile active with the London
merchants in presenting a petition to Parliament on
the worsening relations with the colonies. On January
23 both the London merchants and the Society of Merchants Venturers of Bristol petitioned the House of
Commons in behalf of reconciliatory measures toward
America, but with no positive result. (25) Subsequently David Barclay is reported to have declared in a
meeting of the London merchants in early February that
"however lightly and contemptuously their petition was
treated...the Americans would to a man die, if the act
in his hand, which he held up, was not repealed."(26)

About the same time Dr. Fothergill and David Barclay informed Franklin that the "Hints" were again under consideration. Several conferences had been held
and the Ministry seemed to be well disposed toward them.
Some of the suggestions they contained were thought to
be reasonable, and others might be accepted with small
amendments. The one point on which there could be no
compromise, however, and the one without which Franklin
declared no accommodation could be arranged, concerned
the principle of parliamentary authority to legislate
internally for the colonies. (27)

After further discussion with Lord Hyde as to
those points in the "Hints" to which the Ministry objected, David Barclay presented Franklin with a modified version he had formulated, entitled "A Plan,

which it is believed, would produce a permanent Union between Great Britain and her Colonies". The first item, that the tea destroyed be paid for, for which the port of Boston would be reopened, was finally accepted by Franklin despite his expressed reservations. It was then agreed that a petition be presented to the King by a colonial agent or a delegation of colonial agents, requesting that when the payment for the tea had been made, a commissioner would be sent to America with authority to reopen the port of Boston.(28) Although Franklin felt that a mere suspension of the Boston Port Act was insufficient and that all the Coercive Acts affecting Massachusetts should be repealed, he promised to draft such a petition.

The draft which Franklin later presented to David Barclay and Dr. Fothergill contained a provision for the repeal of all the Coercive Acts. In view of the Government's sure rejection of any such provision, this initiative proceeded no further.

Despite the failure to reach any agreement on conditions for the settlement of the colonial issue, the discussions and negotiations which had taken place over the past two months, together with various petitions presented to Parliament, seemed to have had some effect on the Ministry. In mid-February, Lord North introduced a resolution in Parliament designed to promote reconciliation with the Colonies. Parts of Franklin's plan as presented by David Barclay and Dr. Fothergill were included, such as: Parliament to refrain from taxing the colonies if the latter agreed to raise such sums for the common defense as their condition and circumstances permitted; the colonies to provide for their own civil government and administration of justice; and duties levied in the colonies for the regulation of commerce and trade to be carried to the account of the respective colonies. According to Franklin, certain proposals made by David Barclay and originally contained in the resolution were withdrawn shortly before its introduction. (29)

Notwithstanding the positive aspects of the resolution, the British Friends felt they should withhold support because of its very limited nature. Consequently they warned the American Friends not to "be allur'd thereby, or (by) any other of the present Plans intended to Devide". It was at this point that Barclay, who was writing to James Pemberton, referred to the Testimony issued by the Philadelphia Meeting for Sufferings

119

as being "made a handle of, to the disadvantage of ye community - the language of the Court being that they have the Quakers' Approbation of their Measures:...in Particular the Testimony of 24th 1:st Mo..." (30) As already indicated, the British Friends were much disturbed that their American brethren should appear to be supporting the Government just when the British Quakers were exerting their utmost efforts to induce the Cabinet to modify its colonial policies.

Subsequent meetings between Franklin and Lords Hyde and Howe made it only too obvious that there was no hope of reaching a satisfactory resolution of British oppostion to Franklin's proposition that all the Coercive Acts against Massachusetts be withdrawn and that Parliament disclaim authority to legislate on internal colonial affairs. As a result, on March 18 Franklin set sail for America, having given up hope of Parliament's taking sufficiently far-reaching steps for conciliation with the colonies. A few days before he departed he met David Barclay and Dr. Fothergill at the latter's home. In the course of their conversation the two Quakers requested Franklin "to assure their Friends (in America) from them" that it was their "fixed opinion that nothing could secure the privileges of America, but a firm and sober adherence to the terms of the Association made at the Congress..." (31)

Here again the difference of opinion between the London Friends and the Philadelphia Quakers became obvious. The Londoners were advocating support of a colonial measure which the Philadelphians had condemned, and for compliance with which they later disowned recalcitrant members. The advice of the British Friends carried little weight at this point.

By this time the policy of the Government had abruptly changed, doubtless because of chagrin over recent developments in the colonies. Instead of further pursuing conciliatory measures, a coercive policy became the order of the day. The so-called Fisheries Bill was introduced in Parliament. This provided that all trade of the New England colonies should be confined to Great Britain and the British West Indies, and all trade with the other American provinces was forbidden. The severest part of the bill was the provision barring the New Englanders from their fishing grounds off Newfoundland. (32) The effect of the bill would be to starve out New England by depriving it of one of its most lucrative occupations and by cutting off its regular sources of supply in the other colonies.

The English Quakers were among the foremost in opposition to this measure. When David Barclay and Dr. Fothergill heard of the introduction of the Fisheries Bill they went directly to Lord North and plead with him in vain for two hours not to support the measure. Shortly afterward they served with Daniel Mildred and others on a committee of the London Meeting for Sufferings in drafting two addresses, one to the House of Commons on behalf of the Island of Nantucket, and the other to the King requesting a peaceful adjustment of the dispute with the colonies. (33)

In their address to the House of Commons the Friends explained that nine-tenths of the inhabitants of Nantucket were Quakers. Because of the island's barrenness, the population depended chiefly on obtaining produce and other necessities from the neighboring mainland and on profits from the whaling industry. The passage of the Fisheries Bill would cut off all their means of livelihood, and since the islanders were entirely innocent of any complicity in the colonial resistance measures, the petitioners requested that the bill be rejected. Seventy-two Friends signed the address. (34) A similar address was presented by the London North American merchants. (35)

On March 1 Mr. Alderman Oliver introudced the petitions to the House of Commons which then went into a committee of the whole to consider them. David Barclay was called to the bar and informed the House that the North American merchants desired him to examine some witnesses. (36) The first to appear was Brooke Watson who gave an account of the state of the fisheries and their value to the kingdom. He was followed by Mr. Stephen Higginson who presented a statement of the probable damage to British trade if the proposed measure were adopted. Finally, Captain Seth Jenkins, a Quaker, was called to the bar, who explained that the inhabitants of Nantucket would suffer patiently as long as they were able to, in hopes that the restrictions, if passed into law, would not continue long.

In conclusion David Barclay summed up the arguments against the bill. He pointed out the unhappy effects of such an act on the New England provinces. Many innocent people would suffer, especially the Quakers on Nantucket whose principles would prevent

121

them from supporting active opposition to Great Britain. The impracticability of carrying on the fisheries from Great Britain and the likelihood of loss of trade to the foreign West Indies would, he hoped, persuade the House not to pass the bill. (37)

Similar petitions against the passage of the proposed measure were subsequently presented in the House of Lords from the London North American merchants and the Corporation of the City of London. (38) Captain Seth Jenkins again testified, presenting much the same argument as he had given in the House of Commons. In behalf of Nantucket, he declared that the island had sent no delegates to the Continental Congress, that the population drank tea and was not a party to its destruction, and, moreover, that the islanders were not involved in politics. (39)

Although the bill was eventually passed into law, the island of Nantucket was exempted from its provisions. This was done, according to David Barclay, not from any consideration for the innocence of the people concerned but solely because of the realization of Britain's need for sperm oil. (40)

On March 15 the Meeting for Sufferings approved the draft of a petition to the King. The day before its presentation by Dr. Fothergill, David Barclay, Jacob Hagen, and Thomas Corbyn, a copy was submitted for the perusal of the Secretary of State. On the day following, the Lord Chamberlain presented the bearers of the petition to the King at a public levée, and the address was "graciously received". (41) It was later published in several of the Pennsylvania and New England papers. (42)

In this petition the English Friends declared that from their correspondence with the American Quakers they were convinced that there were no more loyal subjects than the colonists, and they hoped some means might be found to prevent a war between them and Great Britain. (43) David Barclay was of the opinion that it would not do much good, but at least it would satisfy those who wished to leave no stone unturned in the effort to strengthen the hands of those Ministers opposed to sanguinary measures. (44)

Early in April the Quakers also supported the petition presented by the city of London on the same matter. With regard to this action a London correspondent wrote to America:

> The Quakers in England have petitioned
> the King themselves as a people, and now
> attend the city petition; all join in
> once voice against the Ministry, and are
> all faithful to the people of America.
> The Quakers are the most hearty in the
> cause, and see the dreadful consequences
> of a civil war. (45)

In the meantime, individual Friends had attempted to persuade the King to adopt other measures than those contemplated. In February Dr. Fothergill, David Barclay, and Rachel Wilson wrote to the King but received no answer, while two women Friends were refused an audience. (46) Another Quaker woman, Frances Dodshon, presented an address to the King, entreating him to avoid bloodshed and war. (47)

In commenting on these proceedings, Joseph Oxley of Norwich declared that "very many friends" had bestirred themselves diligently "even amongst the great people and in private capacity" to bring about reconciliation. (48) David Barclay wrote that many English Quakers had stood forth in the American cause and defended them wherever they considered the colonists' conduct defensible. (49) Daniel Mildred felt that although their applications to the King would not be crowned with success, it was a testimony to those in authority of "the steady prudent conduct of our Society in these times of Tumult". (50) And finally Dr. Fothergill expressed his satisfaction that as a body and as individuals, the English Friends had omitted nothing that might tend to prevent Parliament from pursuing such rigorous measures. Despite all their efforts, however, it seemed to him "as if thro' judicial blindness" American and England "were permitted to become each other's scourges". (51)

A year later, even though the colonies were moving rapidly toward independence, Dr. Fothergill did not give up hope for an eventual accommodation between them and Great Britain. When Lord Howe departed for America in May 1776, entrusted with broad instructions for conciliation, Fothergill wrote to the Philadelphia Friends recommending Howe for his interest in America "which gives us hopes", he said, "stronger hopes of reconciliation than anything else that could have been proposed to us". (52) Fothergill also addressed a letter to Henry Strachey, secretary to Lord Howe, applauding the mission and pointing out that "America, its present power, its future greatness, its consequence to the Kingdom, to all the States of Europe, are literally unknown to those who direct our councils". He concluded by soliticting an understanding and magnanimous approach to the colonial position. (53)

At a later time, shattered by the disaster which Britain was facing, Dr. Fothergill vented his bitterness in a letter to Franklin whose friendship and respect he retained until his death. After the colonies had declared their independence, and there was the probability of French intervention on the side of the colonies, he wrote:

> There is...one man in this Kingdom who was permitted to be born for its chastisement, if not destruction. By education, by flattery, by disposition, capable of supposing himself superior to every other mortal - unfeeling - unalterable...Entreaties, petitions are disregarded and their promoters stamped indelibly in the pages of vengeance and disgrace. Vice overlooked, impiety not discouraged, everything overlooked in those who have the will or authority to flatter and support. (54)

In his last letter to Franklin shortly before he died, Dr. Fothergill summed up the matter as follows:

> Much horrible mischief would indeed have been prevented had our superiors thought fit to pay any regard to our humble endeavors. But their ears were shut, their hearts hardened, Kings became delirious and the poor people suffered for it. (55)

(1) Quoted from the Kentish Gazette (Canterbury), April 30, 1774, and the London Packet, April 27, 1774, in Hinkhouse, Fred Junkin, The Preliminaries of the American Revolution as Seen in the English Press, 1763-1775 (New York, 1826), 180.

(2) The London Packet, May 4, 1774, in Ibid.

(3) Hinkhouse, op.cit., 180.

(4) Ibid.

(5) The London Packet, Nov. 21, 1774, in Hinkhouse, op.cit., 181.

(6) In August, 1772, Dr. Fothergill wrote to James Pemberton with regard to Lord Dartmouth:

> I cannot but mention one favourable circumstance for America, which is, that Lord Dartmouth is appointed Secretary for the Colonys...So far as depends upon Lord D. I know he will be in your favour. He has great goodness of disposition, good judgment, desirous of information, dis-interested and will have this one wish predominant; to do every thing in his power, for the good of the whole. (Dr. Fothergill to James Pemberton, Aug. 29, 1772, Pem.Pap., v. 34, 165.)

(7) Ritcheson, Charles R., British Policies and the American Revolution (Norman,1954),178; Bargar, B.D., Lord Dartmouth and the American Revolution (Columbia,S.C., 1965),134. Lord Hyde held an un-official position of elder statesman and was in good standing with both the King and the Prime Minister. (Corner, Betsy Copping and Singer, Dorothea Waley, "Dr. John Fothergill, Peacemaker", Proceedings of the American Philosophical Society, v. 98 (1954),13.)

(8) Corner and Waley, loc.cit., 13.

(9) Franklin, Benjamin, Autobiographical Writings, ed. Carl Van Doren (New York, 1945), 351-352.

(10) Ibid.

(11) The full text of the "Hints" is given in Ibid., 354-355.

(12) Lettsom, Memoirs of Dr. John Fothergill, M.D. (London, 1786), 166,168,171.

(13) Franklin, op.cit., 374.

(14) Ibid., 362.

(15) Corner and Waley, loc.cit., 19.

(16) Donoughue, Bernard, British Politics and the American Revolution (London, 1964), 215.

(17) Ibid.;Sossin, Jack M., Agents and Merchants, Bri-
     tish Colonial Policy and the Origins of the Ameri-
     can Revolution, 1763-1775 (Lincoln, 1965), 212.
(18) Sossin, op.cit.,207; Lee, William, Letters of Wil-
     liam Lee,ed. Worthington Chauncey Ford (3 vols.,
     Brooklyn, 1891; reprint, New York, 1971),v.1,
     21-22.
(19) Lee, op.cit., 23.
(20) Ibid.,24. The failure of the merchants in influ-
     encing Parliament at this time is in sharp con-
     trast with their success in pushing repeal of the
     Stamp Act ten years earlier. This change was due
     both to the greatly altered structure of political
     forces in Parliament at the hands of an energetic
     king and his coterie and the fact that from an
     economic standpoint the development of trade with
     South America and eastern Europe minimized de-
     pendence on the North American markets.
(21) N.H.Gaz., March 24, 1775; Ev. Post, March 20,1775;
     Mass. Gaz.,March 20, 27, 1775.
(22) Dr. Fothergill to the Earl of Dartmouth, Jan. 12,
     1775, Chain of Friendship, 436-437.
(23) Dr. Fothergill to James Pemberton, Jan. 26, 1775,
     in ibid., 440.
(24) Ibid., loc.cit., 438.
(25) Parliamentary History of England from the Norman
     Conquest to the Year 1803,ed. W. Cobbett and
     T. C. Hansard (36 vols., London 1806-1820), v.18,
     168-194.
(26) Robert Barclay to his mother, Jan 25, 1775,
     Barclay Letters, Quaker Collections, Haverford
     College; Pa.Ev.Post, April 22, 1775; Pa.Ldg.,
     April 22, 1775.
(27) Franklin, op.cit., 381.
(28) Ibid.,384-386; David Barclay to James Pemberton,
     Feb. 5 & March 18, 1775, loc.cit.
(29) Franklin, op.cit., 392; David Barclay to James
     Pemberton, Feb. 5 & March 18, 1775, loc.cit.
(30) David Barclay to James Pemberton, Feb. 5 & March
     18, 1775, loc.cit.
(31) Franklin, Benjamin, The Life of Benjamin Franklin,
     Written by Himself,ed. John Bigelow (3 vols.,
     Philadelphia 1874), v. 2, 333.
(32) Fisher, Struggle for American Independence, v. 1,
     287. The full title of the bill as "An Act to
     Restrain the Trade and Commerce of the Provinces
     of Massachusetts Bay and New Hampshire and the
     Colonies of Connecticut and Rhode Island and
     Providence Plantations" (Amer. Arch., 4th Ser.,
     V. 1, 1694-1696).

(33) London M.f.S., Min., v.34, Feb. 24,27, March 15,
1775; <u>Journals of each Provincial Congress of
Massachusetts in 1774 and 1775</u> (Boston, 1838), 746;
"A Chronological Summary of Events and Circumstances...", <u>The Yorkshireman</u> (Pontefract, England),
4 vols., 1835-1836, v.4,280-281.
(34) London M.f.S., Min., v.34, Feb. 27, 1775; <u>Pa.
Mer</u>.,May 5, 1775;"A Chron. Summary of Events",<u>loc.
cit</u>., 281-282;<u>Mass.Spy</u>, May 3, 1775, which give
the Quaker petition in full.
(35) <u>Parl. Hist</u>., v.18, 380-381.
(36) The details of these proceedings are in the <u>Parl.
Hist</u>., v.18, 380-385; <u>N.H.Gaz</u>., May 5, 1775;
<u>Essex Gaz</u>., May 2, 1775; and <u>Mass. Spy</u>, May 5, 1775.
(37) <u>Parl. Hist</u>., v.18, 384.
(38) <u>Ibid</u>., 421-457 gives the petitions and the debates on them.
(39) <u>Ibid</u>., 423-425.
(40) David Barclay to James Pemberton, Feb. 5 & March
18,1775, <u>loc.cit</u>.;London M.f.S., Min., v.34,
March 15, 17, 1775.
(41) David Barclay to James Pemberton, Feb. 5 & March
18,1775, <u>loc.cit</u>.;"A Chron. Summary of Events",
<u>loc.cit</u>., 284. Both the <u>Mass. Spy</u> of May 17, 1775,
and the <u>Essex Gaz</u>. of April 25, 1775, carried the
following comment about the petition to the King:
> It is imagined that among all the numerous
> petitions in favour of the Americans,
> addressed to --, none will be more immedi-
> ately acceptable than that of the Quakers,
> as being couched in terms the most humili-
> ating, breathing nothing but passive
> obedience, abject submission, and an utter
> aversion to justifiable resistance, sounds
> harmonious to the ears of tyranny.
(42) <u>Pa.Pkt</u>., May 8, 1775;<u>Pa. Mer</u>., May 12,1775;
<u>Pa. Ldg</u>., May 13,1775;<u>Prov.Gaz</u>., May 27, 1775;
<u>Nwp.Mer</u>., June 3, 1775.
(43) "A Chron. Summary of Events", <u>loc.cit</u>.,283.
(44) David Barclay to James Pemberton, Feb. 5 & March
18, 1775, <u>loc.cit</u>.
(45) <u>Prov.Gaz</u>., July 1, 1775;<u>Nwp.Mer</u>., July 10, 1775.
(46) <u>Essex Gaz</u>., May 12, 1775.
(47) Armistead, Wilson, <u>Select Miscellanies, Chiefly
Illustrative of the History, Christian Principles,
and Sufferings of the Society of Friends</u> (6 vols.,
London, 1851), v.5, 91-93; <u>Pa. Mer</u>., Aug., 25,
1775.
(48) Joseph Oxley to John Pemberton, Feb. 5, 1775,Pem.
Pap., v.27, 89.

(49) David Barclay to James Pemberton, Feb. 5 & March 18, 1775, loc.cit.

(50) Daniel Mildred to James Pemberton, April 5, 1775, Pem.Pap., v.27,70.

(51) Dr. Fothergill to James Pemberton, Sept. 5, 1775, Pem.Pap., v.24,176.

(52) Dr. Fothergill to James Pemberton, April 30, 1776, Chain of Friendship, 467.

(53) Dr. Fothergill to Henry Stratchey, 1776, in ibid., 469-470.

(54) Dr. Fothergill to Benjamin Franklin, 1777, Chain of Friendship, 477-478.

(55) Dr. Fothergill to Benjamin Franklin, October 25, 1780, quoted in Corner, Betsy Copping, "Dr. Fothergill's Friendship with Benjamin Franklin", Proceedings of the American Philosophical Society, v. 102 (1958), 418.

Chapter VIII

THE FIRST YEAR OF WAR

On April 19, 1775, the battles of Lexington and
Concord initiated the military struggle which soon became a war for American independence. In view of the
Quaker testimony against all war, the chief concern of
the Society of Friends was that members abstain from
participation in the conflict in any manner. Failure
to abide by pacifist principles invariably resulted in
the disownment of the offending member, unless he acknowledged his mistake to the meeting. Regardless of
geographical location and particular local situation,
the Friends maintained a general uniformity of viewpoint and conduct, although there were at times some
differences of opinion as to the extent of the application of their testimonies. Such differences were relatively minor and reflected the position and role of
the Friends in the respective states. As the New England Friends declared at their annual session in the
spring of 1775, they were facing "a tryal both within
and from without which (would) shake the foundations
of all who (were) not Established on the Sure Rock."(1)

In Pennsylvania the internal situation had affected the Society to a much greater extent than was the
case elsewhere. Consequently the policies followed by
the Friends there were at times less neutral than the
actions of the Quakers in other states. The Quakers'
emphasis on the position that Friends could not participate in the pulling down or setting up of governments
conflicted sharply with the democratic doctrine of
popular sovereignty held by the patriots.

According to the patriot idea, all citizens should
make their respective contribution to the civil life
of the community, quite apart from the mere acceptance
of a patriot authority. (2) When the patriots did assume the governing authority the following year, not
only the Quaker refusal to perform military service
but fully as much their abstention from any civic responsibilities brought down upon them the wrath of the
new rulers. The position of the Friends put them in
the category of those opposed to the American cause,

129

increased suspicions as to their true intents, and caused the patriots to consider them Tories.

With the outbreak of hostilities, the first serious problem to be faced in Pennsylvania was that of defense. During the colonial period Pennsylvania never had a militia law. In 1756 at the time of the French and Indian War, the legislature passed a voluntary militia law which the Privy Council in London vetoed as being insufficient. (3) This lack of military defense now became one of the radicals' chief points of attack.

When the news of the military events in New England reached Philadelphia, the inhabitants of the city met at the State House and resolved "to associate together, to defend with arms their property, liberty, and lives against all attempts to deprive them of it." Enrollment began at once, the associators forming military companies and starting immediately to drill. (4) Shortly afterward, a group of residents of the City and Liberties of Philadelphia petitioned the Assembly to appropriate the sum of ₤50,000 for the purpose of defense. The Assembly then sitting was the same which approved the resolutions of the First Continental Congress, and the influence of the Quaker members seemed apparent in its grant of only ₤2000. (5)

In June the city Committee of Safety presented a similar petition to the Assembly, requesting financial aid for the Military Association. At the same time a resolution of the Continental Congress requesting two companies of riflemen was laid before the Assembly. (6) In reply to the petition, a committee was appointed to put the city and province in a state of defense on which two Quakers served, Isaac Pearson and William Rodman. (7) Shortly afterward, in compliance with the report of this committee, and probably also responding to pressure from the Continental Congress, the Assembly passed resolutions approving the formation of the Military Association and appointing a provincial Committee of Safety fully empowered to act in case of invasion. It also ordered the issue of ₤35,000 in bills of credit for the use of the Committee of Safety and levied taxes to sink them. As a gesture in behalf of the pacifist elements it recommended that the Association "bear a tender and brotherly regard" toward those who could not bear arms on account of religious scruples, urging the latter at the same time to assist the public cause according to their abilities. (8)

During the summer the movement for military preparations gained ground. In July the Continental Congress passed resolutions encouraging the colonists to
arm, while at the same time exhorting those who were
conscientious objectors to render all services to "their
oppressed Country, which they (could) consistently with
their religious principles". (9) By this time deviations
of a military nature began to occur among the Friends.
A number joined military associations, and reports circulated that several companies exclusively of Quakers
were being formed. Among the leaders of this movement
were Thomas Mifflin, Samuel Marshall, and a previously
disowned Quaker, Joseph Copperthwaite, the commander of
the so-called "Quaker Blues". Other Friends who assumed
military stations were Clement Biddle and John Cadwalader. (10)

Rumors of the actions of these Quakers spread
rapidly throughout the colonies. John Adams informed
his wife that "whole companies of armed Quakers" were
drilling. (11) Roger Sherman of Connecticut and Richard
Caswell of North Carolina wrote home in a similar vein,
and a letter containing such an account was read in
the Massachusetts House of Representatives. (12) The
reports that the Friends were actively supporting the
revolutionary movement led many people to a misconcep-
tion of their real attitude. In writing to Israel
Pemberton, Edward Stabler of Virginia related how
Richard Bland, recently returned from the Congress in
Philadelphia, was attempting to make the people believe
"that a large majority of the Friends in Philad? had
taken up arms". (13)

Meanwhile the Society was taking active measures
to purge its ranks of those who were failing to uphold
its peace testimony. In May, Chester Quarterly Meeting
learned that some of its members had deviated from
their religious testimony by joining the current "Commotions and Tumults", and it appointed a committee to
assist the subordinate monthly meetings in such cases.(14)
In August Philadelphia Quarterly Meeting received similar reports. (15) At the Yearly Meeting sessions in
September 1775, the answer to the query regarding the
Society's testimony against war declared:

> All the accounts except that from Shrewsbury
> lament the sorrowful deviation which has
> lately appeared in many Members from our
> Peaceable Profession, and Principles, in
> joining with the Multitude in warlike

                    Exercise, and instructing themselves
                    in the Art of War...(16)

A subsequent letter from the Meeting for Sufferings to
the English Friends indicated that young men were the
chief source of trouble. (17)

     In order to promote the effective and expeditious
handling of this problem, the Yearly Meeting appointed
some Friends to confer on the matter with visiting
Friends from North Carolina and New York. Their report
urged the monthly meetings to take proper action against offenders and recommended that the quarterly meetings
appoint committees to assist in this work. Friends in
general were advised to avoid all acts, even such as
being spectators at training grounds, which might in
any way compromise their principles. (18)

     The Yearly Meeting also directed each quarterly
meeting to nominate four Friends to join with the
Meeting for Sufferings in considering the problems
which they faced in acting on behalf of the Yearly
Meeting. (19)

     In carrying out the decisions on the employment of
sanctions to assure the maintenance of the Quaker peace
testimony, the official bodies of the Society spared
no one. Not only direct military involvement, but any
action considered as having an "indirect" bearing on
the war came under the ban. As the war progressed,
the application of "indirect" to the various requirements
of the state intensified the hostility of the authorities
to the Friends and contributed to the harshness of the
execution of the laws in many cases.

     By the end of 1775, 163 members were dealt with in
Pennsylvania of which 65 were disowned. Some submitted
acknowledgments of misconduct and were pardoned by their
meetings, the remainder being carried over to the following year. Of these deviations, 144 were for military
action, 6 were for accepting public offices, and 13
were for a combination of both offenses. From the Philadelphia meetings there were 66, and from the meetings in
Chester and Bucks Counties there were 93 deviations.(20)

     In the two neighboring provinces of Delaware and
New Jersey which were both within the jurisdiction of
Philadelphia Yearly Meeting, the Quakers were not seriously affected until a year or so later. In New Jersey
there were only 14 deviations in 1775, all military, of

which seven were disowned that year. (21)   In Delaware
6 out of 8 dealt with were disowned for the same reason. (22)

It was actions and activities not strictly military which posed the most problems for the Friends,
since in such situations a decision had to be made as
to whether the qualification "indirect bearing" on the
war applied to that particular case.   A question in
this category which came before the Yearly Meeting of
1775 was the validity of accepting bills of credit or
other paper monies issued to finance the war.   Some
considered that accepting such notes was indirectly
aiding the prosecution of the war and should therefore
be prohibited.   In the end, however, no final rule was
established.   Each individual was allowed to act as he
saw fit, and all Friends were advised to be tenderly
considerate of each other's motives and conduct.   Spiritual and moral support was promised to any who conscientiously followed the stricter interpretation. (23)

It was not long before the more conscientious
Friends began to feel the brunt of patriot disapproval.
In December John Cowgill of Delaware was summoned before
a Committee of Safety of which Caesar Rodney was chairman for refusing to accept the Continental currency.
Because of his persistence in this stand he was advertised in the newspapers as an enemy to his country,
and all intercourse with him was interdicted under
threat of a similar penalty.   A few weeks later he was
again apprehended on his way to Meeting with his family.
This time he was drummed through the the town of Dover,
a paper on his back bearing the inscription: "On the
Circulation of the Continental Currency Depends the
Fate of America". (24)

Another problem for the Friends had to do with
financial assessments on conscientious objectors for
the prosecution of the war.   Naturally those who supported the war would resent the Quakers' exemption from
any responsibility for its conduct and would demand an
equalization of the burden.   Accordingly two memorials
were laid before the Assembly when it reconvened in
September, one from the officers of the Military
Association of Philadelphia and the other from the
Committee of Safety.   Both groups requested that contributions be prescribed in lieu of military service
for those whose religious and conscientious scruples
prevented them from participating in any military
activity.   The Committee of Safety pointed out that

"where the Liberty of all is at stake, every Man should
assist in its support, and that where the Cause is
common, and the benefits derived from an Opposition are
universal, it is not consonant to justice or Equity that
the Burdens should be partial". (25) It suggested that
the contribution of those who could not bear arms be
pecuniary, and for that purpose their property should
be assessed an amount equivalent to the loss of time
suffered by the associators. Since a new Assembly was
to meet shortly, both memorials were laid on the table
to await further consideration.

        The Assembly which convened in October was the
last one to sit under the old constitution. There were
three new Quaker members which made a total of twelve
Friends, chiefly from Chester and Bucks counties, comprising less than a third of the assemblymen. (26)
Soon after the new Assembly met, the Continental Congress presented a request for another battalion for the
Continental army. (27) Two days later the city Committee of Safety petitioned the Assembly that this request
be granted by an act including terms for the exemption
of conscientious objectors, thus equalizing the contributions of all for the welfare of the state. (28)

        By this time the Friends had taken alarm. The day
on which the city Committee of Safety laid its petition
before the Assembly, the Meeting for Sufferings met to
discuss "certain matters being agitated in the House
of Assembly...which, if adopted, would greatly affect
the Friends & others Conscientiously Scrupulous of
bearing Arms..." (29) Between the meeting's morning
and afternoon sessions, some of the members interviewed
several assemblymen, and having learned of the petitions
presented, procured copies which were read to the meeting
the next day. After some deliberation an address was
drafted, defining the rights and privileges of the Friends,
and about a week later, on October 27, it was laid before
the Assembly. (30)

        This statement pointed out the provision in the
charter of the colony providing for freedom of conscience,
and it declared that if the recommendations of the memorials which had been presented were adopted, the rights
and privileges cited would be infringed on. The statement concluded with a recommendation, urging that conciliatory measures be pursued in order to prevent a
lasting breach with the mother country. This address
was immediately answered by three memorials from the

Committee of Safety, the officers of the city Association, and the committee of the privates of the city Association, contending that no attempt was being made to deprive anyone of freedom of conscience. (31)

The Assembly finally surrendered to the demands for a more vigorous military policy. In a series of resolutions it approved the Association formed for the defense of the province, recommended that all males between the ages of sixteen and fifty join it, and urged that those unable to do so because of conscientious scruples contribute an equivalent to the value of the time spent by an associator in training. It also appointed a committee to frame a set of rules and regulations for the provincial Military Association and to draft a plan for an assessment on non-associators. (32) An act embodying the regulations subsequently agreed on was passed in late November, accompanied by a measure providing that in addition to the regular provincial taxes the sum of £2 10s. was to be paid by every non-associator between the ages of sixteen and fifty. (33)

The Friends were deeply disturbed over this outcome. John Reynell wrote to a friend in England explaining the critical situation in which the Pennsylvania Quakers found themselves. Since they could neither fight nor pay the extra tax prescribed by the legislature for those who did not, he feared that "a time of suffering" would be their lot. (34) The patriots deeply resented the attitude and position of the Friends. In a letter to Robert Morris, Charles Lee declared:

> ...did every impudence and cant match
> that of the Quakers, to enjoy all the
> blessings of liberty without contributing
> a single mite towards the acquiring or
> preservation of that blessing is a degree
> of iniquity which none but the disciples
> of Jesuitism can arrive at -. (35)

When the English Friends learned of the course of events, they were gravely apprehensive. In a letter to Humphrey Marshall, Dr. Fothergill stated his conviction that the public disaster which was befalling America "must soon, in some shape, come home to ourselves". He saw a war in the offing and feared and dreaded that in the near future

we may be rendered a severe scourge to

each other...Many lives will be lost,
many fine fabrics demolished, the labour
of ages ruined; all of this chiefly at
the instigation of some proud discontented
people, who have been in office in America;
and I am sorry to join with them the
generality of the Scotch, many of whom,
high in authority here, and seeing the King
rather set against you urge on these violent
councils...(36)

To James and Israel Pemberton he declared that
there was "no schème, however contrary to the principles
of religion and humanity, that should not be offered
as likely to subdue America that would not be accepted".
For Friends in America, he feared it would be a time of
"great sifting". "For you, our brethren as a Society,
I lament every day, and many amongst us deeply sympa-
thize with you in your affecting situation." As for
the outcome of a military conflict, he firmly believed
that "it is more than probable that we shall never
subdue you". (37)

In November 1775 the Continental Congress took
steps to clear away the colonial forms of administration.
New Hampshire, South Carolina and Virginia were advised
to establish new governments. (38) Independence was in
the air, and the Quakers exerted their utmost efforts
to stave it off. Israel Pemberton and other leaders in
the Society addressed themselves "with great assiduity
to all members of Congress whom they could influence,
even to some of the delegates from Massachusetts, but
most of all to the delegates of South Carolina". (39)
According to John Adams, Arthur Middleton from the
latter province became their hero. As for Adams himself, when it was rumored that he was for independence,
the Quakers represented him "as the worst of men;...
and avoided him, like a man infected with leprosy". (40)
John Dickinson worked with the Friends to prevent over-
hasty action, and Charles Thomson accused them of having
"intimidated Mr. Dickinson's mother and his wife, both
Friends, who were continually distressing him with
their remonstrances". (41)

In a letter to his brother Samuel on New Years
Day 1776, Thomas Wharton expressed the hope of many
Friends when he said he prayed for a change of heart on
the part of those in power in England so that they might
agree "from a principle of justice and right to withdraw their armies and treat with the Americans on terms

136

becoming both them and us. I mean that we should be considered as freemen having rights and privileges inherent and belonging to us..." He believed the colonies would make a contribution to the general cause of the empire "when it was applied for in a constitutional manner..." (42)

The support of Pennsylvania was vital to the success of any step toward independence. By the latter part of 1775 the radicals were employing all their efforts to capture the province for this cause, and their drive continued into the next year with increasing force. The conservatives, led by Dickinson, who were in control of the Assembly, desired above all the retention of the colonial charter. Although they were forced to make concessions to the popular demand, they kept two aims in mind; first, to preserve the charter under whose authority the legislature acted; and second, to postpone final separation from the mother country until the charter was safe. (43) On these points the Quakers, Dickinson, and the conservatives were in general agreement. In addition, the Friends opposed the move for independence at this time because it was being achieved by war, and the Meeting for Sufferings decided to make a public statement of the Quaker position. This action was no doubt also influenced by the appearance on January 10, 1776, of Thomas Paine's Common Sense which was a rousing appeal to the colonies to take the step to break with Britain. (44)

Ten days later, on January 20, the Meeting for Sufferings, having taken under special consideration the condition of affairs "as well in a religious, as civil aspect", issued "The Antient Testimony and Principles of the People Call'd Quakers renewed with respect to the King and Government, and touching the Commotions now prevailing in these and other parts of America, addressed to the People in General". (45) This action was the last public step taken by the Friends to avert what they considered a major calamity, and it was intended to strengthen the hands of the conservatives in preventing Pennsylvania from supporting the radical cause.

The Ancient Testimony contended that the current difficulties were the result of a departure from true religion and righteousness. If those in power would conduct affairs on the principles which they had deserted, peace and reconciliation would be possible. The benefits and favor enjoyed under the King's govern-

137

ment throughout the past called for "the greatest circumspection, care and constant endeavors, to guard against every attempt to alter, or Subvert that dependence and connection". The setting up and pulling down of kings and governments was God's special prerogative, and it was not the business of the Quakers to join in plots and contrivances to overturn them. The address concluded with the exhortation to all Friends:

> May we therefore firmly unite in the
> abhorrence of all such Writings and
> measures, as evidence and design to break
> off the happy connection we have heretofore
> enjoy'd, with the Kingdom of Great Britain,
> and our just and necessary subordination
> to the King, and those who are lawfully
> placed in authority under him; and thus
> the repeated solemn declarations, made
> on this subject, in the Address sent to
> the King, on behalf of the People of America
> in general, may be confirmed and remain
> to be our firm and sincere intention to
> observe and fulfill.

The publication of the Ancient Testimony profoundly affected the attitude of the public toward the Quakers. A week after it appeared it was printed in the Pennsylvania Ledger and was immediately the subject of a bitter attack. (46) Samuel Adams assailed the Friends in the Pennsylvania Evening Post under the pseudonym "Candidus". He bluntly advised them not to give offense by "endeavoring to counteract the measures of their fellow citizens for the common safety". If they professed to be only pilgrims here, they should "walk through the men of this world without interfering on either side. If they would not pull down Kings, let them not support tyrants: ...whether they understand it or not, there is, and every had been an essential difference in the characters". (47) In another address to the "People in General" Adams confuted the Quaker statement that God alone set up and put down kings and that men must accept the authority placed over them. He also declared that the Revolution was part of the omnipotent plan and that the time had come for the establishment of a new commonwealth in the West. (48)

An anonymous writer, The Forester, also attacked the Friends. He was amazed to hear with "what unanswerable ignorance many of that body wise in other matters,

will discourse on the present one." He attributed their
folly "to that superabundance of wordly knowledge which,
in original matters, is too cunning to be wise". He
concluded his tirade with the following exhortation:

> Back to the first plain path of nature,
> friends, and begin anew, for in this
> business your first footsteps were wrong.
> You have now traveled to the summit of
> inconsistency, and with such an accelerated
> rapidity as to acquire autumnal ripeness
> by the 1st of May. Now your rattling time
> comes on. You have done your utmost, and
> must abide the consequences. (49)

One of the most influential opponents of the Quakers was Thomas Paine, supposedly born into the Society,
but if so, for many years past an exile from its ranks.
At this time he addressed an epistle "To the Representatives of the Religious Society of the People called
Quakers, or to so many of them as were concerned in
publishing a late Piece entitled, 'The Ancient Testimony...'."(50) He reproached them for acting as a
political rather than a religious body, "dabbling in
matters, which the professed quietude of their principles instructed them not to meddle with". He charged
them with not abiding by their own statement that the
setting up and pulling down of kings and governments
was God's peculiar prerogative, and he considered that
in their actions the Friends had unwisely mingled religion and politics. If they refused to be a means on
one side, they should in like manner not meddle on the
other. Since the Ancient Testimony declared that the
Quakers should accept the "government which God is
pleased to set over us", he called on them to practise
what they preached.

The Ancient Testimony also influenced the attitude
of the Continental Congress toward the Friends in the
months that followed. Its members judged the Society
as a whole by what happened in Philadelphia, and the
radicals in the other provinces tended to take their
cue from Pennsylvania. Although many agreed with
Thomas Paine that the Friends were dabbling in politics
which were beyond their proper sphere, local conditions
often caused state and subordinate governments to pursue a more friendly policy toward them than was approved
by the patriot zealots. Under the circumstances it cannot be denied that the Ancient Testimony was a politically charged document and its issuance was bound to affect

139

the situation of the Friends, especially in Pennsylvania, for some time to come. (51)

NEW ENGLAND

Since New England was the first battleground of
the War for Independence, the Friends there were the
first to find themselves in the theater of conflict.
The urban center of New England Quakerism was Newport,
Rhode Island. The majority of Friends, however, lived
in the rural areas and a substantial proportion of them
in the neighboring provinces of Massachusetts and New
Hampshire. The Quakers had dominated the government in
Rhode Island at times during the preceding century, although the origin and conduct of the colony had had no
official connection with the Society. (52) By the time
of the controversy with Great Britain, the Friends were
of far less political significance than formerly, but
still numerous enough to be influential.

Throughout New England, with the exception of Newport, the Quaker constituency included little of the
mercantile element so prominent in Pennsylvania. Consequently the Friends there played no important role
aside from the activities of Stephen Hopkins in the
pre-revolutionary controversy. When war broke out they
were neither politically nor economically involved as
were their Pennsylvania brethren, and consequently they
assumed a more genuinely neutral stance than the latter,
a position generally recognized by their compatriots.

The outstanding New England Quaker at this time
was Moses Brown of Providence. Until 1774 when he
joined the Friends he was active in political and commercial circles. (53) A close friend of Stephen Hopkins
and many other political leaders, he served several
terms in the Rhode Island Assembly and in 1772 he was
appointed to the colony's Committee of Correspondence.(54)
In the decade before the war he was a member of the more
radical group and in 1768 he roundly denounced British
colonial policy in his correspondence with James Warren. (55).

When Moses Brown became a Friend his leadership in
the Society decidedly influenced its direction while at
the same time he employed his wordly connections in its
behalf. Evidence that he carried his former political
convictions with him is apparent in his statement to
his brother in 1775 that he had as "great regard for
his country's Rights, Liberties and Happiness as the

140

most sanguine Wigg". (56) He was strongly opposed to
the disciplinary measures adopted by the mother country
and declared "that the Measures now taking to Force
America are so Rong that its out of my power to Restrain
my Self from wishing Success to the Country in which I
was Born". (57)

Moses Brown believed that making public pronouncements about the imperial conflict was contrary to the
peace testimony. Several times he cautioned Israel
Pemberton and other Friends in Pennsylvania against
taking sides in the revolutionary controversy. He
urged moderation among Friends and counseled against
airing their differences of opinion publicly. (58) He
himself used his best offices whenever possible to promote conciliation. As Captain Wallace, a British officer, said of him before the conflict began: "Moses is
meek and recommends moderation but his advice is ridi-
culed by the warm partisans..." (59)

Despite their pacifist principles the New England
Quakers maintained a good repute with their neighbors.
In February 1775, a gentleman in Boston wrote to his
friend in Philadelphia that he had had not heard "the
least unfriendly or uncivil expression uttered by any
of the inhabitants of this town against them, as a
people, for many years". On the contrary they were always "and on all occasions, treated with full as much
(and I think more) catholic tenderness, friendly and
neighbourly kindness and affection, than persons of any
other sect or denomination amongst us". (60)

Soon after the decisive events at Lexington and
Concord in April 1775, the Yearly Meeting of Friends
for New England met in annual session at Newport. On
the suggestion of the Philadelphia Meeting for Sufferings and in view of the difficulties which they realized lay ahead of them, the Yearly Meeting appointed
a committee to operate as a Meeting for Sufferings.(61)
In July, shortly after its establishment, the new
Meeting was confronted with two important problems closely related to the war. One was the peculiarly unfortunate situation of the island of Nantucket, and the other
was the case of some Friends in Lynn, Massachusetts,
who were assisting in a city watch. (62)

The island of Nantucket was in a difficult position. The Massachusetts Restraining Act passed by Parliament the preceding spring, restricting the trade and
commerce of Massachusetts to Great Britain and the West

Indies, exempted Nantucket from its provisions, as already indicated. (63) This exemption had caused the Americans to fear the island would become a provisioning point for the British fleet. Consequently the Continental Congress had passed a resolution prohibiting the exportation of any supplies to the island except from Massachusetts. (64) On the other hand the Massachusetts Provincial Congress resolved that no supplies should be allowed to go to the island until sufficient evidence was given that they would be used solely for domestic consumption. (65)

Nantucket was largely inhabited by Friends who were in complete control of the local government. (66) In order to extricate themselves from their perplexing difficulties the selectmen of the town sent two Quakers, William Rotch and George Barker, with a petition to the Provincial Congress, requesting its advice as to a course of action which would be acceptable to all sides. (67) Christopher Starbuck wrote Moses Brown requesting his opinion as to the consistency of this action with their peace testimony and informed him that vessels had just arrived from Maryland and Virginia which, however, brought them no food because of the resolves of the Continental Congress. (68) Moses Brown presented the matter to the Meeting for Sufferings, of which he was a member, and the meeting declared that "Friends may safely in all cases of grievance, from what body of people soever, apply to such Bodies, or individuals, and remonstrate the same, & in a peaceable Suffering Spirit by argument or persuasion, endeavor (to obtain) Relief..." (69)

Meanwhile the delegation to the Provincial Congress succeeded in clearing the island of any charges of illegal trading, but it was unable to obtain the restoration of its former freedom of communication. (70) By October lack of supplies had become acute and the islanders appealed to the Meeting for Sufferings for provisions from the mainland. Since Rhode Island was already badly off and the season of the year made transportation over land difficult, the meeting suggested that the Massachusetts authorities be applied to for permission to obtain supplies directly from that province by water. The islanders were also to inform the British Admiral at Boston of their intentions and request free passage to prevent any "just occasion of offense" from being given to either side. (71) This advice was adopted and by December the Nantucketeers had obtained permission from the Massachusetts Assembly for the importation of

142

the needed supplies. (72)

Another way in which the war threatened the welfare of Nantucket was in its effect on the whaling industry. The Massachusetts Congress had resolved that no ship should sail from any port in the province without obtaining the permission of the General Court. (73) The islanders asked the Meeting for Sufferings whether they could comply with this provision, especially since it required a bond promising to land the oil and bone in some part of the colony. The meeting replied that such compliance in no way compromised the religious principles of the Friends, and since it did not infringe on the act of Parliament relating to the fisheries, the islanders might "without being justly charged with joining in opposition to the Authority of the Crown, give such bonds". (74)

The island of Rhode Island was in an even more difficult situation than was Nantucket. For a time the Rhode Island Assembly, with the concurrence of the Massachusetts Provincial Congress, had allowed Newport to furnish supplies to the British vessels stationed there, as failure to do so would have subjected it to bombardment. This intercourse with the British kept the port open and through it came communications and supplies for the Americans. The permission to supply the British ships was to expire on the second Monday in January 1776, and apprehension over the town's fate stirred its inhabitants to action. (75)

In December 1775, the town sent a memorial to the Continental Congress, petitioning for the continuation of its present status. At the same time Mary Callender, a Newport Quaker, wrote to Israel and John Pemberton, pointing out the precarious situation of the town and asking them to have William Redwood, a Newport resident who was then in Philadelphia, enlist the aid of Stephen Hopkins and Samuel Ward, Rhode Island representatives in the Continental Congress. (76)

On receipt of this letter the Pembertons gathered together a number of Philadelphia Friends to see what could be done. Several volunteered to approach various members of Congress, acting as private individuals and not as Friends. They were courteously received and in their interviews they stressed the fact that they were appealing as members of civil society and not as Quakers in order to prevent any misinterpretation of their motives. (77)

143

When the Newport memorial came before Congress
most of those speaking in the debates favored allowing
the British ships to be supplied with necessaries, provided that their squadrons in other ports did not
profit thereby. The matter was finally referred to the
Rhode Island Assembly which voted to concur with this
procedure. (78)

It was during this period that the question of the
consistency of Lynn Quakers serving on the town watch
was referred to the Meeting for Sufferings. In this
case the Meeting unhesitatingly informed Lynn Preparative Meeting that such service was inconsistent with
the peace testimony of the Society, it "being mixed with,
if not wholly for Military purposes". It requested
Salem Monthly Meeting, whose constituency included the
Lynn Meeting, to extend its care in the matter. (79) A
few months later, however, the Salem Friends informed
the Meeting for Sufferings that a change had been made
in the method of watching and that since then no Friends
had been called upon. (80)

Two questions which were uppermost in the minds of
the New England Quakers during the first year of the
conflict were whether or not they could consistently
pay taxes to the Revolutionary authorities, and whether
they could accept the paper currency issued to finance
the war. At the outset there was some diversity of
practice and opinion. Moses Brown was especially
anxious that official decisions in such matters "be di-
vested of every bias arising from opposite political
sentiments". In the case of the newly issued currency
some Friends had scruples about accepting it when it was
first issued, and the matter was referred to Smithfield
Monthly Meeting for its advice. Most Friends, however,
felt free to accept it. The one exception was an issue
of notes made by the Province of Massachusetts Bay bearing the effigy of a soldier. Those refusing to accept
this new currency declared they considered it in the
same category as currency issued for the support of a
foreign war. According to Moses Brown this was the only
tenable position, since any other reason would "involve
(the Friends) in the idea of Party which cannot be
right". (81)

The Meeting for Sufferings made no pronouncements
on this question until it had heard from the Yearly
Meeting in Philadelphia. Then it adopted the same
official position as the Pennsylvania Quakers, that of
pledging moral support to those who refused to accept

144

the currency but leaving the decision to the individual Friend. (82) Shortly afterward, in January 1776, Giles Hoosier of Newport reported to the Meeting for Sufferings that he had suffered the forcible seizure of his goods for refusing to accept paper money in payment of a debt. (83)

The issue of paying taxes in wartime proved to be a source of much greater difficulty. Differences of opinion ultimately led to the formation of a small separatist group in New England, as happened later in Pennsylvania. (84) The issue arose over the Society's position that no Friend could consistently pay taxes levied for the conduct of a war. There were some Friends who disagreed with this position, and in July 1775 Moses Brown received an anonymous letter arguing for the payment of all taxes to the authorities in power. The writer pointed out that with the exception of tithes the British Friends had paid all taxes regardless of the changes in government and declared:

> ...if we received advantage from civil
> government, we ought to bear our part of
> the charge of maintaining it, or else we have
> no recourse to it in any case whatsoever. (85)

If the government used force in defensive measures that was beyond the responsibility of the individual.

Those Friends who approved the acceptance of the newly emitted paper money were of a similar mind and advocated the payment of taxes levied to create a sinking fund for its redemption. They argued that refusing to pay taxes to the local government for the conduct of the war while Friends in Britain continued to pay taxes which would be used in part for the support of the war against the colonies would render them a party to the dispute and they would be treated accordingly. Therefore taxes must be paid in both cases or refused in both cases. (86)

With regard to the argument that the English Friends paid mixed taxes, part of which went for civil and part for war purposes, Moses Brown was in agreement. Although he could not accept the extreme position that war taxes should be paid, he felt that the Friends could not "Raise their Testimony so high as to refuse paying Taxes mixt with Civil Government" and that there was not much difference however much was the proportion for war. (87)

145

Later the same year Timothy Davis of Sandwich
Monthly Meeting in Massachusetts, who one suspects was
the author of the anonymous letter to Moses Brown, published <u>A Letter from One Friend to Some of his Intimate</u>
<u>Friends on the Subject of Paying Taxes</u>. (87) In the
same vein as in the anonymous letter, Davis, although
he agreed that Friends could not actively participate
in a war, contended that they should pay all taxes to
the ruling authorities, both war and civil. The
Quakers had paid taxes to the colonial governments in
the past when a great part went for military purposes
and to cease paying them now would be an act of partial-
ity. In support of his argument he referred to Christ's
dictum to "render unto Caesar that which is Caesar's" (89)

Inasmuch as Davis had not submitted his essay to
the Meeting for Sufferings before its publication, the
meeting immediately started proceedings against him
and directed the suppression of the pamphlet lest it

> ...have a Tendency to suppress Tender &
> Religious Scruples, in the Minds of those
> who are or may be exercised respecting
> the payment of Taxes, for the purposes
> of War. (90)

Subsequently Davis was disowned both because he published writings concerning the testimonies of the Society without the approval of the Meeting for Sufferings and because his ideas were considered to be in
disagreement with the official position of the
Society. (91)

An important indication of the position of the New
England Friends regarding the revolutionary movement
was evident in Moses Brown's comments concerning actions
taken by the Pennsylvania Quakers. He and other Friends
considered the manner of issuing the Ancient Testimony
of January 1776 to have been unwise and somewhat extreme.
In a letter to John Pemberton he wrote:

> Some of us should have liked it better
> had (it) been directed as usual, and not
> to the people in General, thereby taking
> away the handle people made use of ag^t
> friends, by a public answer (which, already
> spread about, had) confirmed the people
> generally, that we meddle beyond and
> Contrary to our Profession...(92)

146

The New England Quakers were as strict as any in dealing with members for involvement in the war. Eighteen deviations were dealt with in 1775, of which thirteen were disowned by the end of the year. All cases concerned military service, except one which was for mending guns. Eight each were in Massachusetts and Rhode Island and two were in New Hampshire. (93) It should be noted that there is no indication of Friends serving on public committees. There is no evidence to show whether this was acutally the case or whether the attitude of the New England Friends on this matter differed from that of the Quakers elsewhere.

NEW YORK

In the months following Lexington and Concord, the problem of Friends serving on public committees in New York City seems to have intensified. On May 1 a new Committee of One Hundred, more widely representative of the various groups in the city, replaced the former Committee of Sixty. On it were not only Lancaster Burling and Lindley Murray but also Walter Franklin a prominent New York merchant and a member of the Meeting for Sufferings. (94) About the same time Franklin was also elected a delegate to the New York Provincial Congress. (95)

The situation was considered serious enough to be referred to the Yearly Meeting which convened at the end of May. That body not only approved of the steps already taken by the Meeting for Sufferings but it also advised the subordiante meetings to appoint committees to assist the overseers in dealing with such cases. (96) In its epistle to the New England Friends, the Yearly Meeting expressed its deep concern over the unsettled state of affairs and urged that

> ...you and we be careful not to engage in
> too familiar conversation concerning the
> present commotions which now abound, but
> study to seek an inheritance in the Kingdom
> which is not of this World...(97)

The Meeting for Sufferings was especially concerned about the action of one of its own members and finally persuaded Franklin to desist attending until he had thought the matter over. Evidently its remonstrances had the desired effect since Franklin attended the sessions of the Congress only from May 23 to 31 and thereafter his name no longer appears on the list of dele-

147

gates. Subsequently he refused to sign the Continental
Association and he was not again elected to the Provincial Congress. (98)

As for the Committee of One Hundred, both Murray
and Franklin attended less than half of the time, and
when a new committee was chosen in July neither appeared in the list of the members. Only Lancaster Burling
continued to serve and, as already indicated, he was
subsequently disowned. (99)

The heavy concentration of Friends on the western
end of Long Island accounts for the conservative attitude of that area. At both Islip and Huntington in
Suffolk County the Friends refused to sign the Association and a meeting of freeholders at Islip refused to
send a deputy to the Provincial Congress. Although the
townsmen promised to abide by the decisions of the
other representatives from the county, they declared
that since some of them were "of the People called
Quakers", they meant to act no further "than is consistent with our Religious Principles". (100)

Several of the towns in Queens County also refused
to send delegates to the Provincial Congress and instead reaffirmed their allegiance to George III. (101)
Among them was the town of Hempstead which in April 1775
passed a resolution affirming its loyalty to the King,
urging that the imperial dispute be settled on constitutional grounds and that the union with Britain be
maintained. The town also declared its opposition to
the calling of a provincial congress and refused to
send a deputy since the legally constituted legislature
had already taken all necessary and appropriate action. (102)

In May, Queens County elected delegates to the
Provincial Congress and Thomas Hicks, a Quaker from
Hempstead,was among them. Since Hicks did not appear
when the Congress met it sent him a letter requesting
the reason for his non-attendance, thereby leaving the
town unrepresented. In his reply Hicks explained that
he had been elected without his consent and that subsequently he had consulted several of the leading
citizens of Hempstead who all agreed that in view of
the former resolution of the town he should not serve
in the Congress. Therefore he had declined "taking
a seat in the Congress, from a persuasion of the im-
propriety and even injustice of transacting business
of so much consequence for people who disavowed my

authority". (103)

Under these circumstances it was not surprising
that the feeling against the Quakers was quite strong
in this area. In October 1775 the towns of Great Neck
and Cow Neck petitioned the Provincial Congress to be
set off from the town of Hempstead "so long as the general conduct of the people is inimical to freedom."(104)

Ultimately the Provincial Congress took action with
regard to the disaffected towns in Queens County. Because of their opposition to resistance measures and
their opposition to electing a delegate to the Congress,
thereby leaving those towns unrepresented, the Congress
resolved that all the persons involved should appear
before a committee of the Congress to explain their actions. (105)

When the persons listed in the resolve did not
appear as directed the Congress interdicted all intercourse with them. (106) In February 1776 it further
resolved that certain men of Queens County, among them
three Friends, should be confined until an investigation could be carried out with regard to their conduct. (107)

Early in the fall of 1775 the Friends in New York
City received a request from the Committee of Safety
for a list of all male Quakers between the ages of
sixteen and sixty who were resident in the city and
county of New York. The Meeting for Sufferings, to
which the matter was referred, decided that compliance
with the order would be inconsistent with the Quaker
peace testimony. In its reply to the Committee of
Safety the meeting explained that its action was not
"the effect of an obstinate disposition, but...of a
truly conscientious Scruple". (108)

The question of accepting the Continental currency
did not affect the New York Friends to any great extent
at this time. There was only one instance of a Friend,
William Rickman, Clerk of the Meeting for Sufferings,
who "came to believe he would not be easy in accepting
it, at least for the time being", when he learned of
the position taken by some of the Philadelphia Quakers. (109)

There were only three deviations in connection
with the revolutionary movement among New York Friends
in 1775. Two of them, already referred to, were

serving on public committees. The third was a case of
military training in Oblong Monthly Meeting which resulted in disownment before the end of the year.(110)

It is obvious that New York Friends adhered faithfully to the peace testimony as they interpreted it,
but at the same time they took pains whenever possible
to make it clear that their actions were based solely
on religious principles.

THE SOUTH

The major military campaigns of the war did not involve the south until the later years of the struggle,
and the experiences of the southern Friends reflected
this situation. Late in the spring of 1775 Maryland
Yearly Meeting informed the Virginia Quakers that Friends in Maryland had generally abstained from participating in the prevailing commotions. (111) Four Friends were disciplined in the course of the year, all
for military service, and one of them was disowned. (112)

Some criticism was leveled at the Quakers in Virginia for their refusal to support the colonial cause,
and Robert Pleasants served as their apologist. In defending their position he said they had always "declin'd
the use of the Sword". The community would not be injured by their action because they could fight neither
for nor against the state. As a society, the Friends
had suffered much in the past from arbitrary power,
and therefore how could they be "disaffected to the
cause of Liberty"? In conclusion of one of his statements Pleasants struck a significant note which was
stressed repeatedly by the southern Quakers throughout
the war, the implication of the American battle
for freedom as applied to the institution of slavery.
If the colonists would do the same for their dependents
as they demanded of the mother country, he argued, their
action would "speak louder than Cannon, mortars or any
other instrument of death". (113) As for Virginia, he
felt the same applied with regard to the treatment of
dissenters.

Accepting paper bills of credit and paying taxes
to sink them were serious concerns of the Virginia
Quakers. In December 1775 a committee of the Yearly
Meeting met to discuss these matters and decided to
ask advice from the Philadelphia Meeting for Sufferings,
so that the Friends throughout the colonies might manifest "a oneness in practice, as well as Principle."(114)

150

In its reply, the Meeting for Sufferings did not deline-
ate any specific policy, although it referred to the
fact that many Friends in New Jersey had considered it
inconsistent to pay a tax lately levied there for the
conduct of the war. (115)

There were comparatively few deviations among
the Quakers in Virginia at this time. Four were chosen
as committee men but declined to serve. (116)   In
September, Edward Stabler informed Israel Pemberton
that they had "kept pretty steady except a few young
Persons in a particular Quarter". (117)   The quarter
referred to was evidently Henrico where five members
were dealt with, four for military activity and one
for serving on a public committee.   The latter resigned
his position and submitted an acknowledgment to his
meeting, but the other offenders were disowned.   Five
other Friends in the upland areas of the province also
committed offenses of a military nature, and three of
them were disowned by the end of the year. (119)

In October 1775, North Carolina Yearly Meeting
took a stand on the war similar to that of Philadelphia
Yearly Meeting.   It issued an epistle of advice to
the subordinate meetings in North and South Carolina
and Georgia, declaring against all plottings and agitations in the putting down and setting up of kings and
governments, which was God's prerogative alone.   Friends were exhorted not to be "Bussie Bodies" in such
matters, but were to "Pray for the King and for the
Safety of our Nation".   Although the intentions and de-
sires of those engaged in the dispute with Great Britain
were sincere, the Yearly Meeting was "apprehensive that
a Conformity to their Resolves and Requests" would be
a contradiction of the principles of the Friends, and
it cautioned its members not to "Interfere, Meddle or
Concern (themselves) in those Party affairs". (119)

Evidently the Georgia Friends considered that the
Yearly Meeting statement did not represent their
position fairly with regard to the measures taken to
resist the policies of the British Government.   Wrightsboro Monthly Meeting therefore submitted an address to
the governor of the province explaining the Friends'
testimony against war in general in a manner "suitable
to our disposition and behavior". (120)

Only three Friends were dealt with in the Carolinas for deviating from the Society's position.   Two
of these cases were for miltary service in North

151

Carolina, and one was for joining in public resolutions in South Carolina. All three were disowned by the end of the year. (121)

(1)   N.E.Y.M., Min., v.1 (1638-1787), 312. For a suc-
      cinct account of the role of the Quaker pacifist
      testimony during the Revolutionary War see Peter
      Brock's Pioneers of the Peaceable Kingdom (Prince-
      ton, 1970), chap. 4.
(2)   James, Sydney V., "The Impact of the Revolution on
      Quaker Ideas About their Sect", loc.cit., 372.
(3)   Stillé, Life of John Dickinson, 153-154; Statutes
      At Large of Pennsylvania, from 1682-1801 (18 vols.,
      Philadelphia and Harrisburg, 1896-1909), v.5, 197-
      198.
(4)   Scharf and Westcott, Hist. of Phil.,v.1, 295.
(5)   Votes and Proceedings, Pa. Arch. 8th Ser., v.8,
      7230, 7233.
(6)   Ibid., 7237-7241.
(7)   Ibid., 7242.
(8)   Ibid., 7245-7249.
(9)   Journals of the Continental Congress, 1774-1789,
      ed. Worthington Ford, Gaillard Hunt, Roscoe P.
      Hill, (34 vols., Washington, D. C., 1904-1937),
      v.2, 189.
(10) Graydon, Alexander, Memoirs of a Life Chiefly Pas-
      sed in Pennsylvania within the Last Sixty Years
      (Edinburgh, 1822), 122,123n.; Gilpin, "Memoir of
      Thomas Gilpin", loc.cit.,324-325; Curwin, Samuel,
      Journal and Letters of Samuel Curwin, ed. George
      Atkins Ward (New York, 1842), 26; Documents Re-
      lating to the Revolutionary History of New Jersey,
      New Jersey Archives, 2nd Ser., ed. Francis B. Lee,
      William Nelson, Austin Scott (5 vols., Trenton,
      1903-1917), v.1, 170n., 279n.; Phil.M.f.S. to Lon-
      don M.f.S., Nov. 30, 1775, London M.f.S., Min.,v.34.
(11) John Adams to Abigail Adams, June 2, 1775, Adams,
      John, Familiar Letters of John Adams and His Wife
      Abigail Adams, during the Revolution, ed. Charles
      Francis Adams (New York, 1876), 60.
(12) Richard Caswell to his son, May 11, 1775, Col.Rec.
      of N.C., v.9,1249; Roger Sherman to Joseph Trumbull,
      July 6, 1775; Letters of Members of the Continental
      Congress, ed. Edmund C. Burnett (8 vols., Washing-
      ton, D. C., 1921-1936), v.1, 154; A Journal of the
      Honorable House of Representatives of the Colony of
      the Massachusetts Bay, 1775-1776 (Watertown, 1776),
      202.
(13) Edward Stabler to Israel Pemberton, June 19, 1775,
      Pem.Pap., v.24, 172.

(14) Chester Q.M., Min., 1768-1813, May 8, 1775.

(15) Phil.Q.M., Min., 1772-1826, Aug. 7, 1775.

(16) Phil.Y.M., Min., v.3, 320.

(17) Phil.M.f.S. to London M.f.S., Nov. 30, 1775, Phil.
M.f.S., Min., v.2, 43.

(18) Phil.Y.M., Min., v.3, 328.

(19) Phil.Y.M. to London Y.M., September, 1775, Epistles
to London Y.M., v.4, 412-413.

(20) The dealings and disownments analyzed are in the
following monthly meetings minute books: Abington
M.M, Min., 1774-1782, 40-55, passim:Buckingham
M.M., Min., 1763-1780, 132; Chester M.M., Min.,
1745-1778, 422-429, passim;Concord M.M., Min.,
1757-1776, 435-437,438; Darby M.M., Min., 1763-
1783, 191-206, passim; Exeter M.M., Min., 1765-1785,
245 (S); Falls M.M., Min., 1767-1788, 160,163,
164; Goshen M.M., Min., 1766-1788, 197; Middletown
M.M., Min., 1755-1800, 351,352; Nottingham M.M.,
Min., 1766-1778, 346-357, passim (S);Phil.M.M.,
Min., 1771-1777, 298-346, passim;Phil.M.M.No.Dist.,
Min., 1772-1781, 166-183, passim;Phil.M.M.So.Dist.,
Min., 1770-1780, 82-113, passim; Sadsbury M.M.,
Mins., 1737-1783, 259, 260 (S); Uwchlan M.M., Min.,
1763-1776, 349-369, passim; Warrington M.M., Min.,
1747-1785, 429-443, passim (S); Wrightstown M.M.,
Min., 1734-1790, 231,234.

(21) Chesterfield M.M., Min., 1756-1786, 356-367, passim;
Haddonfield (and Gloucester) M.M., Min., 1762-1781,
279,281,287; Salem M.M., Min., 1740-1788, 359-363.
passim;Shrewsbury M.M., Min., 1757-1786, 351.

(22) Duck Creek M.M., Min., 1705-1800, 262,264 (S);
Wilmington M.M., Min., 1750-1776, 498-518,passim(S);

(23) Phil.Y.M., Min., v.3, 328-329.

(24) "Account of sufferings in Duck Creek Monthly
Meeting", Delaware, June 27, 1778, Phil.M.f.S.,
Misc.Pap., bx. 14 (1774-1778).

(25) Votes and Proc.,7259-7262. See Jack D. Marietta's
"Wealth, War and Religion", loc.cit.,237-238 for
a discussion of the patriots' arguments.

(26) The new Quaker members were David Twining, Thomas
Jenks and Joseph Pyle. Thomas Mifflin had previously been disowned. For a full list of the members
of the assembly see Votes and Proc.,7301-7302.
Twining and Jenks were later disowned for their
active support of the revolutionary cause. (Middletown M.M., Min., 1755-1800, 378,381; Wrightstown
M.M., Min., 1734-1790, 246-247.

(27) Votes and Proc., 7306-7308.

(28) Ibid., 7311-7312.

(29) Phil.M.f.S., Min., v.2, 25.

(30) Ibid.,25-26; Votes and Proc.,7326; Pa. Gaz.,
     Nov. 1, 1775; Pa. Mer.,Nov. 3, 1775, Pa. Pkt.,
     Nov. 13, 1775.
(31) Votes and Proc.,7334-7343.
(32) Ibid., 7351-7352.
(33) Ibid., 7369-7384.
(34) John Reynell to Joshua Williams, Nov. 25, 1775,
     Letter Book, 1774-1784.
(35) Charles Lee to Robert Morris, Nov. 22, 1775,
     Charles Lee Papers, (Collections of the New York
     State Hist. Soc., v. 2-4, New York, 1871-1874),
     v.1, 219.
(36) Dr. Fothergill to Humphrey Marshall, August 23,
     1775, Darlington, Memorials of John Bartram and
     and Humphrey Marshall, 514.
(37) Dr. Fothergill to James Pemberton, August 23, 1775,
     Chain of Friendship, 453; Same to Israel Pemberton,
     Sept. 15, 1775, in ibid, 455.
(38) Fisher, Struggle for American Independence, v.1,380.
(39) Adams, Diary, 408.
(40) Ibid., 408,513n.
(41) Ibid., 408.
(42) Thomas Wharton to Samuel Wharton, January 1, 1776,
     "Selections from the Letter Books of Thomas Wharton
     of Philadelphia, 1773-1783", PMHB,v. 34 (1910),
     52-53.
(43) Stillé, op.cit., 175-176.
(44) Paine, Thomas, The Complete Writings of Thomas
     Paine, ed. Philip S. Foner (2 vols., New York,
     1945), v.1, xiii.
(45) Phil.M.f.S., Min., v.2, 53-59, gives the Ancient
     Testimony in full.
(46) Pa. Ldg., January 27, 1776.
(47) Pa. Ev. Post,Feb. 3, 1776.
(48) Wells, William V., The Life and Public Services of
     Samuel Adams (3 vols., Boston, 1865), v.2, 369-370.
(49) Amer. Arch.,4th Ser., v. 5, 392-393.
(50) Paine, Thomas, Common Sense (London, 1776), 49-54.
(51) Hermann Wellenreuter characterizes the Ancient
     Testimony along with the Testimony issued on
     January 1775 as "highly political actions". See
     Wellenreuter , Glaube und Politik, 413-421,426.
(52) For a full account of Quaker politics in Rhode
     Island in the colonial period see Jones et al.,
     Quakers in the American Colonies, chap. 8.
(53) Jones, Augustine, Moses Brown; A Sketch (Provi-
     dence, 1892), 37.
(54) R.I.Col.Rec., v.7, 190
(55) James Warren to Moses Brown, Oct. 28, 1768, Moses
     Brown Papers, v.1, 88, in the Rhode Island Hist.Soc.

(56) Moses Brown to John Brown, June 16, 1775, Moses Brown Pap., v.2, 35.

(57) Same to same, June 21, 1775, Moses Brown Pap., v.2, 36.

(58) Thompson, Mack, Moses Brown, Reluctant Reformer (Chapel Hill, 1962), 130.

(59) Captain Wallace to Vice-Admiral Graves, May 4, 1775, Great Britain Public Records Office, Admiralty Section, v. 485, pt.2, in letters April 1774 - June 1775 (Transcripts in the Library of Congress), 238.

(60) Pa. Pkt., Feb. 20, 1775; Amer. Arch., 4th Ser., v.1, 1210.

(61) N.E.Y.M., Min., v.1, 310; Mekeel, Arthur J., "New England Quakers and Military Service in the American Revolution", Children of Light, ed. Howard H. Brinton (New York, 1938), 244-245. The Meeting for Sufferings was not established in its final form until the following year. (Mekeel, loc.cit.)

(62) N.E.M.f.S., Min., v.1 (1775-1793), 3-4.

(63) See above, Chap. 7.

(64) Journals of the Cont. Cong., v.2, 70-71.

(65) Starbuck, Alexander, "Nantucket in the Revolution", New England Historical and Geneological Register, v. 28 (1874), 273-274; Journals of each Prov. Cong. of Mass.,314,447,470.

(66) It has been estimated that three-quarters of the inhabitants of the island were directly or indirectly connected with the Society of Friends. (Nantucket Hist. Assoc., Minutes, 1908, Proceedings, v. 14, 10.)

(67) Starbuck, loc.cit., 274;Moses Brown to John Pemberton, Aug. 29, 1775, Pem. Pap., v.28, 41.

(68) Christopher Starbuck to Moses Brown, July 14, 1775, Moses Brown Pap., v.2, 39.

(69) N.E.M.f.S., Min., v. 1, 4.

(70) Moses Brown to John Pemberton, Aug. 29, 1775, loc. cit.

(71) N.E.M.f.S., Min., v.1, 10.

(72) Bos. Gaz.,Dec. 18, 1775.

(73) Starbuck, loc. cit., 275.

(74) N.E.M.f.S., Min., v.1, 11.

(75) William Ellery to William Redwood, Dec. 29, 1775, Phil.M.f.S., Misc. Pap., bx. 14.

(76) Journals of the Cont. Cong., v.4, 35; "Diary of Richard Smith", American Historical Review, v.1 (1895), 304,305; Mary Callender to Israel and John Pemberton, Dec. 26, 1775, Pem.Pap., v.28,13.

(77) Minutes of meetings on the Newport situation, Jan. 5,6, 1776, Phil.M.f.S., Misc. Pap., bx. 14; sundry Friends to Joseph Jacobs, in ibid.;Marshall, Diary,

Jan. 7, 1776; Israel Pemberton to Joseph Jacobs, Jan. 16, 1776, Pem.Pap., v.28, 154.

(78) Journals of the Cont. Cong., V.4, 36;"Diary of Richard Smith", loc.cit.,299,300; Nicholas Cooke to General Lee, Jan. 21, 1776, Sparks MSS, v.70, sub-vol. 1, 13-14; same to General Washington, Jan. 21, 1776, in ibid., 1-2.

(79) N.E.M.f.S., Min., v.1, 3-4.

(80) Ibid., 12.

(81) Moses Brown to James Pemberton, Sept. 26, 1775, Pem.Pap., v.28, 79.

(82) N.E.M.f.S., Min., v.1, 21-22.

(83) Ibid., 27.

(84) For a full account of this separation see Mekeel, Arthur J., "Free Quaker Movement in New England in the American Revolution", BFHA, v.27 (1938), 72-82.

(85) Anonymous to Moses Brown, July 16, 1775, Moses Brown Pap., v.2, 40.

(86) Moses Brown to James Pemberton, Sept. 26, 1775, loc.cit.

(87) Ibid.

(88) This tract was published at Watertown, Mass., and the only known copy is in the Ridgeway Branch of the Library Company of Philadelphia.

(89) Davis, Timothy, Letter from a Friend to some of his Intimate Friends on the Subject of Paying Taxes (Watertown, Mass., 1775), 2-3,7.

(90) N.E.M.f.S., Min., v.1, 34-35.

(91) Sandwich M.M., Min., 1755-1795, Dec.4, 1778.

(92) Moses Brown to John Pemberton, March 20, 1776, Pem.Pap., v.29, 2. The answer referred to was probably Thomas Paine's Epistle to the Friends, according to later references in this letter.

(93) Acoakset (Westport), Mass., M.M., Min., 1766-1787, 77; Dartmouth M.M., Min., 1770-1792, 89-93; Dover M.M., Min., 1750-1784, 117; Greenwich M.M., Min., 1751-1806, 58-61; Nantucket M.M., Min., 1772-1789, 68; R.I.M.M., Min.,1773-1790, 54-61; Salem M.M., Min., 1677-1788, 204; Smithfield M.M., Min., 1763-1780, 117, 122; Swanzey M.M., Min., 1732-1788, Oct. 3, 1775.

(94) Becker, History of Political Parties in the Province of New York, 107n., 108,198n. gives lists of members; Amer. Arch., 4th Ser., v.1, 468; Mather, Frederick Gregory, The Refugees of 1776 from Long Island to Connecticut (Albany, 1913), 1049.

(95) Amer. Arch., 4th Ser., v.2, 1241. Franklin had been one of the founders of the New York City

Chamber of Commerce in 1768 and a member of the Committee of Inspection to enforce the non-importation agreement of 1769. (Becker, op.cit., 61n., 75n.)

(96) New York M.f.S., Min., v.1, 17-25, passim; N.Y.Y.M., Min., v.1, 78,81.

(97) Epistle from N.Y.Y.M. to N.E.Y.M., May, 1775, So. Kingston Pap.

(98) N.Y.M.f.S., Min., v.1, 26,27; Amer. Arch., 4th Ser., v.2, 1241-1348, passim; Becker, op.cit., 232-233,233n.

(99) Becker, op.cit.,198,198n.; Amer. Arch., 4th Ser., v.2, 1645; v.3, 19.

(100) Calendar of Historical Manuscripts relating to the Revolution in the Office of the Secretary of State, Albany, New York (2 vols., Albany, 1868), v.1, 53-55; Mather, op.cit.,1062,1064.

(101) Amer. Arch., 4th Ser., v.1, 1191-1192, v.2,273,838.

(102) Ibid., v.2,273-274.

(103) Ibid., v.2,1246,1114-1115; Ross, Peter, A History of Long Island (3 vols., New York & Chicago, 1903), v.1, 190.

(104) Thomas, Benjamin F., History of Long Island (3 vols., New York, 1908), v.1, 295.

(105) Amer. Arch., 4th Ser., v.4, 372-373, 406. The names given on the list of offenders are all of prominent Quaker families.

(106) Ibid., 372-373,434,535.

(107) Ibid., 1119.

(108) Journals of the Provincial Congress, Provincial Convention, Committee of Safety and Council of Safety of the State of New York (2 vols., Albany, 1842), v.1, 141; N.Y.M.f.S., Min., v.1, 29,30.

(109) William Rickman to John Pemberton, Sept. 9, 1775, Pem.Pap., v.28, 55. William Rickman was at that time clerk of the New York Meeting for Sufferings. (See N.Y.M.f.S., Min., v.1, passim.)

(110) Flushing, M.M., Min., 1771-1776, 85; Oblong M.M., Min., 1757-1781,356.

(111) Epistle from Md.Y.M. to Va.Y.M., 1775, Va.Y.M., Misc. Pap.

(112) Gunpowder M.M., Min., 1768-1784,136.

(113) Robert Pleasants to Robert Bolling, Jan. 10, 1775, Robert Pleasants Letter Book, 1754-1797, 33-34. The argument on slavery was even more fully set forth in a letter from Robert Pleasants to John Thomas, May 30, 1775, Letter Book, 35. Both letters have been published in Adair P. Archer's "The Quakers' Attitude Towards the Revolution", WMQ, 2nd Ser., v.1 (1921), 170-176.

(114)Paper entitled "At a Meeting of the Yearly Meeting
      Committee, Dec.22, 1775", in Va.Y.M., Misc.Pap.;
      Phil.M.f.S., Min., v.2, 60.
(115)Phil.M.f.S., Min., v.2, 71-72. This was probably
      the so-called powder tax which Haddonfield M.M.
      advised its members not to pay. (Haddonfield M.M.,
      Min., 1762-1781,279.)
(116)Robert Pleasants to his brother, Sept. 16, 1775,
      Letter Book, 36.
(117)Edward Stabler to James Pemberton, Sept. 5, 1775,
      Pem.Pap., v.28, 49.
(118)Henrico M.M., Min., 1757-1780,231-236,passim;
      Hopewell M.M., Min., 1759-1776, 316,322; Fair-
      fax M.M., Min., 1745-1776, 465-473,passim. A
      digest of Hopewell M.M. disownments ig given in
      Hopewell Friends History 1734-1934, Frederick
      County, Virginia,comp. by a joint committee of
      Hopewell Friends assisted by John Wayland (Strass-
      burg, Va., 1936), 496-521.
(119)N.C.Y.M., Min., v.1 (1704-1793), 141-142.
(120)Wrightsboro M.M., Min., v.1, 14-15.
(121)Symonds Creek M.M., Min., 1699-1785,604,605; Wells
      M.M., Min., 1774-1794, 10; Bush River, S.C.,M.M.,
      Min., 1772-1783,63,66. The analysing of disown-
      ments for North and South Carolina is incomplete
      since three minute books for North Carolina and
      one for South Carolina in this period are missing.

Chapter IX

THE QUAKERS UNDER THE NEW ORDER

As the first year of the war drew to a close, it was becoming obvious that the colonies would soon declare their independence from Great Britain. Several had already replaced royal with lcoally elected officials and no longer recognized the imperial relationship. Pennsylvania, the key to any final action for independence, was most hesitant to take any drastic steps. In the Assembly elections of May 1776, the moderates and conservatives retained firm control of the government, despite the greatly increased representation which had been assigned to several western counties. Led by John Dickinson on whose influence the Quakers now relied, this alliance sought to delay any move toward independence, much to the consternation of the radicals, until arrangements could be made to guarantee the continuation of the charter system of government. (1)

Largely as a result of this situation and urged on by the New England delegates, the Continental Congress passed a resolution on May 15 calling upon all the colonies which had not already done so to establish new governments capable of safeguarding the public welfare. (2) The Pennsylvania radicals now took steps to implement this directive. In June a provincial conference met in Philadelphia to consider the resolution, and arrangements were made for a constitutional convention to meet in Philadelphia in July and establish a new government. All inhabitants of the province qualified to vote for the assembly were eligible electors, but to this qualification was added the requirement of a test oath or affirmation abjuring the authority of the King of Great Britain and a pledge not to interfere with the establishment of a free government. (3) Although the Quakers had for some time abstained from taking part in such political activities, the requirement of a test of abjuration boded ill for the future.

The constitutional convention convened in Philadelphia shortly after independence had been declared and proceeded to establish the framework of a new state

160

government. The result was what the Quakers had feared, the demise of their beloved charter government, and with its demise Pennsylvania was no longer the province of Penn's men. As one historian has stated, a revolutionary transfer of authority took place which was "nowhere in 1776 so sudden and so stark". (4)

One of the first acts of the constitutional convention was to adopt a "Declaration of the Rights of the Inhabitants of the State of Pennsylvania". The eighth article declared that every member of society had a right to be protected in life, liberty and property, and he was therefore obliged "to contribute his proportion to the expense of that protection, and yield his personal service, when necessary, or an equivalent thereto". However, no one conscientiously opposed to bearing arms should be compelled to do so, provided he compensated in some other manner. (5) The Convention subsequently implemented this article with an ordinance requiring every person between the ages of sixteen and fifty who did not join the military association to pay 20 s. per month until the end of the next Assembly. Moreover, every non-associator over the age of twenty-one was to be assessed 4 s. per Ł on the annual value of his estate. (6) It was now obvious that a conflict was inevitable between the demands of the new regime and a strict observance of the Quaker peace testimony.

Another problem which faced the Quakers, not only in Pennsylvania but throughout America as well, resulted from the action of the Continental Congress in issuing paper money, the so-called Continental currency, to finance the war. Peter Thomson, a well known Philadelphia Quaker printer, had been hired to print the currency, for which action he was subsequently disowned. (7) In order to assure the acceptance of the new currency, the Congress had resolved that anyone found guilty of refusing it "should be ... treated as an enemy to his country and be precluded from all trade or intercourse with the inhabitants of these colonies". (8)

It was not long before individual Friends felt obliged to refuse the Continental notes since they were issued for the conduct of the war, although the Society had as yet taken no official position on this issue. In February 1776 the Philadelphia Committee of Safety closed the shops of John Drinker and of Thomas and Samuel Fisher for non-acceptance of the new currency. Other Friends suffering similar penalties for a

161

like offense were Joseph Surman, Benjamin Sharpless, and Townshend Speakman. (9)

The attitude of the patriots toward the rejection of the new currency soon found expression. Nathaniel Greene and Edward Rutledge both lashed out against those Friends who refused to accept the Continental notes. "If they make a point of it", Rutledge declared to Robert Livingston, "we must make a point of hanging them, which will bring on a storm that will take the wisdom of all our wise men to direct." (10) According to Greene, the Quakers were "almost to a man disaffected. Many have the effrontery to refuse the Continental currency. This line of conduct cannot fail of drawing down the resentment of the people upon them." (11) Samuel Adams declared that although non-resistance was their professed principle, "the Religion of many of them is to get money and sleep, as the Vulgar Phrase is, in a whole skin". (12)

The separation from Britain, the dissolution of the old charter government, together with the serious problems facing many Friends prompted the Meeting for Sufferings to appoint a committee to consider the recent developments. In its report the committee urged that the situation be laid before the approaching Yearly Meeting for "such suitable advice and counsel" as might tend "to promote and maintain union of sentiment & conduct among the members of our Religious Society".(13)

Considering the tenor of the times, the Yearly Meeting which met in Philadelphia in the fall of 1776 was the most crucial and determinative of any yet held in America. All of the other American yearly meetings, except New York where military activity was now centered, were represented. (14) Early in its sessions the Yearly Meeting appointed a committee representative of all the yearly meetings participating to consider "the Conduct that ought to be observed by our Society throughout the Continent in these times of Probation, & Difficulties". (15)

The recommendations of this committee, as approved by the Yearly Meeting, contained precise directions on maintaining and observing all aspects of the Quaker peace testimony as it related to the current war. Specifically, all members of the Society were enjoined to withdraw from any activity in civil government, even in elections to public office, since the authority

162

exercised at the time "was founded, & supported in the Spirit of Wars, & Fighting". Those who refused to comply with this admonition would be acting contrary to their religious principles and were to be disowned. In maintaining their testimony against supporting military measures of any kind, Friends were to pay no fine, penalty or tax in lieu of personal military service either openly or by connivance, nor were they to allow their children, apprentices or servants to do so. Moreover, they were to avoid engaging in any trade or business likely to promote the war, and they were not to partake of its spoils through buying or vending prize goods of any kind. In conclusion the advices reminded Friends of the distress and suffering throughout the continent and urged them to contribute liberally to the relief of the suffering of the members of all societies and denominations. (16)

Before adjourning, the Yearly Meeting took two other important actions. In view of the fact that a number of Friends had already been subjected to harassment and persecution for adhering to their convictions, the Yearly Meeting instructed the monthly meetings to keep regular accounts of sufferings of their members to be submitted annually to the Meeting for Sufferings for consideration by the Yearly Meeting when necessary. This step was taken "agreeable to the antient practice of Friends in Great Britain in times of general persecution, and the Sufferings of Friends since that time". (17)

It also directed an epistle to the subordinate quarterly and monthly meetings, recommending to their earnest consideration the actions and decisions of the Yearly Meeting and especially emphasising the admonition to avoid being "concerned in electing or being elected to public Places of Honor, Trust or Profit".(18)

The conclusions reached and the actions taken . during the sessions of this Yearly Meeting were of major significance for the Society of Friends in America, since they established and assured a fairly consistent and uniform standard of conduct to be adhered to by all Friends. Just as resistance to Great Britain had produced colonial unity on a scale hitherto unknown, so the common difficulties facing the Quakers reinforced the already close bonds between the various American Quaker groups.

At the same time, as far as their relations to

society were concerned, the complete withdrawal of the
Quakers from participation in the political developments which were transpiring had eliminated their
ability to influence events. As John Pemberton explained to Dr. John Fothergill:

> Amongst these Confusions ffrds in general
> remain silent spectators, no opportunity
> offering wherein we can be instrumental
> to promote the peace, & good of our
> Country...(19)

When the state governments were established, one
objective was to assure loyalty to the new regime and
thereby encourage a successful prosecution of the war.
Test oaths or affirmations of abjuration and allegiance
were the chief means of achieving this end, which
would also serve to ferret out those who were still
loyal to the British Crown. Reports that such a procedure was beginning to be employed came to the attention of the Meeting for Sufferings in December. (20)
It thereupon addressed an epistle to the members of
the yearly meeting, instructing them to

> refuse to submit to the arbitrary injunctions
> & ordinances of men who assume to themselves the power of compelling others, either
> in power or by other assistance, to join
> in carrying on war, and of prescribing
> modes of determining concerning our religious
> principles, by imposing tests not warranted
> by the precepts of Christ or the laws of
> the happy constitution under which we and
> others long enjoyed tranquility and peace.(21)

This epistle was later printed in the New York Gazette
and the Newport Gazette, both loyalist newspapers. (22)

A few days after the epistle was issued, a meeting
of the inhabitants of Philadelphia presented a memorial
to the Committee of Safety condemning it. The memorial
also urged the committee to prosecute the signer, John
Pemberton, clerk of the Meeting for Sufferings, and
any other persons connected with its issuance if, on
examination, the paper proved to be of a treasonable
nature. However, no further action seems to have
been taken. (23)

The reading of the epistle in the monthly meetings
in New Jersey caused the imprisonment of two Friends,

Mark Miller of Woodbury and Thomas Redman of Haddonfield. (24) Haddonfield Monthly Meeting and the Meeting for Sufferings appointed committees to visit them
and assist them in court. In the trials which ensued,
both defendants were fined five shillings each which
they contended they could not conscientiously pay
since they were innocent of any legal offense. At this
point the deputy sheriff left the court and soon returned with the announcement that the penalties assessed
had been paid. In recording this minute on the affair,
Haddonfield Monthly Meeting stated that "no Friend had
any hand in the said Payments". (25)

The epistle was also not without its public critics.
In the second number of The Crisis published in January
1777, Thomas Paine attacked it vigorously. The Quakers,
he said, were

> ...continuously harping on the great sin
> of our bearing arms, but the king of Great
> Britain may lay waste the world in blood and
> famine, and they, poor fallen souls, have
> nothing to say. (26)

In the next number which appeared in April, he assailed
the Friends in even stronger terms. Although the union
of the states bade fair to extirpate the use of arms
from one quarter of the world, such was

> ...the irreligious politics of the present
> leaders of the Quakers, that for the sake of
> they scarce know what, they would cut off
> every hope of such blessing by tying this
> continent to Britain, like Hector to the
> chariot wheel of Achilles, to be dragged
> through all the miseries of endless European
> wars. (27)

"O', ye fallen, cringing, priest and Pemberton-ridden
people'," he taunted, "What more can we say of ye than
that a religious Quaker is a valuable character, and a
political Quaker a real Jesuit." (28)

Paine charged that the epistle was intended "to
promote sedition and treason, and to encourage the
enemy". The Friends claimed that their principles
were peace, but they acted the opposite. Although
they were not as they had been formerly, they tried
to deceive themselves into believing they had not
altered. Continuing, he sneered:

> ...like antiquated virgins, they see not
> the havoc deformity has made upon them,
> but pleasantly mistaking wrinkles for
> dimples, conceive themselves yet lovely,
> and wonder at the stupid world for not
> admiring them. (29)

He urged that they be roundly taxed to compensate for their actions.

By this time the new government, dominated by the patriots, was firmly established and was exerting every effort in support of the war. New laws imposing discriminatory taxes on those who did not contribute their bit to the common cause, more extensive military provisions, and stricter requirements of allegiance to the new régime, followed each other rapidly.

In February 1777 the Assembly enacted a new militia law, providing that all males between the ages of eighteen and fifty-three be enrolled in the militia. (30) There was no exemption for persons with pacifist convictions, and fines were prescribed for those refusing or neglecting to attend the required musters and reviews. In case of invasion or rebellion, or if the Continental Congress asked for assistance, the Executive Council of the state was empowered to call the militia into service by classes. Anyone so summoned might hire a substitute, but failure to do so or serve personally called for a fine sufficient to pay for one, the sum to be levied by distraint on the estate of the delinquent if he refused to pay.

In June the legislature passed another act, still more threatening for the Quakers. This law prescribed that an oath or affirmation of abjuration and allegiance be administered to all males over eighteen, renouncing the authority of the King of Great Britain and promising faithful adherence to the Commonwealth of Pennsylvania. (31) All citizens refusing to subscribe were prohibited from "holding any office or place of trust" in the state, including "serving on juries, sueing for any debts, electing or being elected, buying, selling or transferring any lands, tenements, or hereditaments..." Anyone moving out of his city or county of residence, or coming from another state, without a certificate of subscription to such an oath or affirmation, was to be required to do so on pain of imprisonment.

166

Not only did the institution of the new regime result in legislation potentially oppressive to the Quakers, but also much suffering was endured by the Friends through the action of local agencies. In 1776 this took the form of seizure of property and the occupation of meeting-houses for the use of the army, and individual instances of imprisonment, ridicile and assault for refusal to comply with military requisitions. Several meeting-houses were utilized for soldiers quarters, hospitals, and other military purposes. Those at Radnor and Fairhill were so badly damaged that extensive repairs had to be made subsequently. American soldiers on their way to New York from Maryland broke open and occupied the Market Street Meeting House. When the Friends remonstrated with the officer in charge, he allowed them to use the house for their meetings for worship, although the army retained possession of it.(32)

When the theater of warfare shifted from New England to New York and nearby New Jersey in 1776, there was a consequent increase in the tempo of military activities in Pennsylvania. Requisitions of all kinds were made on the inhabitants to gather supplies for the army, and in many cases the Friends felt they had been singled out by the authorities for such levies. One of the chief items taken was blankets. Many Quakers had the leaden weights taken from their window frames. Others had their houses sequestered and soldiers quartered on them, for all of which they refused to accept any compensation. Quaker shop keepers suffered broken windows for refusing to close their stores on public holidays celebrating military victories and the anniversary of independence. One of the worst of such instances occurred on July 4, 1777. (33)

A number of Friends were imprisoned or made the butts of jeering mobs for refusing to perform military service. Edward Wells, Christopher Smith, and William Compton all spent varying lengths of time in the city jail for this reason. Thomas Masterman, William Brown and William Dayne were drummed through the streets of Philadelphia by a company of soldiers for persisting in maintaining their pacifist position. Still others were fined as much as Ł20 for rejecting appointments to public office. (34)

As the war progressed and many more Friends felt the impact of maintaining their pacifist testimony, they began to relate their experiences to the sufferings

167

of the English Quakers who underwent heavy persecution
during the Restoration period in the preceeding century.
This sense of identity in their ordeal prompted the
New York and Philadelphia Meetings for Sufferings in
the spring of 1777 to reprint and distribute to all
their subordinate meetings the letter of William Penn
addressed to the British Friends in 1668. Originally
written as an encouragement to the British Quakers in
the midst of heavy persecution and entitled: "To the
Children of Light in this Generation", the letter contained Penn's exhortation to

> stand as the heavenly seed of righteousness
> and shine unto others, in these uneven and
> rough times that are to come...We are
> the people above all others that must stand
> in the gap, and pray for the putting away
> of wrath, so that this land may not be
> made an utter desolation. (35)

Somewhat later Anthony Benezet expressed the conviction of many faithful Friends as to the reason for
the unhappy times which were being visited upon their
land when he declared that "the hand of God" had been
"lifted in Judgment" and "multitudes have been hurried
into eternity and yet the people do not appear humbled
nor care to inquire into the true cause..." He then
exhorted his fellow countrymen and fellow Quakers to
"look nowhere but in ourselves for the cause of our
miseries". (36)

Coupled with the sense of divine judgment there
went an increasingly firm belief that the trials to which
they were being subjected were destined as a purifying
process to free them from the material lures of this
world. One Friend, when prosecuted by the commissioners
of Chester County for refusal to pay war taxes and to
execute a public office to which he had been appointed,
exemplified this attitude held by many Friends by declaring:

> ...during a long period of peace,
> tranquility, and outward Ease, we have too
> much forgot God and disesteemed his mighty
> Acts,...Blessed be his Name he is turning
> many of our Hearts to. the Rock from
> whence we were hewn and to the Hole of the
> Pit from whence we were digged...(37)

The first year of independence brought with it a

168

new ruling power and a full commitment to the war against Britain and resulted not only in unprecedented
difficulties and sufferings for the Quakers but also
cost the Society the loss of many members who either
felt an obligation to support the new order or could
not face the test of official penalty and social oppro-
bium resulting from refusal to cooperate. There were
168 disownments, the largest number of any year of the
war. Of these, 148 were for military deviations, eight
for joining the military association, seven for serving
as a public committee man or a public official, two
for making guns and bayonets, one for sailing on a
privateer, and five for a combination of various war-
supporting activities. In this as well as in the
previous year, the city meetings sustained the heaviest
losses. (38)

(1) Thayer, Pennsylvania Politics, 177. See also Hawke, David, In the Midst of Revolution (Philadelphia, 1961), chap. 1.

(2) Ibid., 180-184 decribes the role of Pennsylvania in the move for independence.

(3) "Proceedings of the Provincial Congress", Statutes at Large of Pennsylvania,from 1682-1801 (18 vols., Philadelphia and Harrisburg, 1896-1901),v. 9, 473-474.

(4) Wood, Gordon S., The Creation of the American Republic, 1776-1789 (Chapel Hill, 1969), 84.

(5) Journals of the House of Representatives of Pennsylvania, 1776-1781 (only one volume printed, Philadelphia, 1782), v.1, 66.

(6) Statutes at Large, v.9, 23.

(7) Phil.M.M. No. Dist., Min., 1772-1781, 342,361.

(8) Pa. Gaz., Feb. 14, 1776.

(9) Pa. Gaz., Feb. 14, April 24, 1776; Marshall, Diary, Jan. 30, Feb. 5, March 20, April 9, 1776; Drinker, Elizabeth, Journal,Feb. 9, 15, 1776 at the HSP.

(10) Edward Rutledge to Robert Livingston, Oct. 2, 1776, Letters of Members of the Cont. Cong., v.2, 113.

(11) General Green to Governor Cooke, Dec. 12, 1776, Amer. Arch., 5th Ser., v. 3, 1342.

(12) Samuel Adams to James Warren, Dec. 12, 1776, Warren-Adams Letters (Collections of the Massachusetts Hist. Soc., v. 72), 213.

(13) Phil.M.f.S., Min., v.2, 97.

(14) Phil.Y.M., Min., v.3, 338; N.E.M.f.S., Min., v.1, 53-54. The Friends from New England were Moses Brown, Joseph Mitchell, and Thomas Lapham, Jr. Those from Maryland were Robert George, James Berry, John Thomas, John Mason, Joseph Hopkins, James Mastin, John Stuart, John Thomas, Jr., George Lamb and William Amos, Jr. Virginia Yearly Meeting sent Robert Pleasants, Samuel Hargrave, James Ladd, Thomas Draper, Samuel Parsons, Amos Ladd and Edward Stabler. North Carolina Yearly Meeting was represented by Thomas Knox, Thomas White, William White, Joseph Henley, Zachariah Nixon and William Robertson.

(15) Phil.Y.M., Min., v.3, 349-350.

(16) The report of the committee is in ibid, 356-357. The question of paying taxes levied for defense purposes was laid before the Yearly Meeting by Chester Quarterly Meeting which in turn had re-

ceived a query from Wilmington Monthly Meeting
whether Friends could pay such a tax levied by the
Levy Court of New Castle County (Chester Q.M.,
Min., 1768-1813, Aug. 12, 1776; Wilmington M.M.,
Min., 1750-1776, 538; MS. copy of an "Order of the
Levy Court of New Castle County", Nov. 28, 1776,
Wilmington M.M., Misc. Pap.; Phil.Y.M., Min., v.3,
343-344,358).

(17) Phil.Y.M., Min., v.3, 358.
(18) Ibid., 359-362.
(19) John Pemberton to Dr. Fothergill, Oct. 25, 1776,
Pem.Pap., v.34, 177.
(20) Phil.M.f.S., Min., v.2, 113.
(21) Ibid., 114-115; Amer. Arch., 5th Ser., v.3, 1309.
(22) N.Y. Gaz.,Feb. 17, 1777; Nwp. Gaz., March 13, 1777.
(23) Paine Thomas, The Crisis (Philadelphia, 1854), 46,
48,49.
(24) Phil.M.f.S., Min., v.2, 117; Hunt, John, "Diary",
New Jersey Hist. Soc., Proceedings,v.53 (1934), 225.
(25) Haddonfield M.M., Min., 1762-1781, 326,327; Phil.
M.f.S., Min., v.2, 117,121.
(26) Paine, op.cit., 18.
(27) Ibid., 37.
(28) Ibid., 38.
(29) Ibid., 46,49,54.
(30) Statutes at Large, v.9, 75-94.
(31) Ibid., 110-113.
(32) Phil, M.f.S., Min., v.2, 178.
(33) Ibid., 174.
(34) Ibid., 175. For accounts of sufferings during this
period see also Phil, M.M., Min., 1777-1781, 65;
Phil. M.M. No. Dist., Min., 1772-1781, 277-278,
284-287; Phil. M.M. So. Dist., Min., 1770-1780,
204; Report of Phil. M.M. No. Dist. on sufferings,
July 29, 1777, Phil. M.f.S., Misc. Pap., bx. 14;
Drinker, Journal, July 16, 1776, June 5 and July
4, 1777.
(35) James, Sydney V., "Impact of the American Revolution on the Quakers' Ideas about their Sect", WMQ
3 Ser.,v.19(1962),371n.; Penn, William, "To the
Children of Light in this Generation", London, 1678,
Broadside in the QCHC.
(36) Quoted in Brooks, Anthony Benezet, 496.
(37) Quoted in Marietta, Jack D., "Wealth, War and
Religion", Church History, v.43 (1974), 239. For
further discussion of this point see Marietta,
loc.cit., 240-241.
(38) Abington M.M., Min., 1774-1782, 56-97, passim;
Bradford M.M., Min., 1765-1781, 185-194, passim:
Buckingham M.M., Min., 1763-1780, 134-149,passim;

Chester M.M., Min., 1745-1778, 436-440, _passim_;
Concord M.M., Min., 1757-1776, 443-466, _passim_;
Darby M.M., Min., 1763-1783, 202-219, _passim_;
Exeter M.M, Min., 1765-1785, 248-288, _passim_;
Falls M.M., Min., 1767-1788, 181,183; Goshen M.M.,
Min., 1766-1788,205-222, _passim_; Gwynedd M.M., Min.,
1757-1779, 210-230,_passim_;Kennet M.M., Min., 1739-
1791, 577-598, _passim_;Middletown M.M., Min., 1755-
1800, 354-370, _passim_; Newgarden M.M., Min., 1768-
1778, 295,300; Nottingham M.M., Min., 1766-1778,
378-397, _passim_; Phil.M.M., Min., 1771-1777, 351-
427, _passim_;Phil. M.M. No.Dist., Min., 1772-1781,
188-246, _passim_; Phil.M.M. So. Dist., Min.,
1770-1780, 125-173, _passim_;Radnor M.M., Min.,
1772-1782, 83-99, _passim_;Richland M.M., Min.,
1767-1786, 83-99, _passim_;Sadsbury M.M., Min.,
1737-1783, 262,263; Uwchlan M.M., Min., 1776-
1795, 1,10,14; Warrington M.M., Min., 1747-1785,
451,452,458; Wrightstown M.M., Min., 1734-1790, 244.

Chapter X

SUSPICION OF QUAKER TREACHERY, AND

THE VIRGINIA EXILES

In the summer of 1777 the theater of warfare moved
to Pennsylvania, and the resulting military situation
greatly increased the problems of the Quakers. The
British army had been manoeuvering in the Jerseys in
the spring of that year, and many expected it to march
on Philadelphia. In July General Howe embarked large
forces at New York and disappeared for some time. On
the 30th the British fleet appeared off the mouth of
the Delaware, and Washington hurried to Philadelphia
with his army. But the anticipated attack failed to
materialize and instead the British fleet disappeared.
Not till August 21 was it finally sighted sailing up
the Chesapeake, and the Americans then realized that
the long awaited offensive was to take place from the
south. (1)

Under these circumstances the Quakers were in a
situation in which, in view of their conduct and attitude with regard to the war, they could easily be
wrongfully suspected of treasonable actions and thus
become the object of repressive measures. On August 24
General Sullivan wrote to General Washington that one
of his officers had gone over to the enemy. In his
effects was found an account of the position and forces
of the American army, apparently sent from the spurious-
ly designated Quaker Yearly Meeting at Spanktown. (2)
In a letter to John Hancock, president of the Continental
Congress, Sullivan denounced the Quakers as

> the most Dangerous Enemies America knows &
> such as have it in their power to Distress
> the Country more than all the Collected Force
> of Britain while they are themselves
> in no kind of Danger being always Covered
> with that Hypocritical Cloak of Religion
> under which they have with Impunity So Long
> Acted the part of Inveterate Enemies of
> their Country. (3)

173

Fearing that the country could never be defended while
such a channel of intelligence was open to the enemy,
the General called upon the "Guardians of American Freedom" to attend to the matter. In conclusion he declared:

> I have a great aversion to Interfering
> with the Religious principles of any Set
> of men, but when we find That their Religious
> meetings are Prostituted to the Base pur-
> poses of betraying their Country Every
> principle of Policy & the Laws of Self
> preservation Dictate That Those pernicious
> meetings Should not be Suffered in Future
> at Least while we are at war with a people
> whose cause They Espouse & to whom they
> openly profess the most Sincere Friendship.(4)

This letter had the effect of creating great consternation in the midst of the deliberations of the
Congress. Sitting in the Quaker city, expecting a
British attack at any time, and already laboring under
suspicion of the dire motives of the Friends, the delegates lost little time in acting. The letter and
papers submitted by Sullivan were referred to a special
committee whose subsequent report reviewed briefly the
actions of the Quakers since the outbreak of the war
and recommended that immediate action be taken to deal
with them. The report declared that the testimonies
published by the Friends, and the tenor of conduct and
conversation of a number of their membership of considerable wealth, rendered it "certain and notorious
that those persons are, with much rancour and bitterness, disaffected to the American cause". (5)

Congress thereupon resolved that the Supreme Executive Council of Pennsylvania take into custody twelve
of the leading Friends of the city together with all
papers of a political nature in their possession. It
also resolved that since the persons indicated maintained a correspondence highly prejudicial to the public
safety both in and outside Pennsylvania, the executives
of the various states should apprehend all Quakers and
other persons whose attitude seemed inimical to America.
Finally, it recommended that the papers of the Meetings
for Sufferings of the Quakers in the respective states
be seized and examined and that those found to be of a
political nature be transmitted to the Congress. (6)

In compliance with these resolutions, the Supreme
Executive Council of Pennsylvania immediately ordered
the arrest of the accused Quakers along with a number

174

of other suspected persons and had them confined in
the Free Masons' Lodge in the city. The authorities
also seized the papers of the Meeting for Sufferings,
all but a few of which, however, were later returned at
the request of a committee of Friends. (7)

In reporting to the Congress on the actions taken,
the Supreme Executive Council pointed out that the imprisoned Quakers declined to make any promises concerning their future conduct, and it requested Congress'
advice on sending them to Augusta or Staunton in Virginia. In reply Congress recommended Staunton and the
Council ordered that the apprehended Quakers with several others of the detainees be exiled to that place.(8)

Meanwhile the unwilling tenants of the Free Masons'
Lodge had drafted memorials to both the Congress and
the Supreme Executive Council in which they denied the
charge of correspondence with the enemy, and maintained
that they were not legally bound to subscribe tests of
allegiance. Since they were not guilty of any offense,
they were entitled to all the rights of citizenship of
which they were being deprived. (9)

There was now a back-and-forth between the Congress
and the Council as to how these memorials should be
handled. In the end, since the accused Friends refused
to take an affirmation to "be faithful and bear true
allegiance to the Commonwealth of Pennsylvania as a
free and independent State", the Congress directed that
the prisoners be forthwith sent to exile in Virginia
according to the original decision. (10)

When the news of this decision reached the prisoners, they denounced the proceedings of the government
in An Address to the Inhabitants of Pennsylvania. (11)
One hundred and five Philadelphia Friends also submitted
a final remonstrance to the President and Supreme Executive Council of the state. (12)

The Supreme Executive Council gave the affair the
widest possible publicity, since it understood that
the persons affected intended to publish their side of
the case "and raise a ferment". (13) Newspapers in
Pensylvania, Maryland, New York and New England carried
excerpts from the official actions of both the Pennsylvania Council and the Continental Congress, some of
them also publishing the "Testimony" issued by the Philadelphia Meeting for Sufferings in January 1775 as evidence

of Quaker loyalism. (14) On the other hand, loyalist newspapers in New York and Newport espoused the cause of the Quakers and published excerpts from their remonstrances, an action tending to increase suspicion of the Friends. (15)

Most members of the Continental Congress agreed that the Friends deserved severe treatment, although a few held more charitable opinions. Henry Laurens of South Carolina felt they should receive no quarter. In his eyes they had given the strongest proofs of their attachment to the cause of America's enemies, and since they had refused to take an affirmation of allegiance, they were entitled to no hearing. Congress had spent five hours, he complained, debating "one silly point whether certain persons chiefly Quakers...should have a hearing in their own defense". In summing up the matter, he said:

> I am much mistaken if by this shifting
> ground the Cry of persecution would not
> be raised ten times higher, and that
> Congress and Council will eventually make
> ridiculous figures...(16)

James Lovell of Massachusetts was of a similar frame of mind. He was convinced that the safety of the Union called for the steps taken. The Quakers were willing enough to support oppression at the time of the Paxton riots, but they were now calling loudly upon the state for their own rights. "Wretches who will not affirm themselves faithful Subjects and who since the Declaration of Independence complain, in the Registries of their Meetings for Sufferings, that they are forced to aid in a War against Government" deserved little mercy. (17)

According to Richard Henry Lee of Virginia, "The Quaker motto ought to be 'Nos Turba sumus', for if you attack one the whole society is roused". (18) Their testimonies indicated "a uniform, fixed enmity to American measures" and had resulted in the imprisonment of "old Pemberton and several others, to prevent their mischievous interposition in favor of the enemy" when the latter was threatening Philadelphia. Lee feared that the Pennsylvania Friends might try to raise a commotion in Virginia through the Quakers there and advised Patrick Henry, the Governor, to be on his guard and to make secure the "Quaker Tories" whom Congress had just resolved to send to Staunton. (19)

176

John Adams, as usual, launched out against the Friends. He informed his wife that the Americans had been obliged to "humble the pride of some Jesuits, who call themselves Quakers, but who love money and land better than liberty or religion". In his opinion their interest in western lands had been an important factor in their oppostion to independence. (20)

The New Hampshire delegates were somewhat more lenient than their fellow Congressmen. They notified the President of New Hampshire of the discovery of the supposed Quaker plot and transmitted the resolves of Congress recommending state action. They expressed the hope, however, that the state legislature would "act with their own prudence and caution in the affair".(21)

In Virginia and New Hampshire the authorities implemented the advice of Congress concerning the records of Friends meetings. The Virginia Council requested the governor to order the magistrates of Henrico, Loudon, Hanover, Nansemond and any other counties where there were Quaker meetings to seize their records and arrest any persons responsible for treasonable activites. The record books of Cedar Creek Monthly Meeting were sequestrated early in October but were returned shortly afterward. (22) Although the New Hampshire legislature authorized similar steps to be taken in towns where there were Friends meetings, there is no record of any such action being taken. (23)

Meanwhile the Continental Congress's directive for the exile of the suspected inmates of the Free Masons' Lodge had been put into effect. When the party of prisoners reached Reading on September 14, writs of habeas corpus issued by Chief Justice Thomas McKean were served on the officers in whose charge they were. The Pennsylvania legislature, when apprized of this action, passed a law on September 16 suspending the writ of habeas corpus in this particular case. Despite the fact that this was an ex post facto law, the Supreme Executive Council ordered it to be put into effect. (24)

Although the "patriots" believed steps should be taken to deal with the Quakers, "many of the warmest Whigs" did not approve of the extreme measures adopted by the government. According to James Allen, there were many who believed that sending the Quakers to Virginia was "an instance of oppression" and that the action of the Pennsylvania Assembly was "the very extreme of tyranny". Consequently, as the smoke began to clear, there was a general feeling that the affair had gone too far. (25)

It was at this time that Philadelphia Yearly
Meeting convened in annual session "under a sense of
the judgments on our land". There was deep concern
and anxiety over the recent developments and over the
increasingly prejudiced reputation of the Society which
was spreading rapidly throughout the country. In order
to clear the Quakers of the calumnies and aspersions
raised against them, the Yearly Meeting issued a Testimony, refuting the accusation that the Friends were
acting inimically to the American cause and that they
had departed from their pacific principles. This statement declared that they were still "led out of all
Wars & Fightings by the Principle of Grace & Truth"
by which they were restrained as private members and as
official bodies from holding correspondence with either
army. It pointed out that there was no such body as
the Spanktown Yearly Meeting and that therefore no
documents could have been issued by it, nor had any
such papers ever been written by any Friends or by any
of their meetings. (26)

The Testimony further contended that the ascription
of the Spanktown Yearly Meeting documents to the Quakers
was done either with the intention of injuring the good
name of the Society, or in order to conceal the identity
of the person or persons who drafted it. As for the
Friends who had been banished to Virginia as a result
of this incident, they had committed no act which merit-
ed the forfeiture of their liberty. (27)

A deputation from the Yearly Meeting then visited
both General Howe whose headquarters were in recently
captured Germantown, and General Washington to present
them with copies of the Testimony and to protest the
banishment of their fellow Quakers to Virginia. At
the American headquarters they were "kindly entertained
by General Washington and his officers", and the delegation reported its satisfaction in having cleared
the Society of the aspersions cast upon it. (28)

By now fully aware of the difficulties and trials
which the Society must be prepared to face, the Yearly
Meeting also took steps to strengthen, invigorate and
guide the subordinate meetings in facing this crisis.
Believing that a requisite for success in this effort
was an inner reformation of the Society, it recommended that the quarterly meetings appoint committees
to work toward this goal in their respective subordinate

178

meetings. (29) The effect of this recommendation was
the eventual appointment by each monthly meeting of a
committee charged to visit the members and impress upon
them their obligation to maintain plainness of life
and dress and to withdraw as far as possible from the
baneful influence of the world. (30)

In the meantime the banished Quakers had reached
Winchester in Virginia where they ultimately remained.(31)
Their notoriety had preceded them, for on their arrival the Lieutenant of the county had some difficulty in
preventing attacks on them by the local patriots. The
latter were persuaded to desist on condition that the
exiles be removed elsewhere. The lieutenant immediately informed the governor of the situation and requested instructions as to what measures should be
undertaken. (32)

The exiles on their part drafted addresses to
Governor Patrick Henry and the Virginia Council and
despatched them to Robert Pleasants and Edward Stabler,
two well known and highly respected Virginia Quakers,
for transmission to the designated authorities. These
Friends immediately went to Williamsburg where they
presented the addresses to the Governor who, they found,
had been prejudiced against the exiles and Friends in
general by the accounts in the northern newspapers.
The two Friends also visited several members of the
Council, "not without some effect", as the subsequent
action of the Governor and the Council indicated.(33)

In response to the address of the exiled Quakers,
the Governor explained that he would have to receive
directions from either the Continental Congress or the
Pennsylvania authorities before he could act. (34)
The Council, however, commended the Lieutenant of
Frederick County in which Winchester was located on
the manner in which he had protected his Quaker charges
and authorized him to allow the exiles to walk for
their health in any part of the town during the day. It
also requested the Governor to warn the people that any
violence offered the prisoners would be considered "as
highly derogatory and dishonorable to this government",
and it urged him to persuade the Pennsylvania Council
to direct the removal of the banished Quakers to
some other part of the state. (35)

Meanwhile the British had occupied Philadelphia
where they remained for the next six months, the Pennsylvania state government moving to Lancaster and the

Continental Congress to York. The report soon spread
through the country that the British were gladly received by the Quakers, New England being the chief
source of such rumors. In Boston, Providence, Newport
and Portsmouth, New Hampshire, the newspapers carried
accounts to this effect. (36) In November it was further
reported that a spy wearing the Quaker garb had been
sent out by General Howe. The Pennsylvania Council of
Safety ordered the lieutenant of Chester County to
watch all the meetings of the Friends closely, especially
the quarterly meetings, and immediately arrest any subversive agents. (37) Toward the end of the month even
more exaggerated stories circulated concerning the
relations between the Friends of Philadelphia and the
British forces there. New York and Massachusetts
papers declared they had made General Howe a "free Gift
of Ł6000 on his entrance into Philadelphia" and that
subsequently the Quakers had been ordered to pay Ł20,000
more. (38)

At this time several Friends who crossed state
or county lines without certificates of abjuration and
allegiance as required by the law of the previous June
were imprisoned for refusing to take such an affirmation. One member of a delegation sent by Sadsbury
Monthly Meeting to petition for the release of the
prisoners was turned over to the magistrates on a
similar charge. (39) During the first half of 1778 more
Quakers suffered the same treatment, some of them for
teaching school without taking the required affirmation. (40)

To make matters even worse, in December, prompted
by the urgency of the military situation and increasingly impatient with the non-cooperation of the pacifist
sects, especially the Quakers who were the most obvious
in number and wealth, the Pennsylvania legislature enacted a law double taxing anyone not performing military service unless a substitute were hired. (41)
Shortly afterward the penalty was raised to Ł40, the
sum to be collected by distraint, and in default of
seizable property the penalty to be four months imprisonment. (42)

Not only did the new Pennsylvania government have
to deal with the Quaker problem, so did General Washington and the American army who found themselves in Quaker
country during that harsh and unhappy winter of the
Valley Forge encampment. Doubtless prejudiced by the
official pronouncements of the Friends and their policy

of non-cooperation with the current military activities, Washington had come to idenfity the Quakers as a dis- affected element. (43) His ire was especially aroused by the refusal of the Quaker farmers to sell grain to or grind it for the army. He believed the trouble arose either from disaffection or the unwillingness of many Friends to accept the Continental currency in payment. He therefore urged the Pennsylvania Council of Safety to treat such millers as the "worst enemies of their country". (44) When the Continental Army was in dire straits, Washington singled out the Friends along with other dissidents for the impressment of supplies.

The intense suspicion with which the activities and movements of the Quakers were now viewed was mirror- ed in Washington's orders to prevent Friends from passing the lines into Philadelphia to attend a general meeting, since "the plans settled at those meetings are of the most pernicious tendency". (45) One of his gener- als indicated the extreme feelings of some of the patriot officers when he acknowledged the receipt of the orders declaring: "I have ordered...if they refuse to stop when haled to fire upon them, and leave their corpses lying in the road." (46)

As the year drew to a close, George Churchman, the venerable Quaker preacher, noted in his Journal on December 27:

> This endeth the year 1777, a year which
> exhibited a new scene of trials such as
> were hitherto never experienced by the
> People called Quakers in Pennsylvania or
> other parts of the American continent. (47)

The winter of 1777-1778 was indeed a dark time, both for the American army encamped at Valley Forge and for the Pennsylvania Friends as well. Not only were the Quakers subjected to requisitions of property by the contending armies and to distraints and imprison- ments for refusing to comply with militia and draft laws, but also the fate of their banished leaders hung heavily over them.

Early in December letters of some of the exiles were seized which, it was claimed, implicated Owen Jones, Jr. in "traffic with sundry persons at Lan- caster highly injurious to the credit of the Continen- tal currency". (48) The matter was reported to the Continental Board of War in York which thereupon ordered that the exiles be transferred to Staunton, Virginia,

181

where Owen Jones, Jr., was to be imprisoned. (49)

Both the exiles and various members of Philadelphia
Yearly Meeting took immediate steps to clarify the
charges and to urge the discharge of the detainees.
The exiles submitted memorials to the Continental Congress and the Supreme Executive Council of Pennsylvania,
denying the charge of manipulating the Continental
currency and requesting their freedom. Consequently the
Board of War, now under the direction of a new president,
General Horatio Gates, ordered a delay in the execution
of the order for transfer until the Congress and the
Pennsylvania Council could consider the applications
of the exiles. (50)

Meanwhile a deputation of five Pennsylvania Friends
headed by Isaac Zane journeyed to York to present the
cause of the exiles to the Continental Congress. (51)
As a result of their solicitation, urging that the
banished Quakers be freed or at least be heard by the
Congress, the order for the removal of the exiles to
Staunton was suspended. The Congress resolved that
the detained Quakers be set at liberty, provided they
took an affirmation of allegiance to the state of Pennsylvania, a conditon with which the exiles could not
conscientiously comply. (52)

The Friends now turned to the Pennsylvania authorities. In February 1778, a deputation from the Conference on Distressing Cases of Western Quarterly Meeting
visited the President and Council of the state at
Lancaster, who referred them to the Assembly. The
Assembly allowed the deputation to state its case only
after answering two questions: whether they acknowledged the present Assembly to be the representatives
of the state, and whether they believed the people of
the state were bound to observe the laws passed by it.
To the first question the Quakers replied that they
believed the present Assembly to be the representatives
of "a body of the people of Pennsylvania" who had been
chosen to be a legislature. To the second question they
answered that it was their duty to "obey the Principle
of Grace and Truth" in their own hearts, that they
were bound to bear testimony against all unrighteousness,
and that it had always been their principle and practice
"either Actively or passively to submit to the power
which in the Coarse of Providence" they lived under. (53)

The deputation then laid its case before the Assembly, contending that the imprisonment and banishment of

the accused Quakers to Virginia was contrary to the
Declaration of Rights in the state constitution and
that the passage of the recent test laws infringed on
freedom of conscience. Friends could not subscribe to
such affirmations or oaths because the universal love
of God led to peace with all men. Therefore, they
could take no part, directly or indirectly, in the war,
and the instant they took a test affirmation they took
sides. The deputation further pointed out that the
recent militia law requiring the bearing of arms or
the payment of a fine had caused many Quakers great
distress and had resulted in the imprisonment of several. (54) No action resulted from this appeal.

In March the solicitation of another delegation of
Friends resulted in the appointment of a joint committee
of three, named jointly by the President and Supreme
Executive Council and the Assembly, to consult the Continental Congress with regard to the Quaker exiles. The
delegation was subsequently informed that the state
authorities would release them if they found they had
the authority to do so. (55)

During the early months of 1778 the health of the
exiled prisoners deteriorated, and in March two of them
died, Thomas Gilpin and John Hunt. By now both the
Congress and the Pennsylvania authorities were becoming
increasingly embarrassed. On March 10 the Congress received a letter from the Supreme Executive Council of
Pennsylvania requesting the return of the exiles to
Pennsylvania since

> ...the dangerous example which their longer
> continuance in banishment may afford on
> future occasions, has already given un-
> easiness to some good friends to the
> independency of these states. (56)

Consequently on March 16 the Congress resolved that
the Board of War should deliver the Winchester prisoners
to the authority of the State of Pennsylvania. (57)

The Pennsylvania Assembly, moved by the various
applications in behalf of the prisoners, now advised
the Council to close the case. On April 10 the Council
ordered that the exiles be returned to Shippenburg,
a destination later changed to Lancaster at the request
of a delegation of four wives of the exiles who had
journeyed to Lancaster to plead the case of their hus-
bands. (58) On arriving in Lancaster the returned pri-

183

soners appealed to the Supreme Executive Council for
their freedom which was forthwith granted. (59)

Although the early spring of 1778 brought this unhappy ordeal of the Quaker exiles to a conclusion, the
suffering and anxiety of the experience were not easily
forgotten. The problems facing the Friends were by no
means diminishing and, indeed, promised continued trial
and tribulation.

(1) Fisher, Struggle for Independence, v.2, 11-13,17-19.
(2) General Sullivan to General Washington, Aug.24,1777,
     Sullivan, Major General John, Letters and Papers
     of Major General John Sullivan (ed. Otis G.
     Hammond, 2 vols., Concord, N.H., 1930-1931),v.1,
     442-443.
(3) General Sullivan to John Hancock, Aug.24,1777,
     ibid., v.1, 443-444.
(4) Ibid.
(5) Journals of the Cont. Cong., v.8, 694.
(6) Ibid., 694-695.
(7) Phil,M.f.S., Min., v.2, 129,130; John Adams to
     Adrian van der Kemp, May 20, 1813,loc.cit., 70.
(8) Pa. Arch., 1st Ser. (ed. Samuel Hazard, 12 vols.,
     Philadelphia 1852-1856), v.5, 582; v.9, 574;
     Journals of the Cont. Cong., v.8, 707-708. By a
     second series of arrests the total number taken
     into custody was forty-one, all being Friends or
     members of the Church of England. Twenty-nine
     were confined in the Free Masons' Lodge. Somewhat
     over half were subsequently released (Gilpin,
     Thomas, Exiles in Virginia (Philadelphia, 1848),
     67,72,101.
(9) Pa. Arch., 1st Ser., v.9, 589; Journals of the
     Cont. Cong., v.6, 509-510; Gilpin, op.cit.,77-81,
     82-85; Phil.M.f.S., Min., v.2, 145-148.
(10) Pa. Arch., 1st Ser., v.9, 593,596; Journals of the
     Cont. Cong., v.8, 718-719, 722-723.
(11) This was published at Philadelphia in 1777. See
     Gilpin, op.cit.,86-115.
(12) Pa. Arch., 1st Ser., v.6, 509-510; Gilpin, op.cit.,
     115-117.
(13) Pa. Arch., 1st Ser., v.9, 586.
(14) Pa. Gaz., Sept. 10, 1777; Pa. Ev. Post, Sept. 6,9,
     1777; Md. Gaz., Sept. 18,1777; N.Y. Jnl., Sept.29
     1777; Prov. Gaz., October 4, 1777.
(15) N.Y. Gaz., Sept. 19,1777; Nwp. Gaz.,Sept.29,16,1777.
(16) Henry Laurens to Lewis Gervais, Sept. 5, 1777,
     Letters to Members of the Cont. Cong., v.2, 476.
(17) James Lovell to Joseph Trumbull, Sept. 7,1777, in
     ibid., v.2, 484.
(18) Richard Henry Lee to Governor Patrick Henry of
     Virginia, Sept. 8, 1777, in ibid., v.2, 486-487.
(19) Ibid.
(20) John Adams to Mrs. Adams, Sept. 8, 1777, in ibid.,
     v.2, 487.

(21) The New Hampshire Delegates to the President of New Hampshire, Sept. 2, 1777, in _ibid._, v.2, 471-472.
(22) Resolve of the Virginia Council, Sept. 30, 1777, Pem.Pap., v.30, 151; Cedar Creek M.M., Min., 1775-1789, 28,34.
(23) Documents and Records relating to the State of New Hampshire 1776-1783 (Prov. and St. Paps. of N.H.,v.8, ed. Nathaniel Bouton, Concord, 1874), passim.
(24) Gilpin, op.cit., 41, 135. The number of prisoners in the transport was 20, of which 17 were Quakers (Gilpin, op.cit., 42.).
(25) Allen, James, "Diary of James Allen, Esquire, of Philadelphia", PMHB, v.11 (1885), 293.
(26) Phil.Y.M., Min., v.3, 379,382-384.
(27) Ibid.
(28) Ibid.,382,385,415. The members of the delegation were William Brown, James Thornton, Nicholas Waln, Warner Mifflin, Joshua Morris, and Samuel Emlen. For an account of this episode see Hilda Justice's Life and Ancestry of Warner Mifflin (Philadelphia, 1905), 158-164.
(29) Brookes, Anthony Benezet, 496.
(30) Tolles, Meeting House and Counting House, 239.
(31) The story of the exiles' journey to Virginia, their sojourn there and their final return home is given in Gilpin, op.cit., 133-233, and in the Drinker Letters in the Haverford College Quaker Collections. Phil.M.f.S., Min., v.2,175-177 gives a succinct account of the arrest and exile of these Friends. Robert F. Oaks gives an extensive account of the experience of the exiles as recounted in their letters in his "Philadelphians in Exile: The Problem of Loyalty During the American Revolution", PMHB, V. 9 (1972), 298-325. Elizabeth Grey Vining gives the story in novel form in her Virginia Exiles. The Friends thus prosecuted were John Hunt, Israel Pemberton, James Pemberton, Edward Pennington, Thomas Wharton, John Pemberton, Henry Drinker, Samuel Pleasants, Thomas Gilpin, Thomas Fisher, Samuel R. Fisher, Miers Fisher, Charles Jervis, Charles Eddy, Owen Jones, Jr., Thomas Affleck, Elijah Brown and William Smith.
(32) Col. Smith to Governor Patrick Henry, Oct.3,1777, Va.Y.M., Misc.Pap.
(33) Israel Pembemton et al. to Robert Pleasants and Edward Stabler, Oct. 3, 1777, Va., Y.M., Misc. Pap.
(34) Robert Pleasants and Edward Stabler to Israel Pemberton et al., Oct., 1777, in _ibid_.
(35) Order of the Virginia Council,Oct. 15, 1777, in _ibid_.

(36) Boston Ind. Chron.,Oct. 16, 1777; Bos. Gaz.,
     Oct. 20, 1777; Boston Cont. Jnl., Oct. 30, 1777;
     Prov. Gaz., Oct. 18, 1777; Frmn. Jnl.,Oct.17,1777;
     Nwp. Gaz., Nov. 20,1777.
(37) Pa. Arch., 1st Ser., v.6, 4.
(38) Cont. Jnl., Nov. 27, 1777; Bos. Gaz., Dec.1, 1777;
     Mass. Spy, Nov. 27, 1777; Riv. N.Y. Loy.Gaz.,
     Nov. 29,1777.
(39) The Friends involved were Jehu Hollingworth of
     Delaware, Thomas Ruckman of Maryland and James
     Smith of Pennsylvania. The members of the dele-
     gation from Sadsbury Monthly Meeting were William
     Downey, Abraham Gibbons, Joshua Brown and Ellis
     Pusey, the last of whom was prosecuted. See Thomas
     Ruckman's Case, and James Smith's "Account of the
     Treatment I rec.[d]" in Phil.M.f.S., Misc.Pap., bx.19
     (1779-1780); Marshall, Diary, Nov.25,1777; New
     Garden Q.M. Conference Committee on Suffering
     Cases, Min., Feb. 1, 1779-August 7, 1780.
(40) The Friends imprisoned were Charles Dingee, William
     Tomlinson,Benjamin Wright, Evan Hughes, Robert
     and George Stephens, Stephen Howell, George Rush
     and Joshua Bennett, the last of whom was prosecuted
     for teaching school without having taken the affirm-
     ation of allegiance. See various documents dealing
     with the prosecution of these Friends in Phil.M.f.S.,
     Misc. Pap., bx 19; Marshall, Diary, Jan. 17, 1778.
(41) Statutues at Large, v.9, 167-169.
(42) Ibid., 186-187.
(43) George Washington to Governor William Livingston,
     May 11, 1777, Washington, George, The Writings
     of George Washington (ed. John C. Fitzpatrick,
     39 vols., Washington, D.C., 1931-1944) v.8, 44-45.
(44) Young, Henry J., The Treatment of the Loyalists in
     Pennsylvania (unpublished Ph.D. thesis, Johns
     Hopkins Univ., 1955), 126-127.
(45) George Washington to Brigadier General John Lacey,
     Jr., March 20, 1778, Washington, op.cit., v.11,114.
     Although Washington respected their scruples with
     regard to military service, he could not under-
     stand the Quakers' refusal to cooperate in other
     ways. In later years he expressed great respect
     for the Friends and considered them as one of the
     best supporters of the new federal government.
     (Washington to the Pennsylvania Council of Safety,
     January 19, 1777, Washington, op.cit., v.7, 35;
     Brissot de Warville, J.P., New Travels in the
     United States of America (2 vols., London, 1797),
     v.1, 357.
(46) Brigadier General John Lacey to General Washington,

187

March 21, 1778, The American Clipper, May 1940, 74.

(47) Churchman, George, Journal 1766-1788 (10 vols., in QCHC),v.3, 20.

(48) Marshall, Diary, Dec. 11, 1777; Gilpin, op.cit.,186. Another accusation was that "since the Tories of the Quaker Society" had been allowed to live at the Quaker homes in Winchester, the Quakers there had generally refused to accept the Continental currency (Pa. Arch., 1st Ser., v.6, 75).

(49) Pa. Arch., 1st Ser., v.6, 74; Gilpin, op.cit.,186.

(50) Journals of the Cont. Cong., v.10,8; Israel Pemberton to Robert Pleasants, Dec. 22, 1777, Va. Y.M., Misc. Pap.; Marshall, Diary, Feb.8,1778; Thayer, Israel Pemberton, 227-228. Israel Pemberton engaged a young lawyer, Alexander White, to represent the exiles with a memorial from them to the Congress.

(51) Journals of the Cont. Cong., v.10,85,96; Marshall, Diary, Jan.30,1778; Gilpin,op.cit., 205.

(52) Journals of the Cont. Cong.,v.10,98; N.E.M.f.S. to Phil.M.f.S., Min., v.2,143.

(53) Conference on Distressing Cases of Western Q.M., Min., Feb.18,19,1778; Questions of the Assembly at Lancaster; William Cox to Israel Pemberton, March 6, 1778, all in Pem.Pap., v.31,138,147,161.

(54) Pa. Arch., 1st Ser., v.9, 426-427.

(55) Drinker, Journal, March 21, 1778.

(56) Journals of the Cont. Cong., v.10,238.

(57) Ibid., v.10,260.

(58) Pa. Arch., 1st Ser., v.6,404; Drinker, Journal, April 9,10,1778; Marshall, Diary, April 10,13,25, 26,1778. A first hand account of the experiences of these women is contained in the Elizabeth Drinker Letters in the Quaker Collections at Haverford College.

(59) Pa. Arch., 1st Ser., v.6, 510-511.

Chapter XI

THE LATTER YEARS OF THE WAR IN PENNSYLVANIA

The British evacuated Philadelphia in the late spring of 1778, and the scene of warfare during the next three years shifted primarily to the southern states. However, war demands remained high both in money and men, and resentment against the pacifist position of the Quakers, due partly to the recent episodes, was even greater than before, especially among the more radical patriots who were in control of the government. So it is not surprising that many considered the Quaker stance of non-cooperation as tantamount to loyalism.

As a result of the British incursion into Pennsylvania and the activities of the loyalists at that time, the Assembly resorted to increasingly harsh laws aimed at extirpating any remnants of loyalism. The scope of these enactments seems to indicate that they were to a certain extent targeted to bear down on the recalcitrant Quakers.

In April 1778 the Pennsylvania legislature enacted a law requiring all males over 18 years of age to take an oath or affirmation of allegiance to the state before June 1. Among the penalties for non-compliance were the forfeiture of the right to sue in courts of law, to act as a guardian of a child or estate or as executor or administrator of any person, to receive any legacy, or to make a will. Offenders were also liable to pay double the taxes of those subscribing to the test. The most onerous part of the act related to daily business and occupations. According to its provisions:

> all trustees, provosts, rectors, professors,
> masters and tutors of any college or
> academy, and all schoolmasters and ushers,
> merchants and traders; and every person who
> shall act as sargeant at law, counsellor at
> law, barrister, advocate, attorney or notary,
> ...apothecary or druggist, and every person
> practicing physic or surgery in any manner
> for fee or reward,...

189

who refused to conform to its requirements were forbidden to engage in these occupations under a £500 penalty plus costs, half of this amount accruing to the state and half to the respective informer. (1)

The Friends had already begun to bear the brunt of similar but more limited legislation passed earlier. With the restoration of free communication between Philadelphia and the surrounding country on the departure of the British, the Meeting for Sufferings could again function normally. One of its first undertakings was to investigate the situation of a number of Quakers who had been imprisoned for refusing to subscribe a test affirmation of allegiance. In July it sent a delegation to Lancaster to visit the prisoners and interview the authorities. In a letter presented to one of the magistrates to clarify the position of the Friends, the delegation said:

> ...Thou will certainly agree with us
> that taking of a test cannot change the
> Principle of any Man & that men who are
> Enemies to the Government & will seek
> its Overthrow will without hesitation
> take the Test & observe it no longer
> than suits their Conscience & may under
> that Cloak undermine your proceedings
> in an Unsuspected manner...(2)

As a result of these solicitations two Friends were shortly afterward released. (3)

The Meeting for Sufferings also drafted a memorial to the Assembly, which was presented to the Speaker explaining the position and attitude of the Friends. The memorial opened with the argument that "the government of the consciences of men is the prerogative of God", and every encroachment on this prerogative was an offense to Him. Several Quakers who had been imprisoned either for refusal to pay military fines or to take an affirmation of allegiance had acted from "a religious scruple and not...from obstinance or any motive but the desire of keeping a Conscience void of Offense towards God". This appeal concluded with the hope that the present government would continue the tradition of civil and religious liberty established under the former colonial charter and urged that those in bondage for the testimony of a good conscience be set at liberty. (4)

Such appeals by the Friends were attacked and ridi-
culed in some of the New England newspapers. Both the
Boston Independent Ledger and the Massachusetts Spy declared that the "restless Quakers" were again addressing
the Assembly for the repeal of certain laws they considered oppressive. They further charged:

> In short, they want to enjoy all the privi-
> leges and immunities of citizens, without
> contributing either by personal service,
> or an adequate advance of cash to the
> support and defence of them. (5)

The Quakers were accused of playing their "usual sly
card" and of having "acted a base part". They were
sarcastically reminded that "christianity flourished
most when most persecuted", and since virtue was at a
low point among them, their difficulties might "possibly
be a political stroke to encrease it".

Since a number of Friends remained in prison, the
Meeting for Sufferings requested the meetings in and
near Lancaster to have a special care for them. (6)
In November the committee in charge of these cases had
further interviews with the magistrates concerned and
with the Governor and Council, and by the end of the
year these Friends were released. (7)

It was in such an atmosphere that Philadelphia
Yearly Meeting convened in the early fall of 1778,
with representatives from the other American yearly
meetings in attendance. The two chief questions uppermost were taxes and affirmation of allegiance. Some
division of opinion had already become apparent in
the Society over the relation of the peace testimony
to the payment of taxes. Earlier in the year Isaac
Grey of Newgarden Monthly Meeting had published A
serious Address to Such of the People Called Quakers
on the Continent of North America, as profess Scruples
relative to the Present Government. In this tract
Grey contended that the current revolution was the work
of the Lord and supported his argument of the "safety
and propriety of a submission to the powers which rule"
by references to the writings of early Friends concerning the proper attitude toward revolutions. He
pointed out that the Friends in England had paid taxes
and taken test affirmations of allegiance under changing
governments, and he particulary cited their subscription
to the affirmation of allegiance to William and Mary
after the Revolution of 1688. Moreover, the only taxes

they had refused to pay were levies in lieu of personal
military service. Although the Friends could not promote and encourage revolutions, they should beware of
becoming parties by opposing and discouraging the payment of taxes and the performance of other civil
duties. (8)

Grey's views were contrary to the position already
taken by the Society with regard to the payment of war
taxes. This fact together with his publication of the
tract without reference to, or the approval of, the
Meeting for Sufferings led to his disownment by his
monthly meeting a few months later. (9)

The issue of payment of taxes was the occasion
of much soul searching among the Friends because of
its threefold nature. There were the taxes levied
wholly for purposes of war which the large majority of
Quakers agreed could not be paid consistently with their
pacifist testimony. Secondly, there were the mixed
taxes whose proceeds would be used for both civil and
military purposes, the payment of which had thus far
been left to the individual conscience, with strong
moral support given to those who could not conscientiously
pay them. Finally, there were those taxes assessed
for wholly civil purposes which most Friends believed
could and should be paid, although there were those
who maintained that these taxes should not be paid
either since such payment signified recognition of a
government established by war.

The issue was brought before the Yearly Meeting
by both Chester Quarterly Meeting and the Meeting for
Sufferings which requested the Yearly Meeting's direction as to the consistency of paying poor and road
taxes to the new authorities in power. (10) The
Yearly Meeting referred the matter to a committee which
included representatives from the other yearly meetings.
The report of this committee, which was accepted by
the Yearly Meeting, made no final pronouncement on the
question. Instead it urged all members of the Society
to take "care to avoid complying with the injunctions
and requisitions made for the purpose of carrying on
War" as the most effective means of preserving their
Christian testimony, thereby leaving the ultimate decision to the individual conscience. (11) It may
well be that the opinions of Friends attending from
other yearly meetings, especially New England, had a
moderating influence in this instance.

An even more serious problem which came before the Yearly Meeting for consideration was the recent legislation requiring affirmations of allegiance. According to these laws many Friends, if they remained faithful to their testimonies, would be deprived of their means of livelihood, and the whole Quaker school system would be closed down. Despite these threatening consequences, the Yearly Meeting decided that no Friend could comply with the requirements of such laws or pay any fine imposed for non-compliance. (12) One result of this decision was that the Quaker schools were forced to close for a time.

Before the end of the year a shadow fell over the Society with the execution of two members for treasonable relations with the British. They were John Roberts of Merion and Abraham Carlisle of Philadelphia. Roberts had been deeply affected by the banishment of the Quaker exiles to Virginia. He had attempted to obtain the intervention of the British when they were advancing on Philadelphia, and he was later forced by them to act as a guide and informer. During the occupation of the city Carlisle had, against the advice of Friends, accepted an office whose function was the granting of permits for passage into and out of the city. (13)

After the British evacuation, the Americans prosecuted all those who had had traffic with the enemy. Roberts and Carlisle were arraigned for high treason, declared guilty by a jury and sentenced to be executed, their property to be confiscated by the government. On November 4 the sentence was carried out on the city common. One of the judges in the case, Cadwalader Dickinson, was soon afterwards disowned by Philadelphia Monthly Meeting both for this action as well as for his support of the American cause in holding public office. (14)

Since the principles involved were Friends, the Meeting for Sufferings investigated the affair in order to clear the Society of charges of inconsistent action. The committee appointed to this service labeled the proceedings of the government as of "great severity and rigour" and declared that a fair examination of the evidence would not have led to the conviction of the defendants. It also stated, however, that the two men concerned had not lived up to their principles, and therefore the Meeting for Sufferings had not interceded officially in their behalf. (15)

The record of dealings and disownments for the two
years 1777 and 1778 gives some indication of the trend
of events. In these years the problem of deviation
from the Quaker position became less preponderantly
military as the scope of war time legislation was
broadened. In 1777 there were one hundred and four
dealings and eight-two disownments. Sixty-seven of
these cases were military deviations, nineteen were
assisting the army, seven were accepting public office,
four were paying military fines, one for paying a war
tax, and one for sailing an armed bessel, presumably
a privateer. (16) In 1778 the record was one hundred
forty-six dealings and eighty-three disownments. Military deviations accounted for only fifty-five of these
cases, paying military fines rose from four the previous
year to forty-two, fifteen were for taking tests of
allegiance, an offense which had not appeared the year
before, eighteen were for assisting the army, four
for accepting public office and one for being concerned
in an armed vessel. (17) In the second year deviations
for paying military fines ran a close second to military deviations, and dealings for paying such fines
together with those for taking tests of allegiance sur-
passed military deviations.

Two Friends dealt with in 1778 for holding public
office were also charged with signing paper bills
for carrying on the war. Early that year Uwchlan Monthly
Meeting requested the advice of Chester Quarterly Meeting
on the treatment of such cases. The Quarterly Meeting
replied that such action was a violation of Quaker principles. Subsequently the monthly meeting disowned a
member for this offense, and Darby Monthly Meeting proceeded against one of its members for the same reason.(18)

In both years deviations for assisting the army
in the form of carting supplies, loaning horses and
wagons, receiving pay for provisions and forage constituted a significant problem. Such deviations occurred
mostly in Chester County where the American forces
were stationed in the winter of 1777-1778. In 1778
Chester Quarterly Meeting, on a query from Uwchlan Monthly
Meeting, declared that receiving compensation for army
requisitions was contrary to the peace testimony, and
a number of disownments followed. (19)

Since most of those disowned were dealt with for
assisting the American forces, many began to think,
or felt confirmed in their suspicion, that the Quakers'
sympathies were with the British. Evidence of this
impression was apparent in a letter in the Pennsylvania

<u>Packet</u> in June 1778, accusing the Friends of acting from loyalist motives. (20) There is no indication, however, that disciplinary proceedings were not applied with the same rigor in the case of anyone charged with assisting the British. Since the large majority of the Quakers lived in American-controlled territory, the bulk of the disownments would obviously take place there. The British on their part, when occupying Philadelphia, did not require military service, levy war taxes, or prescribe test affirmations of allegiance, and there was therefore no cause for disownments for deviations on such counts.

In the gloom of events culminating in the execution of Roberts and Carlisle, the Society of Friends in Pennsylvania faced the year 1779. As long as the war continued the situation would in all probablility grow worse without any hope for betterment. Evidence of this trend was the enactment of an amendment to the militia law in April 1779, increasing the penalty for refusing to perform military service from the previous Ł40 to Ł100, a sum subsequently raised to not less than Ł100 nor more than Ł1000. For other infractions of the militia laws the fine was increased sixfold for all citizens of the state except residents of Philadelphia who were subject to an eightfold increase. (21)

Another imposition which affected the Friends were fines assessed for refusal to serve as tax collectors. It may well be that Quakers were at times singled out for such appointments, since the increasing number of fines incurred on this account prompted the Meeting for Sufferings to direct the monthly meeting committees on suffering cases to investigate such instances and lodge protests with the appropriate authorities. (22) It also appointed a special committee to work with the monthly meetings on the problem.

At the Yearly Meeting sessions of 1779 which, as in the previous year, were attended by representatives from the other American yearly meetings, one of the most important issues was the application of the peace testimony to various situations faced by Friends. Western Quarterly Meeting had referred a query received from its conference on suffering cases whether the Friends could consistently accept the Continental currency. (23) Chester Quarterly Meeting had forwarded a query from Wilmington Monthly Meeting concerning the consistency of importing goods or dealing in imported goods "in these Times of public commotion". It also asked the Yearly Meeting's advice as to the propriety of grinding grain and feeding cattle for the army or of selling it provisions and forage. (24)

In response to these requests for advice the Yearly Meeting declared that any Friends concerned in importing or shipping goods in armed vessels should be dealt with, and that Friends should not purchase such goods through "prospects of Gain and increasing their Wealth". Grinding grain for or selling provisions to the army was as grave an offense. As for the acceptance of the Continental currency, the Yearly Meeting expressed full agreement with Western Quarterly Meeting that Friends should seriously consider whether such action was in accord with Quaker peace principles, leaving the final decision, however, to the individual's conscience. (25)

In October 1779, shortly after the conclusion of the Yearly Meeting, the Assembly passed a new test law providing that anyone refusing to take an affirmation of allegiance would be "forever excluded" from participation in the government and from keeping schools, except in private homes. Non-subscribers would forfeit all privileges and benefits enjoyed by citizens complying with the law. (26)

The provision with regard to schools especially disturbed the Friends, and the Meeting for Sufferings soon addressed a memorial to the Assembly. The statement declared that those principles which forbade Friends to participate in violent proceedings of any kind also restrained them from complying with laws requiring tests and declarations of fidelity to either party in the war. It insisted that Friends were not actuated by political motives and pointed out that many Quakers had been seriously affected and even threatened with total ruin as a result of recent enactments. In conclusion the memorial appealed for the repeal of those laws which penalized persons with tender consciences and urged the restoration of their civil rights so that the education of their youth might not be obstructed. (27) The Assembly promised action on the memorial at its next sitting. In the meantime the Meeting for Sufferings undertook the assembling of accounts of suffering cases for presentation to the legislature at a later date if called upon. (28)

During the early months of 1780 an extended

controversy on this issue took place between the Meeting
for Sufferings and the Assembly. The Meeting submitted
to President Reed and the Assembly a list of instances
where harsh treatment had been accorded Friends in the
execution of the laws. It called upon the government
to restrain "men of avaricious disposition from making a
prey of, and plundering the peaceable and industrious".(29)

At the request of the Assembly's Committee of
Grievances, four of the Friends who had presented the
memorial attended a conference with the committee. At
that time they were given seven questions to answer
about their attitude toward the current authorities
and regarding the dispute with Britain. One question
concerned Friends' characterization of the Continental
currency as having been issued for military rather
than civil purposes, and another asked why they looked
upon it any differently from earlier emissions of
the colonial government. Finally, they were ordered to
surrender to the committee all testimonies and letters
issued by the general and quarterly meetings in the
city for the past seven years. (30)

The Meeting for Sufferings considered these
questions unworthy of a direct answer and couched its
reply in the form of an address. This stated that the
memorial and other papers presented had given a
sufficient account of the attitude of the Friends
from the beginning of the dispute with Britain. It
denied that their meetings carried on any political
activities, insisted that they were purely religious,
maintained that government was divinely instituted for
the suppression of vice and immorality and for the
protection of the innocent from oppression, and declared that no laws should be adopted which infringed
on freedom of conscience. The address then explained
that many Friends had refrained from contributing to
the support of the war since such activity was opposed
to the very nature and spirit of the Gospel, and that
by the same token some Quakers had refused to accept
the Continental currency issued to carry on the war.
With regard to letters issued by the Society in past
years, it had been the custom of the Society from its
origin to send out epistles of advice to its members,
and when the authorities had examined the epistles in
question in 1777, no evidence of sedition had been
found. (31)

On receiving this address, the Assembly adopted
the recommendation of the Committee on Grievances and

197

indefinitely postponed the matter. The following
September the committee closed the case by declaring
that "the laws of this commonwealth should be made
for the good of the whole people, without partial
distinctions in favor of any particular society of
men". (32)

Meanwhile the President and Council had been
considering the memorial previously presented by the
Friends. In the end the Council followed the example
of the Assembly by resolving that the laws in force
were sufficient remedy against the abuses cited, and
that such cases would be prosecuted if the aggrieved
parties took them into court. It also declared that
the collection of taxes to finance efforts to repel
the enemy was an indispensable duty and that it was
therefore highly incumbent on the public authorities
to enforce the relevant laws. (33)

During the remainder of the year the Friends were
deeply involved both in efforts to obtain the release
of two Quakers who had been imprisoned in Lancaster
jail for refusing to perform military service and in
actively defending themselves against newspaper
attacks. In June 1780 the Meeting for Sufferings had
made unsuccessful representations in behalf of the
prisoners, and in November a committee of the Meeting
for Sufferings transmitted petitions from the prisoners
to the Assembly. Despite this and subsequent attempts
to obtain their release, the imprisoned Quakers were
not finally liberated until the end of 1781. (34)

The persistent protests of Friends against what
they considered as a form of legal persecution had
aroused the ire of many of the more enthusiastic patriots.
In August 1780 an article appeared in the Pennsylvania
Packet accusing them of sedition and disaffection. Included in it were copies of the Testimony of January
1775, the epistle of November 1775, the epistle of
November 1776, excerpts from various meeting records
on the sufferings of the Friends, and the letter from
General Sullivan to Congress of August 24, 1777. The
writer maintained that these items proved "what a
consumate degree of impudence and toryism is engrafted
on their meek natures" and charged the Friends with putting forth under the mask of innocence the violent spirit
of sedition and opposition to our righteous cause". (35)

The Meeting for Sufferings, especially concerned
over the possible effect of this attack on the reputation

of the Society, published a reply in the same newspaper the following month. (36) This explained each of the items which had been cited, putting them in their respective historical settings. It pointed out that even the Continental Congress in 1775 had reaffirmed its allegiance to the King. The statement declared that the Spanktown Yearly Meeting papers were spurious and presented evidence to prove that the charge of the Friends' complicity in that affair was baseless. In concluding, the Meeting expressed its convinced opinion that "the Prejudices excited by this evil Device would long since have subsided had not great Industry been used by Persons of a malevolent Disposition to kindle jealousies, by Insinuations against our religious Society". (37)

A little over a year later Cornwallis' surrender at Yorktown brought an end to active fighting. The last outbreak of patriot resentment against the Friends occurred at this time. When the news reached Philadelphia there was a scene of wild rejoicing, and the city was brilliantly illuminated on the night of its reception. The Friends refused to participate and suffered considerable property damage and even personal assaults. Subsequently the Meeting for Sufferings presented a remonstrance on these occurrances to the President and Council and the Assembly, in which it explained that since the Friends could not "fight with the fighters, neither could they triumph with the conquerors". Therefore they had not illuminated their windows, had followed their lawful occupations, and had kept their shops open. (38)

Despite the cessation of the war in the fall of 1781, the prosecution of the Quakers for disobeying the militia laws continued. Early in 1782 the conference on suffering cases of Western Quarterly Meeting addressed the Assembly on this subject, calling attention to the injustice wrought on many by legislation imposing fines for non-compliance with military demands and by assessing extra heavy taxes for refusal to take tests of allegiance. (39) During the year three Quakers were imprisoned, two for about one year and one for about two years, for non-payment of war taxes. Both Goshen and Bradford Monthly Meetings of which these men were members, as well as the Meeting for Sufferings, exerted every effort to secure their release. (40)

The trend in dealings and disownments as well as of sufferings indicated the course of wartime legislation.

The number of dealings for deviations from the peace
testimony reached the highest point in the years 1779
and 1780, although the number of disownments resulting
never attained the peak number in 1776. For the respective years 1779-1783, dealings for payment of war fines,
taking tests of allegiance, and performing military
service were as follows:

	1779	1780	1781	1782	1783
Payment of fines	105	143	51	27	4
Tests of allegiance	105	49	20	10	5
Total combined	210	192	71	37	9
Military service	19	28	32	28	15

It is obvious that the problem of military service played only a secondary role in the latter years of the
war. (41)

The total number of dealings and disownments for
Pennsylvania during the Revolution was 1287 and 948
respectively which would be approximately 25% and 19%
of adult male Quakers subject to military service and
requisitions. (42) Military deviations accounted for
537 dealings resulting in 515 disownments, or 54% of
total disownments. For paying war taxes and fines there
were 365 dealings resulting in 165 disownments, or 17% of
total disownments. The total for test affirmations of
allegiance, some combined with other war-related deviations, was 185 dealings and 144 disownments, or 15% of
total disownments. Other types of deviation from the
peace testimony were: assisting the armies in various
ways (74 dealings and 32 disownments), and being concerned in privateers and armed vessels (24 dealings
and 22 disownments).

It is to be noted that 95% of dealings for military service and 78% of dealings for taking test affirmations of allegiance resulted in disownments, as compared with only 45% of dealings for paying war taxes
and fines. The decision to join the military or to
take a test affirmation of allegiance to the new government indicated a complete commitment to the revolutionary cause and involved an open breach with the Society's
basic testimony as it was interpreted. In the case

200

of paying taxes there was much difference of opinion within the Society as to the scope of application of the peace testimony, and neither that action nor the payment of war fines necessarily indicated a complete commitment to the Revolution and support of the war. It was therefore in all probability easier for offenders to acknowledge their error, and by the same token the meetings may have been less demanding in the scope of the acknowledgements required in such cases.

The Friends who were disowned can be classified generally in two groups. In the first place there were those marginal and nominal Friends, especially younger men, who were not strongly held by religious commitments and easily espoused the cause of the Revolution. Many in this group were also guilty of non-war-related offenses such as marrying a non-Friend, non-attendance at meeting, frolicking, and other types of conduct inconsistent with Quaker principles. The excision of such members promoted the goal of the reformers whose chief aim was the spiritual revitalization of the Society. The leaders of this movement called for a clear witness to the pacifist testimony, a rejection of mammon in the form of the display of wealth and luxury which characterized many prominent Friends in the decades preceding the Revolution, and a strict adherence to the peculiar from of dress, speech and manners which they considered a necessary evidence of the true Christian life as exemplified by Friends.(43)

A second type of Friend disowned was one who differed in principle from the position taken by the Society. He considered the Society's attitude toward the Revolution and the new state regimes a mistaken one, and although he might not advocate personal military service he generally supported the Revolutionary cause. The loss of these Friends cost the Society a number of well-educated and more progressively minded members of maturer years. A few, notably Owen Biddle, were received back into membership at a later date.(44)

For many of those who remained faithful to the Quaker peace testimony there was a heavy price to pay. In addition to social obliquy, imprisonment, and personal abuse, there were heavy material losses through distraints of property for refusal to pay war taxes and fines. and in the requisitioning of food, housing, horses, wagons, cows and oxen by the contending armies, for which a consistent Quaker could accept no compensation. In the Abington-Byeberry area in 1782, the Friends suffered more losses in distraints for taxes than the total they had paid in taxes under the colonial government, a not inconsiderable sum, even taking into consideration inflationary factors. Of twelve paupers in prison for inability to pay military fines distrained on them, eleven were Friends. (45)

During the first year, 1777, in which accounts of sufferings were systematically kept, the total for distraints and requisitions was at least Ŀ4522, many cases not being listed and damage inflicted often being undeterminable. (46) The British army requisitioned goods valued at Ŀ449, and the American army supplies to the amount of Ŀ1236. Chester County, since it was the chief scene of the Pennsylvania campaign that fall and the location of the American encampment that winter, suffered most heavily, a total of Ŀ3300.

The following year, 1778, was the most severe of the war in terms of sufferings for the Quakers. The total recorded sum for Pennsylvania was Ŀ10,043, of which Ŀ8304 were for war fines. Chester County's proportion was again the highest, Ŀ7717, of which Ŀ1635 were in requisitions for the American army.

From 1779 through 1783 distraints for war fines decreased steadily, while distraints for war taxes increased from Ŀ858 in 1779 to Ŀ2380 in 1782, probably because new tax laws raised the levies considerably, aside from the effects of inflation. For the whole period of the war, the total of recorded sufferings in Pennsylvania was Ŀ38,550, Chester County Friends bearing slightly over half of this burden, namely Ŀ19,469.

The system of distraints was especially onerous since the forced sales usually resulted in low returns. Moreover, it encouraged ruinous seizures and invited official corruption, on account of which complaints to the government had been made as above mentioned. Obviously the prejudice against Friends often expressed itself through this procedure.

The incidence of pecuniary losses on the part of the Quakers had no consistent pattern and was partly a regional and individual matter, determined in large part by the course of the war and the particular situation of individual Friends. In some areas such as Chester County, financial losses were much heavier than elsewhere, and while some Friends were practically ruined, others were very little or not at all affected.

On the other hand, in the eyes of those working for the spiritual reformation of the Society, these material losses were welcomed as a purifying experience, since it was hoped that thereby many Friends would be detached from devotion to their worldly possessions.(47)

(1) The provisions of this law are in <u>Statutes at Large</u>, v.9, 238-245.

(2) Phil.M.f.S., Min., v.2, 153-156; John Perry et al. to Joseph Miller, July 25, 1778, Phil.M.f.S., Misc. Pap.bx.19.

(3) Phil.M.f.S., Min., v.2, 159.

(4) <u>Ibid</u>., 156, 161-164.

(5) <u>Ind. Ldg.</u>, Sept.21, 1778; <u>Mass.Spy</u>,Sept. 24, 1778.

(6) Isaac Zane et al. to Joseph Penrose et al., Sept. 12, 1778, Phil.M.f.S., Misc.Pap., bx.19.

(7) Phil.M.f.S., Min., v.2,191; Abram Gibbons et al. to the Meeting for Sufferings, Nov.6,1778, Phil. M.f.S., Misc.Pap., bx.19; An Account of the Discharge of Jehu Hollingsworth & others from Lancr: Prison, Newgarden (Western) Q.M. Conference Committee, Min., Feb. 1, 1779-Aug.7,1780.

(8) Grey, Isaac, <u>A Serious Address to Such of the People Called Quakers</u>...(Philadelphia, 1778),6,8,12,14-15. In the course of his argument Grey drew upon Timothy Davis' <u>Letter from a Friend</u> published two years earlier in New England (see chap.8). See Peter Brock's <u>Pacifism in the United States</u> (Princeton, 1968), 209-222 for an extensive discussion of the problem of payment of taxes in which the author refers at length to Samuel Allinson's unpublished tract,Reasons against War, and paying Taxes for It, written in 1780. Allinson's treatise is a full and logical justification for his thesis. A number of Friends, including Moses Brown, read and strongly endorsed this statement. There were grounds for Grey's thesis regarding the position taken by 17th century British Friends (See Wellenreuter, <u>op.cit.</u>,9-15).

(9) Newgarden M.M., Min., 1768-1788,409,418. An associate in this enterprise seems to have been Samuel Wetherill, Jr., who was a leader in the establishment of the Free Quaker Meeting a few years later (Phil.M.M., Min., 1777-1782,131,133). Grey had earlier joined with Samuel Wetherill,Jr., Christopher Marshall and others in establishing a textile manufacturing plant which subsequently supplied the American army (<u>Amer. Arch</u>., <u>4th Ser</u>., v.2,140).

(10) Chester Q.M., Min., 1768-1813, May 11, 1778; Phil.M.f.S., Min., v.2, 163.

(11) Phil.Y.M., Min., v.3,400,406,414.

(12) Ibid., 405-406.
(13) For the details of this affair see a report of
a committee of the Meeting for Sufferings dated
Aug. 4, 1779, Phil.M.f.S., Misc.Pap., bx.19; also
Pa. Arch., 1st Ser., v.7,21-58.
(14) Phil.M.M:., Min., 1777-1782, 100,116; Drinker,Journal
Nov.4,1778.
(15) Report of a committee of the Meeting for Sufferings,
Aug.4, 1779,loc.cit.;Phil.M.f.S., Min.,v.2,186-187,
209.
(16) Abington M.M., Min., 1774-1782,100-136 passim;
Bradford M.M., Min., 1765-1781,198,210; Buckingham
M.M., Min., 1763-1780,150-163 passim;Chester M.M.,
Min., 1745-1778,442-453 passim: Concord M.M., Min.,
1777-1795,7-38 passim;Darby M.M., Min., 1763-1783,
222-243 passim:Exeter M.M., Min., 1765-1785,272,
295,299; Falls M.M., Min., 1767-1788,195-200 passim;
Goshen M.M., Min., 1766-1788,223-243 passim; Gwynedd
M.M., Min., 1757-1779,234-256 passim:Kennet M.M.,
Min., 1739-1791,600-616 passim;Middletown M.M., Min.,
1755-1800,376-394 passim;Newgarden M.M., Min.,1768-
1778,330-360 passim;Phil.M.M., Min., 1771-1777,
436-468 passim;ibid.,1777-1782,5-22 passim;Phil.
M.M.No.Dist., Min., 1772-1781,256-297 passim; Phil.
M.M.So.Dist., Min., 1770-1780,176-223 passim;Radnor
M.M.,Min.,1772-1782,112,121,124;Richland M.M.,Min.,
1767-1786,April 17,1777;Uwchlan M.M.,Min.,1776-1795,
19,30;Warrington M.M.,Min.,1747-1785,488,489,490;
Wrightstown M.M.,Min.,1734-1790,246-253 passim;Not-
tingham M.M.,Min.,1766-1778,406-452 passim.
(17) Abington M.M., op.cit., 144-173 passim; Bradford
M.M.,op.cit., 225-268 passim; Buckingham M.M.,
op.cit.,164-176 passim;Chester M.M., op.cit., 457-
463 passim;ibid.,1778-1802,5; Concord M.M., op.cit.,
49-76 passim;Darby M.M., op.cit.,247-259 passim;
Falls M.M., op.cit.,202-216 passim;Goshen M.M.
op.cit., 253-261 passim;Gwynedd M.M., op.cit.,
262-278 passim;Kennet M.M., op.cit.,644-652 passim;
Middletown M.M., op.cit.,401-425 passim;Newgarden
M.M., op.cit.,396-420 passim: Nottingham M.M., op.
cit.,455-465 passim;ibid., 1778-1792,1-41 passim;
Phil.M.M.,Min., 1777-1782,30-100 passim;Phil.M.M.
No.Dist., op.cit.,305-342 passim;Phil.M.M.So.
Dist.,op.cit.,238-266 passim;Radnor M.M.,op.cit.,
128; Richland M.M., op.cit.,Sept. 17,1778;Sadsbury
M.M., Min., 1737-1783,280-296 passim;Uwchlan
M.M., op.cit., 48;Warrington M.M.,op.cit.,492-525
passim;Wrightstown M.M., op.cit.,255-259 passim.
(18) Chester Q.M., Min., 1768-1813, Feb.10,1777;Uwchlan
M.M., Min., 1776-1795,19,30;Darby M.M., Min., 1763-
1783,233,243.

(19) Chester Q.M., op.cit., Feb.9,1778.
(20) Pa.Pkt., June 17,1778.
(21) Statutes at Large, v.9,381-382,441-442.
(22) Phil.M.f.S., Min., v.2,203-204.
(23) Meeting for Conference on Suffering Cases of
     Western Q.M., Min., 1779-1780,Aug.2,1779;Western
     Q.M., Min., 1779-1818,4;Phil.Y.M.,Min.,v.3,431
(24) Chester Q.M., op.cit.,May 10,1779;Phil.Y.M., Min.,
     v.3,431.
(25) Phil.Y.M., Min., v.3,431,433-434.
(26) Statutes at Large,v.9,405-406.
(27) Phil.M.f.S., Min.,v.2,232-236,243;Journals of the
     House of Rep.,1776-1781,521-522.
(28) Phil.M.f.S., Min., v.2,244.
(29) Ibid., 253-254;Journals of the House of Rep.,
     522.
(30) Phil.M.f.S., Min., v.2,255,263-265.
(31) Ibid., 265-267;Journals of the House of Rep.,523-524.
(32) Journals of the House of Rep., 501-520.
(33) Ibid.,522-523.
(34) The details of the affair are in Phil.M.f.S.,Min.,
     v.2,273,277,293,295,302,307,334,and the Pa.Ev.Post,
     January 26,1781. The members of the committee were
     Isaac Zane, John and James Pemberton, Nicholas
     Waln and John Drinker.
(35) Pa.Pkt., Aug.12,1780.
(36) Phil.M.f.S., Min., v.2,278.
(37) Ibid., 278-283;Pa.Pkt., Sept.12,1780.
(38) Phil.M.f.S., Min., v.2,326-333; Pa.Arch.,lst Ser.,
     v.9,450-454;Drinker, Journal, Oct.24,1781.
(39) Conference on Suffering Cases of Western Q.M.,
     Min., 1780-1782,Jan.7,April 1,1782.
(40) Phil.M.f.S., Min., v.2,384,389,422-423,434;
     Bradford M.M., Min., 1781-1788,68,74. The Friends
     involved were George Harris, Nathan Lewis, and
     William McCoy of Goshen and Bradford Monthly
     Meetings in Chester County.
(41) Abington M.M., Min., 1774-1782,174-335 passim;ibid.,
     1782-1797,4,10;Bradford M.M., Min., 1765-1781,271-296
     passim;ibid., 1781-1788,4-72 passim;Buckingham
     M.M., Min., 1763-1780,187-235 passim; ibid.,
     1781-1790,238-289 passim; Chester M.M., Min., 1778-
     1808,6-133 passim;Concord M.M., Min., 1777-1795,
     70-242 passim;Darby M.M., Min., 1763-1783,259-356
     passim:Exeter M.M., Min., 1765-1785,338-493 passim:
     Falls M.M., Min., 1767-1788,228-359 passim;Goshen
     M.M., Min., 1766-1788,269-377 passim;Gwynedd M.M.,
     Min., 1779-1786,1-170 passim;Kennet M.M.,Min.,
     1739-1791,658-780 passim;Middletown M.M., Min.,
     1755-1800,432-542 passim;Newgarden M.M., Min.,

1779-1790,1-186 _passim_;Nottingham M.M., Min.,
1778-1792,23-269 _passim_;Phil.M.M., Min.,1777-1782,
104-351 _passim_;_ibid._,1782-1789,7-174 _passim_;Phil.
M.M.No.Dist., Min., 1772-1781,361-518 _passim_;_ibid._,
1782-1789,2-99 _passim_;Phil.M.M.So.Dist., Min.,
1770-1780,226-348 _passim_;_ibid._,1781-1793,11-71
passim;Radnor N.M., Min., 1772-1782,165-261,_passim_;
ibid., 1782-1784,8,11;Richland M.M., Min., 1767-
1786,Jan.21,1779-July 17,1783,_passim_;Sadsbury M.M.
Min., 1737-1783,313-353 _passim_;Uwchlan M.M., Min.,
1776-1795,51-112 _passim_;Warrington M.M., Min.,
1747-1785,525-672 _passim_;Wrightstown M.M., Min.,
1737-1790,266-335 _passim_. Nineteen of the offenders
were dealt with twice which makes the total 1268.

(42) See Appendix I for estimates of the Quaker
population in Pennsylvania on the eve of the
Revolution and the method of estimating percentages
of disownments.

(43) James, "Impact of the Revolution", _loc.cit._, 370.

(44) Phil.M.M., Min., 1782-1789,May 30,1783.

(45) Young, _op.cit._, 105,110.

(46) The accounts of sufferings are in Phil.M.f.S.,
Min., v.2, _passim_ and in _ibid._, Misc.Pap., bx.14-19.

(47) Marietta, "Wealth, War and Religion", _loc.cit._,
239-241.

Chapter XII

NEW JERSEY AND DELAWARE

In New Jersey the Revolution brought a change of
government somewhat similar to that in Pennsylvania,
but with the important difference that it was not preceded by a conflict between the Quaker and non-Quaker
elements. The New Jersey Quakers were within the jurisdiction of Philadelphia Yearly Meeting and helped formulate its official policies. As in Pennsylvania, the
chief source of difficulty was legislation with regard
to military service, taxes, and affirmations of allegiance. But even though these laws often bore heavily
upon the Friends, there seems to have been a disposition
on the part of the authorities to temper their effect.

When the war broke out, the military situation
was much the same as it was in Pennsylvania. Quaker
opposition and the absence of frontier problems had
combined to bring about lax militia regulations, and
throughout the colonial period no effective militia
law had been passed. (1) In October 1775 the Provincial
Congress took steps to remedy this deficiency. It
passed an ordinance directing the captains of the
militia throughout the colony to list all males capable
of bearing arms in their districts, except persons whose
religious principles proscribed military service.(2)

It was not long before such exemptions were carefully qualified. A new militia law early in 1776 provided that males between the ages of sixteen and fifty
having religious scruples against military service should
pay a fine of 10s. for each absence from the required
musters and reviews. This assessment was considered
to be their equitable portion of the burden of public
defense. In addition, whoever for the same reason
was unable to sign the General Association of the colony
unconditionally, promising to defend it against its
enemies, was required to sign with the proviso: "I agree
to the above Association as far as the same is consistent with my religious principles". Those who persisted
in not signing were to be disarmed and were required
to give sufficient security for their peaceable behavior. (3)

208

The following September the newly constituted
Assembly met for its first session and soon passed an
act for the security of the government. This law required all civil and military officials to take an oath
of allegiance to the state accompanied by an abjuration
of the authority of the king of Great Britain. (4)
Within a short time similar legislation of a wider scope
was passed. In October the Assembly approved the
far more inclusive "Act to punish traitors and disaffected Persons". (5) This act empowered any two
justices of the peace to administer the oath or affirmation of allegiance and abjuration to any suspect brought
before them. If the latter refused to subscribe, he
was to be bound over with sufficient security to appear
at the next session of the General Quarter-Sessions of
the Peace, and in default of such security to be imprisoned until the court met. If he then persisted
in his refusal, he was to continue bound for good
behavior or be fined or imprisoned.

In view of the refusal of the Friends to participate in the war in any way or to comply with such regulations as had been passed, they were soon subject to
various types of penalties. In January 1776 a number
of Quakers in Burlington were seized and taken to Borden-
town where they were imprisoned. (6) In June Haddonfield
Monthly Meeting reported that Ł49 8s. 6d. had been distrained on the property of Friends at Woodbury for refusing to pay the provincial powder tax. (7) During
the course of that summer the Friends' meeting-house in
Trenton was seized and used for sessions of the Provincial Convention and for soldiers' quarters. (8)

The next year was one of increasing difficulties.
The presence of the British army in the northern part
of the state in the winter of 1776-1777 resulted in
stricter militia regulations and their more effective
enforcement. In March 1777 the militia law was amended
to provide for fines ranging from 7½s. to 22½s. for
non-attendance at musters and reviews. Failure to march
in time of invasion or alarm incurred a penalty of
from Ł5 to Ł30. In both cases the fines, if unpaid,
were to be levied by distraint, and in default of property
for distraint, the offender was to imprisoned. (9)

Already in the previous January several Friends
had been imprisoned for refusing to do military service,
and subsequently other Friends were similarly prosecuted.(10)
On the whole, however, the authorities seem to have shown
a lenient disposition whenever possible. In one case

the captain of the militia at Chester accompanied
several Friends to Haddonfield and procured the release
of a number of them through the interposition of the
Governor. (11) The cases of Mark Miller and Thomas
Redman whose fines were paid by an anonymous non-Friend
have already been cited. (12)

The Quakers were naturally concerned over the situation in which they found themselves, and in September
Burlington Monthly Meeting appointed a committee to investigate instances of imprisonment and to render aid
to the prisoners.(13) Coincidentally, that same month
the Assembly slightly modified the militia law in an
attempt to alleviate the rigidity of its requirements
and passed an amendment allowing the hiring of a substitute or the payment of a sum sufficient to hire one
in lieu of personal military servce. (14) But the
principles of the Quakers prevented them from benefiting
by such measures.

The loyalist newspapers made the most of any instances of seeming persecution of the Friends. The
Royal American Gazette in New York City published an
account of the seizure of "inoffensive Quakers, as they
came out of their meeting-houses" by the military
officials in Burlington and Mount Holly who then attempted to force them "to take up arms in the worst of
causes and against the best of Kings". (15) The Newport Gazette reported that "the poor Quakers within the
reach of the rebel headquarters at Morris Town, have
been dragged to that place to take up arms, which all
of them conscientiously refused". (16)

The general alarm caused by the supposed revela-
tions of the Spanktown Yearly Meeting had immediate
repercussions in New Jersey. In October 1777 the Assembly enacted a law requiring schoolmasters, attorneys-at-
law, and jurors to take an oath or affirmation of allegiance to the state, refusal incurring a penalty of a ₤6
fine. (17) In December the Council of Safety imprisoned
six Friends who refused to subscribe such an affirmation,
but these laws do not seem to have been harshly enforced. (18)

In May 1778 Abel and James Thomas of Maryland made
a religious visit to Friends in the middle provinces.
They were taken before two magistrates in Newark for
passing the enemy lines to Long Island without permits
and were charged with designs injurious to the American
cause. Their case was referred to the Council of Safety

which accepted their assertions of innoncence, discharged them, and granted them permission to visit the
meetings in New Jersey, declaring that the government
was "unwilling to obstruct any Society in the exercise
of their religion". (19)

Throughout the remainder of the war the chief
difficulty for the Quakers resulted from enforcement
of the militia laws. In June 1779 the legislature passed
two acts affecting Friends adversely. The first called
up one thousand of the state militia, those classes
not furnishing volunteers being allowed to hire substitutes. The cost of the substitutes was to be assessed
per capita; anyone refusing to pay his quota was to
suffer distraint of his property to the required
amount, or in default of property he was to be imprisoned. (20) The second law tripled all fines levied by
the previous militia act (21), while another law passed
early in 1780 raised the penalty to six times the
original amount. (22)

Even before these laws were passed, Salem Monthly
Meeting informed the Meeting for Sufferings that two
of its members were in prison for failure to comply
with the militia laws. Both meetings sent committees
to interview the Governor and other magistrates concerned
in the matter. The defendants were soon afterward
granted their freedom through the anonymous payment
of their fines by a non-Friend. (23)

At this time a division of opinion arose among
the New Jersey Friends as to the consistency of accepting the Continental currency and paying fines. At Evesham Monthly Meeting in March 1779 Warner Mifflin gave
a "clear testimony" against passing the currency which
"Some Could hardly bear with". (24) Haddonfield and
Salem Quarterly Meeting experienced some difficulty
over the payment of fines. According to one of its
members, "the Testimony of the Pennsylvanians was
very Clost against paying of fines & that went Down
hard with some". (25) But the New Jersey Quakers
faithfully observed the injunctions of the Society with
regard to maintaining the peace testimony and disowned
those who did not.

The operation of the militia laws continued to
harrass the Friends and finally, in October 1780,
Shrewsbury and Rahway Quarterly Meeting presented a
petition to the legislature, stating that the enforcement of these laws had proven very burdensome to Friends

211

and urging and praying that relief be granted. (26)
The petition was referred to a committee then framing
a new militia law which, although it did not in its
final form exempt Friends from military service, directed those officers appointed to hear and determine
cases of military delinquency "to attend to every just
Complaint or Excuse arising from Inability of Body or
Insanity of Mind; and where no Excuses are exhibited,
owing to Scruples of Conscience,...to make every
reasonable Enquiry of the Cases to those who might
otherwise apply for Exemption or Relief". In the latter
instances they were to act "so that Justice and not
Severity" would characterize those who enforced the
law. (27)

In the course of the war the property loss of
the Quakers in New Jersey, mostly through distraint of
goods and possessions, amounted to Ł16,026 19s. 5d. as
recorded. Specified accounts amounted to Ł11,892 13s.
3d. of which Ł7,503 10s. 2d. were for unpaid fines;
Ł488 2 d. for unpaid taxes; and Ł3,900 12s. 1d. for
the two items combined. From 1776 through 1778 at
least Ł6,327 1s. 11d. were distrained for unpaid fines,
over one-third of the total, and for all offenses Ł8,617
14s. 8d., or over one-half of the total. The heaviest
sufferings from a pecuniary standpoint occurred in
the first years of the war, probably a reflection of
the military activities at that time. (28)

As in Pennsylvania, the incidence of dealings and
disownments reflects the course of events as well as
legislative trends. The two highest years were 1776
and 1779, those in the former year resulting from military deviations and those in the latter from payment of
war fines. In 1775 there were 13 deviations and 7
disownments, all for military service. In 1776 there
were 91 dealings, of which 85 were for military service,
resulting in 70 disownments. In 1779 there were 94
dealings and 42 disownments, the majority of which were
for the payment of war fines and taxes, which no doubt
reflected the controversy at that time over the payment
of taxes.

The other chief cause for dealings and disownments
was the taking of a test affirmation or allegiance.
Dealings on this count first appeared in 1778 and
reached a peak in 1781. The cessation of the war may
have led some Friends to believe that the reason for
the refusal to take such tests no longer existed.

By the end of the war there had been 429 deviations

from the Quaker peace testimony for which 288 Friends or 67% of the total dealt with were disowned. Approximately 1/3 of male Quakers of military age were disciplined and about 22% disowned. These figures are the highest of any of the states where there were a significant number of Quakers. It is to be noted that, as in Pennsylvania, military deviations predominated in 1776, and the proportion of disownments was then the highest, 93%, whereas in 1779, when dealings for the payment of war fines and taxes predominated, only 44% of those cases resulted in disownment. (29)

There were a few Friends in New Jersey who were disowned for active support of the British. Two members of the Society, from Haddonfield and Chesterfield Monthly Meetings respectively, went over to the British when the latter occupied Philadelphia during the winter of 1777-1778. The remaining seven were from Plainfield, Shrewsbury, and Kingwood Monthly Meetings in the northern part of the state, who joined the British in the period 1781-1782. It was at this time that Shrewsbury and Rahway Quarterly Meeting directed Plainfield Monthly Meeting to disown some of its younger members who had gone to Staten Island, returning with British raiding parties. (30) There is no indication of deviations involving joining the British when they occupied the northern part of the state during the winter of 1776-1777.

DELAWARE

The Friends meetings in Delaware, like those in New Jersey, were a constituent part of Philadelphia Yearly Meeting, and consequently the Delaware Quakers were guided by its decisions and injunctions. A chief source of their wartime difficulties was the seizure of property for the use of the armies, especially during the Pennsylvania campaign. The meeting-house in Wilmington was expropriated at various times by both the American and British armies for use as a hospital. Individual Friends had soldiers quartered on them, and many sustained considerable loss by military requisition of provisions, forage, grain, livestock, furniture, and farm gears, for which they could not consistently accept compensation. (31)

It was not until 1778 that the legislature passed an effective militia law. In the colonial period the Quakers had opposed the enactment of militia laws and regulations, and in the first years of the Revolution

the government made few efforts to fill the military
requisitions of the Continental Congress. (32) Finally
in May 1778, the Assembly sent a new militia bill up
to the Council. Despite the efforts of the Council
to insert an amendment in favor of those who held religious scruples against bearing arms, the law as passed
contained no such exceptions and instead levied a fine
of 7s. 6d. for failure to report to militia duty. (33)
A supplementary Act of December 1779 raised the fine
to $10, although later in 1781 the penalty was lowered
to $5. (34)

      In the course of the war 64 Friends were dealt
with, 40 of whom were disowned for deviating from
their pacifist testimony. The highest number was in
1776 when there were 20 dealings and 16 disownments.
Of the 64 Friends dealt with, 35 were for military
service, 13 for taking an affirmation of allegiance,
and 8 for paying war fines, with lesser numbers for
paying war taxes, sailing on a prviateer, etc. One of
the last dealings was for celebrating Independence on
July 4, 1782. (35)

      Aside from the instances of personal abuse which
took place in the first months of the war as already
recounted, the recorded sufferings of the Delaware Quakers were primarily for the distraint of property on
refusal to pay wartime taxes and fines. The Friends
do not seem to have suffered from the type of repressive
legislation which was passed in Pennsylvania. Total
sufferings recorded for the Delaware Quakers amounted
to Ł2,189 12s. 9d. Almost half of this amount, Ł908 13s.
9d., was for refusal to pay war taxes, Ł479 9s. 6d.
was for not paying war fines, and Ł385 16s. was for
the offenses combined. The armies expropriated property valued at Ł415 13s. 6d. (36)

      The contrast in the experience of the Quakers in
New Jersey and Delaware as compared with the Pennsylvania Friends reflects the difference in their relations
with their respective communities. The historic political role of the Quakers in Pennsylvania had much to do
with their situation during the Revolution. In New
Jersey and Delaware the Friends had not held a dominant position in the control of affairs for many years
and had not espoused a particular viewpoint in the development of the opposition movement to Britain. Consequently they did not suffer as sharp a decline in community standing nor did they experience as harsh an application of wartime legislation as did their Pennsylvania
brethren.

Notes for Chapter XII

(1) Fisher, N.J. as a Roy. Prov., 103.
(2) Minutes of the Provincial Congress and the Council
     of Safety, 1774-1776 (Trenton, 1879), 257.
(3) Ibid., 407-408.
(4) Acts of the General Assembly of the State of New
     Jersey, 1776-1783, comp. Peter Wilson(Trenton,1784),
     1-2.
(5) Ibid.,4-5.
(6) Craft, James, "Extracts from the Journal of James
     Craft", History Magazine, v.1 (1857), 302.
(7) Haddonfield M.M., Min., 1762-1781, 304-305.
(8) Chesterfield M.M., Min., 1756-1786, 398-400.
(9) Acts of the Gen. Assy.of the St. of N.J., 1776-
     1777 (Burlington, 1777), 26-36.
(10) Hunt, "Diary", loc.cit., 224-225.
(11) Ibid., 225.
(12) See above 165.
(13) Burlington M.M., Min., 1770-1781, 185.
(14) Acts of the Gen. Assy., 1776-1777, 100.
(15) Roy. Amer. Gaz., Feb. 27, 1777.
(16) Nwp. Gaz., March 6, 1777.
(17) Acts of the Gen. Assy., 1776-1777, 113.
(18) Minutes of the Council of Safety of the State of
     New Jersey, 1777-1778 (Jersey City, 1872), 175.
     The Friends were Joseph Horner, Isaac Clark,
     Benjamin Clark, Thomas Clark, and Robert White.
(19) Ibid., 241.
(20) Acts of the Gen. Assy.of the St. of N.J., 1778-1779
     (Trenton, 1779), 58-63.
(21) Ibid., 115.
(22) Acts of the Gen. Assy. of the St. of N.J., 1779-
     1780 (Trenton,1780), 69.
(23) Salem M.M., Min., 1740-1788,388,392,393; Phil.M.
     f.S., Min., v.2, 199,202-203,211.
(24) Hunt, "Diary", loc.cit., 235.
(25) Ibid.
(26) Shrewsbury and Rahway Q. M., Min., 1757-1828, Oct.
     23, 1780; Votes and Procs. of the Gen. Assy. of
     the St. of N.J., 1780-1781 (Trenton, 1781),264.
(27) Ibid., 22; Acts of the Gen. Assy. of the St. of N.J.
     1780-1781 (Trenton, 1781), 49.
(28) The accounts of sufferings are in Phil.M.f.S.,
     Min., and Misc. Pap., and in the minute books of
     the monthly meetings in New Jersey.
(29) Burlington M.M., Min., 1770-1781, 141-271 passim;
     ibid., 1781-1788,10-30 passim;Chesterfield M.M.,

215

Min., 1756-1786,380-599 passim;Evesham M.M., Min.,
1760-1782,326-529 passim:Great Egg Harbor M.M.,
1726-1797, 291-375 passim:Haddonfield M.M., Min.,
1762-1781,289-457 passim;ibid.,1781-1804,5-45
passim;Kingwood M.M., Min., 1772-1782,29,30,45;
ibid.,1782-1787,5,6;Mount Holly M.M., Min., 1776-
1793,3-183 passim:Plainfield M.M., Min., 1751-1788,
June 19,1776-Dec.17,1783 passim; Salem M.M., Min.,
1740-1788,367-422 passim;Shrewsbury M.M., Min.,
1757-1786,355-489 passim. See Appendix I for
method of computing the Quaker male population.
The much higher incidence of disciplinary action
in New Jersey as compared with any other state
may be due in part to the sharp differences of
opinion over the question of payment of taxes.

(30) Shrewsbury and Rahway Q.M.,Min.,1757-1828,Oct. 29,
1781.
(31) Phil.M.f.S.,Min.,v.2,213.
(32) George Reade to General Washington, Jan.19,1778,
Delaware Papers, Sparks MSS, v.15,51.
(33) Minutes of the Council of the Delaware State,1776-
1792 (Papers of the Hist. Soc. of Delaware,v.6),
253; An Act of the General Assembly of the Delaware State for establishing a Militia (Lancaster,
1778).
(34) A Supplement to an Act ... establishing a Militia,
Dec.25,1779, Acts of the General Assembly of the
Delaware State, 1779-1780 (Wilmington,1780);An
Additional Supplementary Act to an Act ...estab-
lishing a Militia, June 19,1781 (Wilmington,1781).
(35) The accounts of these sufferings are in the Philadelphia Meeting for Sufferings records.
(36) Duck Creek M.M., Min., 1705-1800,268-336,passim;
Wilmington M.M.,Min.,1750-1776,523-546,passim;
ibid., 1776-1792,4-163,passim.

Chapter XIII

NEW ENGLAND

The New England Quaker constituency was confined
almost entirely to the three states of Massachusetts,
New Hampshire and Rhode Island. As has already been
indicated, in contrast to the Pennsylvania Friends the
New England Friends were involved only to a limited extent commercially, and almost not at all politically,
in their particular region of the colonies. The establishment of Quakerism in New England antedated by two
decades the founding of Pennsylvania, and its adherents
were largely indigenous in origin, resulting from Quaker
missionary activities rather than Quaker immigration
from Europe. Although the New England Quakers consulted
closely with the Pennsylvania Friends on critical problems facing the Society and were fundamentally in
complete agreement on basic issues, the New Englanders
pursued their own course in interpretating Quaker
testimonies as applied to their particular situation.
Consequently there were at times noticeable differences
between the two Quaker groups in their relations with
the new state governments, and there were occasions
when the New England Friends were openly critical of
policies and actions of their Pennsylvania brethren.

RHODE ISLAND

In proportion to the population, the Friends were
strongest in Rhode Island, and it was there that war
time legislation affected them earliest as well as
most adversely. In June 1776 the Rhode Island Assembly
passed an act requiring an oath or affirmation of
allegiance to the new regime, to be administered to all
disaffected persons. A special provision exempted the
Quakers if they could produce a certificate of membership from the meeting to which they belonged.(1) When
three Newport Quakers were brought before the Newport
town council and were asked to subscribe to an affirmation of allegiance or present a certificate of membership in the Society of Friends, they appealed to the
Meeting for Sufferings for advice as to whether they
could consistently comply. In reply the Meeting for
Sufferings declared that the monthly meetings could

217

issue such certificates to enable their members to avoid
taking the test affirmations. (2) This cooperation
with the authorities of the new government contrasted
with the policy of Pennsylvania Friends who refused to
allow such compliance, for so doing would indicate
recognition of the new regime.

Two years later, in February 1778, a bill proposing
to establish an oath of allegiance was referred to the
people in their respective town meetings for instructions
to their delegates in the state legislature. The proposed measure was so strenuously opposed on account of
the position in which it might put the Quakers that the
bill was never reported out of committee. (3)

Because of Rhode Island's relatively sheltered
position and its remoteness from the frontier, the
militia laws of the colony were practically in a state
of desuetude at the beginning of the Revolution. The
basic militia law of 1744 had exempted persons of tender
consciences from active service, requiring them instead
to perform certain subsidiary duties as messengers,
scouts, and guards in time of alarm. (4) It was not
until December 1776 that the legislature passed an act
"for the draughting all male persons within this state
subject by law to bear arms". (5) Quite naturally the
Friends were alarmed at the institution of a draft,
and early in 1777 a committee of the Meeting for Sufferings interviewed members of the Assembly. The legislature thereupon amended the law by exempting the Friends
from all military duty on the presentation of a certificate of membership in a Friends meeting. This provision was made retroactive in behalf of any Quakers
who had been fined or imprisoned previously for refusing
to perfrom military servce. (6)

Some of the legislators opposed this alteration
in the law lest it facilitate evasions. Consequently,
when the Meeting for Sufferings informed the respective
monthly meetings of the change in the law, it warned
against granting certificates of membership to "any
whose Life, & Conversation does not well answer to our
profession, (since) we must bear the Reproach, and shall
mar our Reputation as a Society". (7)

There was evidently increasing opposition to the
leniency displayed by the legislature, for in April 1778
it withdrew the exemption it had granted to the Friends.
At that time it passed an amending act, requiring all
persons available for military service to be drafted
regardless of their religious affiliation. Hence-

forth the commanding officer of each regiment was instructed to make a return of all Friends in his district who produced certificates of membership when a
draft was ordered. These lists were to be used by
the town authorities in hiring an equal number of persons, the cost to be assessed on the Quakers listed.
Whoever refused to pay the assessed sums was to have
his property distrained to the required amount. (8)
A factor contributing to this action may well have been
the increasing need for men for the Continental army
and the consequent urgent appeals of the Congress to
the individual states.

When this change was made, the Meeting for Sufferings
advised the monthly meetings to cease issuing certificates of membership to drafted Friends, since they
were now to be used in proportioning men to be drafted.
They were thus now made necessary prerequisites "to
the Execution of the Law, which if admitted, would des-
troy the very principle on which the Original was
founded..." Furthermore, Friends who suffered distraints
of property in the execution of the new law should
not accept overplus monies from the sale of the distrained
goods, since they would thereby "wound the Cause of
Truth, depart from their testimony, and bring a Burden
upon the faithful". (9)

An event which doubtless influenced the militia
legislation was the occupation of Newport by the British
in the winter of 1777-1778, and the subsequent action
of the Newport Quakers. In January 1777, after the
British had taken possession of the town, Rhode Island
Monthly Meeting presented an address to General Clinton,
the commander in charge, declaring that its members
were "the King's peaceable & Loyal Subjects" and
pointing out the disownment of those who bore arms in
violation of their pacifist principles. The address
also requested protection for the persons and property
of the Friends and the enjoyment of their religious
liberties. (10)

It was not till the next August that Friends were
seriously affected by the operation of the new law.
At that time the Meeting for Sufferings was stirred
to action by the imprisonment of David Anthony of
Greenwich for refusing to serve in the militia. A
committee of the Meeting interviewed the colonel of
the regiment concerned but without success, and it finally obtained Anthony's release through the intervention
of the Legislative Council. (11) In its report on the
affair the committee referred to "...the good Disposition

of Both houses of Assembly towards religious liberty
and...Consciencious persons" and suggested the approp-
riateness of presenting an address to the legislature
stating the present law's infringement of civil and
religious liberty. (12)

Acting on this recommendation, the Meeting for
Sufferings laid its case before the Assembly and requested
the repeal of the oppressive sections of the militia
law. However, a bill introduced into the House with
such a provision was defeated by a large majority. In
writing to Moses Brown on this matter, Senator Bowen
probably voiced the attitude of many people when he
accused the Friends of obstructionist tactics in
not accepting such exemptions as they already had. He
himself had been opposed to the present law and had
proposed an alternative one which was rejected, but
because of the pressing affairs of government the one in
force had been accepted. (13)

From other comments in the letter it is obvious
that the attitude of the public had been considerably
influenced by reports of events in Pennsylvania over
the past year. Senator Bowen reminded Moses Brown

> that the Body of your Society are
> reputed to be aginst the American cause,
> (and) that they have by all ways and means
> (but taking up arms) assisted our Enemies
> to the Westward. (14)

Moses Brown agreed that the legislature's attitude was
partly conditioned by charges that the Friends in
Pennsylvania were "in plots and conspiracies against
the Government, Communicating Intelligence &c". (15)
He later complained that the publication of the
Spanktown Yearly Meeting accusations in the New England
newspapers ahd resulted in much prejudice against the
Friends. (16) To counteract such false reports, the
Meeting for Sufferings in March 1779 directed all
the subordinate meetings throughout New England to
read the testimony issued by the Philadelphia Friends
on the Spanktown fraud and thereby clear the Society
of the odium cast upon it by the publication of the
article signed "Spanktown Yearly Meeting". (17)

Despite the unfavorable change in the militia law,
the Quakers do not seem to have been severely dealt
with. After the Anthony case, only one other similar
instance is recorded. In June 1778 a party of soldiers

commissioned to arrest delinquent Quakers seized several of them coming from their meeting for worship. The general in charge, Silvanus Reed, strenuously remonstrated with the men responsible for this action, declaring that notwithstanding their orders "Regard for the Publick worship of God and a Common Rule of defence must have Convenced them that Such Proseding could but be disagreeable to him and every other officer". (18)

Shortly afterward the arrested Friends were brought before a court martial for refusing to do the required military service. Two of them pleaded guilty, contending it was contrary to their religious principles to bear arms. They also declined taking an affirmation of allegiance which was tendered them. The court fined each of the offenders £40 to pay for the hiring of substitutes and ordered their imprisonment until the money was paid. (19)

Moses Brown then sponsored a petition to the legislature requesting the release of the imprisoned Friends. He also wrote Senator Bowen in their behalf, pointing out the leniency shown David Anthony. In order to disprove accusations of Quaker sympathy for the British he quoted the remark of a British general on Rhode Island who had declared that "3/4 of the Quakers was Rebels in their Hearts". (20)

Aside from sufferings due to war time legislation which affected all Friends in the state alike, Friends on the island of Rhode Island, which was the chief battle zone of the area, suffered more severely than those on the mainland. The livestock of many Quakers was seized and driven into Newport by the British. On the other hand, the Americans expropriated their crops of corn and hay. Notwithstanding these difficulties, the faithful members of the Society were "preserved from manifesting a Spirit of party, but quietly submitted to both" as either side prevailed, and for the most part the Friends were treated with respect. (21)

The consistency of the pacifist conduct of the Quakers was demonstrated by an event which occurred toward the end of 1777. At that time several citizens of Newport, among them some Friends, were imprisoned on board the British prison ship Lord Sandwich for refusing to sign an association obliging them to fight against the rebels. (22) Subsequently more Quakers were similarly imprisoned, and Rhode Island Monthly Meeting appointed a committee to investigate the matter.

221

The only reason reported for the detention of these
Friends was indiscreet discourse, and the Monthly
Meeting advised those concerned to be more careful
in the future. (23)

When in October 1779, after a three years occupation, the British evacuated the island and the Americans regained control, the lot of the Quakers was
adversely affected for a time, probably as a result
of the earlier Quaker address to General Clinton. In
November 1779 two Quakers were imprisoned on the general
charge of "being adherent to, aiding, & assisting the
King of great Britain his fleets, & armies". They were
eventually freed on bond to appear in court with sureties
and a promise to fulfill their sentence and adjudica-
tion. (24) Soon afterward two other Friends were similarly prosectued. (25) Even Moses Brown was confined
to his house in Providence because of a report that
on a recent return journey from Philadelphia he had discussed the King's condition with great interest and had
been deeply affected. (26)

These events evoked considerable discussion among
Friends as to the consistency of appealing to the
government for the protection of the law. Moses Brown
strongly advocated such action,but before any decision
was reached the Council took steps to halt further
excesses. (27)

In the closing years of the war two incidents occurred
which affected the Newport Quakers. In July 1780 the
French fleet arrived, and the whole town was illuminated.
According to Ezra Stiles, the Quakers "did not chuse
their Light shd shine before men,& their Windows were
broken - a fine subject for Friends Meeting for Sufferings". (28) The following year the French army took
possession of the Friends meeting-house in the city.
The Meeting for Sufferings appealed to the Governor
who interceded with the French officer in charge, and
the house was soon released. (29)

MASSACHUSETTS

The Mainland

Despite the fact that Massachusetts was the home
of Samuel and John Adams and was the hotbed of much
of the radical revolutionary activity, the Quakers there
received more favorable consideration relative to
their pacifist principles and conduct during the war
than was the case in most of the other thirteen new

states. At the beginning of the war they benefited from previous militia laws which exempted them from bearing arms, and these provisions were renewed in the militia laws of 1776 and 1779. (30) Difficulties which arose were primarily due to special levies of troops ordered by the General Court, which did not contain specific exemptions for the Friends.

The first such instance occurred in September 1776 in response to an urgent appeal from the Governor of Connecticut for military aid. The Massachusetts authorities ordered a fifth of the militia not then in service to be drafted, with the exception of a few towns and counties. Three Friends in Worcester County were called up and immediately petitioned the legislature for release, claiming they could not take up arms because of their religious principles. (31) The General Court then amended the order, exempting from the draft all Friends who had been members of the Society before April 19, 1775, and a committee of the House reported in favor of releasing the petitioners. (32)

A few months later, in December, the legislature ordered a census to be taken of all males of military age in order to ascertain the military resources of the state and provide for a better enforcement of the law. In this census all who had been Quakers before April 19, 1775, were to be so designated. (33) In contrast to the action of the Quakers in Pennsylvania and New York on a similar request, the Massachusetts Friends complied with the law, for according to the resulting enumeration there were 1099 male Friends over fifteen years of age in the province. The principle centers of concentration were Dartmouth, Taunton, and Swanzey in Bristol County; Mendon,Douglas, Bolton, and Uxbridge in Worcester County; and Falmouth, Yarmouth, and Sandwich in Barnstable County, with smaller numbers in other towns. In the district of Maine there were 133 male Friends of military age in eight different towns, with the largest number, 64, in Falmouth. (34)

Despite the new exemption, three more Quakers were imprisoned in Worcester for refusing to do military service. In reply to their petition for release in January 1777, the General Court directed them to take their case into the courts since the law had delineated the powers and duties of the local authorities and of the militia officers in dealing with the Friends. (35) In April six Quakers from Dartmouth were accorded similar treatment, but the General Court ordered their

release on bond to return to jail when so directed. (37)
Subsequently four residents of the town of East Hoosack
in the northwestern corner of the state where there
was a monthly meeting under the jurisdiction of New
York Yearly Meeting were imprisoned for refusing to
comply with the draft. They then petitioned the General
Court for release on the basis of their religious scruples
against bearing arms. A petition in their case from
the local Committee of Safety stated there were certain
persons in the township under the denomination of Friends
but without membership in their meeting who professed
it was against their conscience to bear arms. An application in their behalf from the Friends meeting merely
referred to the petitioners as "attenders". The lati-
tude of the government's consideration was shown in
its granting the release of these men, despite their
lack of actual membership in the Society. At the same
time the legislature directed the militia officers and
Committee of Safety of the town to draft four other men
in their place. (38)

The problem which the non-cooperation of the Friends
presented to local officials was quaintly indicated
in a report from a militia officer of the town of Rutland
in the early summer of 1778. Thomas Eddy of Northbridge
had been assigned to guard some of the prisoners taken
at the time of Burgogyne's defeat. He refused to comply
with the order and was delivered to his company at Rutland. The officer in charge received little benefit
from Eddy's presence and informed the General Court as
follows:

> He has remained here peaceably, but says
> he is a Quaker. That it is against his
> principles to take up arms, or in any
> way contribute to Support the war, he
> appears Stedfast and unmoveable in his
> principles - His Friends of the same perswa-
> sion have applied to me to Release him, -
> I do not Consider my Self otherised to do
> it - beg leave to relate his excuse for
> not Serving, viz. that he is a Quaker -
> has joined their meeting which appears
> from several of that Denomination to be
> a fact, Towit last July he was taken into
> meeting -.(39)

On receiving this account the General Court ordered
Eddy's release, despite his reception into membership
in the Society over two years after the legal date of
April 19, 1775.

224

The considerate treatment of the Quakers in Massachusetts was noted in a letter from the New England Meeting for Sufferings to the Friends in Philadelphia in August 1778. This declared:

> Friends in the Massachusetts are not called upon for personal service; except in a few instances, one of which, a friend lately become a member, was drafted,..., and we hope, as hath hitherto been the Case of those drafted in that Government, he will be released..." (40)

The Friend referred to was Levi Hunt of Swanzey Monthly Meeting who had been drafted and sent to the army at Fishkill, N.Y. After petitions in his behalf from both his monthly meeting and the Meeting for Sufferings, the General Court ordered his release. (41)

In the later years of the war the difficulty of obtaining the required quotas of men prompted the legislature to adopt more stringent regulations with regard to conscientious objectors. In June 1779 the Continental Congress asked the state government for two thousand troops, and the General Court ordered the levy without exempting Quakers. Seth Huddleston of Dartmouth Monthly Meeting was taken into custody for refusing to serve. He immediately petitioned the legislature, and the Meeting for Sufferings intervened in his behalf also. (42).

This case prompted a change in policy on the part of the government. After considering the matter, a committee of the House advocated that Huddleston be discharged on payment of a fine to be levied by distraint if not paid. It also proposed that the exemption for the Quakers be withdrawn and that they be required to hire a substitute or pay a fine, the last to be distrained on their property if refused. (43) This suggestion was later adopted. In June 1780 on receiving requests from both the Continental Congress and General Washington for more troops, the General Court ordered a draft. Quotas were to be levied on the towns according to population, and anyone refusing to hire a substitute or pay a fine within twenty-four hours was to be prosecuted under the law of desertion. (44)

The new procedure resulted in considerable difficulty for towns with large numbers of Quakers. The town of Sandwich ordered Friends of wealth to be applied to for loans if fines were imposed, and to be drafted

if they refused to make them. (45) At the same time
the town petitioned the General Court to reduce its
quota of men, a request which the militia officer of
Barnstable County made for his whole county. The
latter gave as his reason that "the hardship of getting
men among the Quakers is inconceivable & what makes
great uneasiness I cannot say unjustly". (46) A similar request from the town of Rochester in Bristol County
was rejected later in the year. (47)

Subsequently, instances of drafted Friends were
appealed to the General Court from both Barnstable and
Bristol Counties. In the latter county seventeen
Quakers were drafted at one time, and they appealed to
the General Court, while the Meeting for Sufferings
petitioned the Council in their behalf. The Council
reprimanded the muster master of the county for not
fining the Quakers and hiring substitutes instead according to the law. The officer's reply to this communication said in part:

> I Cannot Conceive where the general Cort
> Expected The officer Could find so great a
> number as is required - (from the Town of
> Dartmouth) with Their minds fully accomplish-
> ed for soldiers when more than Half the
> number of the male inhabitants There...: -
> had rather submit To Be Trampled on Like
> the meanest Reptile Than by a vigorous
> Exertion To Defend himself:...-only (an)
> inferior proportion is willing to serve &
> (it is) unfair to levil the proportion
> again (on This inferior number) of a superior
> number who will not Contribit Their mite
> to Defend The Just wrights of mankind and
> who Even Deny The first Law in nature. (48)

About the same time similar cases occurred in Yarmouth, Falmouth, and Sandwich in Barnstable County. In
their petition to the General Court these Friends explained their refusal to do military service as

> not out of obstancy or In Contempt of
> Authority but Realy and Singly from a
> Conscientious Scruple and a firm Perswasion
> that Wars and Larning of War & Blood Shed
> Is Against the Command of Christ Which
> Principle has bin held Ever Sence We Was a
> Society (and) Still Remains...(49)

226

The covering letter of the militia officer who forwarded the petitions said that the Friends could not
be marched by force and would be of no use even if they
were taken to camp. No one would have a hand in drag-
ging them off against their consciences, and the officers
had drafted them reluctantly only because the resolve
ordering the levy had included the Quakers in the enumeration by which the quotas had been apportioned. The
resulting situation had caused "Such uneasiness among sd
poor distressed inhabitants this way that to draft of
the non quakers much more than their proportions would
be drawing the cords so as to break". (50)

On receiving these communications, the Council informed the officers in charge of the respective towns
concerned that the Quakers should not have been drafted
but that an equal number of men who could serve should
have been procured. Because of the difficulties which
had arisen, however, the officer at the head of the
first regiment of Barnstable County was directed to
use his discretion in completing the quota assigned.(51)

The permanent militia law of 1781, passed after
the adoption of the new state constitution. attempted
to solve the Quaker problem. Instead of rendering
personal military service in case of war, Friends were
to be assessed their full proportion of the expenses
of raising men. This amount was to be levied by the
town assessors according to the average cost per man plus
ten per cent to cover the cost of their enlistment. (52)

In the matter of affirmations of allegiance the
Quakers seem to have had comparatively little difficulty in Massachusetts. In May 1776 the General Court
passed an act for disarming disaffected persons or those
refusing to associate in defense of the American cause,
and for punishing persons inimical to the rights of
America. (53) This law required all males over sixteen
to subscribe a declaration promising not to aid the
enemy and to defend the colonies against Great Britain
by force of arms. Nothing in the act was to be construed to disarm, disqualify, or punish the Quakers for
not signing the declaration, provided they signed an
alternative "promise" not to aid or abet the enemy.(54)

In February 1778, the legislature prescribed an
oath or affirmation of allegiance to the state to be
administered to any suspicious person. In this case
the Friends were allowed to affirm and also to omit
the word "defend" in promising to support the govern-

227

ment. (55) In March 1779 the Meeting for Sufferings informed the Quakers in Massachusetts that they could not
consistently comply with this law. At the same time
it urged that since there was no intention on the part
of the authorities to persecute the Friends, as indicated by their lenient interpretation of the militia
laws, all members of the Society should be "peaceable
subjects under every government" where their lot was
or might be case, "avoiding all Plotts, & Conspiracies
against the same -". (56)

Only one instance is recorded of prosecution of a
Quaker as a result of this act. In May 1778 Peleg Chase
of Swanzey Monthly Meeting in Bristol County was imprisoned for refusing to take the affirmation of allegiance. Both the monthly meeting and the Meeting for
Sufferings interceded in his behalf.After the chairman
of the committee which complained against him was
interviewed, the case seems to have been dropped. (57)

Nantucket Island

The fate of the Quakers on Nantucket during the
Revolution was somewhat different from that of their
brethren on the mainland. About four-fifths of the inhabitants of the island were Friends whose chief
occupation was whale fishing, with almost complete
dependence on the London market for disposal of their
whaling products. Very little food could be raised
on the barren sands of the island, and for their sus-
tenance they depended on the nearby mainland. (58)
They therefore viewed an open rupture between the mother
country and the colonies with great foreboding, especially since their pacifist principles would forbid them
to take part on either side.

As already indicated, the Massachusetts Bay Restraining Act exempted Nantucket from the application
of its provisions so that its inhabitants might continue
their whaling industry without interference from the
British navy. On the other hand, both the Continental
Congress and the Massachusetts General Court, in order
to prevent the island from becoming a supply point for
the enemy, passed laws prohibiting Nantucket from trading with the enemy and stipulating that provisions,
supplies, and food could be obtained only from the
mainland. The trade of the island was thus confined
to Massachusetts. (59)

The islanders, whose means of livelihood were

thus seriously threatened, petitioned the Massachusetts legislature and obtained authorization to make whaling voyages on the basis of permits issued out of Falmouth. Vessels granted such permits had to be bonded to return to the mainland ports, with the exception of Boston as long as it was under British control. The result of this situation was that the Nantucket whalemen were liable to having their ships seized by the British on the one hand if they adhered to the American requirements, and by the Americans on the other if they observed the British requirements. At times Nantucket sailors had to run something of a blockade to obtain food and supplies for the island. (60)

William Rotch, a leading whaleman and the most prominent Quaker on the island, played a dominant role in the affairs of its inhabitants. When the Revolution broke out he realized that the most appropriate policy for the islanders was to take part on neither side and, as far as possible, to give no cause of offense to either party. His pacifist principles were, of course, a strong, motivating factor. At the beginning of the war he received an application for some bayonets which had come into his possession along with other goods of a merchant who had defaulted ten years earlier and which had lain forgotten. Rotch believed that compliance with the application would be a denial of the Society's peace testimony, and so he declined to deliver the bayonets. Other applications soon followed, and he finally threw the coveted bayonets into the sea since they were an "instrument...purposely made and used for the destruction of mankind". (61)

This action "made a great noise in the country", and he was called before a committee of the General Court at Watertown and questioned about the affair. When he explained the religious basis for his action he was discharged, but the "clamor over my bayonets", he later said, "long continued against me". (62)

During the years 1776-1778 the Nantucketeers were in despair, since vessels sent out for supplies often came back empty. In addition, in 1779 armed vessels led by loyalists descended on the island from Newport and plundered much property. When it was heard that new raids were being planned, the town appointed William Rotch, Dr. Benjamin Tupper, and Samuel Starbuck to appeal to the British commander, General Prescott, at Newport. A delay of the raids was granted to allow time for the deputation to go to New York and lay the situation before Sir George Collier who was in charge of the British navy in American waters. (63)

The deputation was successful in obtaining an order forbidding all British ships to seize anything in Nantucket harbor. Moreover, all the Nantucket sailors heretofore taken prisoner by the British were released. When the British command later changed hands, Timothy Folger was again sent to New York where he obtained permission for Nantucket whaling vessels to operate without interference by the British navy. (64)

On account of these contacts with the British, one Thomas Jenkins submitted a petition to the General Court, accusing the Quakers William Rotch, Dr. Benjamin Tupper, Samuel Starbuck and Timothy Folger of high treason, inasmuch as they had not first obtained permission from the Massachusetts authorities to make their respective trips to interview the British commanders. In the winter of 1779-1780 the accused were called before a committee of the General Court composed of members from both houses of the legislature to answer the charges. After the examination the House members voted for the acquittal of the accused, while the Senate members wanted to hold them for further questioning. Nevertheless the accused were set at liberty to go home, and no further steps were undertaken against them. (65)

Early in 1783, after active fighting had ceased, the town of Nantucket commissioned William Rotch, Samuel Starbuck, and Stephen Hussey to go to Philadelphia and lay the case of the island before the Continental Congress. In their appeal to the Congress, Rotch and his fellow Quakers emphasized the importance of the whaling industry to the new nation and persuaded Congress to authorize the island's inhabitants to pursue their whaling industry without interference and seizure by American vessels.(66) Within a few months the treaty of peace with Great Britain brought the difficulties to an end, but it was to be some time before the island would recover from heavy losses in property and lives.

NEW HAMPSHIRE

In New Hampshire there were only two Monthly Meetings, at Dover and Hampton respectively, with scattered groups of Friends at Danville, Gilmanton Kensington, Kingston, Nottingham, Richmond, Rochester, and Weare. (67) In 1776 the Provincial Committee of Safety at Exeter adopted the resolution of the Continental Congress requiring all males over twenty-one to sign the Association, promising to resist the British with arms. (68) A total of seventy-three Quakers refused to sign, but no action seems to have been taken against them.(69)

The Quakers in Richmond sent a statement to the Provincial Congress, explaining that they were not against the Congress or American liberties, but that they did not sign the Association because they believed it to be the will of God not to take the lives of their fellow men. Their statement concluded:

> ...Whenever we are convinct to the contrary
> we are ready to join our American brethren
> to defend by armes against the hostile
> attempts of the British fleet and armies".(70)

The Friends at Gilmanton sent up a similar statement in which they declared:

> ...we agree and consent to the Declaration
> of Independence of the British Crown and
> are willing to pay our proportion to the
> support of the United Colonies but as to
> defend with arms, it is against our Re-
> ligious principles and pray we may be
> excused...(71)

These statements clearly indicate the contrast between the attitude of many New England Friends and their Pennsylvania brethren with regard to the newly acquired independence from Great Britain and their relation to the newly established governments.

Nor does there seem to be any evidence of difficulties encountered by the Friends in New Hampshire on account of refusal to perform military service. Shortly after independence was declared, the legislature passed a militia act which exempted the Friends from the training bands which were the basis of the military forces of the state. (72) No doubt important factors in this lenient policy were the distance from the scene of warfare and the small proportion of Quakers in the population. There are no records of sufferings on the part of the Friends for refusal to pay war taxes or fines or contribute in any other way to the war effort.

THE TESTIMONY TESTED

Throughout the war there were several demands of the

new governments of a non-military nature which closely
touched the Quaker peace testimony and caused the Friends
much heart-searching. The New England Friends were no
exception, for already in 1776, as was the case elsewhere,
they had to decide whether or not to accept the new
Continental currency. Although there were those Quakers
who felt they must reject it as issued to support the
war, the Society did not take an official position,
and the majority of the New England Friends accepted
the new currency.

     The popular attitude was quite tolerant of the
Quaker non-conformists. When several of them were
summoned before local Committees of Safety for rejecting
the money, they were discharged after explaining that
their action arose from religious and not from political
principles. (73) When another Friend was advertised
for such an offense, Moses Brown wrote that "the people
generally disapprove, and Individuals are ashamed" of
his prosecution. (74) In order to avoid any possible
justification for complaints against Friends in this
matter, Rhode Island Quarterly Meeting warned its
members not to take "any undue advantage by the deprec-
iation or unsettled state of the currency which now
seems to open a way to injustice..." (75) One meeting
disowned a Friend for "altering and passing several
bills of paper money". (76)

     The controversy over the payment of taxes arose
early in the war in New England, precipitated by
Timothy Davis' Letter from One Friend arguing
that all taxes should be paid to the authorities
actually in power. The issue was subsequently intensified by the publication of Isaac Grey's treatise on the
subject in Philadelphia in 1778. A member of the Continental Congress sent a copy of it to the Rhode Island
Assembly through Jabez Bowen who was then Deputy Governor. Moses Brown, who had also obtained a copy, agreed
with the author as far as submission to the new authorities was concerned. If Friends could be united on
that, he would have no objection to their declaring
that they would be "quiet & peaceable Subjects under
Every Government" where their lot was cast. At the same
time he was worried over the effect which other aspects
of the publication might have both inside and outside
the Society. (77)

     On the issue of paying taxes Moses Brown had no
quarrel with those declining to pay because of their
religious scruples, considering the then unsettled
state of affairs. In his own case, he refused to pay

232

only when the levies were wholly for the support of war.
He was willing to pay civil taxes to the present rulers
as he had to the old government. Although the restoration
of the former political relationships would be the most
satisfactory outcome of the war, he could see no hope
for it. He himself would not "lift a finger against
the present Governors", and he hoped that Friends in
general would be careful in their conduct toward them.
Although some New England Quakers paid only wholly
civil taxes and others refused payment of only wholly
war taxes, there was no censure on the part of either
group. (78)

It was in this connection that Moses Brown expressed
his opinion on the conduct of the Pennsylvania Friends.
He felt their action had often been prompted by a desire
for the continuation of the old constitution under which
they had prospered, and he feared they might persist in
this position too long. The dangers of such a course
would be injury to the "Cause of Truth", opening themselves to the charge of being "party men", and running
the risk of losing those liberties which they might
otherwise enjoy. (79)

It was not until early 1779 that the tax issue
brought the Quakers into a confrontation with the government. In January the selectmen of Northbridge in Worcester County asked the General Court whether they
could tax Friends to hire substitutes for military
service. They received an affirmative reply, and thereafter the town records contain frequent mention of a
"Quaker tax". (80)

When the matter came before New England Yearly
Meeting at its sessions in June 1779, it decided that
no Friend could pay taxes wholly for war. Since there
was considerable disagreement as to the payment of mixed
taxes, no position was taken on that point. (81)

The outstanding proponent of the extreme position
was Job Scott of Portsmouth, Rhode Island. He wrote
"A Truly Conscientious Scruple", arguing against paying
mixed as well as military taxes, and be submitted it
to the Philadelphia Meeting for Sufferings for their
opinion. Although the latter decided not to publish
it since they doubted that it represented the attitude
of the Society in general, it directed the pamphlet's
preservation in the Meeting's records "as a testimony
to posterity". (82)

In his treatise Scott discussed the contention

233

that every citizen should bear his share of the expenses
of the government from which he receives advantages,
and he argued that the citizen can do this only as long
as the conduct of the authorities did not contravene
the precepts of the Gospel. Although Scott desired the
protection of his rights and privileges as far as was
consistent with the Christian spirit, "be it far from
our hearts", he charged, "to desire or consent they
should be defended by the promiscuous shedding of human
Blood in War". (83)

Although the New England Meeting for Sufferings did
not accept Job Scott's extreme position, it advised
the monthly meetings that it was inconsistent with the
testimony of the Society for any Friends to pay taxes
"expressly or especially for the support of war, whether
called for in money, provisions, clothing, or otherwise".
If instances of disregard for this advice arose, the
offenders were to be disowned. (84)

In both Massachusetts and Rhode Island war taxes
were levied on the Quakers, usually by way of distraint
since the Friends could not pay them. In 1780 the
town of Dartmouth reported it had assessed £3011 9s. 11d.
on the Quakers. (85) Two years later the General Court
granted the town of Newbury authority for the town
assessors to levy war taxes on the Friends according
to the law. (86)

Although the universally accepted penalty for refusal to pay war taxes was distraint of property, in
Rhode Island there was one instance of imprisonment
which occurred in the summer of 1781. The Meeting for
Sufferings interceded with both the Governor and the
Council in behalf of the imprisoned Friend. The Council
then requested one of the assemblymen from the prisoner's
home town to bring the matter before the town meeting
there, and that body ordered his liberation. (87)

Throughout the Revolution the New England Friends
refrained strictly from accepting any governmental
position. At the beginning of the war they declared
they could not join in proceedings intended to over-
throw the established authorities, and until the restoration of peace any political activity or acceptance
of a governmental position was viewed in such a light.
Several Friends were consequently dealt with for offenses of this nature.

In April 1778, on a request from Salem Preparative
Meeting, Salem Monthly Meeting stated its opinion

that any Friend accepting public office, especially to assess taxes for the conduct of the war, was no longer to be considered a member in good standing. (88) Three years later Lynn Preparative Meeting reported to the same monthly meeting that one of its members was serving in such a position. The monthly meeting then proceeded to deal with the guilty member who thereupon desisted and submitted a public acknowledgment to the meeting. (89)

A similar instance arose in Rhode Island when Artemus Fish of Portsmouth accepted the position of collector of taxes for the support of the war. After a time he became uneasy over this action and desisted from further collections. Both the monthly and quarterly meetings took the matter up, and it was finally laid before the Meeting for Sufferings. The Meeting for Sufferings responded by issuing a general advice to the Society, cautioning all Friends to

> Strictly adhere to our long professed and
> invariable principle against being con-
> cerned in pulling down and setting up,
> or bringing about Revolutions in outward
> Government, by outward force human Policy
> or contrivances. - And also that they be
> not deceived with the Flattering prospect
> of being cloathed with Secular Authority
> either Legislative, Judicial or Executive,
> knowing these things have a tendency
> rather to brace the mind with Pride and
> expose to various Temptations than humble
> the Creature -. (90)

The question of dealing with and recognizing the new de facto authorities following independence was not a problem for the New England Friends. From the beginning of the conflict they complied with orders and requirements of government officials as long as their conscientious scruples were not affected. It was not until 1780, however, that this recognition was given an official stamp by the Meeting for Sufferings when it recommended that the Friends should recognize the regime which was exercising the powers of government. This action was based on the advice of the seventeenth century Quaker Edward Burrough who exhorted the Friends of his time to "avoid disputing whether the authority itself be absolutely of God or not" and to obey the one acutally in power. (91)

The New England Quakers were as consistent as the
Friends elsewhere in requiring a strict observance of
the peace testimony as interpreted by the official
bodies of the Society. In the course of the war there
were 184 deviations from the peace testimony, of which
162 were ultimately disowned. Ninety-seven occurred in
Massachusetts, 67 in Rhode Island, and 20 in New Hampshire. There were 101 dealings for military service, 48
for sailing on armed vessels and privateers, 16 for
assisting the army, 6 for buying prize goods, and
smaller numbers for miscellaneous offenses such as
hiring substitutes, taking test affirmations of
allegiance, etc. Thirty-eight of those dealt with for
sailing on privateers were from Massachusetts, chiefly
Nantucket and Sandwich Monthly Meetings; the remainder
were from Rhode Island.

The largest number of dealings and disownments
occurred in the first years of the war, 1775-1778. The
high peak for both was in 1777 with 47 dealings and 39
disownments. In the succeeding years the numbers
dropped sharply to only one disownment in 1783.(92) In
the case of Massachusetts it is possible to estimate
the proportion of disownments to the adult male membership of the Society. According to state censuses of
1776 and 1777 there were 1609 male Friends of military
age. Of these, eighty-eight, or about five per cent
were disowned for war related offenses. For New England
as a whole the proportions are approximately 7 3/4% of
male Friends dealt with had 6 3/4% disowned. This reflects the less acute situation faced by Friends in New
England as compared with the difficulties faced by
the Pennsylvania Friends. (93)

The record of sufferings incurred by New England
Friends for maintaining their pacifist testimony as
against the war-related demands of the state is not
complete, since most of the accounts for Massachusetts
and New Hampshire were either lost or were never made.
The accounts from Rhode Island meetings are fairly
complete, and these with the reports from two monthly
meetings in Massachusetts give some basis for conclusions in this connection.

The total amount of sufferings recorded was
₤11,397 18s. 10d.; for Massachusetts ₤1580 6s. 1½d.,
and for Rhode Island ₤9817 12s. 8½d. Distraints for
non-payment of taxes accounted for ₤3096 17s. ½d.,
and for militia fines ₤6189 12s. 5½d. The remaining
₤2111 9s. 4d. was in the nature of army supplies and
other unspecified items. Militia fines reported were

confined to Rhode Island and were only £100 annually
unitl 1777. In that year, following the enactment of
a more stringent militia law, they rose to £1944 14s.,
and in 1778 to £3594 10s. ½d. In 1779 they dropped to
£516 7s., and after 1780, when they stood at £42 12s.,
none were recorded.

Recorded distraints for non-payment of taxes were
also greater in Rhode Island than in Massachusetts,
being £2074 12s. 3d. as compared with £1022 4s. 9½d.
In both states the largest amounts were taken in 1781,
£1243 2s. and £677 6s. 4d. respectively. No sufferings
are recorded after that date for Massachusetts and none
after 1782 for Rhode Island.

The hardest years of the war were 1778 and 1781 when
the total sufferings reached £3709 9s. ½d. and £2032
10s. 4d. respectively . The former year was the most severe
for Rhode Island and the latter for Massachusetts, and
in both cases militia legislation was the primary
cause. (94)

In commenting on their lot during the war, the New
England Quakers informed the London Friends in their
Yearly Meeting epistle of 1780:

> Sufferings on account of our testimony
> against war have been various and consider-
> able the last year, some have been for a
> short time imprisoned, and many distraints
> have been made for taxes and other demands
> for the support of that antichristian
> practice...(95)

Despite the difficulties undergone by the New
England Quakers, the extent and severity of their
sufferings were not comparable with those of the
Friends in Pennsylvania. The New Englanders maintained
good relations with their respective governments and
communities throughout the war. Local officials who
prosecuted Friends often acted as they thought the law
required and were obviously unhappy in doing so. In
such cases the central authorities usually exhibited
commendable understanding and leniency in granting
appropriate remedies.

(1) Proceedings of the General Assembly of the Colony of Rhode Island, in the archives of the Secretary of State, Providence, R.I., v.9,431. Rhode Island Quakers in the American Revolution (Providence, 1976) gives a brief account of the experiences of Rhode Island Quakers at that time with excerpts from monthly meeting and the New England Meeting for Sufferings minute books.

(2) N.E.M.f.S., Min., v.1,49,52-53. The Friends concerned were John Goddard, William Robinson and Thomas Robinson.

(3) Proceedings of the General Assembly of Rhode Island, 1777-1779, in the archives of the Secretary of State, Providence, R.I., v.10,55-56; Arnold, Samuel Greene, History of the State of Rhode Island and Providence Plantations (2 vols., Providence, 1894), v.2, 414-415.

(4) Acts and Laws of His Majesty's Colony of Rhode Island (Newport, 1745), 234; Mekeel, Arthur J., "New England Quakers and Military Service", loc.cit., 247-248.

(5) Acts and Resolves of the Rhode Island Assembly, December Session, 1776 (Providence, 1777), 39.

(6) Rhode Island State Records (R.I.Col.Rec., v.8-10), v.8,122.

(7) N.E.M.f.S., Min., v.1,61-62.

(8) R.I.St.Rec., v.8,204-205.

(9) N.E.M.f.S., Min., v.1,67.

(10) R.I.M.M., Min., 1773-1790,102-103.

(11) N.E.M.f.S., Min., v.1,74-75, post 12. The accounts of sufferings of the New England Friends are recorded in the rear of the Meeting's minutes, v.1, paged from back to front and such references are indicated by post.

(12) Ibid., 75.

(13) Ibid.,76; Jabez C. Bowen to Moses Brown, June 13, 1778, Moses Brown Pap., v.2, 149.

(14) Jabez C. Bowen to Moses Brown, June 13, 1778, loc. cit.

(15) Moses Brown to Jabez C. Bowen, July 1, 1778, Moses Brown Pap., v.2, 92.

(16) Moses Brown to Sarah Dillwyn, Dec.8,1778, in ibid., 83.

(17) N.E.M.f.S., Min., v.1,101-102.

(18) Reed, Silvanus, "Orderly Book of Adjutant Silvanus Reed", Collections of the New Hampshire Hist.Soc., v.9 (1889), 364-414.

(19) Ibid., 373.
(20) Moses Brown to Jabez C. Bowen, July 1, 1778, loc. cit. Moses Brown was clerk of the New England Meeting for Sufferings for the years 1779-1783. (Worrall, New England Quakerism, 123.)
(21) N.E.M.f.S. to Phil.M.f.S., Aug.28,1778,N.E.M.f.S., Min., v.1,88.
(22) A List of Persons taken from the Town of Newport... and put on board the Lord Sandwich, in the archives of the Newport Hist.Soc.
(23) R.I.M.M., Min., 1773-1790,114-115.
(24) N.E.M.f.S., Min., v.1,116-117. The Friends involved were Aaron Chase and Thomas Gould,Jr.
(25) Moses Brown to ?, March 9,1780, Moses Brown Pap., v.2,23. The Friends in this instance were Thomas Robinson and Giles Hoover.
(26) Moses Brown to M. Robinson, Nov.16,1779,in ibid.,16.
(27) Moses Brown to ?, March 9,1780, loc.cit.
(28) Stiles, Ezra, Diary, v.2,454.
(29) N.E.M.f.S., Min., v.1,159-160.
(30) Acts and Resolves Public and Private, of the Province of the Massachusetts Bay, 1692-1780(21 vols., Boston, 1869-1922),v.4,620;v.8,88,460,1123.
(31) Ibid., v.19,558-559; Mass.Arch.,in the old State House, Boston, v.182,28-29.
(32) Acts and Res., v.19,691;Mass. Arch., v.182,29.
(33) Acts and Res., v.19,725.
(34) Mass. Arch., v.161, passim; Mekeel,loc.cit., 259-260.
(35) Acts and Res., v.19,755,762; Mass.Arch., v.182,10; v.222,106-107;v.211,87,87a.
(36) Mass. Arch., v.223,201;Acts and Res., v.19,879.
(37) Acts and Res., v.20,102-104.
(38) Mass. Arch., v.183,263-265,267.
(39) Ibid., v.174,342-344.
(40) N.E.M.f.S. to Phil.M.f.S., Aug 28,1778,loc.cit., 89.
(41) Swanzey M.M., Min., 1732-1788, June 1, 1778; N.E. M.f.S., Min., v.1,87,91,93.
(42) N.E.M.f.S., Min., v.1,110;Acts and Res., v.21, 38-44; Mass. Arch., v.185,383-384.
(43) Mass. Arch., v.185,385-386.
(44) Acts and Res., v.21,519-524,568-572.
(45) "The Annals of the Town of Sandwich", in The History of Cape Cod, ed. Frederick Freeman, (2 vols., Boston, 1862), v.1, 127.
(46) Ibid., 127n.;Mass. Arch., v.202.348.
(47) Mass. Arch., v.229,415.
(48) Ibid., v.202,345-346;v.176,522-523;N.E.M.f.S., Min., v.1,130. In the town of Dartmouth in Bristol County one third of the men of military age were Quakers.

(See Greene, Evarts B., and Harrington, Virginia
D., _American Population Before the Federal Census
of 1790_, New York, 1932 ,35.)

(49) Mass. Arch., v.176,253-255. The Quakers in each
town sent a petition, those from Yarmouth and
Sandwich, from which the above quotation is taken,
being identical.

(50) Ibid.,v.171,250. In Barnstable County one-fourth
of the men eligible for military service in the
town of Falmouth and thirteen per cent in the town
of Sandwich were Quakers. (See Greene and Harrington, op.cit., 35.)

(51) Ibid., 248-249.

(52) _Acts and Laws Passed by the Great and General Court_
of Massachusetts (Boston,1781),chap.21,32-43.

(53) _Acts and Res._, v.5,479-484.

(54) Ibid., 483.

(55) Ibid.,770-772.

(56) N.E.M.f.S., Min., v.1,79.

(57) Ibid., 81-82;Swanzey M.M., Min., 1732-1788,May 4,
1778.

(58) Starbuck, Alexander, _The History of Nantucket, Island
and Town_ (Boston, 1924),196.

(59) _Journals of the Cont. Cong._, v.1,70-71;_Amer. Arch._,
4th Ser., v.3,1495. See above p. 122.

(60) Guba, Emil Frederick, _Nantucket Odyssey_ (Waltham,
Mass., 1965), 150,152.

(61) Rotch, William, "An Autobigraphical Memoir of
William Rotch", _New England Historical and Geneological Register_, v.31,263.

(62) Ibid.

(63) Rotch, William, _Memorandum Written by William Rotch
in the Eightieth Year of His Age_ (Boston, 1916),8-14.

(64) Ibid., 14-15.

(65) Petition of Thomas Jenkins, Mass. Arch., 1779;
Rotch, _Memorandum_, 16,18-19,21.

(66) Guba, op.cit., 156.

(67) _Documents and Records Relating to the State of
New Hampshire, 1776-1783_ (ed.Nathaniel Boulton,
I.W. Hammond, and A. S. Batchellor, 34 vols.,
Nashua, Manchester, Concord, 1867-1933),v.8,_passim_;
Mekeel,loc.cit.,274.

(68) Hammond, Otis Grant, _Tories of New Hampshire in
the War of the Revolution_ (Concord,1917),6.

(69) The figures for the various towns are given in
_Miscellaneous Revolutionary Documents of New
Hampshire_ (Prov. and St. Pap., v.30, Manchester,
1910),41,76,106,130,156; Hammond,op.cit.,7.

(70) _Documents and Records Relating to the Province of
New Hampshire from 1764-1776_ (Prov.and St. Pap.,

v.7), 124.

(71) Misc. Rev. Doc of N.H., 57.

(72) Laws of New Hampshire, 1776-1784, (Laws of New Hampshire, ed. A. S. Batchellor and H. H. Metcalf, 10 vols., Manchester and Bristol, v.4),39-40.

(73) Journals of the House of Representatives of the General Court of the Colony of Massachusetts Bay, 1775-1776 (Boston,1776),154;Moses Brown to John Pemberton, April 30, 1776,Pem.Pap.,v.29,32.

(74) Moses Brown to John Pemberton, April 30,1776,loc. cit. In this letter Moses Brown told of his experience when distributing relief for the re- fugees from besieged Boston. At one town he was giving silver currency to the selectmen, but on hearing that the town had recived orders from the Assembly to collect hard money for the use of the army in Canada, he felt a "stop" in his mind and paid the remaining amount in paper currency.

(75) Epistle of Rhode Island Quarterly Meeting, Jan.8-9, 1778, So.Kingston Pap.

(76) Sandwich M.M., Min., 1755-1795,Aug.7,1778.

(77) Moses Brown to John Pemberton, Oct.21,1778,Pem. Pap.v.32,115.

(78) Ibid.

(79) Ibid.

(80) Mass. Arch., v.183,354; Thurston, John R., "North- bridge", in History of Worcester County, ed. D. H. Hurd (2 vols., Philadelphia, 1889),v.1,437.

(81) Scott, Job, Journal of the Life of Job Scott (New York, 1797), 71.

(82) N.E.M.f.S., Min., v.1,133,135,154; Moses Brown to Anthony Benezet, Oct.2,1780 (copy of the original letter is in QCHC).

(83) Scott,Job, A Truly Conscientious Scruple, in QCHC.

(84) N.E. M.f.S., Min., v.1, 138;R.I.M.M., Min., 1773- 1790,177-178.

(85) Mass. Arch., v.239,543.

(86) Ibid., v.187,302,321.

(87) N.E. M.f.S., Min., v.1, 158,160,161.

(88) Salem M.M., Min., 1677-1788,217.

(89) Ibid., Aug.9,Sept.13,Nov.8,1781,June 6,Nov.7,1782.

(90) R.I.M.M., Min., 1773-1790,184;N.E.M.f.S., Min., v.1,161-163.

(91) James, Sydney V., A People Among Peoples(Cambridge, 1963),246.

(92) Acoakset M.M., Min., 1766-1787,77-144 passim; Dartmouth M.M., Min., 1770-1792,82-233 passim: Dover M.M., Min., 1750-1784, 117-172 passim: Falmouth M.M., Min., 1772-1857,7,10,14; Greenwich M.M., Min., 1751-1806,58-103 passim; Hampton M.M.,

Min., 1758-1804,111-152 _passim_; Nantucket M.M.,
Min., 1772-1789, 68-202 _passim_; Pembroke M.M., Min.,
1741-1801,Jan.1,1777-March 7,1781 _passim_; R.I.M.M.,
Min., 1773-1790,54-213 _passim_: R.I. M.M., Records
and Testimonies and Denials, 1718-1827,53-72 _passim_:
Salem M.M., Min., 1677-1788,204-210 _passim_,Aug.8,
Sept. 10,1782; Sandwich M.M., Min., 1755-1795,Feb.7,
1777-Oct.8,1782 _passim_:Smithfield M.M., Min., 1763-
1780, 117-264 _passim_; _ibid_., 1780-1801,292,299,
308; So. Kingston M.M., Min., 1773-1789,55-184
passim;Swanzey M.M., Min., 1732-1788,Oct.3,1775-
April 5,1779 _passim_.

(93) The census figures on which these estimates are
based were taken in 1776 and 1777 (See Greene and
Harrington, _op.cit_., 31-40.) Since the census
of 1777 did not give figures for Quaker males on
Nantucket eligible for military service as it did
for the other counties of Massachusetts, one must
estimate on the basis of the 1776 figures which
give a total white population of 4412. If
according to the testimony before Parliament
concerning Nantucket cited above four-fifths of
the population was Quaker this would give a figure
of 3500 Quakers. A more conservative figure of
3000 would give 600 male Friends of military age,or
a total of 1609 Friends in this category in
Massachusetts. There is a possibility of a fairly
wide margin of error in all the early census figures
and therefore all computations are only approximate
estimates.

(94) Accounts of the sufferings of the New England
Friends are in N.E.M.f.S., Min., v.1, _post_,_passim_.

(95) N.E.Y.M., Min., v.1,349-350.

Chapter XIV

NEW YORK

Throughout most of the Revolutionary War the British
were in possession of New York City and its environs on
Long Island and neighboring Westchester County. Effective
control of the mainland as far north as Lake Champlain
was in the hands of the Americans. The Quakers therefore
lived under two governments, and their attitude toward
each during the conflict is a good criterion of the
sincerity of their pacifist principles.

On the American side there were the same problems
of military service, affirmations of allegiance, and
taxation as elsewhere. Before the War, the Quakers in
New York had been subject to certain fines in lieu of
militia service which were usually collected by way of
distraint. (1) Early in 1775 the legislature debated
the enactment of a new militia law. A committee of
the Meeting for Sufferings interviewed the Speaker of
the House who promised to use his endeavors to obtain
exemptions for the Friends. The law as finally passed
provided that members of the Society of Friends who
produced a certificate of membership signed by six or
more members of their meeting would be subject to
military service only in case of alarm, invasion, or
insurrection. (2) A few months later, after the outbreak of the war, the Provincial Congress passed a new
law with substantially the same provisions. (3)

When the military campaigns reached New York in the
summer of 1776, several Quakers were drafted in Flushing
and New York City. Only one of them was taken to the
guard house for refusing to serve, hire a substitute,
or pay a fine, and he was soon afterward released. (4)
A similar instance of tolerance for the Quaker position
was shown when the military authorities issued a general
order requiring all the inhabitants of the combat zone
to give bond for security that they would not allow their
cattle to fall into the hands of the British. The Meeting
for Sufferings declared that no Friend could consistently
comply with this order, but there is no record of any
prosecution of the Quakers. (5)

As the war progressed and military needs became

243

greater, many people came to resent the Quakers' exemptions and felt they should bear some part of the responsibility for the common defense, if only in a pecuniary way. There was also the apprehension that able-bodied men were evading their responsibilities by taking illegal advantage of the law as it then stood. In the winter of 1776-1777 the Committee of Safety of Westchester County resolved that the legislature should levy an assessment on the Friends which would be "adequate to the Burthens that Other Members of the State bear in Maintaining their Rights". (6)

When the new state constitution was drawn up in the spring of 1777, the section on the militia provided for exemption for the Quakers from military service, in lieu of which a money payment was required. (7) Accordingly, in July 1777 the militia law was amended by providing that in future drafts all persons subject to military service, exempts included, should be enrolled by the captain in whose beat they resided. Those exempted from acutal service were to be assessed in proportion to the value of that service and their estates. (8) This policy was thereafter followed, and acts of March and April 1778 passed to raise additional forces incorporated such provisions. (9)

The militia law of April 1778 provided permanently for this solution of the Quaker problem. It exempted from personal military service all males between the ages of sixteen and fifty-five "who in judgment of law are or shall be of the people called Quakers". In return for this exemption such persons were to pay ₤10 annually, plus an additional ten pounds yearly when the militia would be called into service. The captain of every beat was to give lists of Friends under his jurisdiction to the supervisor of his district who in turn was to make out separate tax lists for the Quakers. The special levies were to be collected by distraint if not paid, and in default of goods or chattels the offender was to be lodged in the county jail until the required payment was made. (10) In October 1779 these fines were increased five-fold. (11)

The tax lists of Westchester County for the winter of 1778-1779 give good evidence that these laws were put into effect. The Friends were assessed separately, and the following sums were levied: Manor of Phillipsburgh, ₤1680; town of Bedford, ₤300; town of Salem, ₤240; town of North Castle, ₤1980. (12) Succeeding militia laws changed the fines somewhat, that of March 1780 raising them to ₤80 annually, and that of

244

April 1782 returning to the £10 levies. (13)

Only one instance of imprisonment for refusal to do military service is reported. Early in 1779 Purchase Monthly Meeting learned that several of its younger members were in prison for this reason. When approached on the matter the officer in charge indicated his willingness to release the prisoners when presented with proof of their membership in the Society of Friends, and the Meeting immediately took steps to comply with this requirement. (14)

The problem of affirmations of allegiance seems to have been particularly acute in Westchester County because of the proximity of the British lines and the considerable number of British sympathizers who lived there. In December 1776 the Provincial Congress directed that an oath or affirmation of allegiance be administered to all males sixteen years and over in the county. (15) Subsequently a Friend from Oblong Monthly Meeting refused to take the affirmation. The meeting then sent a deputation to interview the Provincial Congress which accepted the Quakers' assurance that they entertained no designs against the government in refusing to take the prescribed affirmation. However, the Congress rejected a request to suspend temporarily the tendering of the affirmation of allegiance to the Friends until they could consider the matter in their next quarterly meeting. The rejection was based on the ground that it would be "an unjustifiable and odious distinction between those of their constituents... who were of the denomination called Quakers, and their constituents of all other denominations in Westchester County". (16)

The Friend in question finally took the affirmation but afterward apologized to the monthly meeting for his error in doing so. Meanwhile the monthly meeting sent up a request for the judgment of the yearly meeting on the matter. The reply of the yearly meeting was that any Friends should be disowned who complied with tenders of affirmations of allegiance "except they manifest unfeigned repentance". (17)

Toward the end of the war this question again caused some difficulty. In 1783 the Meeting for Sufferings learned that some Friends had subscribed the affirmation of allegiance on the basis that the conclusion of peace with England had sufficiently settled matters to justify such action. When this case came before the yearly meeting, it reiterated its former

245

judgment and cautioned all members against taking the
affirmation, since they could "give no greater security
to any government, than by a quiet peaceable demeanor,
consistent with (their) principles". (18)

The Continental currency was also a source of
difficulty for the New York Quakers. In December 1776
a committee of the Provincial Congress, appointed to
try persons considered to be inimical to the American
cause, ordered Jacob Deane, Solomon Haight, and John
Hallock, all of Dutchess County, to be sent out of the
state for declining to pass Continental bills. The
first two were to be confined at Exeter, New Hampshire,
and the last at Litchfield, Connecticut. (19) When
the New England Meeting for Sufferings intervened in
behalf of the prisoners at Exeter, it was informed
they would be released only by order of those who had
originally committed them. On being advised of the
situation by the New England Friends, Nine Partners
Monthly Meeting of which the imprisoned Quakers were
members evidently petitioned for the necessary orders,
for in April 1777 Jacob Deane returned a certificate
of membership which had been sent to him. (20)

Because of the division of the state into two
warring camps, religious visitations and attendance at
yearly and quarterly meetings often necessitated
passage through the lines of both contestants. Since
the Quakers were constantly subject to suspicion because
of their neutral position, they were occasionally charged
with inimical designs as a result of these journeys.
The Yearly Meeting of 1777 was the first one held after
the British occupation of New York City, and the Friends
from the mainland had to pass the lines to attend. On
their return, six Quakers from Dutchess County were
arrested by the Commissioners for Detecting and
defeating Conspiracies at Poughkeepsie. At the direction
of the Committee of Safety they were confined in the
Fleet Prison at Esopus Creek at their own expense until
further orders. A petition and several letters, one
from Melancthon Smith, a former member of the Provincial
Congress, finally persuaded the Committee of Safety to
order their release after taking the oath of allegiance
to the state and paying all fees and expenses occasioned
by their imprisonment. (21) Although the Friends informed the Council they could not comply with these
conditions, they were soon allowed to return home.

In June 1778 the difficulties of the Friends were
increased by the passage of a law intended to facilitate

the apprehension of suspected persons. It empowered
the Commissioners for Detecting and Defeating Conspiracies
to tender the oath or affirmation of allegiance to anyone believed "to have influence sufficient to do mischief".
Those who declined to comply with this requirement were
to be sent within the enemy's lines. (22)

Subsequently several Friends were called before
the Commissioners. They refused to take the required
affirmation, and some of them suffered the prescribed
penalty despite petitions in their behalf. (23) Not
until 1784 was the Meeting for Sufferings finally
successful in persuading the legislature to allow two
of the men who had been exiled to Long Island to return
home. (24)

Throughout the remainder of the war the authorities
kept a watchful eye on the activities of the Friends.
In January 1781 General Heath ordered that only those
Friends who had recommendations from Captain Honeywel, who
was in charge of the Westchester County area, should
be allowed to attend the quarterly meeting at Harrison's
Purchase. (25)

Several months later some Friends who attended
the Yearly Meeting of 1781 in New York City were accused
of having carried papers of a political nature and
carrying some people through the lines under a plain
cloak. On invesitgating this report, both Oblong and
Nine Partners Monthly Meetings found it fallacious, and
two Quakers who had been imprisoned on this charge were
soon released. (26)

Towards the end of the war several Friends in New
York City requested the American authorities through
the intermediation of Purchase Quarterly Meeting for
permission to pass through the lines to make a religious
visit to the mainland. Their request was denied, but
four of them made the journey as far north as Hoosack
in western Massachusetts without the necessary permits.
On their return journey they were arrested at Pines
Bridge in Westchester County, and General Heath sent
the prisoners to Governor Clinton with an accompanying
letter in which he declared that the Quakers

> ...alwaies express much inoffensiveness -
> and that they do not meddle with Politicks
> but I have known some of them to collect
> very good Intelligence if they will do it
> on our side they will on the other. (27)

247

Governor Clinton turned the suspected Quakers over
to the Commissioners for Detecting and Defeating
Conspiracies and replied to General Heath:

> The Quakers have already given us so
> much Trouble & have it in their Power
> to do us so much in Mischief under aspicious
> Cloaks of Religion that some Means must be
> fallen upon to prevent the Intercourse
> with the Enemy which their Attendance
> at their Quarterly & Monthly Meetings
> occasion & perhaps a confinement of the
> present Gentry or a prevention of their
> Return to Long Island may have the desired
> Effect. (28)

As the war drew to a conclusion, the problem of
Friends participating in affairs of government again
arose. It may well be that with the cessation of active
warfare in the area, sympathy with the American cause
and the conviction that the new regime was permanent
caused some Friends to believe the way was now open
for such action. Nevertheless the official position of
the Society had not changed, and in May 1781 the
Committee of Sufferings of Purchase Quarterly Meeting
informed the subordinate meetings that "in the present
Commotions of Publick Affairs friends being in any ways
active in Government is inconsistent with our Principles". (29) The monthly meetings were instructed to
deal with those members who disobeyed this injunction
by attending town meetings or allowing such meetings to
be held in their homes. Only by completely abstaining
from such proceedings could their testimony "against
Wars and Commotions in every Respect...be Maintained
and Supported Inviolate". (30)

Although in general the Quakers fared somewhat
better in the British controlled areas of New York City
and environs, including the western part of Long Island,
they also suffered the consequences of refusal to comply
with military orders and requisitions. The first
encounter with the British authorities occurred in
January 1777. At that time Governor Tryon informed
some of the leading Friends of the displeasure of his
government over the participation of several Friends in
revolutionary activities, and he proposed that the Quakers
raise a sum of money to furnish the British troops with
clothing. In reply the Meeting for Sufferings presented
an address to the Governor, explaining that the Friends
referred to had acted contrary to the advice and principles of the Society. Moreover, the Society must

reject his request since compliance with it would be
a denial of its "Religious Testimony against War &
Fightings". (31)

A chief source of difficulty for the Quakers was
the occupation of their meeting-houses by elements of
the British army. Soon after the arrival of the King's
forces, they requisitioned the meeting-house in Flushing
for the storage of military supplies and the housing of
soldiers. The meeting-house suffered considerable
damage, and in May 1778 the Meeting for Sufferings, on
petitioning the military authorities in New York, eventually succeeded in obtaining its return. (32)

Six months later, in November 1778, the conversion
of the cellar of the new meeting-house on Pearl Street
into a military storage depot led to a long controversy.
The Friends in charge of the property accepted rent
for its use. The Meeting for Sufferings considered
such action inconsistent with Quaker principles and
directed the return of the money. When the Friends
responsible refused to comply, the matter was laid before the Yearly Meeting which decided to refer the
question to Philadelphia Yearly Meeting. It sent a
delegation, of which Elias Hicks was a member, to present
the problem to the Pennsylvania Friends at their Yearly
Meeting in 1779. The latter declared that the money
should be returned and issued an advice to the Friends
in general not to rent or hire out their meeting-houses
for any military purposes whatsoever. (33)

New York Yearly Meeting then appointed a committee
to refund the money to the commissary office of the
British army. When the refund was rejected, an address
was sent to the Commissary General, explaining that the
acceptance of the rent had infringed upon "The Testimony
We as a People believe ourselves called to bear to the
World against Wars and fighting". It requested him
to "undo the Matter if it can be done in such manner,
as to give Relief to our Minds and clear the Society
from an Imputation of an inconsistent Conduct with our
Peaceable Principles". The Commissary General was
unable to grant this petition, since the accounts and
receipts for the date of the transaction in question had
already been sent to England. (34)

The yearly meeting committee next appealed to
the London Meeting for Sufferings for its assistance in
the affair. (35) After some negotiations with the
English authorities, the Meeting finally paid the money
to the Exchequer and received a "Tally" with the follow-

ing inscription, approximately duplicating the entry in
the accounts of the Exchequer:

> Paid by the Society of the People Called
> Quakers, of New York in America, by the
> Hands of Daniel Mildred, being the Money they
> had received for Rent of their Meeting
> House, which had been appropriated for the
> use of the Army, as such they could not
> retain it Consistently with their Religious
> Testimony against War. (36)

In 1781 and 1782 the meeting-houses in New York
and at Flusing and Cow Neck on Long Island were requisitioned by the British army. The Friends remonstrated
with the Commander-in-Chief and Governor Robertson and
requested the restoration of the houses. The authorities
refused to return the first two because they were in
the public service, and both of them remained in the
hands of the British until their departure in 1783.
The Cow Neck meeting-house was, however, soon relin-
quished. (37)

The Quakers were also very careful to refrain from
assisting the British army in any direct or indirect
manner. In July 1778 the Meeting for Sufferings issued
an advisory epistle to the subordinate meetings, cautioning them against allowing army horses to be quartered
on them, receiving pay for forage taken from them, or
carting any military supplies.(38) In November 1779
the committee on suffering cases of Westbury Monthly
Meeting leared that some Friends had disobeyed these
injunctions by carting supplies for the army. In order
to prevent suffering for those whose conscience forbade
them to comply with demands of that nature, the committee
declared this action inconsistent with Friends' testimonies. (39)

The position of the Quakers on this point was made
more difficult the following year. In July 1780 Governor
Robertson issued a general order calling on the inhabitants of Long Island to furnish wood for winter fuel to
the barracks yards in New York. Queens County was to contribute 4500 cords, and teams were to be requisitioned
to cart it. (40) A subsequent order in August promised
that those persons giving two-thirds of their hay to
the army would receive certificates for the hay and its
cartage, the remaining third to be free of all military
claims. (41) In September Westbury Quarterly Meeting
Committee of Sufferings advised both the Flushing and

Westbury Monthly Meetings that no Friends could obey
these orders or accept pay for any articles which were
requisitioned. (42)

Despite this injunction several deviations on
these counts occurred, for three years later Westbury
Monthly Meeting requested the yearly meeting's advice
on disciplining the offenders. The yearly meeting
replied that its members should "be careful to cherish
in themselves, and one in another, their Tender Scruples
against contributing or in any wise giving countenance to
the spirit of War". (43)

It was not until toward the end of the war that the
British made any military demands on the Quakers, and
these were never for active service. In January 1780,
at the request of some inhabitants of the city that they
be armed and embodied, the military authorities ordered
all citizens between the ages of seventeen and sixty to
be enrolled by districts and to obey the orders of the
captains of their respective companies under pain of
imprisonment or banishment. The Quakers and firemen
were exempted, although directed to "exert themselves
in case of emergency". (44)

Shortly afterward the Friends in the city were asked
to form themselves into five classes and assume responsibility for the city watch. They refused to do this
or to submit a list of their members in the city to the
Governor as requested. On the occasion of a second order
that Friends together with the Firemen's Marine Society
take over the watch, the Committee of Sufferings advised
the monthly meeting in New York that "Friends complying
therewith in aiding in or doing something in lieu of
Military Servce" were not supporting their testimony
against war. Before obeying any such demands in the
future they should first refer the matter to their meetings. (45)

Because New York City was the administrative center
of British operations in America, the Quakers there
were in a position to be of assistance to Friends whom
the British captured and brought to the city. The first
case of this kind was that of Nathaniel Delano of Nantucket who sailed for the coast of Brazil in the summer
of 1775 as master of a whaling vessel. The British
seized his ship in the Carribbean and took him to Antigua.
On being released he went to St. Eustatia and there
embarked for Nantucket. He was soon captured again and
this time taken to New York and confined on Staten Island.

251

When his plight became known, his brother set out from Nantucket accompanied by another Friend, carrying a letter of introduction from the New England Meeting for Sufferings to the Friends in New York. The American authorities refused to allow him to pass the lines into the city, and Delano then appealed to the Friends on Long Island to assist his brother. The latter's discharge followed soon afterward. (46)

A similar affair occurred in 1778. When the British raided New Bedford they took several Quakers prisoner, all but one of whom, Elihu Mosher, obtained their freedom by stating their peaceable principles to the commander. Mosher was carried to New York, and Moses Brown solicited the aid of Westbury Monthly Meeting in his behalf. Although the intercession of the Monthly Meeting was unsuccessful, Mosher was soon released through an exchange of prisoners. He then found himself without money for his return home, and the Westbury Friends gave him six pounds for the journey. (47) Somewhat later Uriah Ray of Nantucket was also captured at sea and brought to New York. He soon died of the smallpox, and Westbury Monthly Meeting paid the cost of his nursing. (48)

In assisting such cases, the New York Quakers discovered that a number of their fellow members were engaged in activities contrary to their religious principles. In September 1781 the Committee of Sufferings of Westbury Quarterly Meeting informed the New England Meeting for Sufferings that seafaring Friends often indulged in the practice of clearing vessels for certain ports and then sailing to different destinations, sometimes under the pretence of being captured. Many of the offenders were from New England who, when in distress, turned to the New York Quakers for aid. The New York Friends said they were reluctant to appeal to the authorities in behalf of such persons for fear of weakening themselves "in the eyes of those, whom we have to make application to when those who Honestly suffer may stand in need of our assistance". On receipt of this epistle, the New England Meeting for Sufferings sent copies of it to the subordinate monthly meetings, charging them to consider its contents seriously. (49)

From a pecuniary standpoint the total sufferings of the Friends in New York were £13,280 19s. 9d., of which £998 5s. 7d. were taken by the British in and around New York City for the use of the army. On the American side the sufferings were chiefly for military fines and taxes. In Westchester County the property losses of the Friends amounted to £1721 11s. 3d., in Dutchess

County £5792 2s. 1d., and in the district around Saratoga £4104 9s. 10d., part of the last sum being taken in supplies by the American army. (50)

Toward the end of the war, one of the chief causes of distraint was a Black Rate, levied by a Retaliating Act for the purpose of recompensing Americans for goods stolen by the British and their sympathizers. This tax seems to have been especially onerous in Westchester County, probably because of the depredations of British raiding parties known as Cowboys in the area between the lines. (51) In the northern part of the state the activities of the armies at the time of Burgogyne's campaign caused extensive losses to Friends there. (52)

In the regions of military action the Quakers generally refused to leave their homes and continued to attend their meetings for worship as usual. In 1777 a notable example of this occurred at Saratoga, now Easton, in Washington County northeast of Albany. Toward the conclusion of one of their meetings for worship there appeared

> ...a party of Indians with two Frenchmen,
> and surrounded the House; One of the Indians
> after Looking in, withdrew and beckoned
> with his Hand, upon which a Friend went out,
> and was asked by Signs whether there were
> Soldiers there, the Indians upon being answ-
> ered in the Negative, Shook hands with
> him, and the rest came into the House, they
> were marked, painted and equipt for War.
> And it being about the Conclusion of the Meet-
> ing, they Shook hands with Friends and one
> friend having (a knowledge of) the French
> tongue could confer with them, by the assist-
> ance of the two French Men. When they under-
> stood Friends were at a Religious Meeting,
> they went to one of their Houses,got some
> Victuals, of which a prisoner with them par-
> took, and they quietly departed. (53)

Throughout the war there were 103 deviations for war-related activities and 71 disownments or 9½% and 6½% respectively of Quaker males of military age. Forty-nine dealings were for military service, 24 for assisting the armies, and lesser numbers for taking test affirmations of allegiance, paying a military fine, accepting public office, sailing on privateers, making war materials, dealing in prize good, etc. In British controlled terri-

tory there were 46 dealings, and in American territory
there were 63. Sympathy for the American cause prompted
several Friends to leave New York City and Long Island
to join the patriot forces. (54)

The conduct of the Friends in New York State gives
convincing evidence of the non-loyalist, neutral character of their adherence to the Society's peace testimony.
Whether in the British of the American controlled territory, the Quakers acted unswervingly in conformity with
their religious principles. This is seen not only in
their refusal to obey any requirements in support of
the war, but also in their readiness to intercede with
the authorities on either side for relief from measures
penalizing their pacifist position.

(1) Colonial Laws of New York, from the Year 1664 to the Revolution (5 vols., Albany, 1895-1896), v.3, 1068-1069;v.4, 16-18.

(2) Laws of the Colony of New York, 1774-1775 (Albany, 1888),107;N.Y.M.f.S., Min., v.1,18.

(3) Journals of the Prov. Cong., v.1,115.

(4) William Rickman to John Pemberton, Aug.5,1776, Pem.Pap., v.29,88.

(5) N.Y.M.f.S., Min., v.1,36.

(6) Benedict Carpenter to John Pemberton, Feb.12,1777, Pem.Pap., v.29,140.

(7) Flick, Alexander C., The American Revolution in New York (Port Washington,1967), 92.

(8) Journals of the Prov. Cong., v.1,1023.

(9) Laws of the State of New York, Passed at the Sessions of the Legislature Held in the Years 1777-1801 (5 vols., Albany, 1886-1887),v.1,45-47,54-55.

(10) Ibid., 70-71.

(11) Ibid., 158.

(12) Huffeland, Otto, Westchester County during the American Revolution (Westchester County Hist. Soc. Publications, v.3, White Plains,1926),442.

(13) Laws of the St. of N.Y., v.1, 245-246,449-450.

(14) Purchase M.M., Min., 1772-1785, Feb.11,1779.

(15) John McKesson to the Committee of Westchester,Jan.21, 1777, Calendar of Historical Manuscripts Relating to the Revolution,v.1,604.

(16) Journals of the Prov. Cong., v.1,779;Oblong M.M., Min., 1757-1781,426.

(17) Oblong M.M., op.cit., 428,439;Purchase Q.M., Min., 1745-1793, May 3,1777;N.Y.Y.M., Min.,v.1,94-95.

(18) N.Y.M.f.S., Min., v.1,101;N.Y.Y.M., Min.,v.1,170.

(19) John McKesson to the Committee of Westchester, Jan.21,1777,loc.cit.;Nine Partners M.M., Min., 1769-1779,213.

(20) N.E.M.f.S. to Nine Partners M.M., Dec.9,1776, N.E.M.f.S., Min.,v.1,56-57;Nine Partners M.M., op.cit.,224.

(21) Journals of the Prov. Cong., v.1,972,1027. The Friends involved were Joshua Haight, Benjamin Jacobs, Zaphar Green, Jonathan Dean, Trip Mosher and Paul Upton. See A.Day Bradley's "Friends in the Fleet Prison at Esopus", Quaker History v.55 (1966),114-117 for a full account of this episode. Melancthon Smith was a member of the New York Provincial Congress in 1775 from Dutchess County (Amer. Arch., 4th Ser., v.2,1242).

(22) <u>Minutes of the Commissioners for Detecting and De-
feating Conspiracies in the State of New York</u> (3
vols., Albany, 1909-1910),v.1,18;v.2,784.

(23) Oblong M.M., <u>op.cit</u>., 460,462-464;Purchase M.M.,
<u>op.cit</u>., Jan.14,Feb.11,April 8,Oct.14,1779,July 13,
1780;<u>Journals of the Assembly of the State of
New York,1780</u> (Fishkill,1780),91.

(24) N.Y.M.f.S., Min., v.1,110-111,115. These two Friends
were John Green of Chappaqua and Joseph Mabbett.
See A. Day Bradley's "New York Friends and the
Loyalty Oath of 1776", <u>Quaker History</u>,v.57 (1968),
112-113.

(25) General Heath to Major Woodbridge, Jan.28,1781,
William Heath Papers,v.23,262 (in the Massachusetts
Hist. Soc.).

(26) Oblong M.M., Min., 1781-1788,July 18,Aug.9,1781;
Nine Partners M.M., Min., 1779-1783,June 22,July 20,
1781.

(27) Purchase Q.M., <u>op.cit</u>., Aug.3,1781;General William
Heath to Governor George Clinton, Nov.7,1781, Heath
Pap., v.22, 68; Public Papers of George Clinton (8
vols., Albany, 1900),v.7,489-490;Colonel Sheldon
to General Heath, Nov.6,1781. William Heath Pap.,
v.22,55.

(28) Governor Clinton to General Heath, Nov.10,1781,
William Heath Pap., v.22,104;<u>Pub.Pap. of George
Clinton</u>,v.7,495-496. The Friends involved in this
case were John Wyllys, Silas Downing, William
Rickman and Gideon Simmons.

(29) Purchase M.M., <u>op.cit</u> ., May 10,1781; Saratoga M.M.,
Min., 1778-1782,41. Because of the difficulty of
communications between the areas under American
and British control, the Meeting for Sufferings
was replaced by two Committees of Sufferings in
May 1779. In May 1782 the Meeting for Sufferings
was again reestablished (N.Y.M.f.S., Min., v.1,71;
N.Y.Y.M., Min., v.1,143,146-148).

(30) <u>Ibid</u>.

(31) Governor Tryon to Lord George Germain, Jan.20,1777,
<u>Doc. Rel. to the Col. Hist. of the State of N.Y.</u>,
v.8,696;N.Y.M.f.S., Min., v.1,41-44;N.Y.Y.M., Min.,
v.1,90,95.

(32) N.Y.M.f.S., Min., v.1,52-55.

(33) <u>Ibid</u>., 65,67,68-69;N.Y.Y.M.,Min., v.1,105,108,
114-115; Phil.Y.M., Min., v.3,425,433,441;Hicks,
Elias, <u>Journal</u> (New York,1832),17.

(34) N.Y.Y.M., Min., v.1,123-125,142.

(35) London M.f.S., Min., v.36 (1780-1783),June 21,
1782.

(36) N.Y.Y.M., Min., v.1,142,160,177. For a more extensive

account of this affair see Agnes H. Campbell's
"In This Time of Commotion", Quaker History,v.60
(1971),120-123.

(37) Ibid., 136,153;N.Y.M.f.S., Min.,v.1,74,75,78,82-87.
(38) N.Y.M.f.S., Min.,v.1,58-59.
(39) Westbury M.M., Min., 1767-1782,249.
(40) Riv. Roy. Gaz., July 22,1780,ff.
(41) Ibid., August 5,1780,ff.
(42) Westbury M.M., op.cit.,284;Flushing M.M., Min.,
     1776-1781,71.
(43) N.Y.Y.M., Min., v.1,158-159,165;Purchase Q.M.,
     op.cit.,Aug.1,1783.
(44) Riv. Roy. Gaz., Jan.22,1780,ff.
(45) N.Y.M.f.S., Min., v.1,77-81.
(46) N.E.M.f.S., Min., v.1,55,59.
(47) Ibid., 92-95,97;Westbury M.M., op.cit., 215.
(48) Westbury M.M., op.cit., 223.
(49) Westbury Q.M. Com. of Suf. to New England M.f.S.,
     Sept. 12, 1781, So. Kingston Pap.; Epistle of
     New England M.f.S. to the subordinate monthly
     meetings, Jan.9,1782, in ibid.
(50) The account of these sufferings are in N.Y.M.f.S.,
     Min., v.1, post,passim;Purchase M.M., First
     Register, 1742-1800,passim;Oblong M.M., Record
     Book of Sufferings, 1775-1826, passim; Amawalk
     P.M., Min., 1775-1800,passim, and the various
     quarterly and monthly meeting minute books already
     cited. N.Y.M.f.S., Min., v.1,182-183;Amawalk P.M.,
     op.cit., 19;Bolton, Robert,Jr., A History of the
     County of Westchester (2 vols., New York, 1848),
     v.1,210.
(52) Hall, Rufus, Journal (Byeberry,Pa., 1840),17.
(53) N.Y.M.f.S., Min., v.1,185-186;Hall, Journal,18;
     Hirst, Margaret E., The Quakers in Peace and War
     (New York, 1923),390-391. This account is the
     source of the story "Fierce Feathers" as told in
     L.V. Hodgkin's A Book of Quaker Saints (London,1922),
     chap.15.
(54) Flushing M.M.,Min., 1771-1776,85; ibid., 1776-1781,
     1-83, passim;ibid., 1781-1782,18-57,passim;ibid.,
     1782-1784,38-66, passim;Nine Partners M.M., Min.,
     1769-1779,198-272,passim;ibid., 1779-1783,April 17,
     1779;Nine Partners M.M., Register, 1769-1798,34-105,
     passim;Oblong M.M., Min., 1757-1781,356-486,passim;
     ibid., 1781-1788,69,81;Purchase M.M., Min., 1772-
     1785,May 9,1776-July 10, 1783, passim; Saratoga
     M.M., Min., 1778-1782,6-73, passim; Westbury
     M.M., Min., 1767-1782, 154-313,passim;ibid., 1782-
     1790,14. See Appendix I for method of computation.

Chapter XV

THE QUAKERS IN THE SOUTH

In the southern states the Friends were not the
only sect adhering to pacifist principles. In Maryland,
Virginia and North Carolina there were numerous settlements of Mennonites,Brethren or Dunkards, and Moravians.
All four groups soon found themselves involved in the
issue of war and conscience. Whatever concessions the
Quakers obtained were simultaneously extended to the
other sects, but the Friends supplied the most active
leadership in dealing with the government.

MARYLAND

At the outbreak of the Revolution the position of
the Friends in Maryland was a very favorable one. They
had enjoyed religious freedom for many years, and the
militia laws of the province in no way violated their
principles. The basic law of 1661, continued with some
alterations until the War for Independence, provided
for a militia by enlistment, exempting Quakers and
Moravians from performing any military service.(1)
The Maryland Convention of 1775 continued this policy.
It resolved that all males between the ages of sixteen
and fifty should enroll themselves in some company of
the militia, except persons Who from their religious
principles cannot bear arms in any case". (2)

In 1776 the attitude toward the Friends began to
change. In January of that year the Provincial Convention withdrew the former exemption and required all
males of military age, except ministers of the Gospel
and certain officials, to enroll in the militia under
penalty of a fine of not less than 40s. and not more
than £10 for failure to do so. (3) Another evidence
of this change in attitude was the difficulty experienced
by Thomas Johnson later the same year in procuring from
the Provincial Convention the right of affirmation for
Quakers and other sects with religious scruples against
taking oaths. (4)

Up to this time Maryland Friends had had no query
in their Discipline concerning military service. The

Yearly Meeting of 1776 made an addition to the Fifth
Query, cautioning members against "bearing arms, military Services, or contributing towards the support of
War", and advising the monthly and quarterly meetings
to keep accounts of sufferings resulting from changes
in the militia law. Subsequently Indian Spring Monthly
Meeting appointed a special committee to visit members
who had departed from their religious testimony on war
in joining the military. (5)

In 1777 the legislature passed what became the basic
state militia law throughout the remainder of the war.
This act divided the militia into eight classes, all
males of military age to be enrolled, without any
exception for conscientious objectors. In case of
invasion in Maryland, Virginia, Delaware, or Pennsylvania the Governor and Council were empowered to call
out the militia by draft according to classes. Refusal
to serve, hire a substitute or pay a fine involved
distraint of property for the specified amount or imprisonment not exceeding two months. Failure to attend
muster and reviews incurred a fine of up to 30s. per
day. (6)

Not until April 1778 did the military situation
cause the authorities to resort to this type of draft.
At the time the legislature called for 2900 men for
the Continental Army, the quotas to be raised by draft
if not fulfilled by enlistment. Anyone drafted and
refusing to serve or hire a substitute was to be fined
not exceeding £1000 and not less than £20, this sum
to be collected by distraint if not paid. (7)

Legislation with regard to affirmations of allegiance followed somewhat the same course as the militia
laws, lenient at first and then becoming stricter. In
April 1777 an Act to prevent the growth of Toryism provided that no one could hold office without taking the
oath or affirmation of allegiance to the state or signing
the Association promising to defend it, excepting those
who could not do so for religious reasons. (8) In
December an Act for the better security of the government required all males over eighteen to take the oath
or allegiance, the Quakers, Mennonites, and Dunkards
being allowed to take an affirmation on pain of a treble
tax on their regular assessments. Other provisions
debarred those refusing to subscribe the said test of
allegiance from presecuting suits in courts of law,
practicing law, physic, surgery, or teaching in private
or public schools, from being an apothecary, preaching

259

the Gospel or holding any military or civil offices in the state, or voting in any elections. (9)

This legislation together with the tightening of the military requirements aroused the Quakers to action. At its annual session in 1778 the yearly meeting established a Meeting for Sufferings composed of twelve members from each of the two Quarters, whose duty was "to sit on Cases of difficulty, where the Testimony of Truth may be concerned". (10) Soon afterward both the Meeting for Sufferings and the Quarterly Meeting for the Western Shore declared that no Friends could take test affirmations of allegiance, give in their estates to be taxed, or pay taxes levied for the support of the war. (11)

In September 1778 the Philadelphia Meeting for Sufferings informed Maryland Friends of their remonstrance to the Pennsylvania Assembly on laws infringing freedom of conscience, especially test acts, and suggested that the latter take similar action. (12) The Maryland Meeting for Sufferings adopted the suggestion and presented an Address to the Maryland Assembly in which the Friends stated that it was their "indespensible duty to abstain from all wars and contests" and that they could not, consistently with their religious principles, join with either of the contending parties. Consequently they were unable to take tests of allegiance to either side, for which refusal many of their members had suffered grievously. The Society's repeated cautioning of its members not to join in any plots or conspiracies against the government under which they lived was evidence of the Quakers' sincerity and consistency. In conclusion the Friends solicited the legislature's consideration of their conscientious scruples and urged prompt redress of their grievances. (13)

Although the reputation of the Quakers was at a low ebb in some quarters, there were many people "of the most considerable acco^t" who sympathized with them. (14) The committee presenting the address found many representatives generally favorable to the Friends, who yet felt that a general exemption in their favor would be unprecedented. One argument raised against them was the report that the Philadelphia Quakers had subscribed the test affirmation of allegiance in that state. The committee thereupon secured from John Pemberton a denial that Friends in Philadelphia had taken the test and also procured a copy of a recent Massachusetts militia law exempting Friends. Both items were placed in the hands of some members of the House, but no favorable action followed. (15)

The next year, 1779, the Assembly modified its attitude and in August suspended the collection of treble taxes assessed on non-jurors until November 10. (16) The Friends desired the repeal of the other disabling provisions and presented a second address to the legislature at the following session. This was read before both houses, and a committee of the lower house reported in favor of complete exemption for the Quakers. The majority refused to take such a step at that time, but the following May 1780 the Assembly again suspended treble tax collections on non-jurors until the end of the next session. (17)

In July 1780 the legislature passed an act to secure an extra supply of horses and wagons for the use of the Continental Army. In an attempt to grant some relief to non-jurors, it provided that owners of estates up to Ł4000 who donated a horse with wagon and gears would be exempted from all disabilities and extra taxes, excepting the disbarment from voting and holding office. Non-jurors with estates up to Ł8000 and Ł12,000 respectively were to supply two and three horses and wagons with gears. (18) The Friends felt that compliance with this law would compromise their religious principles, and both Nottingham and Deer Creek Monthly Meetings took steps to prevent deviations on this account. Later reports indicated that few Quakers took advantage of the exemption offered in this act. (19)

As the war drew to a close, the restrictions on non-jurors were gradually removed. In February 1781 the treble taxes on them were completely repealed, and the following January 1782 all the disabilities excepting those referring to voting and holding office were also removed. (20) It was not until 1786, after some controversey between the more liberal House and the conservative Senate, that those provisions were also abolished. The repealing act restored the right to hold office and to vote to those non-jurors who would subscribe to the oath or affirmation of allegiance in the new state constitution. (21)

Aside from the treble taxes mentioned, the Quakers along with the other inhabitants of the state were subject to special war levies from time to time. Because of the refusal of the Friends to pay these taxes,

in December 1777 the legislature directed the commissioners of taxes to collect such unpaid taxes by distraint. (22) In 1778 the Meeting for Sufferings informed
all Friends that giving in accounts for their estates
to be taxed would be a deviation from their religious
principles. In 1780 the yearly meeting repeated this
injunction, warning against the payment of any war
taxes. (23) A number of law suits against Friends
refusing to obey the law followed. This situation was,
however, somewhat alleviated by acts of 1781 and
succeeding years for raising supplies, which exempted
the Quakers from double taxes for declining to give an
account of their property if their refusal proceeded
from conscientious scruples and they were basically
friendly to the government. (24)

    The total of recorded sufferings in Maryland was
Ⱡ7198 2s. 4d., of which Ⱡ2447 12s. 11d. were for taxes
and fines combined, and Ⱡ276 3s. were in goods taken
for the use of the army. In 1777-1778 over two-thirds
of the total specified was for fines, and in 1779-1780
almost one half of the amount specified was for
taxes. (25)

    During the course of the war there were 80 devi-
ations and 65 disownments for war-related activity.
This amounted to approximately 12% and 10% respectively
of the male Quakers eligible for military service. For
military service there were 31 dealings; for taking an
affirmation of allegiance there were 34; and for paying
military fines, 9. The high points for both dealings
and disownments were in 1776 and 1778. In 1776 the
13 dealings and 12 disownments were all for military
service. In 1778 26 of the 33 dealings and 25 of the
30 disownments were for taking test affirmations of
allegiance. (26)

    As far as the new governmental authorities were
concerned, the Maryland Friends did not hesitate to
deal with them as the de facto government. In their
annual Yearly Meeting epistle to British Friends in
July 1777 they recognized their new state of independence
in expressing the hope that "notwithstanding the separation which has now taken place...our affection, one
for another however separated, will stand on a sure
foundation..." (27)

VIRGINIA

During the colonial period the Quakers in Virginia

262

did not enjoy as complete religious freedom or attain
the same prestige as did those in neighboring provinces.
Nevertheless they were a respected part of the population at the outbreak of the Revolution, and many of them
had close ties with the Pennsylvania Friends. (28) Moreover, the Quaker meetings in the northern upland areas
of the colony were included within the confines of
Philadelphia Yearly Meeting since for the most part
the Friends there had migrated from Pennsylvania. It
was only toward the end of the colonial period that
the pacifist position of the Friends was recognized.
Although a law of 1738 allowed the Quakers to furnish
a substitute instead of serving personally in the militia, not until 1766 were they relieved of military duty
entirely. (29) According to this law, the Friends were
granted complete exemption from serving in the militia
on presentation of a certificate of membership in the
Society of Friends, except in time of invasion when a
substitute was to be hired.

The Virginia Provincial Congress which met in 1775
treated the Quakers with greater consideration than
Friends had expected and continued their exemptions
from military service in an ordinance regulating the
militia. (30)   In May 1776 this ordinance was amended.
Henceforth Quakers, Mennonites, and other pacifist
sects formerly exempted from militia service were to be
enlisted in the militia by the commander-in-chief of
their respective counties and were to be subject to
the ordinary rules, regulations, penalties, and
forfeitures. The only exception granted was that they
were not required to attend general or private musters. (31)

Subsequently a group of Quakers from Prince Georges
County presented a petition to the Council of War of
the county, stating their inability to conform to
the clause in the law requiring the payment of a fine
for refusing to serve in the militia when called up.
They pointed out that their refusal did not proceed

> from an obstinate humor or contempt of
> your authority, being purely in obedience
> as we apprehend to the discharge of a good
> conscience. (32)

Opposition soon arose to this limited recognition
of the pacifist position of the Friends and similar
pacifist sects. In June the Committee of Safety of
Frederick County complained to the Provincial Congress

263

that the exemptions granted the Quakers burdened the
rest of the county unduly. It suggested that the county
courts assess annual levies on them in lieu of personal
service, and that when the militia was called into
actual service the Quakers be drafted and then provide
a substitute. (33)

When the British invaded Pennsylvania in the summer
of 1777, the Virginia militia was called out and several
Friends were drafted. Fourteen members of Hopewell
Monthly Meeting in Frederick County were taken from
their homes and marched about two hundred miles to the
American camp outside Philadelphia. Some of the officers
in charge "with drawn swords pushed the Friends into
Rank, threatening they would have their blood if they
did not comply". (34) Four were put on wagon guard, and
endeavors were made to have them bear arms. When these
attempts failed, guns were tied to three of the men with
no better success. Before they reached their destination
seven were discharged, evidently on account of sickness.
When the rest arrived at the camp in Pennsylvania,
Clement Biddle interceded with General Washington on
their behalf, and they were immediately released and
allowed to return home.

Stephen Peebles of Prince George County was also
marched to the camp at Valley Forge at about the same
time. After obtaining a certificate of membership
from his meeting,he appealed to Friends in Pennsylvania
who procured his release through General Arnold. (35)
Several other Friends taken by force when the militia
was called out were set at liberty by the Governor when
they reached Williamsburg. (36)

In the fall of 1777 the Virginia House of Burgesses
passed an act which embodied the policy thereafter adopted
with regard to the pacifist sects. Instead of actual
service on the part of Quakers and Mennonites, substitutes were to be hired and the cost assessed upon them by
counties according to the number of tithables in each
family. Whenever payment of these levies was not forth-
coming within ten days, the sheriff of the county was
to collect the same by distraint. (37) Subsequent
militia laws included similar provisions for Quakers
and Mennonites on presentation of a certificate of
membership in their respective. groups, provided a substitute was hired in case of invasion. (38) In 1781
the question of granting such certificates in order to
avoid the draft came before Fairfax Monthly Meeting which
decided that since this action contributed to the con-

264

duct of the war, it was not permissable. (39)

Soon after the war, in 1784, the Virginia legislature passed an act exempting Quakers from attending
musters on producing a certificate of membership from
a monthly meeting. (40) This ended any difficulty for
the Friends in that state with regard to military service.

Not until 1777 did the problem of affirmations of
allegiance arise. In May a law was passed requiring
an oath or affirmation of abjuration and allegiance
of all males over sixteen under penalty of being rendered incapable of holding office, serving on juries, sueing
for debts, electing or being elected, or buying lands,
tenements or herditaments. Persons coming from other
states were to take this test on pain of imprisonment
or to depart immediately on giving a bond and security. (41) In October an act to raise money for public
exigencies levied a double tax on the regualr assessment of all persons refusing to take the test affirmation, and this was raised to a treble tax in October
of 1778. (42)

After the passage of the militia and test acts in
1777, the Friends presented an address to the legislature stating their position on both matters. They
declared their principles prohibited them from "being
Active in fighting and sheding of Blood,...or holding
correspondance with or giving inteligence to the prejudice of either of the contending Powers". They could
subscribe to no affirmation of allegiance and requested
that they not be forced to act contrary to their religious principles. (43)

In May 1778 the yearly meeting advised the Quakers
in Virginia not to take any affirmations of allegiance
and directed the subordiante monthly meetings to deal
with and disown those who persisted in doing so. (44)
The same year a proposition for banishing from the
state those refusing to take such affirmations prompted
Friends to address the legislature again on the subject,
and the matter was then dropped. (45)

In 1779 the government showed itself more favorably
inclined to the Quakers and repealed the treble tax
law. At that time Edward Stabler expressed the opinion
that the severity of the Pennsylvania legislation had
influenced the Virginians to do what they might not
otherwise have done. (46) Events in Pennsylvania such
as the Spanktown Yearly Meeting affair had doubtless
also influenced the legislators.

When the war ended the difficulties experienced by the Friends in the matter of affirmations of allegiance ceased. A law enacted in 1783 removed the disabilitities formerly imposed on non-jurors as far as Quakers and Mennonites were concerned. It also validated all land purchases made by them when such provisions were in effect. (47)

The problem of war taxes was closely linked to that of affirmations of allegiance. When the law was passed levying special taxes on those refusing to take the affirmation of loyalty to the state, the Committee of Sufferings of Warrington and Fairfax Quarterly Meeting took up the matter. It subsequently advised Friends not to hand in accounts of their estates to be taxed and not to pay such taxes. (48) The yearly meeting of 1779 received and adopted a minute of Philadelphia Yearly Meeting urging its members not to pay any taxes levied in support of the war. (49)

In 1781 the state legislature enacted a law requiring the submission of an account of certain lands and property for the assessment of a war tax on pain of heavy fines. Since the Quakers could not comply with this law, Fairfax and Hopewell Monthly Meetings appointed a joint committee to interview the commissioners and magistrates of their respective districts and explain the Quaker position. The delegation was kindly received, but the law continued to be enforced. (50)

The total amount of sufferings in Virginia was £11,221 11s. 11 3/4d. Almost half of the distraints, £5191 12s. ¼d., was levied on the members of Fairfax and Hopewell Monthly Meetings in the upland sections of the state. The accounts begin in 1777, and the highest figures are from 1780 to 1783. (51) The comparatively tolerant treatment of the Quakers by the populace in general was attested to by Edward Stabler who wrote James Pemberton that they had not suffered personal insults or unreasonable seizures of property. He also stated that although Friends had not joined in the illumination celebrating Cornwallis's surrender, "there was not the least disturbance, not one pane of Glass broke". (52)

Deviations and disownments numbered 104 and 69 respectively for the period of the war or approximately 12% and 8% of male Quakers of military age. The largest number of dealings was for military service 48, followed by test affirmations of allegiance 21, hiring

266

substitutes 10, and lesser numbers for paying military fines, accepting public office, and serving on a privateer. The highest number of deviations occurred in 1779, a total of 36, which included 13 each for taking a test affirmation of allegiance and for military service. The next highest number was in 1777, when there were 23 dealings, seven for military service and eight for publicly protesting the draft. In the latter years of the war there were few deviations from the pacifist position except in 1781 when there were 17. (53)

The highest number of disownments occurred in 1779 and 1781 with fifteen and ten respectively. A total of 41 were disowned for military service, ten for taking an affirmation of allegiance, five for hiring a substitute and lesser numbers for combinations of these offenses.

THE CAROLINAS

Although the Friends in North Carolina did not wield the influence they had in the early days of the colony, they did hold a position of respect and standing in their respective communities. They had always enjoyed religious liberty and had been exempted from personal service in the militia, in lieu of which they were expected to pay a special fine. An act of 1770 had granted them complete exemption, except in the case of invasion when they were required to hire a substitute or pay a fine. (54) The Provincial Congress of 1775 continued this provision, but in 1776 it was somewhat altered so that all able bodied men excepting certain officials were required to serve in the militia or furnish a substitute under penalty of a Ł10 fine. (55)

When the Assembly of the new state government met in April 1777, one of its first acts was the establishment of a state militia. This law repeated most provisions of the former one, adding a provision that those refusing to serve, furnish a substitute, or pay a fine, should be imprisoned until they found security for appearance at the next court martial. At this next session in November, however, the legislature passed an amendment to the law which altered this requirement by releasing members of the pacifist sects from military service on presentation of a certificate of membership and payment of a Ł25 fine, under penalty of distraint of goods and chattels to that amount. (56)

The Friends seem to have suffered considerable

267

losses on account of these acts. In Guilford County
many of them had horses and other possessions seized
as distraint for fines. They refused to take the overplus from the sales of such property, and a sizeable
sum accrued to their credit. In November 1777 the
Assembly directed that these monies, which were deposited
in the hands of the sheriff of the county, should be
paid into the hands of Charles Bruce and Robert Lindsey
for the use of the proper owners. (57)

In the spring of 1778 the legislature ordered the
raising of recruits to complete the state's quota for
the Continental army. The Quakers, Dunkards, and
Moravians in each county were required to furnish men
in proportion to their membership, in default of which
substitutes were to be hired and the cost distrained on
the delinquents. (58) The following August Rich Square
Monthly Meeting in Perquimans County appointed a
committee to collect the sufferings of its members, since
they would be "Subjected to a Severe Penalty for not
furnishing a Certain Proportion of Men to act as Substitutes in carrying on of Carnal Wars, and Sheding
Human Blood,...a number haveing already Suffered very
considerably on that account..." (59)

Later in the year several Friends were drafted,
probably for an expedition to South Carolina. Nine of
them obtained certificates of membership and requested
their discharge. A tenth, Joseph Newby, applied for
a like indulgence on the basis of religious scruples
against war, although he was unable to present a
certificate of membership with the Friends because of
a previous disownment for marrying out of the meeting.
A dispute arose between two of the officials involved
over the interpretation of the militia law, one of them
contending that the £25 substitute fine did not apply
when a draft was made for an expedition. General Skinner
who was in charge of the men finally wrote to Governor
Caswell for his opinion. The governor, after laying
the matter before his Council, replied that the Quakers
concerned, including Newby, should be discharged on
payment of the prescribed fine. (60) Subsequently
this policy of proportional requisitioning was applied
to the regular militia.

In 1778 the government initiated a new policy of
granting exemption from military service to pacifist
sects, accompanied by increased taxes. Since such taxes
were as objectionable as the military service in lieu of
which they were assessed, Western Quarterly Meeting ad-

vised its members not to pay them. Subsequent laws,
passed during the remaining years of the war, raised
the rate of taxes in money and kind levied on the
pacifist sects. (61)

In May 1778 a requisition of clothing for the army
was ordered. The Quakers, Mennonites, Dunkards, and
Moravians were required to furnish lists of those members on whom the levy fell, on pain of having their
property distrained to purchase their proportion of
the supplies. (62) The legislature also passed an
act assessing the Quakers and the other pacifist sects
a three-fold tax and requiring them to return an
inventory of their taxable property under penalty of
an additional four-fold tax. (63)

When the **Yearly Meeting** convened the following
October, the question of paying the taxes arose. After
careful deliberation the meeting sent out a general
epistle of advice recommending that members take into
"a close and solid consideration whether the payment
of taxes under the present Commotions be Consistant
with our Peaceable Principles". (64) Since the government continued this method of taxation for the duration
of the war, it was a constant source of distress for
Friends. (65)

Since the Yearly Meeting did not issue a clear-cut
pronouncement on the matter and individual meetings
were left to proceed as they saw fit, some differences
of opinion soon arose. In December 1779 Robert Pleasants
wrote to Thomas Nicholson of Perquimans County urging
a uniformity of conduct. He felt that Friends could no
more pay such taxes than take affirmations of allegiance,
since both were "calculated to promote the same ends
and make us parties in the destruction, the Violence &
the confusion consequent to such intestine commotions".
Differences in conduct would "tend to weaken & discourage those who (conceived) it to be their duty to
suffer the loss of life and liberty & property, rather
than violate the Testimony of a good Conscience". If
Friends, especially those in the same state, failed
to act uniformly on such matters, it would strengthen
the hands of their persecutors. Those refusing to
comply with the law would be considered obstinate and
would suffer more severe punishments. In conclusion
he urged all Friends to "endeavor to walk in the just
mans path, so as that our lights may shine, and in all
things (we may) be preserved from giving just cause of
Offence to Jew, Gentile, or the household of faith".(66)

269

Although the Quakers in the eastern part of the
state were inclined to pay taxes levied for war purposes,
the Standing Committee of the Western Quarterly Meeting
issued a statement to members calling for consistency
of action in the matter. While admitting that differences
of opinion existed as to whether or not they should
give an account of their estates to be taxed and pay
the levies accordingly assessed, the committee urged
Friends to consider carefully whether such action was
not inconsistent with their religious principles and
urged them not to disregard their pacifist testimony
when the tax collectors appeared. (67)

The next year, 1780, the legislature ordered a
requisition of supplies for the army, the Quakers,
Mennonites, Dunkards, and Moravians to be assessed in
proportion to the prevailing tax laws, a three fold
amount. Western Quarterly Meeting again issued an
epistle of advice urging the subordinate monthly meetings
to maintain their "peaceable Testimony by an Honest
refusal to Act or Willingly (comply) with any Requisitions
or Demands made by men in Supporting or Carrying on
wars, or the sheding of blood". (68)

These three-fold and four-fold taxes combined imposed a heavy burden on the Friends and others subject
to them. In January 1781 Wayne County Quakers laid a
remonstrance before the legislature petitioning for
relief from the grievances under which they suffered.
This was referred to a joint committee of both Houses
which subsequently reported that the laws had been
construed greatly to the prejudice of the Friends and
that they ought not to pay more than four times the
taxes or ordinary citizens. The House concurred in
the report and sent a resolve to this effect to the
Senate. The latter did not agree, however, and drafted
an alternative resolve raising the amount to seven-
fold the ordinary rate of taxation with which the
House finally concurred. (69)

Nevertheless, the authorities were anxious that
the laws be justly executed. An act of 1781 to raise
troops for the militia included a provision tax for
all men not serving in the Continental army. Quakers
subject to the three-fold tax were exempted from this
payment. (70)

When the war was over the legislature took immediate steps to relieve the Friends and other religious
groups subject to special taxation for refusal to
participate in the conflict. By an act of 1783 both

270

the three-fold and the four-fold taxes were repealed, provided that all persons who had not taken an oath or affirmation of allegiance to the state and did not do so within the next six months should pay a double tax. (71)

The problem of test affirmations of allegiance did not arise till the middle of 1777. In May of that year a law was passed defining treason and prescribing an oath or affirmation of abjuration and allegiance to be administered to any persons considered disaffected to the state. The following October the Yearly Meeting decided that its members could not consistently comply with this law and presented an address to the Assembly explaining its position. In part it said:

> As we have always declared that we believe
> it to be Unlawfull for us, to be Active
> in War, and Fighting with Carnal Weapons,
> and as we conceive that the proposed
> affirmation Approves of the present measures,
> which are carried on and Supported by
> Military force, we cannot engage or join
> with either party therein; being bound by
> our Principles to believe that the Setting
> up & pulling down Kings & Governments, is
> Gods peculiar prerogative,...and that it
> is not our Work or Business to have any
> Hand or Contrivance therein, nor to be busy-
> bodies in matters above our Stations:...
> We hope that you will consider our principles
> a much Stronger Security to any State than
> any Test that can be Required...(72)

As a result of this petition, the next session of the Assembly made some modifications in the prescribed affirmation. It replaced the word "allegiance" by "fidelity" and provided that all who subscribed to the altered affirmation before the beginning of its session in May 1779 should be restored to all their previous privileges of citizenship, while those remaining obdurate were to be banished from the state.(73) Some Friends took the revised affirmation, but their action did not accord with the viewpoint of the Society. In September 1778 the Standing Committee of the Western Quarter warned its fellow members not to deviate from their princicples in this manner and advised the monthly meetings to deal with those who did. The Yearly Meeting which met in October declared that the alterations in the law made it no more acceptable. (74)

Soon after the passage of the above act, the County
Court of Perquimans County ordered the banishment and
the forfeiture of the estates of all who after sixty
days had not complied with the law. In January 1779
the Standing Committee of the Eastern Quarter
addressed the legislature, thanking it for its attempt
to mitigate the difficulties of the Friends by altering
the former test law but pointing out that the existing
requirment was much the same in substance as the previous
one. In part it said:

> If our Conscientious and tender Scruples
> in this Respect should have a tendency to
> bring great Sufferings upon us and terminate
> in the Ruin of many Honest Familys, we Submit;
> but Ardently desire that you will not Consider
> us as Enemies to our Country because we
> Scruple taking the afores^{d} Test...

In conclusion the committee requested the authorities
to extend to the Quakers those privilges they had
hitherto enjoyed until their conduct should justify
their withdrawal. Later in the same year the Yearly
Meeting informed its members that they could not consistently take the test as long as the situation remained
unsettled and was still to be determined by military
force. (75)

The order of the Perquimans County Court was nevertheless carried out with consequent great suffering and
loss for many Friends. Almost every Quaker plantation
in the county was taken over, and the Standing Committee
of the Eastern Quarter finally appealed to the government for relief. The legislature immediately passed
an act declaring that any Quakers, Dunkards, Mennonites,
or Moravians who had previously been legally possessed
of their estates should remain in possession of them,
and that all entries against their properties should
be deemed null and void. (76)

After the war the Yearly Meeting revised its position with regard to affirmations of allegiance and put
the Friends at liberty to take or reject such a test
as the individual thought best. Since the form prescribed by the state was not satisfactory for some, it
drew up an alternative one. (77)

In the neighboring province of South Carolina
similar laws were in effect. In 1778 three Friends from
Pennsylvania, North Carolina, and Virginia who were there

272

on a religious visit were arrested near Ninety-Six and tendered a test oath of allegiance under penalty of £10,000 security to leave the state and not return without the permission of the legislature. Since giving the security demanded would imply guilt on their part, they refused to do so and were searched and committed to prison. On hearing of the matter, the Philadelphia Friends persuaded Henry Laurens who represented South Carolina at the Continental Congress to write to the President of South Carolina and others in authority in behalf of the imprisoned Quakers. The monthly meeting at Bush River, South Carolina, issued certificates of membership for the three men, and the Friends in Charleston obtained a writ of habeas corpus and interviewed the President and Council. The prisoners were then released and allowed the liberty of the limits of Bush River Monthly Meeting. Soon afterward a special act of the legislature granted their complete freedom, and they then proceeded homeward. (78)

Throughout the war the southern Quakers remained aloof from the political affairs of the provinces in which they resided. Late in 1776 Bush River Monthly Meeting had some trouble with a few members who voted delegates to the Provincial Convention. The matter was referred to the quarterly meeting which declared that "all (Friends should) be Cautioned..., not to be found medling in those party affairs". This advice was sent to both Bush River Monthly Meeting in South Carolina and Wrightsborough Monthly Meeting in Georgia. (79)

Somewhat later similar difficulties arose in North Carolina when some Friends accepted offices as magistrates and assessors. In March 1778 the Standing Committee of Western Quarterly Meeting urged the subordinate monthly meetings to keep their members from accepting such positions "under the present Commotion and Confusion that now abound", and advised them to deal with those who did. (80)

The total recorded sufferings for the North Carolina Friends was £10,094 5s. 6d. None were reported until 1778, and all but £1479 2s. were incurred between 1778 and 1781. (81) For the most part, the accounts of these sufferings are not specified, although most of the distraints listed were for unpaid fines and taxes.

In North Carolina there were 59 dealings and 35

273

disownments. Military service accounted for 26 dealings
and 23 disownments, affirmations of allegiance for 18
dealings and 2 disownments, and sailing on privateers
and armed vessels for 5 dealings and 4 disownments.
There were also dealings for hiring substitutes, paying
war fines, holding public office, and allowing a son
to go to war (82), all of which evidently terminated
in acknowledgments since there were no disownments on
these counts.

The highest number of dealings and disownments
occurred in 1776 and during the years 1779-1781. Those
in 1776 were all for participating in the military effort.
In the latter years disciplinary proceedings were instituted for military activities and taking test affirmations
of allegiance. As was the case elsewhere, deviations
of a military nature incurred the highest incidence of
disownments in proportion to dealings. There seem to
have been few dealings for the payment of war taxes, a
not unlikely result of the ambiguity of attitude in
this matter on the part of many Friends and certain
sections of the Society in North Carolina.

In South Carolina there were twenty-one dealings
and nineteen disownments, all for military involvement
in the war. (83) The highest numbers occurred in 1776
and 1780-1782, the latter years being the most active
period of the war in the south.

GEORGIA

In Georgia the Friends were subject to the tides
of war as the British and Americans were alternately
in control. In all cases the Quakers refused to take
part in the conflict on either side. Under the new
state government, militia laws were passed exempting
the Friends from military service on the payment of
a twenty-five per cent increment in the general war
tax, a condition which was completely unacceptable.(84)
It was not until 1778, however, that the Quakers began
to feel the brunt of war when the state assembly passed
a law to facilitate the apprehension of loyalists. This
act provided that all the inhabitants should subscribe
to an oath or affirmation of allegiance to the state
and abjuration of the authority of the King of Great
Britain on pain of confiscation of their estates. (85)

Early in 1779 the British took Savannah and for
the next three years controlled that part of the state,
reinstituting royal government wherever they held the

authority. When this occurred, some of the more violent
of the American patriots descended on the suspected
Quakers and "took what they pleased, some plundering
openly, some stealing privately, being encouraged
therein by the colonels". Five Friends were sent to
South Carolina where they were imprisoned for five
months and finally released by order of General Lincoln.
Some Friends in the upper part of the state were imprisoned for several days and then released on court
order. (86)

It was at this time that test affirmations of
allegiance were administered to many Friends in the
American-controlled areas of Georgia. Several Quaker
families were banished to British-held Savannah on
refusing to take the affirmation. Other Friends, subjected to plundering by the Americans, fled to Savannah
for refuge. (87)

Because of the difficulties they were experiencing
at the hands of the Americans, and believing that the
British were going to reconquer the province, Wrightsborough Monthly Meeting presented an address to the
King's commanding officer at Augusta in the early
part of 1779, attesting to their peaceable behavior.(88)
A year later, in July 1780, the royal governor and council
granted a petition from the inhabitants of Wrightsborough
requesting to be restored to the King's peace and protection and setting forth their distressed situation.(89)
Conditions did not improve much thereafter, however, as
seen in a report to the British Governor, Sir James
Wright, in March 1781 concerning the plundering of
Wrightsborough by an American party. According to
Col. Grierson, "the principal and best inhabitants"
of the town feared there would be a dangerous insurrection, and unless they were protected they would have to
quit the settlement. (90)

Naturally the Quakers were looked upon with favor
by the British since they were not participating in
the war. Those who took refuge in Savannah were granted
allowances of beef and rice by the royal authorities.
In the spring of 1781 the loyalist assembly passed an
"Act for the Relief of the People Called Quakers",
granting them the right to sit in the Commons House of
Assembly and to serve on juries in civil cases by taking
an affirmation instead of an oath. (91)

One cannot deny that there would be some justification for considering the Georgia Friends as loyalist

sympathizers because of their relations with the British installed government during the period 1779-1781. However when the British eventually withdrew from the south and evacuated Savannah only two Friends went with them, Joseph Maddox and Jonathan Sell. (92) It is notable, moreover, that there was no confiscation of Quaker property on grounds of loyalism following the war, a fact which would indicate that their community accepted the pacifist stance of the Friends.

In the course of the war twenty Friends were dealt with by Wrightsborough Monthly Meeting for military activities, of which fifteen were disowned. (93)

(1) Proceedings and Acts of the General Assembly of
Maryland,1638-1664 (Archives of Maryland ed. W.H.
Browne et al., 63 vols., Baltimore, 1883-1946,
v.1), 412-413; Mereness, Newton D., Maryland as a
Proprietary Province (New York, 1901), 283-284,288;
Proceedings and Acts of the General Assembly,1775-
1756 (Arch. of Md., v.52), 468.

(2) Journal of the Maryland Convention, July 26 -
August 14, 1775..., (Arch. of Md., v.11),19; Amer.
Arch., 4th Ser., v.3, 109.

(3) Journal of the Maryland Convention, 1776,Amer.
Arch.,4th Ser., v.14, 733.

(4) Delaplaine, Edward S., "The Life of Thomas Johnson",
Maryland Historical Magazine, v.17 (1922,203; Laws
of Maryland, ed. Virgil Maxcey (3 vols., Baltimore,
1811), v.3, 16.

(5) Md. Y.M., Min., v.3,20,87-88; Indian Spring M.M.,
Min., 1772-1817,19.

(6) Laws of Md.,1777 legislative session, 64; 1783
legislative session, 30, in the Hall of Records,
Annapolis.

(7) Ibid., 1778 legislative session,178,180-182.

(8) Ibid., 1777 legislative session, 64.

(9) Ibid., 154-158. Compare this law with similar
Pennsylvania law of April 1778.

(10) Md. Y.M., Min., v.3, 99,102-103.

(11) Md. M.f.S., Min., v.1 (1778-1841),2; Gunpowder M.M.,
Min., 1768-1784,206; Indian Spring M.M., Min.,
1772-1817,26.

(12) Phil.M.f.S., to Md. M.f.S., Sept. 17,1778, Phil.
M.f.S.,Min., v.2,166; Balt.M.f.S., Min., v.1,3-4.

(13) Md. M.f.S., Min., v.1,4-5.

(14) Thomas Lightfoot to John Pemberton, Oct. 26,1778,
Pem.Pap., v.32,120.

(15) Committee of Md.M.f.S. to John Pemberton, Nov. 13,
1778, Pem.Pap., v.32,127-129; Md. M.f.S., Min.,
v.1, 6-7.

(16) Laws of Md., 1779-1781,173, in the Hall of Records,
Annapolis.

(17) Ibid., 223; Md. M.f.S., Min. v.1,14-16.

(18) Laws of Md., 1779-1781,314,316-317.

(19) Nottingham M.M., Min., 1778-1792, 187, 190,197;
Deer Creek M.M., Min., 1776-1782, Feb.1, March 1,
1781.

(20) Laws of Md., 1779-1781,457; ibid., 1781-1785,105,
in the Hall of Records, Annapolis.

(21) For the story of this controversy see Votes and Proceedings of the House of Delegates of the State of Maryland, 1783-1785 (n.p.,n.d.), 106-107,114-116; Laws of Maryland, 1786 (Annapolis, 1786), chap.14.

(22) Laws of Md., 1777-1778, 146, in the Hall of Records, Annapolis.

(23) Md. M.f.S., Min., v.1,2; Md. Y.M., Min., v.3,114-115.

(24) James Berry to John Pemberton, Feb.14,1781,Pem.Pap., v.35,9; Laws of Md., 1781-1785,72,225-226,347.

(25) The accounts of sufferings are in Md.M.f.S., Min., v.1,passim, and in the monthly meeting minutes cited.

(26) Cecil M.M., Min., 1689-1779,March 1776-November 1779, passim;Deer Creek M.M., Min., 1776-1782, April 29, 1779-July 4,1782, passim;Gunpowder M.M.,Min., 1768-1784,136-309, passim;Indian Spring M.M., Min., 1772-1817, 23-52, passim; Pipe Creek M.M., Min., 1772-1801,59,60; Third Haven M.M., Min., 1771-1797, 92-162, passim.
According to the method of computation employed in Appendix I, there were approximately 660 male Friends of military age in Maryland. Of these 80, or 12%, were disciplined and 65, or approximately 10%, disowned.

(27) The Yearly Meeting in Maryland to London Yearly Meeting, July 6-11,1777, Epistles to London Y.M., v.4,454-455.

(28) Statutes at Large, being a Collection of all the Laws of Virginia, (ed. William Walter Henig, 13 vols., New York, Philadelphia, Richomnd, 1819-1823), v.5,16-17, hereafter cited as Stat. of Va. This law also applied to Mennonites, Brethren and Moravians.

(29) Ibid., 242-243.

(30) Proceedings of the Convention of Delegates...in the Colony of Virginia, 1775 (Richmond, 1816),38; Edward Stabler to James Pemberton, Sept. 5,1775, Pem.Pap., v.28,49.

(31) Stat. of Va., v.9,139.

(32) Petition to the Council of War of Prince Georges County, Va.Y.M., Misc.Pap.

(33) Amer. Arch., 5th Series, v.5, 1579.

(34) The Friends taken were Thomas McClun, James Steer, James Gawthrop, Moses Walton, Richard Ridgway,Jr., Aaron Gregg, Thomas Fawcett, Joseph Steer, Jr., Richard Fawcett, Jr., William Wickersham, Thomas Fawcett, Jr., Henry Williams,John Berry, Jr., and Samuel Bevan. A complete account of this affair is given in "A Narrative of the sufferings of Thomas McClun et al"., Phil.M.f.S. to London M.f.S., Feb. 26,1778,Phil.M.f.S., Min., v.2,146 and in

Phil.M.f.S., Misc.Pap.,bx.14. See also, Gilpin,
Exiles, 181.

(35) Statement of Stephen Peebles,June 7,1778,Phil.M.f.S.,
Misc.Pap.,bx.14;Israel Jacobs to Samuel Hopkins,
July 27,1778, in ibid.

(36) Edward Stabler to one of the Pembertons, Oct.9,1777,
Pem.Pap.,v.30,177.

(37) Stat. of Va., v.9,345.

(38) Ibid., v.11,18,175,389,493;v.12,24.

(39) Fairfax M.M., Min., 1776-1802,190.

(40) Stat. of Va., v.11,382.

(41) Ibid., v.9,281-283.

(42) Ibid., 351,549.

(43) "To the Speaker and the House of Delegates in Virginia",Va.Y.M.,Misc.Pap.;Pem.Pap.,v.31,8.

(44) Va.Y.M.,Min.,1702-1843,144;Henrico M.M.,Min.,1757-
1780,278.

(45) Edward Stabler to Israel Pemberton, Jan.26,1779,
Pem.Pap., v.32,159.

(46) Edward Stabler to Abel James, Jan.4,1780, Abel
James Pap.

(47) Stat. of Va., v.11,252-253.

(48) Warrington and Fairfax Q.M., Min., 1776-1787, June
22, 1778. This quarterly meeting was under the
jurisdiction of Philadelphia Yearly Meeting,
Warrington Monthly Meeting being in Pennsylvania
and Fairfax Monthly Meeting being in Virginia.

(49) Va. Y.M., Min., 1702-1843,146-147; Henrico M.M.,
Min., 1757-1780,290.

(50) Fairfax M.M., Min., 1776-1802, 211,215; Edward
Stabler to James Pemberton, March 9,1782, Cox,
Wharton,Parrish Col.

(51) Accounts of these sufferings are in Va. Y.M., Min.,
1702-1843, passim; in the various monthly meeting
minutes; and for Hopewell and Fairfax Monthly
Meeting in Phil.M.f.S., Misc. Pap. Because the
sufferings did not assume critical proportions
until the latter part of the war, a meeting for
sufferings was not set up for the yearly meeting
until 1782 (Va. Y.M., Min., 1702-1843,150-151).

(52) Edward Stabler to James Pemberton, Dec. 12,1781,
Pem.Pap., v.26,36.

(53) Blackwater M.M., Min., 1779-1795, 2-48, passim;
Cedar Creek M.M., Min., 1775-1789,29-72,passim;
Fairfax M.M., Min., 1745-1776,465-500, passim;
ibid.,1776-1802,11-259, passim;Henrico M.M., Min.,
1757-1780,231-296, passim;ibid., 1780-1781,
March 3-Oct.7,1781,passim; ibid., 1781-1866,2,27;
Hopewell M.M., Min., 1749-1776,316-355; ibid., 1777-
1791,2-246,passim.
See Appendix I for method of computation

according to which there were 880 Virginia
Quakers of military age. Of those 104 or approximately 12% were disciplined and 8% disowned.

(54) Laws of North Carolina, 1715-1776 (Colonial and
State Records of North Carolina, ed. William Saunders and Walter Clark, 26 vols., Goldsboro,N.C.,
1886-1907,v.23),787-788.
(55) Proceedings of the Prov. Cong. of N.C. (Col. and
St. Rec., v.10),200,563.
(56) Laws of North Carolina, 1777-1788 (Col. and St.
Rec., v.24),1-5,116-117.
(57) Ibid., 137.
(58) Ibid., 156.
(59) Rich Square M.M., Min., 1760-1799,156.
(60) Thomas Nicholson to Israel Pemberton, Nov.24,1778,
Pem.Pap., v.32,136; General William Skinner to
Governor Caswell, Nov.13, 1778,Jacob Wilson et al.
to Colonel Thomas Harvey, Nov.11,1778, Thomas
Newby et al. to Colonel Thomas Harvey,n.d., St.
Rec. of N.C., 1778-1779 (Col. and St. Rec., v.13),
274-275; Governor Caswell to Colonel Thomas Harvey,
Nov. 19,1778, Governor Caswell to General William
Skinner, Nov. 19,1778,ibid., 289-290. The Quakers
involved were Humphrey Park, Thomas Elliott, Job
Smith, Miles Elliott, Benjamin Albertson, Forster
Toms, Thomas Draper, Silas Draper and Joseph Medlin.
(61) Laws of N.C., 1777-1788, 190,193,413,716; Western
Q.M., Min., 1760-1900,137-138.
(62) State Records of N.C., 1777-1778 (Col. and St.
Rec., v.12),640.
(63) Laws of N.C., 1777-1788,204.
(64) N.C. Y.M., Min., v.1,166.
(65) Laws of N.C., 1777-1788,222,282,318,390-392,435.
(66) Robert Pleasants to Thomas Nicholson, Dec.5,1779,
Robert Pleasants Letters.
(67) N.C. Y.M., Min., v.1,186-187.
(68) Ibid., 187-188.
(69) State Records of N.C., 1781-1785 (Col. and St.
Rec., v.17),636,642-644,716,725,728-729.
(70) Laws of N.C., 1777-1788, 386.
(71) Ibid., 492.
(72) N.C. Y.M., Min., v.1,157-158.
(73) St. Rec. of N.C., 1777-1778,809; Miscellaneous
Revolutionary Documents (Col. and St. Rec., v.22),
168; Laws of N.C., 1777-1778,86,219.
(74) N.C.Y.M., Min., v.1, 164; Cane Creek M.M., Min.,
1751-1796,74.
(75) Thomas Nicholson to Israel Pemberton, Nov.24,1778,
Pem Pap.,v.32,136; N.C. Y.M., Min., v.1,176,178-179.
(76) N.C.Y.M., Min., v.1,185-186;Laws of N.C.,1777-1788,

329; Edward Stabler to John Pemberton, May 25,1780, Cox, Wharton, Parrish Col.

(77) N.C.Y.M., Min., v.1,210.

(78) Phil.M.f.S., Min., v.2,172-175,289; Bush River M.M., Min., 1772-1783,107;"Life of Joshua Brown", The Friend (Philadelphia),v.20 (1846-1847),348,356. The Friends were Joshua Brown of Pennsylvania, Achilles Douglas of Virginia and Uriah Corson of South Carolina.

(79) Western Q.M., Min., 1760-1900,132.

(80) Cane Creek M.M., Min., 1751-1796,71

(81) The accounts of sufferings are in N.C.Y.M., Min., v.1,passim, and the various monthly meeting minute books.

(82) Cane Creek M.M., Min., 1751-1796,58-108,passim; Core Sound M.M., Min., 1733-1791,130-131,148; Deep River M.M., Min., 1778-1808,20-48,passim; New Garden M.M., Min., 1776-1782,7-111,passim; Symonds Creek M.M., Min., 1699-1785,604-702, passim; Wells (Perquimans) M.M., Min., 1774-1794,10-117, passim. These figures are incomplete because of the missing minute books for this period. For this reason it is not feasible to compute the proportion of dealings and disownment of the Friends in the Carolinas.

(83) Bush River M.M., Min., 1772-1783,63-166,passim.

(84) Baker Pearl, The Story of Wrightsborough (Thomson, Ga., 1965), chap. 5.

(85) Revolutionary Records of the State of Georgia (ed. Allen D. Candler, 3 vols., Atlanta, 1908), v.1,48, 207.

(86) Joseph Williams, Joseph Maddox and others to London Meeting for Sufferings, Jan.2,1782, Epistles to London Y.M., v.5,133-137.

(87) Strickland, Reba Carolyn, Religion and the State in Georgia in the Eighteenth Century (New York, 1967), 155; Joseph Williams et al. to London M.f.S., loc.cit.

(88) Strickland, op.cit., 155.

(89) Colonial Records of the State of Georgia, Original Papers (comp. Allen D. Candler, W.P.A., Project No. 350,v.38,pt.2,n.p., 1937),381-382.

(90) Col. Grierson to Sir James Wright, March 4, 1781, in ibid., 480.

(91) Col. Rec. of the St. of Ga., 480,487.

(92) Hitz, Alexander M., "The Wrightsborough Quaker Town and Township in Georgia", BFHA, v.46 (1957), 17. Both Maddox and Sell had been appointed Commissioners of Roads for St. Paul's Parish in June 1780 under the temporarily restored British

administration of Georgia. (<u>The Proceedings and Minutes of the Governor and Council of Georgia</u>, October 4, 1774 through November 7,1775, and September 6, 1779, through September 20,1780, <u>Collections</u> of the Georgia Hist. Soc., v.35,204-205.)

(93) Wrightsborough M.M., Min., 1772-1793, <u>passim</u>.

Chapter XVI

THE FREE QUAKERS

As we have already indicated, there were strong
differences of opinion among the Friends, especially
in Pennsylvania, in the years immediately preceding
the War for Independence as to the appropriate attitude
for the Society to adopt toward the anti-British policies
and actions of the colonial radicals. A minority felt
that the official bodies of the Society went too far
in their opposition to colonial resistance, and some
called for outright support of the radical position.

When the war finally broke out, these tensions
could no longer be contained, and many Friends whose
sympathies were strongly in favor of a firm resistance
to the repressive actions of the British government
joined in military measures. There were also other
war-related problems which had evoked sharp differences
of viewpoint, especially the question of payment of
taxes and subscribing tests of allegiance. These issues
assumed an acute form in Pennsylvania and New England
and resulted in the establishment of a small splinter
group in each area as indicated above. (1)

Although the controversy over the Society's position
on taxation arose first in New England, dissent over
the Society's stand on both taxation and subscribing
tests of allegiance was more widespread and substantial
in Pennsylvania. The leader of the Pennsylvania dissenters was Samuel Wetherill, Jr., a recorded minister
in the Society who was disowned in 1779 for taking an
affirmation of allegiance to the new state government
and for assisting in the publication of a treatise causing
difficulty to the Society, probably Isaac Grey's discourse on taxation. Just before the war, he, Isaac Grey,
and Christopher Marshall had cooperated in establishing
the first weaving factory in Pennsylvania which subsequently furnished cloth to the Continental army. (3)

Other important members of the Pennsylvania separatist group were William Crispin, Commissary in Washington's army, disowned by Philadelphia Monthly Meeting
in 1776 for military activity; Clement Biddle, Quarter-
master under Gates at Valley Forge and elsewhere, dis-

283

owned by Philadelphia Monthly Meeting in 1776 for entering military service; the physician Benjamin Say, disowned by Philadelphia Monthly Meeting for the Northern
District in 1780 for taking the test and paying military
fines; Peter Thomson, who was employed by the Congress
to print the Continental currency and disowned for
that action in 1779; and two women famous for their part
in the Revolution, Lydia Darragh and Elizabeth Griscom
Ross, known as Betsy Ross. (4)

Wetherill's concern over the position taken by the
Society arose early in 1775. At that time he took
strong exception to the opposition expressed by the
Meeting for Sufferings to the resistance measures under
way. (5) The following year Christopher Marshall, a
member of the Committee of Public Safety, had also become very critical of the attitude being displayed by
the Quakers. Although he had been disowned many years
before he followed the course of the Society closely
and counted among his friends a number of prominent
members. He now accused Friends of worshipping their
Book of Discipline and of having strayed from their
original doctrine of the light within. In strong terms
he railed:

> How formal in crying out the Discipline,
> yet how covetous...and uncharitable you
> are...

Many of their leaders had attained eminence in the Church
through pretence of keeping the Discipline, he declared,
and would oblige all the others"to pay a great reverence
to this mighty Pope".(6)

During the course of the war these men and women
were joined by many others with similar ideas,and by
1781 a sufficient number had consolidated their interests and ideas to form a new organization distinct from
the traditional body of Quakers. Many of those who
were disowned were unable to ally themselves with other
religious groups which were different from the Friends
in church polity and mode of worship. But, they desired some religious affiliation and struck out on
their own. The Free Quakers as finally established included only those motivated by common religious opinions
and constituted but a part of those who had been disowned. They were joined in the new project by a number
of people of no previous religious persuasion who were
attracted by their expression of Quaker idealogy. (7)

In February 1781 a group of those interested in
the undertaking met at the home of Samuel Wetherill, Jr.,
in Philadelphia. Their discussion centered about the
formation of a new religious society based on the fundamental principles and beliefs of the Friends and "such
catholic and liberal sentiments as are consistent with
the enlarged benevolence of the Gospel Dispensation".
At a second meeting two months later it was decided to
hold weekly meetings for worship at the home of Timothy
Matlack. Shortly thereafter the group accepted an offer
from the trustees of the University of Pennsylvania
to hold their meetings in one of its halls. (8)

The next step was to invite other disowned Friends
to join the new venture. The invitation was issued
in the form of a broadside entitled <u>An Address to those
of the People called Quakers</u>, who have been disowned for
Matters religious and civil . It was subsequently
printed in the <u>Providence Gazette</u> in Rhode Island,
probably at the instigation of the separatists in
New England. (9) The <u>Address</u> contended that the
separation had been brought about by the pride and folly
of "former churches, vainly attempting to abridge the
rights of conscience". The promoters of the new organization declared they had no new doctrines to teach, no
designs of prompting schisms in religion, and no intention of setting forth new "creeds or confessions of
faith". Their only desire was to worship free "from
every species of ecclesiastical tyranny", and they intended to pay due regard to the principles of their
forefathers as far as they applied to current conditions.

The new meeting then proceeded to frame a Discipline.
It also appealed to the monthly meetings in Philadelphia
for some share in their properties and issued a circular
letter stating the basis of its claims in this respect.(10)

The Discipline differed sharply from that of the
parent Society in a few aspects. The meetings for
worship and business were to be conducted in the
ancient fashion, and the general doctrines, organization,
and mode of conduct and living set forth were supposed
to contain all that was best in Quakerism adapted
to the changed times. The outstanding differences were
the ommission of any theological statement of belief,
the abolition of all offenses in matters such as
marriage, the absence of any provision for disownment,
and the insertion of an encouragement to participate in
civil affairs and the military defense of the country.

It also diverged from the traditional Discipline in per-
mitting appeals to civil tribunals where differences
arose, although it encouraged the settlement of disputes
privately, if possible. (11)

Upon the refusal of the city monthly meetings to
grant the use of one of their meeting-houses and
the burial ground, the Free Quakers requested the
Assembly to take action in their behalf. The Meeting
for Sufferings thereupon presented a counterpetition,
defending the Society's proceedings against the
disowned members and protesting against any attempt on
the part of the authorities to intervene in the affair.
In the end the legislature decided to take no action.(12)
The new group then erected their own meeting-house at
the corner of Fifth and Arch Streets with the inscription
over the lintel, "Built in the Year of the Empire Eight".
The cornerstone was laid on June 29,1783, and in June
of the following year the first meeting for worship
was held there. (13)

The controversy in Pennsylvania had some repercussions in Virginia, and Friends there were somewhat fear-
ful that it would have a bad effect on their standing.
Rumors were current that a large separation had taken
place among the Pennsylvania Quakers over the question
of paying taxes. Edward Stabler obtained some documents relative to the matter which he presented to
members of the legislature. He later wrote James Pemberton that this had put the situation in the proper
light. (14)

By 1800 there were well over one hundred members
affiliated with the new meeting. About thirty-five
had been disowned by the Philadelphia Monthly Meetings,
sixteen by the meetings in Bucks County, and thirteen
by those in Chester County. One member had been disowned by Burlington Monthly Meeting in New Jersey.(15)
The group did not continue to grow, and after the turn
of the century it began to decline. The last regular
meetings for worship were held in the 1830's. It was
reported that John Price Wetherill, Samuel Wetherill,
Jr.'s son, was the last to attend the meeting in
1836. (16)

In New England the controversy over the payment of
taxes arose in the first months of the war, centering
about Timothy Davis' Letter from One Friend to Some
of his Intimate Friends on the subject of Paying
Taxes. (17)In this treatise Davis contended that all

286

taxes should be paid to the authorities actually in power, citing the writings of George Fox and Isaac Pennington to support his argument. Davis and his associate Caleb Greene were soon identified. The latter apologized for his action and promised to stop the circulation of the pamphlet. Davis, however, remained unmoved in his position. The Meeting for Sufferings then referred the matter to Sandwich Monthly Meeting of which Davis was a member. The monthly meeting was unable to reach a decision as to his guilt and appealed to the quarterly meeting for its judgment. (18)

When the quarterly meeting failed to settle the case, the Yearly Meeting took up the matter and appointed a committee to confer with representatives from Sandwich Quarter. On the recommedation of this committee the Yearly Meeting issued a testimony against Davis' pamphlet and requested his monthly meeting to disown him. This was done in December 1778, and Davis and his followers soon began to hold separate meetings. (19)

Disturbances in Rochester Meeting where Davis was a member and where he insisted on holding meetings at the same time as the usual ones resulted in an investigation of the situation. This revealed that twenty-nine Friends were frequenting his gatherings. Sandwich Monthly Meeting then began a purge of his supporters, in the course of which thirty-five Friends were dealt with and thirty were disowned. (20) Dartmouth Monthly Meeting was similarly affected and disowned nine members. (21)

As in Philadelphia, the question of property rights soon arose. One of the dissenters, formerly Register of Sandwich Monthly Meeting, refused to surrender the meeting's records. (22) At this juncture the separatists began holding meetings in various meeting-houses where they had formerly attended, often simultaneously with the Friends. In an attempt to obtain legal rights in these properties, they sent a petition to the Massachusetts General Court in support of their claims, but the General Court went no further than returning a sympathetic answer. (23)

Somewhat later, in 1784, Joseph Taber published a pamphlet defending Davis and his followers against the condemnation of the Society. He traced the cause of the controversy, attempted to show the injustice of the actions of the Meeting for Sufferings and the Yearly Meeting, and presented an apology for Davis' thesis, referring to statements of prominent 17th century English Friends to substantiate his viewpoint. (24) This public-

287

cation does not seem to have produced any difficulty
for the Society nor to have furthered the cause of the
dissenters.

By the middle of 1781 Davis' party had established
a new monthly meeting at Dartmouth. It was soon in
correspondence with the similar dissenting group in
Pennsylvania, and several of its leaders visited
their Philadelphia counterparts. Despite their points
of agreement and the friendly communciatons which took
place, certain differences in viewpoint soon became
apparent. This was especially so with regard to the
Book of Discipline issued by the Philadelphia Free
Quakers, as they named themselves. The New Englanders
criticised the lack of any criteria for membership in
the Philadelphia group as well as the abandonment of
disownment for any reason. (25)

In 1782 Timothy Davis and Cornelius Wing visited
the Philadelphia Free Quakers. They held meetings
in the city and at Springfield in Chester County and
Richland in Bucks County. Accompanied by Samuel
Wetherill, Jr., they also proceeded to Maryland where
they met with some dissenters at Deer Creek and West
River. As early as 1779 the meeting-house at Sandy
Spring was reported to have been broken into by some
people "claiming a right to the House", but the Maryland group never assumed an organized form, and aside
from a visit to Philadelphia by some of the dissenters
there, nothing is subsequently heard about them. (26)

The following year, 1783, Timothy Matlack made
a religious journey to New England, and in 1785 Benjamin Bumpus went to Philadelphia. Bumpus held meetings
at Gloucester and Longacoming in New Jersey as well
as at Philadelphia. (27)

The New England separatists never became strong
enough to build their own meeting-house. For some time
they were allowed the use of a part of the meeting-house
at Acushent, and after altering their time of meeting
they were granted the same privilege at Long Plain. It
would therefore seem that there was not as strong a
feeling of alienation among the New England Friends
as prevailed in Philadelphia. (28)

Evidently a number of the New England dissenters
finally rejoined the main body of the Society. In
1795 Samuel Wetherill, Jr., visited the Free Quaker
group at Long Plain to persuade Timothy Davis not to

288

take such a step. He also held meetings at the Rochester
meeting-house where Benjamin Bumpus was the leading spirit
in the separatist group. (29) Subsequently nothing
is heard of the New England Free Quakers other than
that Samuel Wetherill, Jr., was issued a certificate
by the Philadelphia Free Quakers in 1802 to make a
visit to the New Englanders. (30)

Although the dissident groups in New England and
Pennsylvania had a common origin in issues raised by the
Revolution and maintained mutually sympathetic relations
with each other, they had distinctive characteristics.
The New Englanders were much more conservative. Aside
from their position on the question of payment of taxes,
they followed much more closely the pattern of belief
and discipline of the body of the Society. They emerged
as a group on a single issue and they dissolved relatively soon when the issue ceased to exist.

The Pennsylvania dissenters, on the other hand,
consisted of a more complex constituency and established
their organization on principles distinctly different
from those of the original Society of Friends. The name
Free Quakers is justifiably applicable to them, since
they based their rule of conduct and action on freedom
from the restraints which characterized the main body
of the Society. Not only did they welcome into their
ranks all former Friends who had been disowned for any
reason at any time, but they also rejected the employment of any disciplinary procedure, stressing freedom
of conscience as the individual guide. They maintained
that thereby they were fulfilling the original meaning
of the "inner light" as held by early Friends.

Along with the New England separatists, they
eventually suffered the fate of outdated causes. With
the passage of time and the fading into history of
their immediate raison d'être, together with the
progressive diminution of the ranks of the founders,
the life of the new Society gradually waned and finally
expired.

(1)   This subject has been dealt with in Charles Wether-
      ill's History of the Religious Society of Friends
      called by Some the Free Quakers, in the City of
      Philadelphia (Philadelphia, 1894); Wetherill Web-
      ster King's "The Fighting Quakers", Phildelphia
      Numismatical and Antiquarian Society Proceedings,
      v.29 (1921),69-81; Sharpless, History of Quaker
      Government, v.2,chap.9; and Mekeel "Free Quaker
      Movement in New England", loc.cit., BFHA.

(2)   Timothy Matlack had been disowned in 1765 for
      what the meeting considered unsound business
      practices (Phil.M.M., Min., 1765-1771,47). Chris-
      topher Marshall had been disowned in 1751 for
      associating with men suspected of engaging in
      counterfeiting and the passing of false currency.
      (Phil.M.M., Min., 1745-1751,March 31,1775). In
      the case of Samuel Wetherill, Jr., Anthony Benezet
      exerted every effort to avoid his disownment by
      keeping the controversy out of the meeting and
      in the hands of the overseers in hopes "it would
      be easier to settle the matter by a tacit acknow-
      legement of his mistake". Thereby he managed to
      have action against Wetherill postponed four times,
      but eventually he had to give way and Wetherill
      was disowned (Anthony Benezet to George Dillwyn,
      April 8, 1779, Brooks, Anthony Benezet, 334-335);
      Phil.M.M., Min., 1777-1782,131,133; Wetherill,op.
      cit., 18; Sharpless, op.cit., v.2,209.

(3)   Amer. Arch., 4th Ser., v.2,140; Wetherill, op.cit.,
      16.

(4)   Phil.M.M., Min., 1771-1777,331,346,351,358; Phil.
      M.M. No. Dist., Min., 1772-1781,342,361,376,430.
      Lydia Darragh notified Washington of an attack
      planned by the British when they were occupying
      Philadelphia (see Bakeless, Katherine and John,
      Spies of the Revolution (New York, 1966). She
      was disowned in October 1782 for not attending
      meeting and for "joining with a number of Persons,
      associated under a pretense of religious Duty,
      so far as to attend their Meeting". (Phil.M.M.,
      Min., 1782-1789,47,101,102.)
          Betsy Ross, who is reputed to have made the
      first American flag, was disowned in 1774 for
      marrying a person of another religious persuasion.
      (Phil.M.M.No. Dist., Min., 1772-1781,88,90-91.)

(5)   See p. 130 above.

(6) Christopher Marshall to T. H., March 28,1776,Letter
     Book, 176-177, at the HSP; same to John Baird,
     Jan.30,1776,ibid., 162.
(7) Sharpless, op.cit., v.2,207-208; Wetherill,op.cit.,
     18.
(8) Extracts from the Free Quaker M.M., Min., Feb. 20,
     April 19, 24,1781, in the Free Quaker Pap.
(9) Ibid., April 24, 1781; Prov. Gaz., June 16, 1781. A
     A copy of the Address is in the Free Quaker Pap.
(10) Free Quaker M.M., Min., May 7, June 4, July 9,
     1781; Marshall, Diary, July 6,8,1781.
(11) A copy of the Discipline of the Free Quaker Meeting
     is in the Free Quaker Pap.
(12) Phil.M.f.S., Min., v.2,338-345,374-379;Phil.Y.M.
     to London Y.M., 1782,Phil.Y.M., Min., v.4,53;
     Drinker, Journal, Sept.14,16,18,1782; Sharpless,
     op.cit.,v.2,209.
(13) Marshall, Diary, July 29,1783; Wetherill,op.cit.,
     37-39. The house still stands at its original
     location. It is the headquarters of the Phila-
     delphia Junior League which maintains it.
(14) Edward Stabler to James Pemberton, June 26, 1782,
     Pem. Pa., v.36,159.
(15) Those disowned by the Philadelphia Monthly Meetings
     were: Moses Bartram, Clement Biddle, Owen Biddle,
     Nathaniel Browne, George Chandler, Thomas Coates,
     Samuel Crispin, Thomas Crispin, William Crispin,
     Cadwalader Dickinson,Edward Evans, Evan Evans,
     James Fisher, William Fisher, Jr., Joseph Covett,
     Thomas Hopkins, Isaac Howell, Samuel Howell,
     William Milnor, John Morris, Samuel Morris, Jr.,
     Joseph Ogden, Jr., John Parrish, Jr., Samuel Morris,
     Benjamin Paschall, Edward Pole, Thomas Renshaw,
     Samuel Robbins, Abraham Roberts, Benjamin Say,
     Abraham Shoemaker, William Thomas, Peter Thomson,
     Joseph Warner, William Warner and Samuel Wetherill,
     Jr. (Phil.M.M., Min., 1771-1777,299-404, passim;
     ibid.,1777-1782,49-247, passim;Phil.M.M.No.Dist.,
     Min., 1772-1781,113-148,passim;ibid.,1782-1789,30;
     Phil.M.M.So.Dist., Min., 1770-1780,137-242,passim.)
         Those disowned in Bucks County were: Enoch
     Betts, Abner Buckman, John Buskman, Jr., John
     Chapman, Thomas Dyer, Nathaniel Ellicott, Samuel
     Foulke, Isaac Heston, Robert Jones,Thomas Ross,Jr.,
     Jonathan Scholfield, Samuel Smith, Stacey Taylor,
     Timothy Taylor, and Thomas Wright (Buckingham M.M.,
     Min., 1763-1780,138-283,passim; Falls M.M., Min.,
     1767-1788,241-281,passim; Gwynedd M.M., Min., 1757-
     1779, 235,290;Richland M.M., Min., 1767-1786,
     Dec.. 16,1779,May 18,1780;Wrightstown M.M., Min.,

1734-1790,231-304,passim).

Those disowned in Chester County were:
Matthew Ash, James Bartram, John Bartram, Jonathan
Bonsall, David Evans, Nathan Gibson, Henry Hays,
J(oseph) Musgrave, Jonathan Pascall, John Pearson,
Joseph Pearson, John Richardson, and William Warner
(Chester M.M, Min., 1745-1778,425,427;Darby M.M.,
Min., 1763-1783,192-313, passim:Kennett M.M., Min.,
1739-1791,651,669;Radnor M.M., Min., 1772-1782,
99,195,200.).

The disownment of the New Jersey Friend,
Isaac Collins, is in Burlington M.M., Min., 1770-
1781,192,196. Owen Biddle has been claimed as a
Free Quaker, but since he returned to the original
Society in 1783 he cannot have been very active
in the new group (Phil.M.M., Min., 1782-1789,75.).
A complete list of the members of the Free Quaker
Monthly Meeting is found in Wetherill,op.cit.,
app.XII,111-114. This includes non-Friends who
joined, as well as some Friends who had been
disowned for non-war related offenses.

(16) Wetherill, op.cit., 42.
(17) Mekeel, "Free Quaker Movement in New England",
     loc.cit., 74.
(18) N.E.M.f.S., Min., v.1,41,46,50;Sandwich M.M.,Min.,
     1755-1795, March 7,28,1777;Sandwich Q.M.,Min.,
     1686-1804,96.
(19) N.E.Y.M., Min., v.1,329-330;Sandwich M.M.,op.cit.,
     Dec. 4,1778,June4,Sept.30,1779,March24,1780-
     Oct.3,1783,passim.
(20) Those disowned were: George Allen, George Braley,
     Benjamin Bumpus, Nathan Davis Jr., Nicolis Davis,
     Richard Davis, Abraham Devol, William Eastis,
     Barnabas Hammett, Stephen Hathaway, Isaac Hiller,
     Moses Hiller, Seth Hiller, Seth Hiller, Jr., Marck
     Jenne, Savory Londes, Stephen Merrihu, Lectious
     Runnels, Silas Swift, Bartholomew Taber, Benjamin
     Taber, Joseph Taber, Peter Taber, Thomas Taber,Jr.,
     William Taber, Peleg Trip, Barnabas Wing., Jr.,
     Daniel Wing, Josephus Wing, and William Wing.
(21) Dartmouth M.M., Min., 1770-1792,143-201,passim.
     Those disowned were Caleb Hathaway, Joshua Sherman,
     Jr., Amaziah Smith, Eleashib Smith, John Smith,
     Joseph Smith, Edward Taber, William Taber and wife
     and daughter, Nicholas Taber.
(22) Sandwich M.M., Min., op.cit.,May 3, 1780;Moses
     Brown to James Pemberton, May 22, 1782,Pem.Pap.,
     V.36,121.
(23) Sandwich M.M., op.cit., Dec. 5, 1783;N.E.M.f.S.,
     Min., v.1,191;Moses Brown to James Pemberton,

Sept. 19,1783,Free Quaker Pap.

(24) Taber, Joseph, _An Address to the People Called Quakers Concerning the Manner in which They Treated Timothy Davis_, Boston, 1784. Copies of this treatise are in the Massachusetts Hist.Soc., Boston, and the American Antiquarian Society, Worcester, Mass.

(25) Free Quaker M.M., Min., Aug.6,Sept.3,Dec., 1781.

(26) Certificates of Timothy Davis and Cornelius Wing dated Rochester, March 4,1782, and one for Samuel Wetherill,Jr., dated Philadelphia, March 11,1782, Free Quaker Pap.; James Pemberton to Moses Brown, June 5,1782,in _ibid_.;Indian Spring M.M., Min., 1772-1817,31-32.

(27) Marshall, Diary, July 3,1783, May 15,22,25,June 1, 12,13,1785.

(28) Taber, Mary Jane Howland, "Friends Here and Hereaway", Old Dartmouth Hist. Soc., _Proceedings_ (December,1904),18; Moses Brown to James Pemberton, April 21,1783,Pem.Pap., v.38,131.

(29) Hull, Henry, _Memoirs of the Life and Religious Labours of Henry Hull_ (Philadelphia,1858),68-69.

(30) Certificate of Samuel Wetherill,Jr., dated Philadelphia, June 17,1802,Free Quaker Pap.

Chapter XVII

QUAKER RELIEF WORK

Although the Quakers maintained a strictly non-cooperative position throughout the war, they were not insensitive to the needs and sufferings of their fellow citizens, war prisoners, and any others adversely affected by the conflict. In 1790, in the second session of the first Congress of the United States, Elias Boudinot payed a moving tribute to their relief activities. He had served as Commissary General of Prisoners and had had to work with almost non-existent resources. The prisoners were reduced to "the very depths of distress, without food, or raiment, without blankets or firing, (and) suffered everything that human nature could bear". It was in this situation that

> many Quakers of this city (Philadelphia) exercised such humanity towards them as did honor to human virtue, The miserable prisoner not only felt the happy effects of their exertions in his favor, but participated in their money, their food, and clothing.](1)

In many other areas the same concern for human welfare was also evident.

The first Quaker relief project was the assistance offered to the inhabitants of Boston when it was held by the British in the fall and winter of 1775-1776. Friends in Pennsylvania, Delaware, New Jersey, and Maryland financed the undertaking which was administered by the New England Quakers. When some citizens of Philadelphia first began subscriptions to aid the New Englanders in the summer of 1774, the Friends had refused to cooperate since they considered "it safest for us to contribute when they may be more in need of it than we apprehend they can be as yet, & to promote a subscription among ourselves when it appears necessary."(2) The Quakers also feared that their subscribing with others might be construed as approval of the conduct of the Bostonians. (3)

The situation of those Friends who lived in

Boston had already become a matter of concern to the
New England Quakers. Salem Monthly Meeting contributed
₤8 for their relief and sent a committee into the city
to investigate their condition. The committee reported
that although the inhabitants of Boston were deprived of
many fresh provisions, they had a sufficiency of brew
and salt foods, and that the committee had given aid
to such as were in need. (4)

At this time Johnn Pemberton was on a religious
visit to New England, and he consulted with Moses Brown
on the possibility of providing assistance to persons
of all denominations. The chief concern was that any
such step should in no way contribute to the conduct of
the war or benefit those who were active in its prosecution. For this reason they concluded it was inadvisable
to cooperate with any of the committees in operation,
since they were likely "to favor the violent party". (5)

Not until the following June, in 1775, was further
action undertaken. The newly established New England
Meeting for Sufferings appointed a committee to visit
Friends in Boston and ascertain their condition. The
committee went into the city by water from Lynn. The
British Admiral, having heard that the Quakers in
Philadelphia had formed a regiment to fight against the
King, received them cooly. When he learned that those
who had taken up arms were disowned, he allowed the
delegation to proceed on its mission. It found that
most Friends in the city, as well as those who had
left, were in low circumstances, and this information
was immediately sent to the Philadelphia Meeting for
Sufferings. (6)

Meantime the Meeting for Sufferings in Philadelphia
was laying plans for extensive relief to the sufferers
in New England. The June sessions of the meeting were
mostly devoted to this question, and two of its members
just returned from a visit to those provinces, John
Hunt and Nicholas Waln, reported on the situation
there. (7) Since the New England Meeting for Sufferings
now furnished a reliable agency through which to work,
the Philadelphia Friends decided to raise a subscription
throughout their yearly meeting, and the Meeting for
Sufferings sent subscription papers to all the subordinate monthly meetings. (8)

This action received widespread publicity, and
the letter to the monthly meetings appeared in newspapers from Virginia to Massachusetts. (9) For fear the
New England Friends might misinterpret this undesired

295

publicity, the Philadelphia Quakers informed them that
for some time they had desired to undertake such action,
but that this had not been possible until the establishment of the New England Meeting for Sufferings. They
asked that the meeting send them a complete account of
the prevailing conditions for the guidance of the
Pennsylvania Friends in planning the project and soliciting funds. (10) When the English Quakers heard of the
relief actions they approved of it as a Christian,
humane act, although they feared lest it be misconstrued
"at the other end of town". (11)

The Maryland Friends had also desired to aid the
sufferers in New England, but they had not as yet
called for contributions. Now that the Philadelphia
Meeting for Sufferings had opened the way for such
assistance, both quarterly meetings in Maryland initiated
collections to be forwarded to Philadelphia for this
work. (12)

According to the request from Pennsylvania, the
New England Meeting for Sufferings made a survey of the
conditions of those in distress and submitted a full
account of their findings to Philadelphia. In this report they warned that the task of relief would be a
heavy one and that it could be done only if a considerable amount of money were donated. Moreover , great
care would have to be taken both to prevent their intentions from being misconstrued as they already had
been, and to "stop the Mouths of the Censorious of
both parties". (13)

In November 1775 the Philadelphia Meeting for Sufferings sent Ь2000 to New England by David Evans and John
Parrish, and it also assigned Ь200 due from the New
England Friends for books for the same purpose. It
authorized the New Englanders to draw on Philadelphia
for more funds if needed, and it stipulated that the
distribution was not to be limited "to the Members of
our own or any other Religious Society, nor to the place
of their present or former residence". On the other
hand the money was not to be "bestow'd on those who
are Active in carrying on or prosecuting Military
Measures, of either part,...that we (may) preserve our
Religious Testimony against War's & Fighting pure-".
Sufferers both inside and outside Boston were to be
recipients, and the distributors were requested to make
a complete census of all persons and families with which
to refute any misinterpretations which might arise
later. (14)

296

When the money and the accompanying communication were received, the New England Meeting for Sufferings appointed a committee to go to Boston with addresses to both General Washington and General Howe to explain its mission and request permission to pass the lines. The Meeting also commissioned Moses Brown and five other Friends to investigate the needs of people in the towns outside Boston who might come within the intention of the donation. (15)

On arriving at Boston, the committee interviewed Washington who allowed it to pass the American lines under a flag of truce. General Howe, however, would not allow it to confer with the Boston Quakers, but permitted the sheriff, Mr. Loring, to transact their business. Through him the committee sent a draft for Ŀ100 to James Raymer and Ebenezer Pope to be distributed "without Regard to religious Sects, or political parties". (16)

When their mission to Boston had been discharged, the committee moved on to Lynn, Salem, Marblehead, and other towns. At Marblehead and Salem they distributed aid with the assistance of the selectmen, canvassing the town of Salem house by house. Four members of the committee then proceeded to Cape Anne where conditions were worse than in many other places. The whole number of families aided on this trip was four hundred. (17)

Within the next few months further distributions were made in other towns and villages in Massachusetts. Thomas Hazzard and Moses Brown visited Medfield, Bolton, Lancaster, Marlborough, Sudbury, Weston, Woborn, Reading,Sherborn, Holiston, Northbury, Waltham, and Monotoma, assisting one hundred and forty-one families and distributing Ŀ229. David Buffum and Ezekiel Comstock made distributions in Sutton and Worcester, and Jacob Mott, Jr., and Isaac Lawton performed a similar mission to Newport on Rhode Island, Jeremiah Hacker of Lynn was authorized to draw up to Ŀ200 for the relief of the inhabitants of Falmouth in Casco Bay and the towns between there and Cape Anne. Eber Chase and Theophilus Shore, Jr. were commissioned to make investigations and donations in Swanzey, Bridgewater, and other towns in that area. About one hundred and sixty families who had removed from Boston and Charlestown to those places were thus assisted. (18)

Meanwhile the Philadelphia Friends sent Ŀ500 more

for distribution. They also decided to distribute
relief to any who might remove from New England to
Pennsylvania because of the war situation. (19)

In April 1776 the New England Meeting for Sufferings
sent the Philadelphia Meeting for Sufferings a full
account of the money distributed, together with a census
of the families assisted. According to this report
5220 persons had been assisted in the amount of Ł1968
5s. 2½d., the number of families being 1472. (20) The
Philadelphia Friends thereupon appropriated Ł500 more
and expressed the hope that their efforts would not
only relieve the sufferings of the poor, but that they
would also "make good impressions on the minds of some
who have been prejudiced against Friends". (21) Before
the New England project was finished, assistance was
extended to Portsmouth and the Isle of Shoals in
New Hampshire, Hull and Plymouth in Massachusetts, and
Nantucket and Newport in Rhode Island. (22) In all,
Ł2540 proclamation money or Ł3196 Pennsylvania currency
was sent to New England. (23)

The situation on the islands of Nantucket and
Rhode Island was also especially acute during the
winter of 1775-1776. Although the Massachusetts government had finally allowed the Nantucketers to procure
supplies from the mainland, they had difficulty in
obtaining enough for the island's needs. The cessation
of trade greatly increased the number of the poor, and
the scarcity of firewood obliged numbers of families
to resort to the use of peat. (24) On hearing of this
situation, Moses Brown sent part of the Philadelphia
donation to Christopher Starbuck with instructions as
to its distribution and requested that the selectmen
of the town furnish a list of the most needy poor. (25)

In April 1776 several Friends from Nantucket
attended some sessions of the New England Meeting for
Sufferings and reported that many inhabitants were
without money to purchase supplies. The meeting thereupon donated Ł70 to procure wood for the poor, wherewith
some fifty families were assisted. (26) Subsequently
the increasing poverty resulting from the disappearance
of the whaling business and the rapid decline of the
cod fisheries for lack of salt prompted another
appropriation of Ł50. (27)

In the case of the island of Rhode Island, not only
had the military operations in the area resulted in
much want and harship, but many families had also been

298

driven from their homes. In October 1775 Rhode Island
Quarterly Meeting sent some Friends to visit the island
and assist any Quakers there who were in need. (28)
As a result of this mission the Meeting for Sufferings
sent a part of the Philadelphia fund to Philip Wanton
of Newport for distribution there. The recipients of
this assistance went far beyond Quaker circles, and
Wanton was daily besieged by needy people who had
heard of the Philadelphia donation. (29)

The need was obviously great, and Wanton and Mary
Callendar appealed to Moses Brown for more aid. The
Meeting for Sufferings then sent Isaac Lawton and Jacob
Mott, Jr., to the island where they distributed over
₤300 to 1267 persons in 330 families in Newport. (30)
Moses Brown himself, in February 1776, loaned the Town
Council of Newport ₤100 for poor relief. Subsequently,
in the winter of 1776-1777, at the direction of the
Philadelphia Friends, ₤100 in money and ₤60 worth of
wood were also distributed there. (31)

Although in the course of 1776 military operations
moved out of most of New England, the British retained
control of Newport until 1779. Dislocation of trade
and commerce and the general effect of wartime conditions
resulted in continuing poverty and hardship for many.
Consequently in January 1779 Rhode Island Quarterly
Meeting appealed to the subordinate monthly meetings for
aid "to Relieve the Distress of all Denominations" who
had been forced to leave "their own Habitations and Seek
Shelter from the Present Inclement Season among Straing-
ers". The situation had been caused by the flight of
a large number of people from their homes on the island
of Rhode Island to the mainland for refuge. In response
to this appeal the monthly meetings raised ₤222 for
the relief of the refugees. (32)

At the time when the New England Friends were distributing relief to the needy in the Boston area, Friends
in Virginia and New York were also active in relief
programs. In January 1776 the British fleet with which
Governor Dunmore of Virginia had found asylum bombarded
and burned the town of Norfolk, which put many of the
inhabitants in a distressing situation. In February,
Henrico Monthly Meeting raised ₤26 to assist the suffering and sent Edward Stabler and Robert Pleasants to
distribute the money. The two Friends interviewed the
Governor on the warship Dunmore and requested him to
allow the inhabitants of the town to move up the rivers
with their effects. If this could not be granted, they

asked him for at least permission to take them relief
supplies by water since the conditions of the roads
and remoteness of that part of the country made travel
by land almost impossible. The latter request was granted, and passports were issued to the Friends to take
provisions to the sufferers. However, General Lee of
the American forces objected to the action, and the
supplies were temporarily stored at Four Mile Creek on
the James River pending further arrangements. (33)

Already in September 1775 the New York Meeting
for Sufferings called upon the monthly meetings to
support the raising of a fund for the distress likely
to befall many people. (34) The next year the British
ocupied New York City and adjacent portions of Long
Island which thereafter became the center of British
operations in America throughout the war. The inhabitants of the region, including nearby Westchester
County which now became the area separating the British
from the American forces, suffered greatly from the
ensuing military operations.

In November 1776 Purchase Monthly Meeting in
Westchester County initiated a collection in money and
kind for relief purposes. Two funds were raised, one
for Friends and one for non-Friends, the former netting
₤61 and the latter ₤57. A similar subscription undertaken in December 1777 for non-Friends brought in a
total of ₤71, and in addition to the money, Chappaqua
Monthly Meeting contributed 21 bus. of wheat, 2 bus.
of corn, 168 lbs. of pork, and 80 lbs. of beef. A
third collection was made in the winter of 1778-1779.(35)

Early in 1777 the Friends in New York City accepted
a part of the surplus of the New England relief fund
from the Philadelphia Meeting for Sufferings. At the
same time they launched a subscription of their own,
as a result of which Flushing and Westbury Monthly
Meetings raised ₤31 and ₤34 respectively, probably only
a portion of the total. (36)

In the winter of 1776-1777 the British, now ensconced
in New York, carried their campaigns into northern New
Jersey with the usual impoverishing effects on the inhabitants of the area. In July 1777 the Philadelphia
Meeting for Sufferings directed the committee in charge
of the New England fund to enquire of Friends in and
around Rahway and Plainfield as to the conditions there
and to furnish such sums as were necessary to relieve
distress. The New Jersey Friends replied that from 30

to 40 families needed assistance, and the meeting sent
Ł100 to them for distribution. Two years later, in
the winter of 1778-1779, Shrewsbury Monthly Meeting
raised a relief fund from among its members, and the
Meeting for Sufferings donated Ł100. (37)

The arrival of the British forces in Pennsylvania
in the summer of 1777 created the first widespread
suffering of the war in that region. The progress of
the armies through the northern counties of Delaware
and the eastern section of Pennsylvania left much
distress in its wake. In September, Kennett Monthly
Meeting in Chester County urged its members to render
such aid to the needy as they could personally, and it
appointed a committee to assist in this work. (38)

According to Crevecour, the Quakers sent the
necessitous all they had "and shed tears over the fate
of those whom they were unable to help". Many of the
"Anciens" traveled over the country from plantation to
plantation collecting all the bacon, flour, and other
provisions they could procure. Quantities of money,
clothing, and other useful articles were thus gathered
and distributed. (39)

Philadelphia and the immediate vicinity were the
chief scene of relief work. In January 1777 Friends
of Lampeter Preparative Meeting in Lancaster County
proposed sending several barrels of meal to the city
for the use of the needy,but the project did not materialize. (40) After the British occupation of the city,
Philadelphia Monthly Meeting and Philadelphia Monthly
Meeting for the Southern District both appointed
committees to assist persons of all denominations, and
they distributed all but six of the Ł416 raised for
that purpose. The Meeting for Sufferings appropriated
Ł400 for the relief of those who had taken no part in
the war, and the meeting-house on High or Market Street
was opened to the poor of the city and suburbs who
were turned out of the public houses by the British
soldiers. (41) Falls Monthly Meeting in Bucks County
collected money for the benefit of the distressed inhabitants of the province, especially those in
Philadelphia. (42) Two attempts to obtain permission
from General Washington to send food in from the country
were unsuccessful, since he felt unable to grant such
favors without the approval of Congress. (43)

Individual Friends were also active in the cause
of mercy. After the battle of Germantown the Quakers
in the city were allowed to take food and other necessar-

301

ies to the wounded Americans, and members of Elizabeth
Drinker's household carried coffee and whey to the
wounded Americans at the State House. (44) Such
incidents continued throughout the war. The loyalist
Benjamin Marston, captured and imprisoned at Philadelphia in 1781, especially mentioned the great kindness
of the Quakers in supplying provisions, clothing, and
comforts of various kinds to the sick and destitute.(45)

In England the English Quakers became involved in
relief activities also, both in assisting American
prisoners of war who were incarcerated in Britain and
in contributing to the relief of those suffering from
the effects of the war in America. On December 24,
1777, a group of Quaker merchants met at the King's
Arm Tavern in Cornhill, London, to consider means for
the relief of American prisoners of war at Portsmouth
from whom a petition had been received, indicating
they were in need of warm winter clothing. A subscription
was immediately undertaken and by December 29 ₤1486
had been raised. (46)

On January 3, 1778, a committee of merchants attended the Lords of Admiralty to intercede on behalf of
the prisoners. Lord Sandwich, to whom they presented
their concern, not only approved of their action but
he also gave orders for the erection of a temporary
building for the prisoners. Shortly afterward the
merchants solicited a subscription for relief funds in
Bristol, Nottingham, and in Yorkshire, as well as in
London. By February ₤4647 had been received from the
country in addition to ₤3700 from the city itself. (47)

It was during this winter of 1777-1778 that the
British occupied Philadelphia, and all communications
between the country and the city were severed at the
orders of the Continental Congress and the state governments of New Jersey and Pennsylvania. Heavy penalties
were decreed for anyone attempting to disobey these
orders. Therefore, in December 1777 several of the
Philadelphia Friends met to consider ways and means
of getting supplies into the city. A committee was
appointed to ask the English Quakers to send a shipload
of food and other necessities, the Philadelphians
agreeing to pay for the shipment as soon as circumstances allowed. (48)

Meanwhile Thomas Gawthrop who was in England on a
religious visit informed the London Friends of the
situation in Philadelphia. This prompted the formation

of a committee of London Quakers to raise money and
send a cargo of food to Philadelphia. The sum of Ł5000
was soon collected, individual subscriptions running
from Ł50 to Ł100. These supplies were to be sold at
prime cost, the Philadelphia Friends to pay for them
when they could. (49) The London committee also sent
a circular letter to the Quakers in Britain and Ireland,
soliciting an additional Ł5000 to Ł6000 for American
relief, and authorized the Philadelphia Friends to
draw on that fund up to Ł500 if necessary. (50)

When the Quakers in Bristol heard of the difficulties of their American brethren, they sent a shipload
of flour, peas, grits, and barley, two-thirds to be
paid for by the Philadelphia Friends and the other third
to be a gift. This cargo, valued upwards of Ł2100
never reached its destination. It was captured by an
American privateer and taken into the port of Boston. (51)

Soon after receiving the British appeal and the
letter from Philadelphia, the Irish Friends held their
Half Yearly Meeting in Dublin. They immediately began
a subscription to assist the Americans and instructed
the Philadelphia Quakers to draw on this fund up to
Ł1000. At their next semi-annual session in November
1778, they wrote the Pennsylvania Friends via Robert
Murray of New York that Ł2000 had been raised, and
authorized them to draw up to that amount if it were
found necessary. (52) Subsequently English Friends
added Ł3000 to this sum, and the Quakers in Cornwall
raised Ł75 separately for the same purpose.(53)

When the news of what British Quakers had done
reached America it was printed in both the partiot and
loyalist newspapers. The Freemans Journal and New Hampshire Gazette reported that the English Friends were
raising "a subscription towards carrying on the war in
America", while the loyalist Pennsylvania Royal Gazette
informed its readers correctly that the money was being
collected for both needy Friends and others in Pennsylvania. (54)

The provisions sent from London were shipped on
board the Mary and Charlotte, Captain Besnard. When
the cargo, valued at Ł4666, reached Philadelphia in
June 1778, much of the shipment had been damaged by
heat, the voyage having taken seventeen weeks. It
was divided into three allotments, one for each monthly
meeting in the city, each of which agreed to distribute
its share and pay for it when called upon, regardless

of the damage. (55) Subsequently a controversey arose
as to what extent the Philadelphia Friends should assume
the cost of the loss incurred by the shipment. Eventually the Philadelphia and London Friends decided to
share the loss equally.

In the south the Friends also responded to needy
situations resulting from the war. In 1778 the Western
Shore Quarterly Meeting Committee on Suffering Cases in
Maryland urged the subordinate monthly meetings to raise
funds "for the Support of the Poor of all Denominations",
and Gunpowder Monthly Meeting alone collected ₤107 for
this purpose. (56) The worst ravages of the war were
not felt in Maryland, however, and when the Philadelphia
Friends offered funds for relief in 1782, the Maryland
Quakers replied that such assistance was not needed
at that time. (57)

It was not until the last years of the war that
the Carolinas became the scene of the conflict and situations arose calling for assistance. When the British
took Charleston in May 1780 many people were forced
to leave their homes. According to a contemporary
account the "Quakers from policy or an humane principle"
provided for the unfortunates and "offered their Country
seats for their Accomodation". (58) A year later,
after the battle of Guilford Courthouse in North Carolina, Nathaniel Greene appealed to the Friends there to
succor the wounded, declaring that he knew of "no order
of men more remarkable for the exercise of humanity
and benevolence". The Quakers promised to do all in
their power, although they were already taxed by the
depradations of the armies in the neighborhood and were
caring for over one hundred persons bereft of all provisions in their meeting-house. (59)

Thus far we have discussed Quaker relief efforts
in behalf of the community in general. There were at
the same time extensive relief activities carried out
in behalf of members of the Society which no doubt often
benefited their neighbors as well. In these efforts the
British and Irish Friends were most active, appreciably
supplementing what the Pennsylvania Friends, despite
their own war-caused difficulties, were contributing.
These monies were used in three ways: for Friends on
Nantucket, for Friends in the Carolinas and Georgia,
and for some individual cases of need around Philadelphia and elsewhere.

In New England as already indicated, food shortages

and other privations were ever present during the war.
The English Friends were especially concerned over the
welfare of the Rhode Island Quakers, and in July 1779
Rhode Island Monthly Meeting received a bill of exchange
from them for Ł100. (60) That fall Moses Farnum in
company with Joseph Mitchell of Nantucket made a religious
visit to Philadelphia and reported the suffering condition of many Friends in New England. The Philadelphia
Meeting for Sufferings thereupon donated a draft of
up to Ł315 for aid to the New Englanders and informed
the visiting Friends of the Irish fund. The Philadelphia
donation enabled Moses Brown to distribute much needed
assistance both on Nantucket and on the mainland. (61)

For the Nantucket Friends the winter of 1780-1781
brought particularly harsh conditions. At the request
of the New England Meeting for Sufferings the Philadelphia Friends donated Ł200 for the assistance of
needy Friends, Ł100 of which was to be spent in Philadelphia for supplies and necessities to be shipped
directly to Nantucket. The New England Meeting for
Sufferings also allocated Ł135 of the amount they had
received from the Irish fund for the aid of the Nantucketers. In the summer of 1781 the Philadelphians
further advanced from the Irish fund 15 Half Joannes,
or Ł195, for the assistance of Friends on the island
of Rhode Island and Ł150 to aid Friends on Nantucket.(62)

A year later, in June 1782, the Philadelphia Friends
turned their attention to New York and offered the
Friends there a portion of the English and Irish funds.
The New York Friends declined this offer since they had
already received Ł500 from the English Quakers directly.(63) In addition to this amount the New York Friends
themselves raised over Ł420 which was expended on
various relief projects. (64)

Because of depradations which the war brought
the south, both the English and Philadelphia Quakers
undertook to provide assistance to the Friends in
the Carolinas and Georgia. In the spring of 1781 two
North Carolina Friends visited Philadelphia, bringing
an account of the circumstances of the southern Quakers.
They returned home with Ł500 in gold from the Irish
donation and a letter to the Standing Committee of the
Western Quarter, explaining the origin of the money
and requesting information as to the situation of the
Quakers around New Garden, Cane Creek, and Deep River
Monthly Meetings. (65)

Reports also reached Philadelphia about this time that the Friends in South Carolina were in difficult straits, and the Meeting for Sufferings wrote to Isaac Peace and John Kirk, two Charleston Quakers, and to the Standing Committee of the Western Quarter in North Carolina, requesting a true account of the matter. The information later received was somewhat contradictory. One story was that families of men joining the British were banished to the British lines and so had tken refuge in Charleston where there was much distress. Another report through Edward Stabler from Richard Lushington who had just returned from a trip to North Carolina declared that no Friends had been sent into Charleston, but that other people sent there had been put into the Friends meeting-house. Moreover, the Friends of Bush River Monthly Meeting in South Carolina had been assured by General Greene that they would not be disturbed. (66)

Since the British occupation of Charleston made communication with the Friends there practically impossible, the Philadelphia Meeting for Sufferings turned to Samuel Bowne in New York and asked him to look into the matter and forward to the meeting any information he might obtain on the South Carolina situation. (67) Subsequently a letter arrived from the North Carolina Friends which explained that a few Quakers had quite voluntarily gone to Charleston to escape trouble and that they were therefore not eligible for assistance as members in good standing. The letter also advised the Philadelphia Friends to be cautious "of receiving accounts on so slender Authority", and assured them that the needs of both the North Carolina and South Carolina Quakers had been attended to. According to the letter the chief difficulty was obtaining salt due to poor transportation and the presence of robbers who infested the countryside. (68)

Friends in Georgia had meanwhile appealed to the London Meeting for Sufferings, explaining their situation and requesting assistance. This letter was accompanied by one from Governor Sir James Wright supporting their request. In reply the London Friends authorized Daniel Silsby, Joseph Maddox, and Joseph Williams in Savannah to draw up to Ł500 to relieve the distress of the Quakers in Savannah, Wrightsboro, and other parts of the province. (69)

When the Philadelphia Friends heard of this, they feared that the London Quakers might have been defrauded, and they wrote to North Carolina for information on the matter. An investigation revealed that several Friends had voluntarily gone into Savannah when the British had taken possession of that part of the province. Others who had done likewise because of threats from the Americans were now representing their case as banishment. The North Carolinians further informed that they had sent some of the Philadelphia donation to the Friends in Wrightsboro and that the fund was now nearly exhausted. (70)

Both the North Carolina and Philadelphia Friends then took action with regard to the situation in Savannah. The former warned the Wrightsboro Friends not to accept any of the English donation in the hands of the Savannah Quakers for fear of possible irregularities, but that they should rather apply to the Friends in Charleston for a share of the fund which the Philadelphia Friends had meanwhile transmitted there. The Wrightsboro Monthly Meeting thereupon appointed a committee to join with the Bush River Quakers in obtaining a share of that fund. (71)

In the meantime the Philadelphia Meeting for Sufferings had learned that Joseph Maddox had used the money sent to the Georgia Friends from England in a manner of which Daniel Silsby disapproved and without the latter's knowledge. The meeting proceeded to inform the English Friends of the state of affairs in Savannah and recommended that the London Quakers make no more such donations without first consulting Philadelphia. (72)

On their own part the Philadelphia Friends requested John Drinker & Co. to transmit ₤200 for the relief of southern Friends through Traugott Bagge, a merchant of Salem, North Carolina. In view of the damage wrought on meeting properties on account of the military campaigns, a further donation was later transmitted for the repair of Friends meeting-houses. (73)

Of individual cases assisted by the English and Irish funds, the most noteworthy was that of Benjamin Gilbert, a Quaker from Northampton County on the then Pennsylvania frontier. In June 1780 the Philadelphia Meeting for Sufferings received word that he and his family had been seized by the Indians and carried some distance into the western wilderness and their home and property destroyed. The meeting appointed a committee to inquire into the matter and to use its endeavors to obtain the release of the Gilberts. The

307

President and Council of Pennsylvania refused to
assist these efforts but allowed the committee to write
the Friends in New York to request assistance in re-
covering the kidnapped Quakers. When the Committee
of Sufferings of Oblong and Purchase Quarterly Meeting
received this request which was accompanied by an
instruction to draw on the Philadelphia Meeting for
Sufferings up to the amount of 100 English Guineas as
necessary, it appointed a committee to undertake the
project. (74)

In the spring of 1782, a son of Benjamin Gilbert
who had escaped capture set out for Canada to obtain
the release of his family. He received £120 from
the Irish fund with which to buy a horse and other
equipment for the expedition. In Vermont he obtained
permission from the Governor and Council to cross the
border and go to Montreal to solicit the aid of the
Canadian authorities.

Meanwhile the captives had been scattered throughout the wilderness and adopted by the Indians. By
purchase and persuasion their freedom was finally obtained, and by the time young Gilbert reached Montreal
he found them gathered together, thirteen in all. The
only casualty resulting from this episode was the
father who died on the return journey to Philadelphia
because of the hardships he had endured. Abigail
Dodson who had lived with the family was not retrieved
until two years later, and for her recovery the Meeting
for Sufferings donated £45, this in addition to the
£41 given for the release of the Gilberts, all from
the English and Irish funds. (75)

Through their relief efforts the Quakers demonstrated the positive nature of their religious testimonies. Regardless of their economic status the
Friends had a strong concern for the welfare of their
fellow citizens, to relieve whose distress they contributed liberally even while facing their own difficult
situations. Their action showed that despite refusal
to participate in an armed conflict to terminate the
connection with Britain, there was no question as to
their close identity with the land of their birth.

(1) Boudinot, Elias, <u>The Life, Public Services, Address-
     es and Letters of Elias Boudinot</u>, ed. J.J.Boudinot
     (2 vols., Boston, and New York, 1896),v.2,227.
(2) James Pemberton to Dr. Fothergill,July 1,1774,
     Ett.Pem.Pap., v.2,68.
(3) Phil.M.f.S. to London M.f.S., Nov.5,1774,Phil.M.f.S.,
     Min., v.1,431. For a full account of this episode
     see Henry J. Cadbury's <u>Quaker Relief During the
     Siege of Boston</u> (Pendle Hill Historical Study
     No.4, Wallingford, Pa., 1943); and Mack Thompson's
     "Moses Brown's 'Account of a Journey to Distribute
     Donations 12th Month, 1775', with an Introduction,"
     <u>Rhode Island History</u>, v.15 (1956),97-121.
(4) Salem M.M., Min., 1677-1788,199-200; Jeremiah
     Hacker to John Pemberton, April 14,1775,Pem.Pap.,
     v.27,128;same to same, June 14,1775, in <u>ibid</u>.,165.
(5) John Pemberton to his wife,Nov. 30,1776,Pem.Pap.,
     v.27,28.
(6) N. E. M.f.S., Min., v.1,1;N.E.M.f.S. to Phil.M.f.S.,
     July 15,1775,in ibid., 2-3.
(7) Phil.M.f.S., Min., v.2,3,7,8.
(8) Marshall, Diary, July 9,1775;N.E.M.f.S., Min.,
     v.1,5-7; Phil.M.f.S., Min., v.2,9-12; Phil.M.f.S. to
     N.E.M.f.S., July 27,1775,<u>ibid</u>., 14-16.
(9) <u>Va. Gaz</u>., July 29,1775; <u>Pa. Ev. Post</u>, July 15, 1775;
     <u>Pa. Mer</u>., July 14, 1775; <u>Pa. Gaz</u>., July 12, 1775;
     <u>Pa. Ldg</u>., July 22, 1775; <u>N.Y. Gaz</u>., July 24, 1775;
     <u>Nwp. Mer</u>., July 24,1775; <u>Essex Gaz</u>., July 21,1775.
(10) Phil.M.f.S. to N.E.M.f.S., July 27,1775,<u>loc.cit</u>.
(11) Mildred and Roberts to John Pemberton, Sept.8,1775;
     Pem.Pap., v.28,51.
(12) James Berry to Israel Pemberton, Aug.8,1775,Pem.
     Pap., v.28, 23; Third Haven and Little Creek (South-
     ern) Q.M., Min., 1759-1822, July 26, 1775; West
     River Q.M., Min., 1710-1822,130.
(13) N.E.M.f.S. to Phil. M.f.S., Sept. 12,1775,N.E.M.f.S.,
     Min., v.1,9-11;Phil.M.f.S., Min., v.2,27-28.
(14) N.E.M.f.S., Min., v.1,16;Phil.M.f.S. to N.E.M.f.S.,
     Nov.9,1775, in <u>ibid</u>.,14-16;Phil.M.f.S., Min.,v.2,
     37-40.
(15) N.E.M.f.S., Min., v.1,19-20.
(16) <u>Ibid</u>., 22-24.
(17) <u>Ibid</u>., 25-26. After the distribution, the town
     of Salem passed a vote of thanks for the relief
     sent by the Pennsylvania and New Jersey Friends
     (Felt, Joseph B., ed., <u>Annals of Salem from Its</u>

Settlement, 2 vols., Salem, 1845-1849, v.2,130,399).
(18) N.E.M.f.S., Min., v.1,28-30;N.E.M.f.S. to Phil.
M.f.S., March 11, 1776, in _ibid_., 52; Phil.M.f.S.,
Min., v.2,74.
(19) Phil.M.f.S., Min., v.2,50,65;Phil.M.f.S., to N.
E.M.f.S., Feb.15,1776, in _ibid_., 62.
(20) N.E.M.f.S. to Phil.M.f.S., April 24,1776,Phil.M.f.
S., Min., v.1,37-38. A summary of the distributions
is in N.E.M.f.S., Min., v.1,39-40, while a complete
account and the census of the families aided is in
Phil.M.f.S., Misc. Pap.
(21) Phil.M.f.S. to N.E.M.f.S., May 9,1776,Phil.M.f.S.,
Min., v.2,83-85;N.E.M.f.S., Min., v.1,42-43.
(22) N.E.M.f.S. to Phil.M.f.S., June 15,1776,N.E.M.f.S.,
Min., v.1,44-45;Phil.M.f.S., Min., v.2,89-90.
(23) When the accounts were finally closed, Ł2540 16s.
5½d. proclamation money or Ł3196 6s. Pennsylvania
currency had been sent to New England, and about
Ł670 remained in the hands of John Reynell with
Ł300 still to be collected. The Maryland Quakers
contributed Ł235 9s., those in Delaware Ł160 12s.
6d., those in New Jersey Ł1060 9s. 2½d., and the
Pennsylvania Friends Ł2453 1s. 5d. The Maryland
and Delaware Meetings subsequently raised Ł119 5s.
7d. and Ł141 10s. 6d. respectively, making a
grand total of Ł4427. Over Ł100 of this amount
was eventually used for other relief projects.
For a detailed account of income and expenditure
see Phil.M.f.S., Min., v.2, 100-103,183. Specific
accounts of this Maryland Friends are in Third
Haven and Little Creek Q.M., Min., 1759-1822,
Oct.21,1775;West River Q.M., Min., 1710-1822,131;
and Gunpowder M.M., Min., 1768-1784,134. The
Delaware accounts are in Wilmington M.M., Min.,
1776-1792,58 and Duck Creek M.M., Min., 1705-1800,
279,281.
(24) N.E.M.f.S. to Phil. M.f.S., March 11,1776,_loc.cit_.
(25) Same to same, April 24,1776,_loc.cit._;Joseph
Mitchell to Moses Brown, April 23, 1776, Mitchell
Papers (1916), 139, in the Nantucket Hist. Soc.
The list was supplied as requested.
(26) N.E.M.f.S. to Phil.M.f.S., April 24,1776, _loc.
cit_.,same to same June 15,1776, _loc.cit_.
(27) Same to same, Aug. 11,1777,N.E.M.f.S., Min., v.1,71.
(28) R.I.Q.M., Min., 1746-1791,191.
(29) N.E.M.f.S., Min., v.1,20;Philip Wanton to Moses
Brown, Jan. 24,1776, Moses Brown Pap., v.2,48.
(30) N.E.M.f.S., Min., v.1,28,40;Philip Wanton to Moses
Brown, Jan.24,1776,_loc.cit_.;Mary Callender to
Moses Brown, Jan.24,1776, Moses Brown Pap., v.2,48;

same to John Pemberton, Jan.31,1776, Pem.Pap.,v.28, 165.

(31) N.E.M.f.S., Min., v.1,56,59;Phil.M.f.S. to N.E.M.f.S., Feb. 15,1776,loc.cit.;Mary Callender to Moses Brown, Feb.7,1776, Moses Brown Pap., v.2,50;Edmund Townshend to Moses Brown, Feb.29,1776,in ibid.,52.

(32) N.E.M.f.S., Min., v.1,98,99,102,117;R.I.Q.M. to the subordinate monthly meetings, Jan.7 & 8, 1779, So. Kingston Pap.

(33) Henrico Q.M., Min., 1745-1783,Feb.24,May 15,1776; Robert Pleasants to his brother, Jan.3,March4,1776, Letter Book,36,37.

(34) N.Y.M.f.S., Min., v.1,31-32;Westbury M.M., Min., 1767-1782,146;Flushing M.M., Min., 1771-1776,86.

(35) Purchase M.M., Min., 1772-1785, Nov.14,1776;Dec.11, 1777,May 14,1778;Jan.14,1779.

(36) Phil.M.f.S., Min., v.2,111-112;N.Y.M.f.S., Min., v.1,36,38,45;Flushing M.M., Min., 1776-1781,17; Westbury M.M., Min., 1767-1782,178.

(37) Phil.M.f.S., Min., v.12,124,126-128,193;Shrewsbury M.M., Min., 1757-1786,397.

(38) Kennett M.M., Min., 1739-1791,618.

(39) Ecuyer,W.S. (Hector St. John Crevècoeur), Lettres d'un Cultivateur Americain (2 vols., Paris, 1784), v.1,182.

(40) James Gibbons to Israel Pemberton, Jan.19, March 8, 1777, Pam. Pap., v.29,132,147.

(41) Phil.M.f.S., Min., v.2,136-138;Phil.M.M., Min., 1777-1781, 11,52;Phil.M.M. So. Dist., Min., 1770-1780, 217,259.

(42) Falls M.M., Min., 1767-1788,201-202.

(43) Phil.M.f.S., Min., v.2,140.

(44) Drinker, Journal, Oct. 10,11,1777;Stein, Roslyn, The British Occupation of Philadelphia, September 1777 - June, 1778, (unpublished M.A. thesis, Columbia University, 1937), 78.

(45) Marston, Benjamin, Benjamin Marston of Marblehead, Loyalist (New Brunswick Hist. Soc. Collections, No.7,1907),99.

(46) Gordon, William,The History of the Rise, Progress and Establishment of the Independence of the United States of America (4 vols., London, 1788, reprinted New York, 1969),v.3,99-100.

(47) Ibid., 100.

(48) Phil.Mf.S., Min., v.12,187-188.

(49) Ibid.;Dr. Fothergill to Abel James and sister, March 11, 1778, Jonah Thompson Col. bx.2;Joseph Woods to Dr. Parke, Feb.1o,1778,Pem.Pap.,v.31,114; Robert Barclay to Dr. Parke, Feb.16,1778,in ibid.,

126-128.
(50) Phil.M.f.S., Min., v.2,189;"To Friends in Great
     Britain and Ireland, March 6,1778", Phil.M.f.S.,
     Misc.Pap., bx.14; Etting Scientist Pap., 28, at
     HSP;Robert Barclay to Dr. Parke,Feb.16,1778,loc.
     cit.
(51) Phil.M.f.S., Min., v.2,189;Roy.Amer.Gaz., July 2,
     1778.
(52) Eben Pike et al. to John Reynell et al., May 11,
     1778,Phil.M.f.S., Min., v.2, 185;Coates,Reynell
     Pap., bx. 14; James Forbes et al., to John Reynell
     et al., Nov.4,1778, Phil.M.f.S., Misc. Pap.,bx.19
     (1790-1792);Robert Dudley to Robert Murray, Nov.13,
     1778,in ibid.
(53) London M.f.S. to Phil.M.f.S., March 8,1782,Phil.
     M.f.S., Min., v.2,348;Phil.M.M., Min.,1777-1781;316.
(54) Frmn.Jnl.,March 31, 1778; Pa. Roy. Gaz.,April 14,
     1778.For a detailed account of this episode see
     Kenneth Carroll's "The Maryland and Charlotte Fiasco.
     A Look at 1778 British Quaker Relief for Philadel-
     phia", PMHB, v.102, (1978), 212-223.
(55) Phil.M.f.S.,Min.,v.2,189-180;Phil.M.M.,Min.,1777-
     1781,53;Phil.M.M.No.Dist.,Min.,1772-1781,322;Phil.
     M.M.So.Dist.,Min.,1770-1780,256;"A British Food Ship
     for Philadelphia Quakers",More Books,v.14 (1939),
     64-65; Carroll, loc.cit., 223.
(56) Gunpowder M.M., Min., 1768-1784,206,210.
(57) Phil.M.f.S., Min., v.2,358,382.
(58) Joseph Harrison to Mrs. John Lawrence, June 16,1781,
     PMHB, v.14 (1890), 82.
(59) Snowden, W. H., "General Greene and the Friends at
     Guilford", American Friend v.2 (1895),307.
(60) R.I.M.M., Min., 1773-1790,138.
(61) Phil.M.f.S., Min., v.2,224,258-259;N.E.M.f.S., Min.,
     v.1,117;Phil.M.f.S. to N.E.M.f.S., Oct.18,1779,
     Phil.M.f.S., Min., v.2,242, a copy of this letter
     is also in ibid., Misc. Pap., bx.15; N.E.M.f.S.,
     Min., v.1,119;Moses Brown to Jonathan Macy and
     Jethro Mitchell, Dec. 14,1779,Mitchell Pap.
(62) Phil.M.f.S., Min., v.2,298,428;N.E.M.f.S., Min.,
     v.1,165;N.E.M.f.S. to Phil.M.f.S., Dec.11,1780,
     Phil.M.f.S., Min., v.2,298; James Pemberton to
     Sarah Barney, Jan.23, 1781,Pem.Pap., v.35,81;
     William Rotch to James Pemberton, Feb.18,1781,
     in ibid., 93.
(63) N.E.M.f.S., Min., v.1,96;Phil.M.f.S., Min., v.2,
     392;Phil.M.f.S.to N.Y.M.f.S., June 20,1782,Phil.
     M.f.S., Min., v.2,350; Gathered Leaves, v.1,64
     (a two volume collection of N.Y.M. Misc. Pap.).
(64) Flushing M.M., Min., 1782-1784,36-77;N.Y.M.f.S.,

Min., v.1,74-75,81,88,108-110,115;N.Y.Y.M.,Min.,
v.1,169.

(65) Phil.M.f.S. to Standing Committee of Western
Quarter of N.C.Y.M., May 12,1781,Phil.M.f.S.,
Misc.Pap., bx.16 (1781-1782).

(66) Phil.M.f.S., Min., v.2,320,321; William Matthews
to John Pemberton, Nov.23, 1781,Pem.Pap., v.36,23;
Letter of Edward Stabler, Dec.19,1781,Cox,Wharton,
Parrish Col.

(67) John Pemberton to Samuel Bowne, Dec.31,1781,Pem.
Pap., v.36,27.

(68) Standing Committee of Western Quarter of N.C.Y.M
to Phil.M.f.S., Aug.10,1782,Phil.M.f.S.,Misc,
Pap., bx.16.

(69) Joseph Williams, Joseph Maddox et al. to the
London M.f.S., Jan.2,1782, London M.f.S., Min.,
v.36, June 7,21,1782; Epistles to London Y.M.,
v.5,133-137;Sir James Wright to the London M.f.S.,
Jan.5,1782, Epistles to London Y.M., v.5,138-139;
London Y.M. to Daniel Silsby, June 7,1782, Epistles
from London Y.M.; v.5,229-230,London M.f.S.,
Min., v.36,June 21, 1782.

(70) Phil.M.f.S. to Standing Committee of Western Quarter
of N.C.Y.M., Oct. 26,1782,Phil.M.f.S., Misc.Pap.,
bx.16; Standing Committee to Western Quarter of
N.C.Y.M. to Phil. M.f.S., May 10,1783,in ibid.

(71) Wrightsboro M.M., Min., 1772-1793,77-78.

(72) Phil.M.f.S. to Standing Committee of Western Quarter
of N.C.Y.M., Aug.28,1783, Phil.M.f.S., Misc. Pap.,
bx.16. Joseph Maddox was subsequently disowned by
Wrightsboro Monthly Meeting for his actions (Wrightsboro M.M., Min., 1772-1793,81,85.).

(73) Phil.M.f.S. to the Standing Committee of Western
Quarter of N.C.Y.M., May 18,1783,Phil.M.f.S., Min.,
v.2,432, a copy of the same is in ibid.Misc.Pap.,
bx.17 (1783-1785); same to same, n.d., Phil.M.f.S.,
Misc.Pap., bx.18 (1785-1789).

(74) Phil.M.f.S., Min., v.2,273,277;N.Y.M.f.S., Min.,
v.1,89. A full account of this episode is given in
William Walton's Captivity and Sufferings of
Benjamin Gilbert and his Family (Cleveland, 1904).

(75) Phil.M.f.S., Min., v.2,355,394,426,428;ibid.,v.3,
61,77. For an extensive account of the aid given
by English and Irish Friends see Kenneth L.
Carrol's "Irish and British Quakers and their
American Relief Funds, 1778-1797", PMHB,v.102
(1978), 437-456.

Chapter XVIII

POST-WAR PROBLEMS AND READJUSTMENTS

Although the conclusion of the war brought a cessation to many of the difficulties experienced by the Friends, the years immediately following presented a number of issues which carried over from it. One of the first problems arose early in 1784: whether or not consistent Friends could pay taxes for the liquidation of state debts incurred in the conduct of the war.

In February of that year, the Baltimore Meeting for Sufferings noted that no reports of distraints had come up from the Western Quarter. An invesitgation revealed that many of the members were paying taxes to sink the war debt on the basis that the cessation of the war had lifted the prohibition to do so. The Meeting for Sufferings took a different viewpoint and declared its unanimous judgment that "notwithstanding the effusion of human blood has been stayed, friends cannot be clear, in paying taxes imposed for sinking the debt incurred by the late war." (1) Four years later, in 1788, there were again reports of Friends paying such levies. At that time the Yearly Meeting advised its members to refrain from such action and directed the monthly meetings to disown those who persisted in doing so. (2)

In both Pennsylvania and New Jersey the same question arose. In 1784 Western Quarterly Meeting in Pennsylvania considered the matter and decided against paying any taxes to carry the war debt. Among the New Jersey Quakers there seems to have been some disagreement. At the sessions of Gloucester and Salem Quarterly Meeting in June 1784, the subject came up for discussion and there was "some tite Rubing work so that one of the first rank made an Acknowledgment & Evesham Seemed to be getting through with that Gable about Suffering for taxes". At the next quarterly meeting sessions in September the question again arose, and one of the members recorded:

> We had it up & Down about taxpaying. They
> Seemed Like to Knock Evesham in the head &

314

> throw us by but Warner Mifflin &
> Several others Stood Titely to the
> Testimony and it was Raised over all
> against paying of taxis. (3)

Since the matter at issue touched a fundamental
testimony of the Society, the Yearly Meeting addressed
itself to the question when it met in Philadelphia
shortly afterward. As might have been predicted, it
decided against the payment of such taxes and referred
the quarterly meeting to official statements on the
subject which the Yearly Meeting had issued in 1778
and 1780. (4)

Somewhat later the New York Quakers faced the same
problem. In March 1785 the Meeting for Sufferings
learned that some Friends were paying taxes of this
nature. Although the meeting issued no official statement, it decided that its members as individuals should
encourage and support those who had scruples against
making such payments. The matter was then brought to
the attention of the yearly meeting which convened a
few weeks later and it issued an exhortation to its
members to "preserve from Complyance, with any Tax or
requisition inconsistent" with their peaceable testimony. (5) The New England Friends took a similar position, and a number of Quakers there had their property
distrained for refusal to pay taxes to sink the war
debt. (6)

Another issue which arose as an aftermath of the
war was whether or not a Friend could be concerned
in the sale or purchase of lands confiscated from Tory
loyalists. Before the Revolution the New England
Quakers had faced a similar problem when in 1761 Rhode
Island Quarterly Meeting had queried the yearly
meeting whether it was consistent for Friends to acquire
lands in Nova Scotia which had been confiscated from
the French. At that time the yearly meeting declared
that "no friend nor friends (should) take any such Land
nor be Concerned in taking any Such Land" because it
had been acquired by force. (7)

Throughout the War for Independence the Society
in New England and Pennsylvania had adhered to this
policy. In 1778 William Gorton of South Kingston
Monthly Meeting in Rhode Island was disowned for
hiring confiscated estates. In 1780 Samuel Foulke of
Richland Monthly Meeting in Bucks County, Pennsylvania,
was disowned partly on the grounds of having surveyed
lands confiscated from Joseph Galloway. (8)

315

After the war this problem assumed serious proportions
in New York where many estates lying along the Hudson
were confiscated from their Tory owners. In September
1784 Jacob Underhill, John Griffin, Zephaniah Birdsall,
William Cornell, and some other Friends who had been
tenants on the Frederick Phillipse Manor informed the
Meeting for Sufferings of a difficult perdicament in
which they found themselves. The land on which they
lived had been confiscated by the government and put
up for sale. During the years in which they had occupied
their tracts near Chappaqua they had invested a considerable sum of mony in improving the property. They
therefore inquired whether it would be consistent with
their testimony as Friends to purchase the solid rights
of thse tracts, the value of which was far less than
the improvements. The opinion of the Meeting for
Sufferings was that Friends could not consistently
make any such pruchases, since their "Testimony against
War (was) nearly concern'd therein". The persons involved were advised to make an appeal to the authorities,
explaining their situation and the loss which the
occupiers would suffer if the land were sold from under
them. (9)

Later the same year, Purchase Monthly and Quarterly
Meetings were informed that some Friends had been
buying confiscated lands. The quarterly meeting declared
its united opinion that such purchases were inconsistent
with the Friends' peace testimony since the lands were
spoils of war and that the offenders should be dealt
with. (10) About the same time Amawalk Preparative
Meeting found that three of its members had made
similar purchases, and Purchase Monthly Meeting, on
being informed, appointed committees to deal with the
delinquents. (11)

When the next Yearly Meeting convened in the spring
of 1785, this problem was brought up for discussion. It
advised its members that it had observed "with Sorrow"
that some Friends in one quarter had "made purchases
of Confiscated Lands, which as it is partaking of the
Spoils of War, is an open Violation of our Testimony
in that Respect, and demands the care and exertion of
our Monthly Meetings". (12)

In November 1785 the case of the Friends on the
Phillipse Manor again came before the Meeting for
Sufferings as the date for the sale of the land was
near at hand. The meeting was informed of the possibility of procuring a suspension of the sale and
appointed a committee to assist in making such an

application to the authorities. A petition subsequently presented obtained the desired postponement, although the land was later sold. (13)

The final victory of the Americans in the Revolution necessitated a reorientation of the Society's attitude toward the government in power. Shortly after the signing of the peace treaty, John Thomas, a Friend of West River, Maryland, received a letter from Robert Pleasants of Virginia rejoicing in the cessation of the war and expressing the hope that the future of the new nation would be a bright and prosperous one. Pleasants was especially concerned that the ideals of freedom for which the United States was established should have a beneficent effect on mankind in general. In part he said:

> It clearly appears to me that the dispute between Great Britain and America, has been a means of opening the eyes of Princes, as well as people in most parts of the World, in respect to the proper limits of power in one, or rights of the other; as well as to show the inconsistency of sacrificing the lives of thousands to gratify the ambition of a few...And if the struggles of America have been a means of instruction to the Old World how careful ought we now to be to Act consistent with our own arguments, and allow to others, what we have demanded as a right inherent in every man?...it admits of no doubt with me, that if we consider the natural rights of all mankind...and wholesome laws are enacted to establish those rights, America will be great (and) happy, and not only become the residence of people from all parts of the World, but be a means perhaps of opening a door of Emancipation to many nations who in times past have been held in bondage by the tirany of absolute Monarchs. (14)

Although the Quakers accepted fully the outcome of the conflict, they continued their policy of aloofness from politics in any form. In August 1784 the New York Meeting for Sufferings learned that some Friends had accepted governmental appointments. Fearing that others might follow their example, it issued an epistle of advice to the monthly meetings, warning

317

that the assumption of such positions might lead into
practices inconsistent with the religious principles
of the Society. It urged all members to "stand upon
their Guard against mixing with the Spirit of this World,
which hath a tendency to leaven us into the nature of
it". (15)

Up to this time oaths of allegiance were required
from all persons assuming public offices. Subsequently
the law was changed to allow affirmations instead, and
some Friends took advantage of the alteration to accept
governmental positions. In 1787 the Meeting for
Sufferings again addressed the monthly meetings, re-
affirming the position taken in 1784 and calling
attention to the epistle of that year. (16)

The New England Quakers took a similar stand. In
April 1785 Rhode Island Quarterly Meeting urged the
subordinate monthly meetings to bear in mind the "danger
of being hurt of the Inward man by accepting offices in
Outward government and thereby mixing too intimately
with the people & spirit of the world."(17) In 1787
the Yearly Meeting also issued such advice, especially
urging against the appointment of anyone to positions
of trust in the Society who accepted stations in outward government. Despite this admonition some Friends
proved willing subjects to "those alluring and ensnaring
insinuations which under pretence of greater usefulness
induce some to accept offices of honour and profit".
The next year, 1788, the Yearly Meeting expressed sorrow
that certain members of the Meeting for Sufferings had
failed to heed its advice of the previous year and
offered them the alternative of giving up their secular
offices or surrendering the positions which they held
in the Society. (18)

In Pennsylvania, Virginia, and North Carolina the
Society adopted the same attitude. In 1786 Philadelphia
Yearly Meeting urged its members to "beware of taking
an active part in government, either to elect or
be elected". (19) The following year both Virginia
and North Carolina Yearly Meetings issued similar
admonitions. (20)

Despite their abstention from affairs of government,
the Quakers were very much concerned about the issue
of separation of church and state which arose in Maryland and Virginia in 1784 and 1785. In the latter part
of 1784 a bill was introduced into the Maryland House
of Delegates to provide for a general tax in support

318

of ministers of the gospel of all denominations. Such
a system of religious support was directly opposed to
the principles of the Friends. In February 1785 the
Meeting for Sufferings in Maryland called a special
meeting for the following month in Baltimore to decide
what action should be taken. (21)

At this special session the Meeting for Sufferings
drafted a memorial to the Assembly, protesting against
the proposed legislation. It also appointed a committee
to obtain the signatures of Friends in the various
meetings and counties. After the approval of the Philadelphia Meeting for Sufferings had been obtained, the
memorial was presented to the legislature and read before
both Houses. It served to open the debate on the
question, and in the end the proposed bill was defeated. (22)

The Virginia Friends followed the same procedure
as those in Maryland. In May 1785 Hopewell Monthly
Meeting heard that a bill was before the legislature
which would provide for general taxation for the support
of religion. It reported the matter to the Yearly
Meeting which in turn petitioned the Speaker and the
House of Delegates not to pass the law. The petition
declared that the bill was contrary to the principles of
the Friends and an infringement of both religious and
civil liberty. It would be a denial of the bill of rights
of the state constitution, and would tend to the disadvantage of the community at large. Subsequently this
bill was defeated. (23)

Another aspect of the post-war adjustments was the
migration of a group of loyalist Quakers and their
friends from New York, New Jersey, and Pennsylvania to New
Brunswick. The leaders went for political reasons, while
many who joined them were prompted mainly by economic motives. Early in the summer of 1783, when it became obvious
that the British would soon evacuate New York City where
many loyalists had taken refuge, several loyalist Quakers
met to discuss plans for the establishment of a settlement
in the maritime provinces of Canada. They appointed three
of their number, including Samuel Fairlamb and John Rankin,
as their agents to locate the most desirable lands and
transact the necessary business. A committee of six was
empowered to handle any complaints and controversies which
might arise and to oversee the work of the agents. The
meeting ordered an advertisement to be placed in the New
York newspapers, and it also adopted an agreement regulating the conduct of the projected community. (24)

According to the rules agreed on, a majority vote
of all the members of the new colony twenty-one years
and over would determine all matters of public policy.
Five persons were to be appointed annually to settle
all complaints, three of them to constitute a quorum.
No member of the community could dispose of lands
allotted to him without the approval of the other
members, and no slaves could be bought, sold or kept.

In order to assure the success of the project, Fairlamb and Rankin presented a memorial to Sir Guy Carleton
who was in charge of the British forces in New York,
requesting his support of the plan. Carleton, anxious
to assist all loyalists desiring to emigrate, forwarded
the memorial to Governor Parr in Halifax with a recommendation for assistance to the would-be colonists. (25)
Governor Parr received the memorial favorably, and the
location finally chosen for the colony was Beaver Harbor
in New Brunswick, although the original intention had
been to settle in Nova Scotia. The name adopted for
the new settlement was Penn's Field or Pennfield. (26)

The first settlers arrived at the site of their
new home in the fall of 1783. About two hundred persons,
including sixty-eight men and heads of families, thirty-
one women, seventy children, and thirty-two servants
embarked at New York for the settlement. One hundred
forty-one were from Pennsylvania, fifty-three from New
Jersey, and two from Long Island. Among them were farmers,
merchants, tailors, cord-wainers, blacksmiths, masons,
wheelrights, carpenters, millers, mariners, a hatter,
a tanner, a printer, and a schoolmaster. (27)

The following year the colonists applied to
Governor Parr on behalf of five or six hundred Quaker
families in New York, Pennsylvania, and New Jersey who
desired to emigrate to New Brunswick, obviously for
economic reasons. Since there was no apparent political
motivation for this migration, the Governor referred
the petition to the Secretary of State in London as
it was not within his authority to accept non-loyalist
immigrants without the approval of the British Government. The reply of the Secretary of State was to
authorize grants of lands to individuals who might
emigrate to Canada on their own accord. (28) Evidently
many families took advantage of this opportunity, for
by 1786 the settlement was reported to have three hundred
houses, and a contemporary writer estimated its population
at eight hundred souls. (29)

On June 11, 1785, two years after the establishment

of the settlement, a general election was held. Five
directors were chosen to transact the business of the
community for the ensuing year, as well as two "Masters
of the Roads & Highways", and a clerk. The directors
immediately ordered the men of the settlement to appear
on a specified day to clear the town of brush and rubbish
and eliminate a dangerous fire hazzard. Two days were
appointed for clearing ground for a meeting-house and
cemetary, and for this purpose the company was divided
into two shifts. The meeting also ordered their agent,
Samuel Fairlamb, and the directors to receive applications for new allotments of land from those who had
received plantations incapable of being improved or
too far away from the settlement. (30).

On June 17, 1786, a second general election was
held at which five new directors were chosen. In July
a general meeting of the community agreed to construct
a meeting-house for public worship. (31) From that
time on the records of the colony are almost completely
lacking, probably because of the unfortunate events of
the next few years. In the latter part of 1786 the
town was practically wiped out by fire, and much of
the time there was a shortage of food supplies. Relief
assistance furnished by Friends in Pennsylvania and
England served only as a temporary stimulus. (32) The
town at Beaver Harbor had been built in the expectation
of trade which never came, and forest fires swept the
district in 1790, leaving only one dwelling. The funds
of the settlers were already exhausted, and their
spirits were frustrated by the hardships and disappoint-
ments encountered.

After the last disaster a few inhabitants remained,
but Pennfield was no longer a Quaker colony. Some of
the original settlers moved to Pennfield Ridge, Mace's
Bay, and other localities in the province. (33) A
census in 1803 reported only fifty-four inhabitants in
the parish of Pennfield, most of them Quakers. It was
noted that they were excellent farmers, were located
on good tracts of land, and were in good circumstances. (34)

(1) Md.M.f.S., Min., v.1,38-39.
(2) Md.Y.M., Min., v.3,183-184.
(3) Western Q.M., Min., 1779-1818,87;Hunt, "Diary",
     loc.cit., v.53, (1934),42;v.54 (1935),111. New
     Jersey Free Quaker sympathizers referred to in
     chap. 16 were no doubt supporters of tax payment.
(4) Hunt, "Diary", loc.cit., v.54,111;Phil.Y.M., Min.,
     v.4,99-100,104.
(5) N.Y.M.f.S., Min.,v.1,133-134;N.Y.Y.M., Min.,v.1,
     193-194.
(6) N.E.Y.M. to London Y.M., 1785,N.E.Y.M., Min., v.1,
     402.
(7) N.E.Y.M., Min., v.1,253,258.
(8) South Kingston M.M., Min., 1773-1789,103;Richland
     M.M., Min., 1767-1786,Dec.16,1779,May 18,1780.
(9) N.Y.M.f.S., Min., v.1,123-125.
(10) Purchase M.M., Min., 1772-1785,Oct.14,Nov.11,1784;
     Purchase Q.M., Min., 1745-1793,Nov.4,1784.
(11) Amawalk Preparative Meeting, Min., 1775-1800, 51;
     Purchase Q.M., Min., 1772-1785,Dec.2,1784. The
     Friends involved were David and Jesse Hallock and
     Isaac Lounsberry.
(12) N.Y.Y.M., Min., v.1,191,194.
(13) N.Y.M.f.S., Min., v.1,147-149,324-325.
(14) Robert Pleasants to John Thomas, June 28,1783,Robert
     Pleasants Letters, 1746-1799.
(15) N.Y.M.f.S., Min., v.1,120-122.
(16) Ibid., 199,200-202.
(17) R.I.Q.M. to the subordinate monthly meetings, April
     9, 1785, So.Kingston Pap.
(18) N.E.Y.M., Min., v.1,436;v.2,4.
(19) Hunt, "Diary", loc.cit., v.54,111.
(20) Va.Y.M., Min., 1702-1843,157; N.C.Y.M., Min., v.1,
     233,237.
(21) Md.M.f.S., Min. v.1,43.
(22) Ibid., 44;Phil.M.f.S.,Min., v.2,449,451;Journals
     of the Gen. Assy. of the St. of Md., House
     Journals, 1785, 7; ibid., Senate Journals, 1785,4;
     Evan Thomas to James Pemberton, Nov.23,1785,Phil.
     M.f.S., Misc.Pap., bx. 17 (1783-1785).
(23) Va. Y.M., Min., 1702-1843,156-157;Hopewell Friends
     History, 195.
(24) "A Book of Records of the transactions and proceed-
     ings of the Society of the People Called Quakers,
     who have agreed to settle themselves on the River
     St. John in Novascotia". ed. J. Vroom, New Bruns-
     wick Hist. Soc., Collections, v.2(1899),76-77. The

advertisement appeared in the Roy. Gaz., July 2,1783,
and is quoted in Vroom,loc.cit., 74n.
It reads:

> Notice is hereby given to those of the
> people called Quakers who have entered
> into an agreement to settle together in
> Nova Scotia that they are requested to
> meet at the house of Joshua Knight, No.36
> in Chatham-street, a little above the Tea-
> Water Pump, on the Seventh Day next, the
> 5th of July, at four o'Clock Afternoon,
> in order to conclude upon some matters of
> importance to them, and those who mean to
> join the above-mentioned body are re-
> quested to call at No.188,Water-street,
> between the Coffee-House Bridge and the Fly-
> Market, and have their names entered
> as soon as possible.

Both Joshua Knight and Samuel Fairlamb were disowned by their respective Meetings for activities
connected with the war (Abington M.M., Min.,
1774-1782,95,115; Chester M.M., Min., 1745-1778,
422-424). This migration to Canada is extensively
dealt with in Aruthur J. Mekeel's "The Quaker-
Loyalist Migration to New Brunswick and Nova
Scotia in 1783", BFHA,v.32 (1943),No.2,65-75; and
"Quaker-Loyalist Settlements in New Brunswick
and Nova Scotia", in ibid., v.36,(1947),No.1,26-38.

(25) Sir Guy Carleton to Governor John Parr, Aug.9,1783,
     Report on American MSS in the Royal Institute of
     Great Britain (4 vols., Boston. 1972),v.4,269-270.
(26) Vroom, loc.cit., 77n. In a communciation to the
     Secretary of State in London, dated October 21,
     1783, Governor Parr mentions the surveying of
     land between St. John's and Passamaquoddy for
     the settlement of a company of Quakers (Governor
     Parr to the Secretary of State, Oct. 21,1783,
     Can. Arch., 1894,408).
(27) These data are taken from "A Return of Loyalists
     and Quakers, who embark for the River St. John
     in Nova Scotia, for whom Samuel Fairlamb, John
     Ranken & George Brown are appointed Agents", Gather-
     ed Leaves, v.1,59. A brief account of the settle-
     ment at Beaver Harbor is given in "Glimpses of
     the Past", St. Croix Courrier, St. Stephen,N.B.,
     June 22, 1893,v.28, No.39.
(28) Governor Parr to the Secretary of State, July 24, 1784,
     Can. Arch., 1894,422;Secretary of State to Governor
     Parr, Oct. 5,1784,ibid., 426.
(29) Vroom,loc.cit., 77n.;Siebert, Wilbur H., "The Exodus

of the Loyalists from Penobscott and the Loyalist
Settlements at Passamaquoddy", New Brunswick Hist.
Soc., Collections, v.3 (1914),485-525.

(30) Vroom,loc.cit., 77-78.

(31) Ibid., 78-79.

(32) Phil.M.f.S., Min., v.3,70,73-74. The census list
of persons aided is in Phil.M.f.S., Misc.Pap.,
bx.19. "To the National Meeting of Friends in
Ireland", Aug.31,1789,Phil.M.f.S., Min., 3,107-108;
London M.f.S. to Phil.M.f.S., July 10,1789,ibid.,
109-110.

(33) Vroom,loc.cit., 80; Siebert,Wilbur H., The Loyalists
of Pennsylvania (Ohio State Univ. Bulletin,v.24,
No.23, Columbus, 1920),101-105.

(34) Siebert, op.cit., 103.

CONCLUSION

The War for Independence and the resulting separation of the American Colonies from the British Empire was a severe testing time for the Society of Friends in America. It not only terminated the Quaker role in the political affairs of Pennsylvania, (1) but by the same token it brought to an end the reason for the involvement of the British Friends in colonial American affairs.

During the decade of constitutional controversy which preceded the war, it was mainly the Pennsylvania Quakers who were concerned because of their vital interests in the fate of the colony and the close economic ties of many of them with England. The application of their pacifist principles to affairs of state, a fundamental ideal of the colony's founders, had already met an insuperable obstacle in the military demands of the war with France, a situation which had ended official Quaker participation in the government. Since, however, the Friends still wielded significant influence in the province, they continued to advocate a pacifist approach in public affairs.

Strongly convinced of the wrongness of British conduct of colonial affairs, American and British Quakers cooperated closely in persistent support of colonial attempts to obtain changes in British policies. In taking such action the Pennsylvania Friends exerted every effort to induce their compatriots to eschew violent procedures in protesting what all considered oppressive and unconstitutional acts. As far as Pennsylvania was concerned this approach had some success. However, other colonies pursued their own course of action which, together with British lack of understanding and limited and inaccurate knowledge of colonial affairs and attitudes, inevitably led to rising tensions and increasing obduracy on both sides.

Despite temporary periods of accomodation in the dispute, the actions of the British government ultimately produced a rapid trend toward violent resistance. It was then that many Friends ceased to participate in opposition activities, having concluded that calls for pacific measures were falling on deaf ears. Subsequently the Pennsylvania Friends, impelled by their con-

325

cern for the future of the colony, issued statements
charged with political overtones, urging Friends not to
participate in the resistance movement which leading
Quakers feared was veering toward independence and
internal revolution. (2)

Even after the Friends in America had ceased
their efforts in behalf of peaceful procedures, British
Quakers made a last minute attempt to bridge the gap
between the protest demands of the colonies and the
disciplinary tactics of the British government. But
this effort at peaceful mediation was also in vain. By
then it was obvious that the persistent action of Friends
on both sides of the Atlantic to achieve a solution to
the imperial conflict by peaceful means had failed.

When constitutional debate gave way to military
struggle, the Quakers throughout the colonies were
affected alike. Faithful to their religious pacifist
testimony, they refused to take part in the conflict.
This position of non-cooperation with the war effort
was commonly adhered to throughout the war.

The unity of viewpoint within the Society of Friends
is evident in the universal resort to disciplinary
measures against those who would not maintain the peace
testimony as interpreted by the Society. The total
number of members dealt with for failure to conform
with the testimony was 2350, of whom 1724 or almost
three quarters (74%) were disowned. (3) Almost two-
thirds (63%) of those disowned were disciplined for performing military service, 14% for paying war fines and
taxes, 11% for taking tests of allegiance to the new
states, and 7% for assisting the war effort in various
ways. The remaining 5% of disownments were for miscellaneous marginal deviations such as hiring substitutes,
buying or selling prize goods, watching military exercises, joining a patriot association, celebrating independence, etc.

In national. terms the proportion of Quaker males
of military age who were dealt with can be estimated
at 17% and those disowned at 13%. Males over military
age could well be guilty of paying war taxes and fines
or taking tests of allegiance, and, considering that
we do not have a full accounting of dealing and disownments because of some missing minute books for this
period, the total percentages might rise to 20% and 15%
respectively. (4)

Among those disowned there were quite a number who, although disagreeing with the Society's interpretation of the peace testimony, were strongly attached to its mode of worship and church organization. In Pennsylvania and New England they formed small, independent groups known as Free Quakers which, however, ceased to exist within a few decades after the events which brought them into existence.

The refusal of the Quakers to cooperate with the war effort aroused suspicion in some quarters that they were loyalist sympathizers if not outright loyalists. (5) This was especially the case in Pennsylvania where the outspoken Quaker opposition to the course the radicals took and the idea of separation from Britain had brought upon them virulent attacks. Elsewhere in America there was no inherited political interest to prompt quasi-political pronouncements which would prejudice the position of the Friends. New England Quakers even expressed grave reservations regarding the statements issued by the Friends in Pennsylvania at the beginning of the war. Both in New England and in other states Friends accorded what was tantamount to de facto recognition of the new state authorities and freely dealt with them, although they felt they could not officially recognize them while the war was in progress.

The consistency of the Quaker position is seen in that the Friends' refused as strictly to comply with the British as with the American military requisitions. This became clearly evident when the British controlled northern New Jersey early in 1777 and occupied Philadelphia later that year. (6) Throughout the seven years when New York City was the focal point of British military and naval power in America, the Quaker inhabitants persistently refused to cooperate in any way. Moreover, the few Friends from Pennsylvania, New Jersey, and Maryland who joined the British forces were disowned. (7) Although it cannot be denied that the Quakers would have preferred to retain the imperial relationship rather than undergo military confrontation and internal upheaval, when war broke out they followed a policy of strict neutrality in withholding support from both parties. (8) In carrying out this policy they were the most consistent of all the pacifist sects. (9)

At the conclusion of the war those few Quakers who had been openly loyalist either migrated to Canada or went to England with the returning British forces.(10) The absence of confiscation of Quaker property because of loyalism would argue that state and local authorities conceded the genuinely pacifist neutral position of the Friends.

Naturally the public in general could not understand the absolutist position of the Quakers in refusing to contribute to the war effort in any way. The new state governments considered the provisions allowing the hiring of substitutes or the payment of a special tax in lieu of persoanl military service as a fair concession to the pacifist principles of the Friends and similar religious pacifist groups. In this respect, considering the pressures of war and the struggle for national survival, the states can hardly be condemned for failing to provide fully for particular limitations of action which the principles of certain religious bodies imposed on their members. In fact, the extent to which the Massachusetts authorities accorded favorable treatment to the Friends was in sharp contrast to the unhappy suffering inflicted on the first Quaker missionaries to the Bay Colony in the 1650's and 1660's.

Because of the refusal of the Friends to accept alternatives to personal service or to provide any material support for the war, they brought upon themselves varying degrees of hardship and "sufferings" in all the states, the severity depending on local conditions and attitudes. Total exactions estimated from a pecuniary standpoint, as far as they were recorded, amounted to Ŀ 103,195, taken largely in distraint of property for failure to comply with wartime legislation. The Pennsylvania Quakers were the heaviest sufferers,partly because of the political climate there at the time. The situation of many Friends on whom these sufferings bore heavily evoked comparisons with the earlier period of Quaker persecution in England. In facing these hardships the Friends claimed that a proper observance of the principles of religious freedom and freedom of conscience, cornerstones of both the new Pennsylvania state constitution and the former colonial charter of liberties, would have spared them many of the difficulties visited upon them.

At the same time, throughout America the Quakers exerted their best efforts to assist in alleviating the necessitous circumstances in which many of their

fellow citizens found themselves on account of the war.
These efforts began with relief for the besieged
Bostonians in 1776 and continued through the war period
wherever assistance could be rendered.

In the decades following the war the impact of
the Quaker experience soon became obvious. A basic
change in the relation of the Friends to society was
evident in their complete withdrawal from any political
or governmental activity. This was an outer sign of a
change in the inner direction of the Society whose
energies were now devoted to a strong spiritual emphasis.
One historian has characterized the Revolutionary experience of the Friends as having clarified for them
the relationship between an adherence to their peculiar
testimonies and way of life on the one hand and participation in wordly affairs on the other. (11) Indeed,
one must agree with Wellenreuter that the reform movement within the Society achieved its goal of spiritual
renewal and purification from worldly influences
through the impact of the Revolution. (12)

In spite of their intensified inwardness of direction, the Quakers did not eschew their sense of moral
and social obligation toward their fellow citizens.
They continued and even expanded their efforts in behalf of the anti-slavery movement and such causes as
prison reform, proper treatment of the insane, and
education. (13) When the bitterness of the war period
had passed, the Friends soon acquired a reputation as
exemplary citizens and as a constructive force in their
communities.

Notes for Conclusion

(1)   John Adams, a heated opponent of the Quaker in-
      fluence in Pennsylvania in the period preceding
      the Revolution, speaking in retrospect long after
      the conflict, caustically, and certainly unfairly,
      characterized the Quaker role and its demise on
      the achieving of independence as follows:
            I have witnessed a Quaker Despotism in
            Pennsylvania. The Sovereignty was in
            Quakers. The Revolution destroyed it.
      (John Adams to Adrian Vanderkamp, May 30,1813,loc.
      cit.)

(2)   An eyewitness and early historian of the American
      Revolution has depicted a human reaction of the
      Pennsylvania Friends to the situation they faced:
            Revolutions in government are rarely
            patronized by any body of men who forsee
            that a diminution of their own importance
            is likely to result from the change.
      (Ramsay, David, History of the American Revolution,
      2 vols., Philadelphia, 1789, reissued in 1968,
      v.1,313.)

(3)   See appendices for analyses of dealings and disown-
      ments.

(4)   Approximate estimates of Quaker population at the
      end of the colonial period have been given as
      follows: Maryland 3000, New Jersey 6000,
      Virginia 4000, the Carolinas and Georgia 6000*.
      (Jones, Quakers in the American Colonies,xvi.)
      According to the number of monthly meetings and
      the area of concentration of Friends in New York,
      New England and Delaware, possible estimates are
      New England 12,000, New York 5000, and Delaware
      1000. Added to 24,000 for Pennsylvania the total
      of American Quakers would be approximately 61,000.
            According to census figures for Massachusetts,
      males over sixteen eligible for military service
      constituted 22% of the total population. (See
      Greene and Harrington, American Population,31-40.)
      This does not vary greatly from Young's estimate
      of 20% (males 18 to 53) of the population re-
      gistered in the Pennsylvania militia. (Young,
      Treatment of the Loyalists,399). Applying 22%
      to the national Quaker population at the end of
      the colonial period, there were an estimated
      13,420 male Quakers of military age. Of these
      approximately 17% were dealt with and 13% disowned.
            *This figure is larger than that given in

330

Jones to allow for the Quaker settlement in
Georgia which he did not include.
(5) Judging from the standpoint of the patriots, anyone
who did not actively support the war would be considered a loyalist and some historians accept this
criterion. In their eyes pacifist sects such as
the Quakers were "passive" or "static" loyalists.
(See Young, op.cit., 81-84 and Nelson, William H.,
The American Tory, Oxford, 1961,90).
(6) Calhoun, Robert McCluer, The Loyalists in Revolutionary America, 1760-1781 (New York, 1973),363.
(7) Pennsylvania:
Abington M.M., Min., 1774-1782,148-164,passim;
Bradford M.M., Min., 1765-1781,235,239;Darby M.M.,
Min., 1763-1783,247,251; Falls M.M., Min., 1767-
1788,207-219,passim;Gwynedd M.M., Min., 1757-1779,
275,280;Phil.M.M.No.Dist., Min., 1772-1781,314,
321; Phil.M.M.So.Dist., Min., 1781-1793,41;Richland
M.M., Min., 1767-1786,9/17/1778,1/21/1779;
Uwchlan M.M., Min., 1776-1795,91,93.
New Jersey:
Chesterfield M.M., Min., 1756-1786,422,426;Haddon-
field M.M., Min., 1762-1781,370,372;Kingwood M.M.,
Min., 1772-1782,45;Plainfield M.M., Min., 1751-1788,
1/17/1782,2/21/1782;Shrewsbury M.M., Min., 1757-
1786,443,446.
Maryland:
Gunpowder M.M., Min., 1768-1784,277.
Thirty Friends were disciplined for joining
the British forces, twenty-one from Pennsylvania,
seven from New Jersey, and two from Maryland.
Twenty-nine were disowned, one submitting an
acknowledgement to his meeting. After the war,
another disowned Friend submitted an acknowledgement to his meeting and was reinstated.
(8) A leading authority on the loyalists contends that
the neutralists, which were one-third of the
population according to John Adams, included the
pacifist sects and that the Quakers cannot be
considered as loyalists. (Brown, Wallace, The King's
Friends, Providence, 1965,244,252,268; The Good
Americans, New York, 1969,229). Arthur M. Schlesinger in his Birth of the Nation (New York, 1968),
744, agrees with this conclusion.
(9) Brock, Peter, Pacifism in the United States, chap.
6,7 discusses fully the position of the other
pacifist sects.
(10) Of the 415 loyalist claims presented to the
British government by Pennsylvania loyalists who
went to Britain, only twelve were presented by

Quakers and only two New Jersey Quakers presented
similar claims. (Brown, The King's Friends, 123,
143.)

(11) Baumann, For the Reputation of Truth, 227-228.

(12) Wellenreuter, Glaube und Politik, 402 ff.

(13) James, "Impact of the Revolution", loc.cit., 373,
380,382.

Appendix I

Estimates of the Quaker Population on

the Eve of the Revolution

There is no reliable estimate of the population of colonial Pennsylvania available. The only source of information is Robert Proud's History of Pennsylvania (2 vols., Philadelphia, 1798),v.2,275-276,339. Using his estimates for 1771 and carrying forward to 1775 according to his method of calculating population increase, the population of the areas of Quaker concentration, Bucks, Chester and Philadelphia Counties and Philadelphia City, the total population estimate for those areas may well have been approximately 145,000.

Proud estimates the proportion of Friends to the population of the city of Philadelphia in 1771 as one-seventh. Applying this proportion to the population figure above indicated there would have been about 22,500 Quakers in the Quaker populated areas. Adding an estimated number of 1500 Friends living in the outlying counties of Lancaster, York and Berks, the total number of Friends in Pennsylvania would have been about 24,000. This seems to be approximately substantiated by Jones (Quakers in the American Colonies, 524) who estimates the number at up to 25,000.

When dealing with the question of disownments for war-related offenses, only males are counted. According to the Massachusetts census of 1777, males of military age constituted 22% of the population. (See Greene and Harrington, American Population,31-40.) Applying this proportion to the estimated Quaker population of Pennsylvania, the number of males eligible for military service would be 5280.

The above method of computation has been employed in estimating proportions of disownments for other states. Since there is no way of obtaining an accurate enumeration of Quaker population in any state, all computations are merely plausable estimates.

Appendix II

Dealings

Year	N.E.	N.Y.	N.J.	Pa.	Del.	Md.	Va.	N.C.	S.C.	Ga.	Total
1774	0	2	0	0	0	0	0	0	0	0	2
1775	18	2	13	162	8	4	9	2	1	0	219
1776	38	10	91	168	20	13	9	9	2	1	361
1777	47	19	60	96	9	11	23	3	1	2	271
1778	22	16	36	135	12	33	5	4	2	0	265
1779	17	11	94	232	9	8	36	11	2	1	421
1780	17	7	37	239	3	0	1	11	6	4	325
1781	10	17	54	116	1	8	18	11	2	8	245
1782	14	13	33	96	2	3	2	4	4	4	175
1783	0	6	11	40	0	0	1	4	1	0	63
1784	0	0	0	2	0	0	0	0	0	0	2
1785	0	0	0	1	0	0	0	0	0	0	1
Total	183	103	429	1287	64	80	104	59	21	20	2350

Appendix III

Disownments by Years*

Year	N.E.	N.Y.	N.J.	Pa.	Del.	Md.	Va.	N.C.	S.C.	Ga.	Total
1774	0	2	0	0	0	0	0	0	0	0	2
1775	18	1	7	138	5	1	6	2	0	0	178
1776	30	7	70	190	16	12	5	6	3	1	340
1777	39	11	36	84	4	9	8	3	1	1	196
1778	24	6	25	83	4	30	11	2	1	0	186
1779	14	8	42	128	4	2	15	5	2	1	221
1780	13	3	33	149	2	0	9	3	2	3	227
1781	10	9	38	87	2	6	10	8	5	4	179
1782	14	19	33	54	3	5	2	4	2	4	140
1783	0	5	4	32	0	0	2	4	3	1	51
1784	0	0	0	2	0	0	1	0	0	0	3
1785	0	0	0	1	0	0	0	0	0	0	1
Total	162	71	288	948	40	65	69	37	19	15	1724

*Seventy-four percent of those dealt with were disowned.

Appendix IV

Disownments by Cause

	Military	Naval& Priva- teers	Asst.War Effort*	Fines& Taxes	Test Affir.	Held Pub. Off.	Total
N.E.	90	47	14	0	3	1	155
N.Y.	46	2	15	4	3	1	71
N.J.	165	5	11	71	28	8	288
Pa.	537	22	58	165	101	23	906
Del.	27	2	0	3	6	1	39
Md.	29	1	3	1	31	0	65
Va.	42	1	10	3	13	0	69
N.C.	23	4	4	0	2	2	35
S.C.	19	0	0	0	0	0	19
Ga.	15	0	0	0	0	0	15
Total	993	84	115	247	187	36	1662**

*Assisting in the war effort included such activities as manufacturing or mending arms,furnishing a team for the army, carting supplies for the army, collecting blankets for the army, carrying messages for the army, etc.

**In appendix III the number disowned is given as 1724. The balance of 62 not indicated in this table were involved in such activities as buying and vending prize goods, joining a patriot association, watching military exercises, celebrating independence day, redeeming distrained goods, etc., which are individually too few to be categorized.

Sixty-three per cent of those disowned were disciplined for direct war involvement, both military and

naval; fourteen per cent for paying war fines and taxes;
eleven per cent for taking a test of allegiance; and
seven per cent for assisting the war effort in various
ways.

BIBLIOGRAPHY

Primary Sources

A Manuscript Materials

Archival Collections

The most extensive collection of manuscript materials for this subject is found at the Historical Society of Pennsylvania, as follows:

John Adams Letters, 1781-1825

Thomas Clifford Papers, 1722-1832

Thomas Clifford Letter Books, 1767-1789, in the Thomas Clifford Papers.

Coates, Reynell Papers, 1702-1843

Samuel Coates Letter Book, 1763-1781

Cox, Wharton, Parrish Papers, 1600-1900

Elizabeth Drinker Journal, 1759-1807. Parts of the Journal have been published in Extracts from the Journal of Elizabeth Drinker, 1759-1807, ed. Henry D. Biddle, Philadelphia, 1889.

Etting, Pemberton Papers, 1654-1806

Etting Scientitst Papers, 1762-1876

William Logan Fox Collection

Free Quaker Papers

Abel James Letter Book,1770, in the Jonah Thompson Collection.

James and Drinker Correspondence, 1759-1775,in the Jonah Thompson Collection.

Christopher Marshall Diary, 1773-1793. Part of the Diary has been published as Extracts from the Diary of Christopher Marshall,1774-1781,ed. William Duane, Albany, 1877.

Christopher Marshall, Letter Book

Pemberton Papers, 1641-1880

John Reynell Letter Books, 1762-1770

Jonah Thompson Collection, 1607-1903

Samuel Wharton, Observations upon the Consumption of the teas in North America, London, Jan.19,1773, in the Wharton Papers.

Thomas Wharton Letter Books, 1773-1784. Selections

have been published in PMHB, v.33 (1909),319-339,
432-453;v.34 (1910),41-61.
The Quaker Collection at Haverford College houses the
following:
Samuel Allison, Reasons against War and paying
Taxes for It
The Journal of George Churchman, 1766-1783
The Letters of Elizabeth Drinker
The Letter Book of Robert Pleasants, 1754-1797
The Letters of Robert Pleasants,1746-1799
Job Scott, A Truly Conscientious Scruple
Other manuscript collections are as follows:
The Moses Brown Papers, 1735-1842, at the Rhode
Island Historical Society, Providence, R.I.
Stephen Collins Letter Book,1773-1775, in the
Stephen Collins Papers in the Library of Congress.
The William Heath Papers, 1774-1814, at the Massa-
chusetts Historical Society, Boston. Part of
this collection has been published in the Massa-
chusetts Hist. Soc. Collections, Fifth Series,
v.4 (1878), 1-285; Seventh Series, vols. 4,5
(1904-1905).
Laws of Maryland, Legislative Sessions, 1777,1778,
1779-1781, 1781-1785 in the Hall of Records,
Annapolis, Md.
Massachusetts Archives, 1776-1782, at the Old
State House, Boston, Mass.
Joseph Mitchell Papers (1916) at the Nantucket
Historical Society.
Proceedings of the General Assembly of the Colony
of Rhode Island, 1777-1779, in the archives of
the Secretary of State, the State House, Provi-
dence.
The Jared Sparks Collection of Manuscripts in
American History in the Houghton Library, Harvard
University.

Records of the Society of Friends

Guides to the records of the Society of Friends have
been issued for Maryland, New England and Pennsylvania,
as follows: Quaker Records in Maryland, ed. Phebe R.
Jacobsen, Publication No. 14, The Hall of Records
Commission, State of Maryland, Annapolis, 1966; MS
Guide to the Records of the Yearly Meetings of New
England with their Subordinate Meetings, 1683-1972;
Inventory of Church Archives of New Jersey:The Reli-
gious Society of Friends,prepared by the New Jersey
Historical Survey Project, Works Project Adminis-

tration, Newark, 1941; <u>Inventory of Church Archives</u>;
<u>Society of Friends in Pennsylvania,</u> prepared by the
Pennsylvania Historical Survey, Works Project Administration, Philadelphia, 1941. The records of
the Society of Friends for Pennsylvania and New
Jersey are now, for the most part, deposited in the
Quaker Collection at Haverford College and the Friends
Historical Library at Swarthmore College.
The minute books and papers of the various meetings
of the Society of Friends referred to in the text
are listed below under their respective yearly meet-
ings.
The Yearly Meeting for Maryland (now known as Balti-
more Y.M.).
    The minute books and records of all but one of the
    meetings in this yearly meeting are in the Friends
    Historical Library, Swarthmore College. Micro-
    films are in the Hall of Records, the State House,
    Annapolis, Maryland. Exceptions are so indicated.
Maryland Y.M., Min., v.3 (1765-1789).
                Misc. Pap.
                M.f.S., Min., v.1 (1778-1841).
Cecil M.M., Min., 1689-1782
Gunpowder M.M., Min., 1768-1784
Indian Spring M.M., Min., 1772-1817
Third Haven M.M.,Min., 1771-1797, in the Hall of
    Records, Annapolis, with microfilm at FHLSC.
Third Haven and Little Creek (Southern) Q.M., Min.,
    1759-1822.
West River (Baltimore) Q.M., Min., 1710-1822
New England Yearly Meeting.
    The original minute books, or microfilm copies
    thereof, together with miscellaneous papers and
    records of the meetings in this yearly meeting
    are at the Rhode Island Historical Society, Provi-
    dence, R.I.
New England Y.M., Min., v.1 (1683-1787)
                M.f.S., Min., v.1 (1775-1793)
Acoakset (Westport) M.M., Min., 1766-1787
Dartmouth M.M., Min., 1770-1792
Dover M.M, Min., 1750-1784
Falmouth M.M., Min., 1772-1837, originals at the
    Maine Historical Society, Portland, Me.
Greenwich M.M., Min., 1751-1806
Hampton M.M. Min., 1758-1804
Nantucket M.M., Min., 1772-1789, at the Nantucket
    Historical Society, Nantucket, Mass.
Pembroke M.M., Min., 1741-1801
Rhode Island M.M., Min., 1773-1790
                Testimonies and Denials, 1718-

        1827, at the Newport Historical Society, New-
    port, R.I.
    Rhode Island Q.M., Min., 1746-1791
    Salem M.M., Min., 1677-1788
    Salem Q.M., Min., 1727-1799
    Sandwich M.M., Min., 1755-1795
    Sandwich Q.M., Min., 1686-1804
    Smithfield M.M., Min., 1763-1780;1780-1801
    South Kingston M.M., Min., 1773-1789
                        Misc. Pap.
    Swanzey M.M., Min., 1732-1788
New York Yearly Meeting.
    The minute books and records of the meetings in
    this yearly meeting are in the Haviland Records
    Room, 15 Rutherford Pl., New York City, N.Y.
    New York Y.M., Min., v.1 (1748-1800)
                        Misc. Pap., in Gathered Leaves,
        2 vols.
                        M.f.S., Min., v.1 (1758-1796)
    Amawalk P.M., Min., 1775-1800
    Flushing M.M., Min., 1776-1781
    Nine Partners M.M., Min., 1769-1779;1779-1783
                        Register, 1769-1798
    Oblong M.M., Min., 1757-1781;1781-1788
                Record Book of Sufferings, 1775-1826
    Purchase M.M., Min., 1772-1785
                        First Register, 1742-1800
    Purchase Q.M., Min., 1745-1793
    Saratoga (Easton)M.M., Min., 1778-1782
    Westbury M.M., Min., 1767-1782;1782-1790
North Carolina Yearly Meeting (The Yearly Meeting for
North and South Carolina and Georgia).
    The minute books and records of the meetings in
    this yearly meeting are in the Quaker Collection,
    Guilford College, Greensboro,N.C. with the ex-
    ception of the Rich Square M.M. Minutes which are
    at the Friends Meeting House, Woodlands, N.C. Four
    minute books for the Revolutionary period are
    missing: Fredericksburg Monthly Meeting in South
    Carolina, and Carvers Creek, Centre and Contentnea
    Monthly Meetings in North Carolina.
    North Carolina Y.M., Min., v.1 (1704-1793)
    Bush River M.M., Min., 1772-1783
    Cane Creek M.M., Min., 1751-1796
    Core Sound M.M., Min., 1733-1791
    Deep River M.M., Min., 1778-1808
    New Garden M.M., Min., 1776-1782
    Rich Square M.M., Min., 1760-1799
    Symonds Creek M.M., Min., 1699-1785
    Wells (Perquimans) M.M., Min., 1774-1794

Western Q.M., Min., 1760-1900
Wrightsboro M.M., Min., 1772-1793
Philadelphia Yearly Meeting (The Yearly Meeting for
Pennsylvania, New Jersey and the Provinces Adjoining).
  The minute books and records of the meetings in
  this yearly meeting are mostly in the Friends
  Historical Library, Swarthmore College (designated
  by S) or in the Quaker Collection, at Haverford
  College (designated by H). The location of minutes
  in other depositories is so indicated.
Philadelphia Y.M.,Min.,v.3(1747-1779);v.4(1780-
  1798) (H).
                        M.f.S.,Min.,v.1 (1755-1775);v.2
      (1775-1785);v.3 (1785-1802) (H)
                        Misc.Pap.,bxs. 13-21,1766-1797 (H)
Abington M.M.,Min.,1774-1782;1782-1797 at the
  Abington Friends Meeting House, Jenkintown,Pa.
  A transcription of these minutes is at the HSP.
Bradford M.M., Min.,1765-1781;1781-1788 (H)
Buckingham M.M.,Min.,1763-1780;1781-1790 at the HSP.
Bucks Q.M., Min., 1774-1805 at the National Bank,
  Newtown, Pa.
Burlington M.M., Min., 1770-1781;1781-1788 (H)
Burlington Q.M., Min., 1770-1795 (H)
Chester M.M., Min., 1745-1778;1778-1808 (S)
Chester Q.M., Min., 1768-1813 (H)
Chesterfield M.M., Min., 1756-1786 (H)
Concord M.M., Min., 1757-1776;1777-1795 (H)
Darby M.M., Min., 1763-1783 (S)
Deer Creek M.M., Min., 1776-1782 (S)
Duck Creek M.M., Min., 1705-1800 (S)
Evesham M.M., Min., 1760-1782 (H)
Exeter M.M., Min., 1765-1785 (S)
Fairfax M.M., Min., 1745-1776;1776-1802 (S)
Falls M.M., Min., 1767-1788 (H)
Gloucester and Salem Q.M., Min., 1697-1776;1776-
  1794 (H)
Goshen M.M., Min., 1766-1788 (H)
Great Egg Harbor (and Cape May) M.M., Min., 1726-
  1797 (H)
Gwynedd M.M., Min., 1757-1779,1779-1786 (H)
Haddonfield (Gloucester) M.M., Min., 1762-1781;
  1781-1804 (H)
Hopewell M.M., Min., 1759-1776;1777-1791 (S). Ex-
  tracts from these minutes have been published
  in Hopewell Friends History 1734-1834,Frederick
  County, Virginia, comp. by a joint committee
  of Hopewell Friends assisted by John Wayland,
  Strassburg, Va., 1936.
Kennet(t) M.M., Min., 1739-1791 (S)

Kingwood (Quakertown) M.M., Min., 1772-1782.(S)
The minutes of this meeting have been published
in Records of the Kingwood Monthly Meeting of
Friends, Hunterdon County, New Jersey, comp.
James W. Moore, Flemington, N.J., 1900.
Middletown M.M., Min., 1755-1800 at HSP.
Mount Holly M.M., Min., 1776-1793 (H)
Newgarden M.M., Min., 1768-1778;1779-1790 (H)
Nottingham M.M., Min., 1776-1778;1778-1792 (S)
Philadelphia M.M., Min., 1765-1771;1771-1777;1777-
1782;1782-1789 (H)
Philadelphia M.M. Northern District, Min., 1772-
1781;1782-1789 (H)
Philadelphia M.M. Southern District, Min., 1770-
1780;1781-1793 (H)
Philadelphia Q.M., Min., 1772-1826 (H)
Pipe Creek M.M., Min., 1772-1801 (S)
Plainfield (and Rahway) M.M., Min., 1751-1788, in
the Haviland Records Room, 15 Rutherford Pl.,
New York City.
Radnor M.M., Min., 1772-1782;1782-1784 (H)
Richland M.M., Min., 1767-1786 (S)
Sadsbury M.M., Min., 1737-1783 (S)
Salem M.M., Min., 1740-1788 (H)
Shrewsbury M.M., Min., 1757-1786 (H)
Shrewsbury and Rahway Q.M., Min., 1757-1828 (H)
Uwchlan M.M., Min., 1763-1776;1776-1795 (H)
Warrington M.M., Min., 1747-1785 (S)
Warrington and Fairfax Q.M., Min., 1776-1787 (S)
Western Q.M., Min., 1758-1779;1779-1818 (H)
Conference on Suffering Cases,Min.,
1779-1780;1780-1782(S)
Wilmington M.M., Min., 1750-1776;1776-1792 (S)
Misc. Pap. (S)
Wrightstown M.M., Min., 1734-1790 (S)
Virginia Yearly Meeting.
The minute books and records of the meetings in
this yearly meeting are all in the Quaker Collec-
tion at Haverford College with the exception of
Henrico Monthly Meeting and Henrico Quarterly
Meeting Minutes, part of which are in the Hunting-
ton Library at San Marino, Calif. Photostatic
copies of these minutes are in the Quaker Collec-
tion at Haverford College.
Virginia Y.M., Min., 1702-1843
Misc. Pap.
Blackwater M.M., Min., 1779-1795
Cedar Creek M.M., Min., 1775-1789
Henrico M.M., Min., 1757-1780 (HL);1780-1781,1781-
1806 (H)

Henrico (Upper) Q.M., Min., 1745-1783 (HL)
London Yearly Meeting
    All the record books of the meetings in London
    Yearly Meeting referred to are in the Friends
    Reference Library, Friends House, London.
    London Y.M.,Min.,vols.13-17(1763-1785).Microfilm
        copies are at QCHC.
                    M.f.S., Min., vols. 31-36(1761-1783).
        Microfilm copies are at FHLSC.
                    Epistles from London Y.M.,vols 4,5
        (1756-1790). Microfilm copies are at QCHC.
                    Epistles to London Y.M.,vols. 4,5
        (1758-1801). Microfilm copies are at FHLSC.

Devonshire House M.M.,Min.

B Printed Materials

    Contemporary Books and Pamphlets

Crowley, Thomas, Letters and Dissertations on Various
    Subjects by the Author of the Letter Analysis A.P.
    on the Dispute between Great Britain and America.
    London, 1776.
    ———————————— Observations and Propositions on
    Accomodation between Great Britain and Her Colonies,
    London, 1768.
Davis, Timothy, A Letter from a Friend to Some of his
    Intimate Friends on the Subject of Paying Taxes,
    Watertown, Mass., 1775.
Drinker, John, Observations on the Late Popular Meas-
    ures offered to the Serious Consideration of the
    Sober Inhabitants of Pennsylvania by a Tradesman
    of Philadelphia, Philadelphia, 1774.
An Earnest Address to Such of the People Called
    Quakers as Are Sincerely Desirous of Supporting and
    Maintaining the Christian Testimony of Their An-
    cestors, Philadelphia, 1775.
Fothergill, Dr. John, Considerations Relative to the
    North American Colonies, London, 1765.
Goddard, William, The Partnership, Philadelphia, 1770.
Grey, Isaac, A Serious Address to Such of the People
    Called Quakers on the Continent of North America,
    as profess Scruples relative to the Present Govern-
    ment, Philadelphia, 1778.
Hopkins, Stephen, The Grievances of the American
    Colonies Candidly Examined, London, 1766.

——————The Rights of the Colonies Examined,
Providence, 1765.
Paine, Thomas, Common Sense, London, 1776
——————————The Crisis, Philadelphia, 1854 ed.
Taber, Joseph, An Address to the People Called
Quakers Concerning the Manner in which They Treated
Timothy Davis, Boston, 1784.

Laws, Legislative Proceedings and

Public Archives

Canada
  Report on Canadian Archives, 1894, ed. Douglas
    Brymer, Ottawa, 1895.
Continental Congress
  Journals of the Continental Congress, 1774-1789,
    ed. Worthington Ford, Gaillard Hunt, Roscoe P.
    Hill, 34 vols., Washington, D.C., 1904-1937.
  Letters of Members of the Continental Congress,
    ed. Edmund C. Burnett, 8 vols., Washington,
    D. C., 1921-1936.
Delaware
  An Act of the General Assembly of the Delaware
    State for Establishing a Militia, Lancaster,
    Pa., 1778.
  Acts of the General Assembly of the Delaware
    State, 1779-1780, Wilmington, 1780
  An Additional Supplementary Act to an Act...
    Establishing a Militia, June 19,1781, Wilmington,
    1781.
  Minutes of the Council of the Delaware State, 1776-
    1792, Papers of the Hist. Soc. of Delaware,v.6
    (1887).
Georgia
  The Colonial Records of the State of Georgia,
    Original Papers, ed. Allen D. Candler, W.P.A.
    Project, No.350,v.38,pt.2,n.p., 1937.
  The Proceedings and Minutes of the Governor and
    Council of Georgia, October 4,1774, through
    November 7,1775, and September 6,1779 through
    September 20,1780, Collections of the Georgia
    Hist. Soc., vols.35,36 (1956,1961).
  The Revolutionary Records of the State of Georgia,
    comp. Allen D. Candler, 3 vols., Atlanta, 1908;
    republished New York, 1972.
Great Britain
  Journals of the House of Commons, 1574-1834, print-

ed by order of the House of Commons, 90 vols.,
London,n.d.
Journals of the House of Lords, 1509-1828, printed
by order of the House of Lords, 60 vols., London,
n.d.
The Parliamentary History of England from the Nor-
man Conquest in 1066 to the Year 1803, ed. W.
Cobbett and T.C. Hansard, 36 vols., London
1806-1820.
Public Records Office, Admiralty Section, Letters
April 1774-June 1775. Transcripts in the Library
of Congress.
Report on American Manuscripts in the Royal In-
stitute of Great Britain, 4 vols., Boston, 1972.
Maryland
Archives of Maryland, ed. William Hande Brown,
Bernard C. Steiner, Clayton C. Hall, J. Hall
Pleasants, Raphael Seemes, 63 vols., Baltimore,
1883-1946.
Journal of the Maryland Convention, July 26-August
14,1775, Arch. of Md., v.11.
Journal of the Maryland Convention, 1776, Amer.
Arch., 4th Ser., v.4,711 ff.
Laws of Maryland, ed. Virgil Maxcey, 3 vols.,
Baltimore, 1811.
Laws of Maryland, 1786, Annapolis, 1786
Proceedings and Acts of the General Assembly of
Maryland, 1638-1664, ed. William Hande Brown,
Baltimore, 1883. Also Arch.of Md., v.1.
Proceedings and Acts of the General Assembly of
Maryland, 1755-1756, ed. J. Hall Pleasants,
Baltimore, 1935. Also Arch. of Md. v.52.
Votes and Proceedings of the House of Delegates of
the State of Maryland, 1783-1785, n.p., n.d.
Massachusetts
Acts and Laws Passed by the Great and General Court
of Massachusetts, Boston, 1781.
Acts and Resolves, Public and Private, of the Pro-
vince of Massachusetts Bay, 1692-1780, 21 vols.,
Boston, 1869-1922.
A Journal of the Honorable House of Representatives
of the Colony of Massachusetts Bay, 1775-1776,
Watertown, Mass., 1776.
Journals of Each Provincial Congress of Massachu-
setts in 1774 and 1775, Boston, 1838.
Journals of the House of Representatives of the
General Court of the Colony of Massachusetts Bay,
1775-1776, Boston, 1776.
New Hampshire
Documents and Records Relating to the Province

of New Hampshire, Prov. and St. Pap., v.7.

Documents and Records Relating to the State of
New Hampshire, 1776-1783, Prov. and St. Pap., v.8.

Laws of New Hampshire, 1776-1784, Bristol, N.H.,
1916 (Laws of New Hampshire, ed. A.S. Batchellor
and H.H. Metcalf, 10 vols., Manchester and Bristol, 1904-1922,v.4.).

Miscellaneous Revolutionary Documents of New
Hampshire, Prov. and St. Pap., v.30.

Provincial and State Papers of New Hampshire, ed.
Nathaniel Boulton, I.W. Hammond, and A.S. Batchellor, 34 vols., Nashua, Manchester, Concord,
1867-1933.

New Jersey

Acts of the General Assembly of the State of New
Jersey, 1776-1777, Burlington, 1777.

Acts of the General Assembly of the State of New
Jersey, 1776-1783, comp. Peter Wilson, Trenton,
1784.

Acts of the General Assembly of the State of New
Jersey, 1778-1779, Trenton, 1779.

Acts of the General Assembly of the State of New
Jersey, 1779-1780, Trenton, 1780.

Acts of the General Assembly of the State of New
Jersey, 1780-1781, Trenton, 1781.

Documents Relating to the Revolutionary History of
New Jersey, New Jersey Archives, Second Series,
ed. Francis B. Lee, William Nelson, Austin Scott,
5 vols., Trenton, 1903-1917.

Minutes of the Council of Safety of the State of
New Jersey, 1777-1778, Jersey City, 1872.

Minutes of the Provincial Congress and the Council
of Safety,1774-1776,Trenton, 1879.

Votes and Proceedings of the General Assembly of
the Province of New Jersey, session beginning
January, 1775, Burlington, 1775.

Votes and Proceedings of the General Assembly of
the State of New Jersey, 1780-1781, Trenton,1781.

New York

Calendar of Historical Manuscripts relating to
the War of the Revolution in the Office of the
Secretary of State, Albany, New York, 2 vols.,
Albany, 1868.

Colonial Laws of New York from the Year 1664 to
the Revolution, 5 vols., Albany, 1895-1896.

Documents Relative to the Colonial History of
the State of New York, 15 vols., Albany 1853-
1887.

Journals of the Assembly of the State of New York,

1780, Fishkill, N.Y., 1780.

Journals of the Provincial Congress, Provincial
Convention, Committee of Safety and Council of
Safety of the State of New York, 2 vols., Albany,
1842. Also in Amer. Arch., 4th Ser., v.2,1246-
1347.

Laws of the Colony of New York, 1774-1775, Albany,
1888.

Laws of the State of New York, Passed at the Sessions of the Legislature Held in the Years 1777-
1801, 5 vols., Albany, 1886-1887.

Minutes of the Commissioners for Detecting and
Defeating Conspiracies in the State of New York,
ed. Victor Hugo Pattsits, 3 vols., Albany, 1909-
1910.

North Carolina

Colonial Records of North Carolina (Col. and St.
Rec. of N.C., vols. 1-10).

Colonial and State Records of North Carolina, ed.
William Saunders and Walter Clark, 26 vols.,
Goldsboro, 1886-1907.

Laws of North Carolina, 1715-1776 (Col. and St.
Rec. of N.C., v.3).

Laws of North Carolina, 1777-1778 (Col. and St.
Rec. of N.C., v.24).

Miscellaneous Revolutionary Documents (Col. and
St. Rec. of N.C., v.22).

Proceedings of the Provincial Congress of North
Carolina (Col and St. Rec. of N.C., v.10).

State Records of North Carolina, 1777-1778 (Col.
and St. Rec. of N.C., v.12).

State Records of North Carolina, 1778-1779 (Col.
and St. Rec. of N.C., v.13).

State Records of North Carolina, 1781-1785 (Col.
and St. Rec. of N.C., v.17).

Pennsylvania

Colonial Records of Pennsylvania, 1683-1790,16
vols., Philadelphia, 1852.

Journals of the House of Representatives of Pennsylvania 1776-1781, Philadelphia, 1782 (only one
volume printed).

Minutes of the Provincial Council, Oct. 15, 1762-
Oct. 17, 1771 (Col.Rec. of Pa., v.9).

Pennsylvania Archives, First Series, ed. Samuel
Hazard, 12 vols., Philadelphia, 1852-1856.
—————————————————————Eighth Series, ed. Charles
F. Hoban and Gertrude McKinney, 8 vols.,
Harrisburg, 1931-1935.

Statutes at Large of Pennsylvania, from 1682-1801,

18 vols., Philadelphia and Harrisburg, 1896-1909.
Votes and Proceedings of the House of Representatives of the Province of Pennsylvania, 1683-1776, 6 vols., Philadelphia, 1775-1776, Also in Pa. Arch., 8th Ser.

Rhode Island

Acts and Laws of His Majesty's Colony of Rhode Island, Newport, 1745.
Acts and Resolves of the Rhode Island Assembly, December session, 1776, Providence, 1777.
Records of the Colony (and State) of Rhode Island and Providence Plantations, ed. John Russell Bartlett, 10 vols., Providence, 1856-1865. Vols. 1-7 published as Records of the Colony of Rhode Island and Providence Plantations in New England, 1636-1776. Vols. 8-10 published as Records of the State of Rhode Island and Providence Plantations, 1776-1792. Reprinted New York, 1968.
Rhode Island Colonial Records see Records of the Colony of Rhode Island...
Rhode Island State Records see Records of the State of Rhode Island...

Virginia

Proceedings of the Convention of Delegates...in the Colony of Virginia, 1775, Richmond, 1816.
Statutes at Large, being a Collection of all the Laws of Virginia, ed. William Waller Henig, 13 vols., New York, Philadelphia, Richmond, 1819-1823.

Diaries, Journals, Correspondence and

Published Papers

Adams, John, Diary. (Works of John Adams With a Life of the Author, ed. Charles Francis Adams, 10 vols., Boston, 1856,v.2.)
——————Familiar Letters of John Adams and His Wife Abigail Adams, during the Revolution, ed.Charles Francis Adams, New York, 1876.
Allen, James, "Diary of James Allen, Esq., of Philadelphia". PMHB, v.9 (1185),176-196,278-296, 424-441.
Almon, J., A Collection of Papers, relative to the Dispute between Great Britain and America, London, 1777.
American Archives, see Force, Peter.

Boudinot, Elias, The Life, Public Services, Add-
resses and Letters of Elias Boudinot, ed. J.J.
Boudinot, 2 vols., Boston and New York, 1896.
Brissot de Warville, J.P., New Travels in the United
States of America, 2 vols., London, 1797.
Clinton, George, Public Papers of George Clinton,
8 vols., Albany, 1900.
Craft, James, "Extracts from the Journal of James
Craft of Burlington, New Jersey", History
Magazine, v.1 (1857), 300-302.
Crèvecoeur, Hector St. John, Lettre d'un Cultivateur
Americain, depuis l'année 1770, jusqu'à 1781,
2 vols., Paris, 1784.
Curwin, Samuel, Journal and Letters of Samuel Cur-
win, ed. George Atkins Ward, New York, 1842.
de Berdt, Dennys, "Letters of Dennys de Berdt,
1757-1770", Colonial Society of Massachusetts,
Publications, v.13 (Transactions 1910-1911),
293-461.
Dickinson, John, The Writings of John Dickinson,
Political Writings, 1764-1774, ed. Paul Lester
Ford, Memoirs of the Historical Society of
Pennsylvania., v.14 (1895).
Force, Peter and Clarke, M. St. Clair, American
Archives, Fourth and Fifth Series, 9 vols.,
Washington, D.C., 1837-1853.
Forster, William to his sister Elizabeth, Oct. 7,
1773, Journal of the Friends Historical Society
(London), v.20 (1923), 95,96.
Fothergill, Dr. John, Chain of Friendship, Selected
Letters of Dr. John Fothergill of London, 1735-
1780, ed. Betsy C. Corner and Christopher C.
Booth, Cambridge, Mass., 1971.
Franklin, Benjamin, Autobiographical Writings, ed.
Carl Van Doren, New York, 1945.
Franklin, Benjamin, The Life of Benjamin Franklin,
Written by Himself, ed. John Bigelow, 3 vols.,
Philadelphia, 1847.
Gage, Thomas, The Correspondence of General Thomas
Gage with the Secretaries of State, 1763-1775,
ed. Charles Edwin Carter, 2 vols., New Haven,
1931-1933.
George III, The Correspondence of King George the
Third, ed. Sir John Fortescue, 6 vols., London,
1928.
Graydon, Alexander, Memoirs of a Life Chiefly Passed
in Pennsylvania within the Last Sixty Years,
Edinburgh, 1822.
Hall, Rufus, Journal of the Life, Religious Exer-
cises and Travels in the Ministry of Rufus Hall,

Byeberry, Pa., 1840.

Harrison, Joseph to Mrs. John Lawrence, June 16, 1781, PMHB v. 14 (1890), 82.

Hicks, Elias, Journal of the Life and Religious Labors of Elias Hicks, New York, 1832.

Hopewell Friends History 1734-1934, Frederick County, Virginia, comp. by a joint committee of Hopewell Friends assisted by John Wayland, Strassburg, Va., 1936.

Hull, Henry, Memoirs of the Life and Labours of Henry Hull, Philadelphia, 1858.

Hunt, John, "Diary of John Hunt", ed. Edward Fuhlbreugge, New Jersey Historical Society Proceedings, v.52 (1934), 177-193,223-239; v.53 (1935), 26-34,111-128,194-209,251-262.

Lacey, Brigadier General John to General Washington, March 21, 1778, The American Clipper, May 1940, 74.

Lee, Charles, Charles Lee Papers, New York State Historical Society Collections, vols. 4-7, New York, 1871-1874.

Lee, William, Letters of William Lee, 1766-1783, ed. Worthington Chauncey Ford, 3 vols., Brooklyn, 1891; reprinted New York, 1971.

London Yearly Meeting, Epistles from the Yearly Meeting held in London, 1675-1850, 2 vols., London, 1760, 1850.

Paine, Thomas, The Complete Writings of Thomas Paine, ed. Philip S. Foner, 2 vols., New York, 1945.

Penn, William, To the Children of Light in this Generation, London, 1678. Broadside in QCHC.

Reed, Joseph, "Joseph Reed's Narrative", Charles Thomson Papers, Collections of the New York Historical Society, v.11 (1878), 269-286.

Reed, Silvanus, "Orderly Book of Adjutant Silvanus Reed", New Hampshire Historical Society, Collections, v.9 (1889), 364-414.

Reed, William B. Life and Correspondence of Joseph Reed, 2 vols., Philadelphia, 1847.

Rotch, William, "An Autobiographical Memoir of William Rotch", New England Historical and Geneolgoical Register, v.31 (1877), 262-264;v.32 (1878), 36-42,151-155,271-274,389-394.

——————————— Memorandum Written by William Rotch in the Eightieth Year of his Age, Boston, 1916.

Scott, Job, Journal of the Life of Job Scott, New York, 1797.

Smith, Horace Weymess, Life and Correspondence of

the Rev. William Smith, 2 vols., Philadelphia,
   1879.
Smith, Richard, "Diary of Richard Smith in the
   Continental Congress, 1775-1776", American
   Historical Review, v.1 (1895), 288-310,493-516.
Stiles, Ezra, Literary Diary, ed. Franklin Bow-
   ditch, 3 vols., New York, 1901.
Sullivan, Major General John, Letters and Papers of
   Major General John Sullivan, ed. Otis G. Hammond,
   2 vols., Concord, N.H., 1930-1931.
Thompson, Mack, "Moses Brown's 'Account of Journey
   to Distribute Donations 12th Month, 1775' with
   an Introduction", Rhode Island History, v.15
   (1956), 97-121.
Thomson,Charles,Charles Thomson Papers, New York
   State Historical Society Collections,v.11 (1878).
Vroom, J., ed., "A Book of Records of the trans-
   actions and proceedings of the People Called
   Quakers, who have agreed to settle themselves
   on the River St. John in Nova Scoita", New
   Brunswick Historical Society Collections,v.2
   (1899), 73-80.
Warren-Adams Letters, Massachusetts Historical
   Society Collections, v.71-72 (1917,1923).
Washington, George, The Writings of George Wash-
   ington, ed. John C. Fitzpatrick, 39 vols.,
   Washington, D.C., 1931-1944.

                        Newspapers

Boston Gazette 1719-1798   Bos.Gaz.
Continental Journal and Weekly Advertiser (Boston)
   1776-1787 Cont.Jnl.
Essex Gazette (Salem) 1768-1775   Essex Gaz.
Evening Post (Boston) 1778-1780   Ev.Post.
Freemans Journal or New Hampshire Gazette (Ports-
   mouth) 1776-1778 Frmn.Jnl. See New Hampshire
   Gazette.
Independent Chronicle (Boston) 1776-1820 Ind.Chron.
Independent Ledger (Boston) 1778-1786 Ind. Ledg.
Maryland Gazette (Baltimore) 1778-1792 Md.Gaz.
Massachusetts Gazette; and the Boston Post Boy
   and Advertiser 1769-1775 Mass.Gaz. A continuation
   of the Boston Post Boy 1734-1769.
Massachusetts Spy (Boston) 1770-1775 Mass.Spy
New Hampshire Gazette (Portsmouth) 1765-1820
   N.H.Gaz. Published under various names.
New Hampshire Gazette and Historical Chronicle
   (Portsmouth) 1763-1775 N.H.Gaz.Hist.Chron.

See New Hampshire Gazette.
Newport Gazette 1777-1779 Nwp. Gaz.
Newport Mercury 1758-1820 Nwp. Mer.
New York Gazette and the Weekly Mercury 1768-1783
 N.Y. Gaz.
New York Journal or, the General Advertiser 1766-
 1777 N.Y. Jnl.
Pennsylvania Evening Post 1775-1784 Pa.Ev.Post
 All Pennsylvania newspapers cited were published
 in Philadelphia.
Pennsylvania Gazette 1728-1818 Pa. Gaz.
Pennsylvania Journal; and the Weekly Advertiser
 1766-1793 Pa. Jnl.
Pennsylvania Ledger; Or the Virginia, Maryland,
 Pennsylvania and New Jersey Weekly Advertiser
 1775-1776 Pa. Ledg.
Pennsylvania Mercury, and Universal Advertiser
 1775 Pa. Mer. Also known as Story and Humphrey's
 Pennsylvania Mercury and Universal Advertiser.
Pennsylvania Packet and the General Advertiser
 1771-1790 Pa. Pkt. Also known as Dunlop's
 Pennsylvania Packet, or the General Advertiser.
Providence Gazette; and Country Journal 1762-1820
 Prov.Gaz.
Rivington's New York Gazette 1777 Riv.N.Y. Gaz.
 A continuation of Rivington's New York Gazetteer.
Rivington's New York Gazetteer; or the Connecticut,
 New Jersey,Hudson's River and Quebec Weekly
 Advertiser 1773-1775 Riv.N.Y.Gaztr.
Rivington's New York Loyal Gazette 1777 Riv.N.Y.Loy.
 Gaz. A continuation of Rivington's New York
 Gazette.
Royal Gazette (New York) 1777-1783 Roy.Gaz.
 A continuation of Rivington's New York Loyal
 Gazette.
Royal American Gazette (New York) 1777-1783 Roy.
 Amer.Gaz.
Royal Pennsylvania Gazette 1778 Roy.Pa.Gaz.
Virginia Gazette (Williamsburg, pub. Rind &
 Pinkney) 1766-1776 Va. Gaz.

Secondary Sources

Books, Articles, Dissertations

Alvord, Clarence V., The Mississippi Valley in
 British Policies, 2 vols., Cleveland, 1917.
The American Revolution in New York, prepared by
 the Division of Archives and History of the

353

State of New York, Albany, 1926.

Archer, Adair P., "The Quakers' Attitude Towards the Revolution", WMQ, 2nd Ser. v.1 (1921), 167-182.

Armistead, Wilson, Select Miscellanies, Chiefly Illustrative of the History, Christian Principles, and Sufferings of the Society of Friends, 6 vols., London, 1851.

Arnold, Samuel Greene, History of the State of Rhode Island and Providence Plantations, 2 vols., Providence, 1894.

Bakeless, Katherine and John, Spies of the Revolution, New York, 1966.

Baker, Pearl, The Story of Wrightsboro, Thomson, Ga., 1965.

Bargar, B.D., Lord Dartmouth and the American Revolution, Columbia, S.C., 1965.

Bauman, Richard, For the Reputation of Truth, Baltimore, 1971.

Becker, Carl Lotus, History of Political Parties in the Province of New York, 1760-1776, Bulletin of the Univ. of Wisconsin, No. 286, History Series II, No.1, Madison, 1909.

Beer, George Louis, British Colonial Policy, 1754-1765, New York, 1907.

Biographical Catalogue, Being an Account of the Lives of Friends..., London, 1888.

Bolles, Albert S., Pennsylvania, Province and State, 2 vols., Philadelphia and New York, 1892.

Bolton, Robert, Jr., A History of the County of Westchester, 2 vols., New York, 1848.

Boorstein, Daniel, Jr., The Americans; The Colonial Experience, New York, 1958.

Bowden, James, The History of the Society of Friends in America, 2 vols., London, 1854.

Bradley, A.Day, "Friends in the Fleet Prison at Esopus", Quaker History, v.55 (1966), 144-117.
——————————"New York Friends and the Loyalty Oath of 1776", Quaker History, v.57 (1968), 112-113.

Braithwaite, William C., The Second Period of Quakerism, 2nd ed., Cambridge, 1961.

Brett-James, Norman G., The Life of Peter Collinson, London, 1926.

Bridenbaugh, Carl and Jessica, Rebels and Gentlemen; Philadelphia in the Age of Franklin, New York, 1942.

Brinton, Howard H., Divine-Human Society, Philadelphia, 1938.

"A British Food Ship for Philadelphia Quakers",

More Books v. 14 (1939), 64-65.

Brock, Peter, Pacifism in the United States, Princeton, 1968.

———————— Pioneers of the Peaceable Kingdom, Princeton, 1970.

Bronner, Edwin B., "The Quakers and Non-Violence in Pennsylvania", Pennsylvania History, v.35 (1938), 1-22.

Brooks, George S., Friend Anthony Benezet, Philadelphia, 1937.

Brown, Joshua, "The Life of Joshua Brown", The Friend (Philadelphia), v.20 (1846-1847), 341, 348, 356-357.

Brown, Wallace, The Good Americans. The Loyalist in the American Revolution. New York, 1969.

Brown, Wallace, The King's Friends, Providence, 1965.

Brunhouse, R.L., "The Effects of the Townsend Acts in Pennsylvania", PMHB, v.54 (1930), 355-373.

Cadbury, Henry J., "Intercolonial Solidarity of American Quakerism", PMHB, v.60 (1936), 362-374.

————————————————"Quaker Relief During the Siege of Boston", Colonial Society of Massachusetts Publications, v. 34, 39-179. Also published as Pendle Hill Historical Study No. 4, Wallingford, Pa., 1943.

Calhoun, Robert McClure, The Loyalists in Revolutionary America, 1760-1781, New York, 1973.

The Cambridge History of the British Empire, ed. J. Holland Rose, A.P. Newton, and E.A. Benians, 8 vols., New York and Cambridge, 1929-1959.

Campbell, Agnes H., "In This Time of Commotion," Quaker History, v. 60 (1971), 120-123.

Carroll, Kenneth L., "Irish and British Quakers and their American Relief Funds, 1778-1797", PMHB, v.102 (1978), 437-456.

———————————— "The Mary & Charlotte Fiasco. A Look at 1778 British Quaker Relief for Philadelphia", PMHB, v. 102 (1978), 212-223.

"A Chronological Summary of Events and Circumstances...," The Yorkshireman, pub. at Pontefract, England, 4 vols., 1832-1836, vols. 1-4, passim.

Cole, W.A., The Quakers and Politics, unpublished Ph.D. thesis, Cambridge Univ., 1955.

Corner, Betsy Copping, "Dr. Fothergill's Friendship with Benjamin Franklin", American Philosophical Society Proceedings, v. 102 (1958), 413-419.

Corner, Betsy Copping and Waley, Dorothea, "Dr. John Fothergill, Peacemaker", American Philosophical Society Proceedings, v. 98 (1954),11-12.

Crossfield, George, Memoirs of the Life and Gospel Labours of Samuel Fothergill, Liverpool, 1843.

Darlington, William, Memorials of John Bartram and Humphrey Marshall, Philadelphia, 1849; republished New York and London, 1967.

De Brahm, John Gerar William, History of the Province of Georgia with Maps of Original Survey, 1772,Wormsloe, Ga., 1849.

Delaplaine, Edward S., "The Life of Thomas Johnson", Maryland Historical Magazine, v. 17 (1922), 191-209, 381-405; v.18 (1923), 108-130, 234-248.

Dickerson, Oliver M., The Navigation Acts and the American Revolution. Philadelphia, 1951.

Donoughue, Bernard, British Politics and the American Revolution, London, 1964.

Drinker, Henry, "Effects of the Non-Importation Agreement in Philadelphia", PMHB, v.14 (1890), 41-45.

Écuyer, W. S., see Crèvecoeur, Hector St. John.

Egnal, Marc and Ernst, Joseph A., "An Economic Interpretation of the American Revolution", WMQ, 3rd., Ser., vol. 29 (1972), 3-32.

Fisher, Edgar Jacob, New Jersey as a Royal Province, 1738-1776, Columbia Univ. Studies in History, Economics and Public Law, v. 41, New York, 1911.

Fisher, Sydney George, Pennsylvania: Colony and Commonwealth, Philadelphia, 1897.
————— The Struggle for American Independence, 2 vols., New York, 1908.

Flick, Alexander C., The American Revolution in New York, Port Washington, 1967.

Ford, Paul Leicester, "The Adoption of the Pennsylvania Constitution of 1776", Political Science Quarterly, v. 10 (1895), 426-459.

Foster, William E., Stephen Hopkins, Rhode Island Historical Society Tracts, No. 10, Providence, 1874.

Frost, J. William, The Quaker Family in Colonial America, New York, 1973.

Gilpin, Thomas, Exiles in Virginia, Philadelphia, 1848.
—————"Memoir of Thomas Gilpin", PMHB, v. 49 (1925), 289-328.

Gipson, Lawrence Henry, The Coming of the Revolution, 1763-1775, New York, 1954.

"Glimpses of the Past", St. Croix Courrier, St. Stephen, N.B., June 22, 1893, v.28, No. 39.

Gordon, Thomas F., The History of Pennsylvania, Philadelphia, 1829.

Gordon, William, The History of the Rise, Progress and Establishment of the Independence of the United States of America, 4 vols., London, 1788; re-printed New York, 1969.

Greene, Evarts B. and Harrington, Virginia D., American Population Before the Federal Census of 1790, New York, 1932.

Guba, Emil Frederick, Nantucket Odyssey, Waltham, Mass., 1965.

Hammond, Otis Grant, Tories of New Hampshire in the War of the Revolution, Concord, 1917.

Hawke, David, The Colonial Experience, Indianapolis, 1966.

——————————In the Midst of Revolution, Philadelphia, 1961.

Hinkhouse, Fred Junkin, The Preliminaries of the American Revolution as Seen in the English Press 1763-1775, New York, 1926.

Hirst, Margaret E., The Quakers in Peace and War, New York, 1923.

Hitz, Alexander M., "The Wrightsborough Quaker Town and Township in Georgia", BFHA, v.46 (1957),10-22.

Hodgkin, L.V., A Book of Quaker Saints, London,1922.

Huffeland, Otto, Westchester County during the American Revolution, Westchester County Historical Society Publications, v.3, White Plains, 1926.

Huston, James E., "The Campaign to Make Pennsylvania a Royal Province, 1764-1770", PMHB, v.95 (1971), 28-49.

——————————Pennsylvania Politics, 1746-1770, Princeton, 1972.

Jacobson, David L., John Dickinson and the Revolution in Pennsylvania, 1764-1776, Univ. of California Publications in History, v.78, Berkley, 1965.

James, Sydney, V., "The Impact of the American Revolution on Quakers' Ideas About their Sect", WMQ, 3rd. Ser., v. 19 (1962), 360-383.

——————————A People Among Peoples, Cambridge, Mass., 1963.

Jensen, Arthur L., The Maritime Commerce of Philadelphia, Madison, 1963.

Jones, Augustine, Moses Brown; A Sketch, Providence, 1892. Originally published in New England Magazine, v.6 (1887), 34-42.

Jones, Rufus M., assisted by Isaac Sharpless and

Amelia M. Gummere, The Quakers in the American Colonies, London, 1911.

Justice, Hilda, Life and Ancestry of Warner Mifflin, Philadelphia, 1905.

Keith, Charles P., The Provincial Councilors of Pennsylvania, Philadelphia, 1883.

Kelsey, Raynor W., "Early Books of Discipline of Philadelphia Yearly Meeting", BFHA, v. 24 (1935), 12-23.

King, Wetherill Webster, "The Fighting Quakers", Philadelphia Numismatical and Antiquarian Society Proceedings, v. 29 (1921), 69-81.

Labaree, Benjamin Woods, The Boston Tea Party, New York, 1964.

Lettsom, John Coakley, Memoirs of Dr. John Fothergill, M.D., London, 1786.

Lincoln, Charles H., The Revolutionary Movement in Pennsylvania, Publications of the Univ. of Pennsylvania, Series in History, No. 1, Philadelphia, 1901.

Lovejoy, Davie S., Rhode Island Politics and the American Revolution, 1760-1776, Providence, 1958.

Marietta, Jack D., "Conscience, the Quaker Community, and the French and Indian War", PMHB, vol. 95 (1971), 3-27.

———————————— Ecclesiastical Discipline in the Society of Friends, 1682-1776, unpublished Ph.D. thesis, Stanford Univ., 1965.

————————————"Wealth,War, and Religion: The Perfecting of Quaker Asceticism, 1740-1783", Church History, v. 43 (1974), 230-241.

Marston,Benjamin, "Benjamin Marston of Marblehead, Loyalist", New Brunswick Historical Society, Collections, No. 7 (1907), 79-110.

Mather, Frederick Gregory, The Refugees of 1776 from Long Island to Connecticut, Albany, 1913.

Mekeel, Arthur J., "The Free Quaker Movement in New England in the American Revolution", BFHA, v. 27 (1938), 72-82.

————————————"New England Quakers and Military Service in the American Revolution", Children of Light, ed. Howard H. Brinton, New York, 1938, 243-275.

————————————"The Quaker-Loyalist Migration to New Brunswick and Nova Scotia in 1783", BFHA, v. 32 (1943), 65-75.

————————————"Quaker-Loyalist Settlements in New Brunswick and Nova Scotia", BFHA, v. 36 (1947), 26-38.

Mereness, Newton D., <u>Maryland as a Proprietary
Province</u>, New York, 1901.
Morgan, Edmund S. and Helen M., <u>The Stamp Act
Crisis</u>, Chapel Hill, 1953.
Nelson, Russel Gage, Backcountry Pennsylvania 1709-
1774, The Ideals of William Penn in Action, un-
published Ph.D. thesis, Univ. of Wisconsin, 1968.
Nelson, William H., <u>The American Tory</u>, Oxford, 1961.
Oakes, Robert F., "Philadelphia Exiles: The Problem
of Loyalty During the American Revolution", PMHB,
v. 96 (1972), 298-325.
————————— "Philadelphia Merchants and the
First Continental Congress", <u>Pennsylvania
History</u>, v. 40 (1973), 149-166.
Olton, Charles S., "Philadelphia Mechanics in the
First Decade of the Revolution, 1765-1775",
<u>Journal of American History</u>, v. 59 (1972-1973),
311-326.
Pannell, Ann Gary, The Political and Economic Re-
lations of the English and American Quakers,
1750-1785, unpublished Ph.D. thesis, St. Hughs
College, Oxford, 1935.
Pole, J.R., <u>Political Representation in England and
the Origins of the American Republic</u>, Berkley,1971.
Price, Richard, <u>A Discussion on the Love of Our
Country</u>, London, 1879.
Ramsay, David, <u>History of the American Revolution</u>,
2 vols., Philadelphia, 1789; reprinted 1968.
————————<u>The History of South Carolina</u>, 2
vols., Charleston, 1809.
<u>Rhode Island Quakers in the American Revolution</u>,
Providence, 1976.
Rightmyer, Nelson Waite, "Churches under Enemy
Occupation, Philadelphia 1777-1778", <u>Church
History</u>, v. 14 (1945), 33-60.
Ritcheson, Charles R., <u>British Politics and the
American Revolution</u>, Norman, Oklahoma, 1954.
Romanek, Carl Leroy, John Reynell, Quaker Merchant
of Philadelphia, unpublished Ph.D. thesis, State
Univ. of Pennsylvania, 1969.
Ross, Peter, <u>A History of Long Island</u>, 3 vols., New
York and Chicago, 1903.
Rotherman, Dietmar, <u>The Layman's Progress. Religious
and Political Experience in Colonial Pennsylvania</u>,
<u>1740-1770</u>, Philadelphia, 1961.
Ryerson, Alan, Leadership in Crisis. The Radical

Committees of the Revolution, 1765-1776; A Study
in the Revolutionary Process. Unpublished Ph.D.
thesis, Johns Hopkins Univ., 1972.

Salem, Annals of Salem from Its Settlement, ed.
Joseph B. Felt, 2 vols., Salem, Mass., 1845-1849.

Sandwich, "The Annals of the Town of Sandwich",
in The History of Cape Cod, ed. Frederick Freeman,
2 vols., Boston, 1862.

Scharf, John Thomas and Westcott, Thompson, History
of Philadelphia, 1609-1884, 3 vols., Philadelphia,
1884.

Schlesinger, Arthur M., The Birth of the Nation,
New York, 1968.

————————————— The Colonial Merchants
in the American Revolution, Columbia Univ. Studies
in History, Economics and Public Law, v.78,
No. 182, New York, 1918.

————————————— "Politics, Propaganda, and
the Philadelphia Press, 1767-1770", PMHB, v.60
(1936), 309-322.

Sharpless, Isaac, A History of Quaker Government
in Pennsylvania, 2 vols., Philadelphia, 1899.

Siebert, Wilbur H., "The Exodus of the Loyalists
from Penobscott and the Loyalist Settlements at
Passamaquoddy", New Brunswick Historical Society
Collections, v. 3 (1914), 485-525.

————————————— The Loyalists of Pennsylvania,
Ohio State Univ. Bulletin, v. 24, No. 23,
Columbus, 1920.

Sloan, David, "A Time of Sifting and Winnowing",
Quaker History, v. 66 (1977), 3-22.

Snowden, W.H., "General Greene and the Friends at
Guilford", American Friend, v. 2 (1895), 307.

"The Society of Friends in Pennsylvania and New
Jersey, 1764-1782", The Friend (Philadelphia),
v. 19 (1845-1846), 404-405,412-413; v. 20 (1846-
1847), 6-333, passim.

Sossin, Jack M., Agents and Merchants, British
Colonial Policy and the Origins of the American
Revolution, 1763-1775, Lincoln, Nebraska, 1965.

Stackpole, Edouard A., The Sea Hunters, The New
England Whalemen During Two Centuries 1635-1835,
Philadelphia, 1953.

Starbuck, Alexander, The History of Nantucket,
Island and Town, Boston, 1924.

————————————— "Nantucket in the Revolution",
New England Historical and Geneological Register,
v. 28 (1874), 272-278, 436-442; v. 29 (1875),
48-53, 141-145.

Stein, Roslyn, The British Occupation of Philadelphia, September, 1777-June, 1778, unpublished
M.A. thesis, Columbia Univ., 1937.

Stillé, Charles J., Life and Times of John Dickinson, Memoirs of the Historical Society of Pennsylvania, v.13, Philadelphia, 1891.

Stone, Frederick, D., "How the Landing of Tea Was
Opposed in Philadelphia by Colonel Bradford and
Others in 1773", PMHB, v. 15 (1891), 383-393.

Strickland, Reba Carolyn, Religion and State in
Georgia in the Eighteenth Century, New York,
1967.

Taber, Mary Jane Howland, "Friends Here and Hereaway", Old Dartmouth Historical Society Proceedings, December, 1904, 16-24.

Taylor, Thomas B., "The Philadelphia Counterpart
of the Boston Tea Party", BFHA, v.2, No. 3
(1908), 86-110; v.3, No.1 (1901), 21-49.

Thayer, Theordore, Israel Pemberton, King of the
Quakers, Philadelphia, 1943.
——————————————— Pennsylvania Politics and the
Growth of Democracy 1740-1776, Harrisburg,
1953.

Thomas, Benjamin F., History of Long Island, 3
vols., New York, 1908.

Thompson, Mack, Moses Brown, Reluctant Reformer,
Chapel Hill, 1962.

Thurston, John R., "Northbridge", in History of
Worcester County, ed. D.H. Hurd, 2 vols.,
Philadelphia, 1889.

Tolles, Frederick B., Meeting House and Counting
House, the Quaker Merchants of Colonial Philadelphia, 1682-1763, Chapel Hill, 1948.
——————————————— Quakers and the Atlantic Culture, New York, 1960.

Van Tyne, Claude H., The Causes of the War of Independence (The Founding of the American Republic,
v.1), New York, 1922.

Walton, William, Captivity and Suffering of Benjamin Gilbert and His Family, Cleveland, 1904.

Weeks, Stephen Bureauguard, The Southern Quakers
and Slavery, Johns Hopkins Univ. Studies in
History and Political Science, extra v. 15,
Baltimore, 1896.

Wellenreuter, Hermann, Glaube und Politik in
Pennsylvania 1681-1776, Köln, 1972.

Wells, William V., The Life and Public Services of
Samuel Adams, 3 vols., Boston, 1865.

Wetherill, Charles, *History of the Religious
Society of Friends called by Some the Free
Quakers, in the City of Philadelphia*, Philadel-
phia, 1894.

Wharton, Anne H., *Geneology of the Wharton Family
of Philadelphia, 1664-1880*, Philadelphia, 1880.

Wood, Gordon S., *The Creation of the American
Republic, 1776-1789*, Chapel Hill, 1969.

Worrall, Arthur J., New England Quakerism, 1656-
1830, unpublished Ph.D. thesis, Univ. of
Michigan, 1970.

Young, Henry, The Treatment of the Loyalists in
Pennsylvania, unpublished Ph.D. thesis, Johns
Hopkins Univ., 1955.

162,304,306
Grenville,George 12,23
Grey,Isaac 191,192,204,
232,283
<u>Grievances of the Ameri-
can Colonies Candidly
Examined</u> 16

Haight,Solomon 246
Hagen,Jacob 86,122
Hallock,John 246
Hanbury,Capel 15,21
Harris,George 206
Heath,General William
247,248
Henry,Patrick 92,179
Hicks,Elias 249
Hicks,Thomas 148
Higginson,Stephen 121
Hillsborough,Lord 37,38
"Hints for the Conver-
sation upon...Terms...
between Great Britain and
her Colonies" 116,118
Holy Experiment 6
Hooper,William 99
Hoover,Giles 239
Hopkins, Stephen 16-17,28,86,
140,143
Howe,Richard 117,120,123
Howe,General William 173,
178,180,297
Howell,Isaac 52,56,82
Howell,Samuel 33,51,64,80,82
Howell,Stephen 187
Huddleston,Seth 225
Hughes,Evan 187
Hunt,John 183,186
Hunt,Levi 225
Hussey,Stephen 230
Hyde,Lord 115,117,118,
120,125

Jacobs,John 30,106
James,Abel 33,51ff.,
57ff.
James & Drinker 15,63,68,
103
Jenkins,Capt.Seth 121,122
Johnson,Thomas 258

Jones,Owen,Jr. 72,181,182,
186

Knight,Joshua 323

Laurens,Henry 176,273
Lawton,Isaac 297,299
Lee,Richard Henry 176
Lee, William 117
<u>Letter from One Friend to
Some of his Intimate
Friends</u> 146,232,286
Lewis,Nathan 206
Lovell,James 176

Mabbett,Joseph 256
Maddox,Joseph 77,276,306,307
Marshall,Benjamin 80,82,113
Marshall,Christopher 80-81,
96,204,283ff.
Marhsall,Samuel 131
Marston, Benjamin 302
<u>Mary and Charlotte</u>(ship)303
Massachusetts Circular
Letter 36,37
Massachusetts Restraining
Act 141,228.See also
Fisheries Bill.
Masterman,Thomas 167
Matlack,Timothy 288,290
McCoy,William 206
McKean,Judge Thomas 177
Meeting for Sufferings 4
London 4ff.,10,24
Maryland 4
New England 4
New York 4
Philadelphia 4
Virginia 4
"Memorial and Plan of Union"
70
Mennonites 258,259,263,264,
269ff.
Merchants Venturer of Bristol
21,118
Middleton,Arthur 136
Mifflin,Thomas 33,51,52,71,
80,82,84,90ff.,106,113,131
Mifflin,Warner 211,315
Mildred,Daniel 21,39,43,53,

Tupper,Dr.Benjamin 229,230

THE LIBRARY
ST. MARY'S COLLEGE OF MARYLAND
ST. MARY'S CITY, MARYLAND 20686